Steel and Steelworkers

SUNY series in American Labor History
Robert Asher and Amy Kesselman, editors

STEEL AND STEELWORKERS

Race and Class Struggle in Twentieth-Century Pittsburgh

by
JOHN HINSHAW

STATE UNIVERSITY OF NEW YORK PRESS

Published by
State University of New York Press, Albany

For information, address State University of New York Press,
90 State Street, Suite 700, Albany, NY 12207

Production by Christine L. Hamel
Marketing by Patrick Durocher

Library of Congress Cataloging-in-Publication Data

Hinshaw, John H., 1963–
    Steel and steelworkers : race and class struggle in twentieth-century
Pittsburgh / by John Hinshaw.
        p.   cm. — (SUNY series in American labor history)
    Includes bibliographical references and index.
    ISBN 0-7914-5225-5 — ISBN 0-7914-5226-3 (pbk.)
    1. Iron and steel workers—Pennsylvania—Pittsburgh—History.   2. Iron and
steel workers—Labor unions—Pennsylvania—Pittsburgh—History.   3. Working class—Pennsylvania—Pittsburgh—History.   4. Social class—Pennsylvania—Pittsburgh—History.   I. Title.   II. Series.
HD8039.I52 U545 2002
305.9'672'0974886—dc21

                                                                        2001034868

                    10 9 8 7 6 5 4 3 2 1

Contents

Acknowledgments

When I moved to Pittsburgh in 1987, I thought of the city as part of that economic and political region known as the industrial north. Over the next decade or more that I lived, worked, and engaged in politics in Pittsburgh, I came to understand that in some key ways I was mistaken. Pittsburgh remains one of the most industrialized and ethnically diverse regions in the world—a unique and wonderful place to live. However, as I began to realize through my studies of its industrial history and my experiences in its post-industrial phase, Pittsburgh's economy and especially its politics remained largely under the tight control of a small, tightly knit, and extremely conservative owning class. As a result, the region's civic character resembled the surrounding Appalachian coal fields more than the economically diverse and relatively politically vibrant cities such as Chicago, Philadelphia, or Cleveland.

Of course, my perspective on Pittsburgh has surely been shaped by my experiences of living during an era when capital has reigned supreme and labor has been on the defensive. Big business has regained much of the ground that unionized workers had forced it to concede in the decades following the 1930s. I moved to Pittsburgh in 1987, and in the depths of the post-industrial era, when jobs and hope were scarce, it was difficult to remember that Pittsburgh was a stronghold of the CIO, as bold and vibrant a working-class organization as the Knights of Labor, the IWW, the Socialist or Communist Parties—organizations that also found numerous adherents throughout Western Pennsylvania. Part of my responsibility as a historian has been to understand a region and a working class that contributed so much to working-class history, and also to the profits and power of the owning class. My goal has not been to laud the accomplishments of past heroes; the dead can bury their own. I instead wish to investigate the legacy and unfinished tasks that they left for workers, especially those whom David Montgomery termed the "militant minority," in the present.

In such a solitary task as scholarship, I nonetheless enjoyed the support and solidarity of many people. What follows is simply a token of my appreciation for their contributions to this project and my well-being. Of course, they are not to be held responsible for errors of fact or interpretation. Those mistakes are mine, and mine alone.

My parents, Harold and Vlasta Machala Hinshaw, stimulated my curiosity from my beginning. Through the course of this project, they provided important sources of emotional and material assistance. Although they probably will not recognize its forms, discussions and arguments around the dinner table helped shape my interest in the intersection between power, race, and economics. My siblings, their spouses, and their children provided much-needed distractions from research and writing.

Peter Rachleff sparked my interest in labor history; indeed, he was an inspired teacher, role model, and committed activist. Peter suggested that I might benefit from studying with Joe Trotter at Carnegie Mellon University who proved to be an extremely supportive graduate advisor and a model scholar. In 1998–99, Joe Trotter made it possible for me to rewrite this study through a generous post-doctoral fellowship at the Center for Afroamerican Urban Studies and the Economy. Such support was invaluable to the completion of this project.

While I was a graduate student at CMU, I had the pleasure of working with Judith Modell, who encouraged me and taught me much about anthropology and history. I regret that neither Bennett Harrison nor Eugene Levy lived to see the final version of this project. Barbara Lazarus also stimulated my interest in cultural analysis and provided years of interesting employment. Members of the Working-Class History seminar helped me to understand the dynamics of academic scholarship and debate.

Amongst the many librarians and archivists who helped me, two deserve special thanks. David Rosenberg, at the Archives of Industrial Society, provided access to thousands of documents and hours of enjoyable discussion and debate. Sue Collins, at Carnegie Mellon, helped locate seemingly endless amounts of government documents and other materials in what is really a rather small library. Their aid was invaluable, their professionalism admirable, and their courtesy was especially appreciated when I felt at my wits' end. I am also deeply grateful to the librarians and archivists at the Carnegie Library of Pittsburgh, Penn State, Indiana University of Pennsylvania, Albright College, and Bates College.

It was a pleasure to work with Tony Buba and Ray Henderson on their documentary: *Struggles in Steel: A Story of African American Steelworkers*. At a critical point in my dissertation, Tony and Ray provided numerous tape recordings of interviews that greatly enriched my understanding of the steel industry. This study has benefited enormously from their insights and generosity. I also benefited from working with another working-class hero, Peter Kellman, who helped me to understand the ways that corporations have depended upon government and the law for their survival. Peter also taught me an enormous amount about workers' history of organization and struggle and the possibilities for struggle in our own historical era.

Many people gave generously of their time and knowledge and allowed me to interview them. The Steel Industry Heritage Corporation in Homestead also made available numerous transcripts of interviews and other materials. Many thanks are also due to James Barrett, Larry Evans, Alice Hoffman, and Robert Anderson for their skills as interviewers. The oral histories that they and others helped to collect greatly enriched this book.

On a related note, many thanks are due to the generations of working-class militants whose resolutions, minute books, grievance hearings, and shop-floor papers enriched my understanding of Pittsburgh history. I hope that this study does justice to their struggles. I owe an enormous debt of gratitude to the United Steel Workers of America which has largely opened its historical record to public scrutiny, something that the steel companies have not done. Most of the company records in this study were made available by farsighted workers, such as William Gaughan, and archivists, such as Mark McColloch, who recognized the historical significance of grievances, company reports, and pension files and retrieved them from the ash heap for history. By contrast, U.S. Steel and other steel companies continue to guard their records as if they contain top-secret files. Since 1989, the records of the East German secret police have been thrown open to the public. Why not the records of the old Coal and Iron Police? Or indeed, those of the FBI or the State Police?

The editor of this book and series, Robert Asher, provided exceptionally insightful and helpful comments. In particular I am grateful for the ways that he encouraged me to broaden the scope of my analysis. It has been a pleasure working with him.

A year spent at the University of the Witwatersrand in Johannesburg, South Africa, helped me realize the similarities between its violent industrial history and that of Western Pennsylvania. I am enormously grateful to the then-Director of the Institute for Advanced Social Research, Charles van Onselen, who provided me a much-needed year to revise my manuscript. A brilliant social historian, Charles taught me an enormous amount about the possibilities of social history and the often impoverished political will and imagination of academics. James Campbell provided considerable assistance, inspiration, friendship, and numerous meals with his wonderful family. He graciously provided comments on an earlier draft of this manuscript and urged me to explore what alternative strategies that workers, unions, and companies might have taken.

Caroline Acker generously shared with me her considerable analytical and editing skills. She also shared her love and friendship throughout many months. Caroline also taught me much about the craft of history and the art of activism.

It gives me enormous pleasure to thank Lisa Frank. More than anyone I have known, she helped shape and sharpen my thinking, prose, and appreciation for historical materialism. Lisa Frank and Neal Bisno graciously opened their door to me during a year when I needed housing and found a home. Neal is a gifted union organizer and a perceptive student of labor history, and I benefited from many conversations with him about unions. Each possesses formidable intellectual and political skills that shaped my thinking and analysis in ways too profound and subtle to adequately acknowledge.

Lisa Frank also introduced me to Michael Sprinker, whose bold working-class spirit and razor-sharp wit provided us both with enormous pleasure through the bleak years of the Bush and Clinton Administrations. He is gone, and the university and the ongoing project of Marxism are both the poorer for it. This book is dedicated to his memory and his indomitable spirit.

A Note on Historiography

I have tried to refrain from engaging in overt debates with the findings of other scholars. In part this derives from a desire to keep the focus on the story rather than on defining my place in the historiography or historical profession by contrasting my interpretations with those of other scholars. My reluctance to situate this study into a literature also derives from my acute awareness of, and gratitude towards, the several generations of scholars without whom I could not have completed this study. Some of these scholars I know personally, such as Liz Jones, Mark McColloch, Jack Metzgar, Bruce Nelson, and James Rose; others, such as David Brody, Staughton Lynd, or Judith Stein, I know primarily through their written work. Even though we may disagree on matters of interpretation, I deeply appreciate their contributions to my own understanding of labor and business history. Many scholars have studied the steel industry and steelworkers, and I wish I could thank them all personally; instead I have tried to acknowledge my debts to them via the academic convention of footnotes.

Until recently, historians focused most of their attention on the history of steel and steelworkers in the nineteenth and early twentieth centuries. Most accounts of steel and steelworkers sought to understand the dynamics of the period before the rise of industrial unionism in the 1930s. Gifted scholars such as David Brody, David Montgomery, Francis Couvares, and Paul Krause analyzed the struggles of craft workers to retain their control over the shop floor and maintain their unions against employers who quickly amassed enormous economic and political power.[1] A number of scholars, most notably Staughton Lynd, focused on the process of the re-unionization of steel in the 1930s. Far less attention was paid to the industry and its workforce after the formation of the Steel Workers Organizing Committee.[2] In part, this omission occurred because historians generally viewed the automobile industry as more indicative of the trends and dynamics of capitalism.[3] Certainly the United Automobile Workers enjoyed a more sensational history than the USWA, in large part because the struggles between Social Democrats and radicals remained a real contest in the UAW until the late 1940s. Furthermore, after 1947, when Walter Ruether's coalition of Social Democrats and conservatives consolidated its power in the UAW, it continued to display more imagination and militancy than the leaders of the USWA. By contrast, in steel, the "possibilities for radicalism" that Lynd discovered in the early 1930s were largely lost by 1937 and remained a distant and largely forgotten memory in the USWA thereafter.[4]

Yet the debate begun by Lynd continues. In "The United States Steel Duquesne Works, 1886–1941," James Rose has argued that the Steel Workers Organizing Committee, precisely because of its top-down nature, represented the limits of the possible for steelworkers.[5] After a careful and detailed analysis of U.S. Steel's Duquesne Works, Rose concluded that steelworkers in the 1930s faced a choice not between radical or conservative unionism, but between the SWOC or no unionism at all. Like Rose's study, my own work respects the tight constraints imposed upon workers by the enormous economic, political, and coercive power of steel companies. This study shows that the state played a strong role in disorganizing workers, bolstering capital, and discouraging the development of radical organizations in the steel industry long before, and long after, the consolidation of the SWOC in 1937. For the marketplace for political ideas, no less than the market for steel, was far from free; capital and the state did their best to ensure the appropriate outcome. Throughout the late nineteenth and early twentieth centuries, industrialists and politicians worried that immigrant workers were radicals; by the 1930s, black workers joined the threat. The fact remains that radicalism in the 1930s was a possibility, but only that. That radicalism threatened to reemerge, but failed to coalesce, for instance, in the Sadlowski campaign of 1977, suggests the importance and limitations of workers' agency in any analysis of their political future.

At the turn of the twenty-first century, the history of steel and steelworkers after 1937 is beginning to enjoy an increasingly rich body of scholarship. Much of this work is undertaken in order to understand the causes and consequences of deindustrialization. Insightful books by journalists, economists, and eventually historians on what was generally conceded to be a tragic saga for workers, the industry, and the country as a whole have obviously informed this book, and I have sought to move the discussion forward. The consequences of deindustrialization for steel regions and steel-workers have been nothing short of devastating, and perhaps the tendency by writers to view the process as an aberration of the normal dynamics of capitalism or public policy is natural. One of the most important of these works for the steel industry is John Hoerr's *And the Wolf Finally Came: The Decline of the American Steel Industry*. For Hoerr, the rapid decline of steel-making in the 1980s was the outcome of "forty years of poor management of people and a misdirected union-management relationship." As a labor journalist, Hoerr was a firsthand observer of the bitter rounds of collective bargaining in the early 1980s and the mill closings of those years. Further-more, Hoerr shed valuable light on the generally bitter shop-floor relations between workers and management in the years after World War II. How-ever, Hoerr views deindustrialization as a tragedy, the result of flaws in the character of both management and labor that caused them to fail to coop-erate in the face of foreign competition.[6]

By contrast, I argue that the industrialization of Pittsburgh from the beginning deviated from the allegedly "normal" path of capitalist develop-ment, in which entrepreneurs competed within a free market arbitrated by a neutral state. While government was generally neutral in the competi-tion among capitalists, it refused to grant workers the legal rights that it extended to big business. Furthermore, throughout the nineteenth century, and well into the mid-twentieth century, the steel industry benefited enormously from state assistance, although it was less favored by the late 1950s. Therefore, deindustrialization was less a failure on industrialists' part than a strategy: industrialists did not build steel mills in order to perfect industrial technology, to develop American society, or to provide jobs; they did so in order to make money. Steel was simply a means to an end. Industrialists amassed spectacular profits from steel for many years, but when it became more profitable for steelmakers not to make steel, they invested elsewhere. That is the normal process for capitalists, albeit one that has had disastrous results for many workers and their communi-ties. To put the case thus does not mean that companies did not also invest in steel, or that all managers and supervisors were members of a vast conspiracy. However, it seems to me to be crucial to understand the strategies and trajectory of capital over long periods of time, important both in its own right and as a way to understand deindustrialization.

My work has also benefited from Judith Stein's *Running Steel, Running America: Race, Economics, Policy and the Decline of Liberalism*. Stein argues that because of the enormous importance of steel to policy makers, and vice versa, several Presidents of the United States, as well as several Presidents of U.S. Steel, helped to determine the fate of steel mills and their workers. My work seeks to join Stein's in pushing labor historians to move beyond the old dichotomy of workplace versus community studies, and to understand the ways that politics has shaped the possibilities and limits of corporations and trade unionists. Like Stein's, this study argues that the foreign commitments of political elites shifted public policy away from traditional subsidies to national industries. Furthermore, Stein's work and this study argue that understanding steelworkers and the USWA requires distinguishing between the economic and political pressures on, and strategies of, unionists at the local, regional, and national levels. Like Stein, this study views the question of race as a central political issue, although Stein sees more benign intent on behalf of the leaders of the USWA towards their black members, a point with which this study respectfully disagrees.[7]

Bruce Nelson also analyzed the explosive issue of civil rights within the USWA in *Divided We Stand: American Workers and the Struggle for Black Equality*. Nelson analyzes the struggles of black workers within the steel industry all over the United States and compares their history to that of longshoremen. Like this study, Nelson argues that for black workers, and regarding civil rights in steel more generally, the issue of seniority was critically important. Nelson's analysis of discrimination throughout the steel industry allows him to conclude that as far as job discrimination went, "there was no Mason-Dixon line in steel." The persistence of racial discrimination in the steel industry, upheld in part by the seniority system and ignored in large part by the USWA and its Civil Rights Committee, points to a profound failure of solidarity. However, this study differs from Nelson's in some important ways. For Nelson, white workers proved the most important obstacle to black workers, whereas this study argues that steel companies and government bear greater responsibility. Nelson argues that on questions of civil rights and seniority, the early 1950s, with its relatively full employment, saw enormous progress; by contrast, this study argues that by 1950, the fight for civil rights in steel was dead, killed by the enormous ideological and political restrictions of the Cold War.[8]

Finally, my study of steelworkers has been greatly enriched by Jack Metzgar's *Striking Steel: Solidarity Remembered.* Metzgar seeks to shatter the view that the 1950s were simply a decade of conformity, arguing that this decade saw more strikes by workers, including the marathon 1959 steel strike, than any other in the century. Whatever the limitations of the USWA from the perspective of radicals, the union made it possible for hundreds of thousands of working-class families to move out of poverty, no small achievement. Furthermore, the ability of unions to raise working-class standards of living laid the groundwork not just for consumerism, but for the liberation movements of the 1960s and thereafter.[9] One has only to look at Pittsburgh, Youngstown, Philadelphia, Detroit, or a host of other cities today, to understand how the decline of strong unions has altered life for workers, their communities, and society in general.

Metzgar's work and my own, in somewhat different ways, seek to overcome the schism of radical scholarship regarding the New Deal and the CIO unions. Metzgar points to the fact that radicals enjoy a love-hate relationship to the New Deal, its liberalism, and the unions that promoted both. In broad terms, labor historians since the 1960s have often incorporated major parts of the New Left's perspective towards liberalism when scholars chronicled the fight for unions and reforms in the 1930s and 1940s. Labor historians emphasized the important roles played by radicals and socialists in helping secure the historic victories in those years. Yet many New Left scholars criticized the limits of both the New Deal and the CIO, particularly the former, pointing out that its philosophy was essentially pro-capitalist and its programs were often stunted, especially towards African Americans and workers. For instance, historians often observe that the Social Security Act and the Fair Labor Standards Act did not cover domestics or farm laborers, who made up the majority of black workers. Scholars such as Thomas Sugrue observed that New Deal housing programs like the Federal Housing Authority subsidized private housing in all-white suburbs, while other programs spent relatively little on public housing, and even diverted public and private spending from housing in multi-racial urban neighborhoods. In assessing the impact of the New Deal on workers, many labor historians are justified in qualifying their assessments: were all-white blue-collar suburbs a victory for workers, a partial victory for white workers, banks, and contractors, or a defeat for inter-racial neighborhoods?[10]

When the subject of analysis turns to the years after World War II, the split between radical and liberal scholars' views towards the New Deal and unions becomes most acute. Most labor historians emphasize the extent to which liberals and the majority of the unions joined the anti-communist crusade of the 1950s, to the detriment of union democracy, black workers, and ultimately unionism itself. Scholars have largely ignored the victories won by liberals and trade unionists in the 1950s and 1960s, emphasizing instead the extent to which both embraced the military-industrial complex and white supremacy of the Cold War years. But important victories were won; for instance, in 1956, the labor movement won increases in the minimum wage, and in 1961, it extended the minimum wage to service workers who had initially been excluded from the Fair Labor Standards Act. One can only imagine how many hours a week fast food workers would labor today, and at what wages, had workers not won such a victory during the past. When labor historians analyze the years after 1973, when unions, liberalism, and New Deal programs faced serious threats, and sometimes succumbed to their enemies, scholars emphasize the extent to which unions and government made life bearable for workers. Only when compared to the present, when workers have been forced to defend their unions or New Deal programs, can many radicals appreciate the difference the New Deal made in working people's lives.

Because this book analyzes steelworkers in the non-union and union eras, both before and after the New Deal, it sheds light on the ways that the New Deal contributed to the organization of workers and their quality of life. The USWA led steelworkers to a more affluent life, and it did so within the political and legal context of the New Deal. Before the New Deal, historians would be hard pressed to find a situation where profitable and powerful employers eliminated jobs as a result of new technology, but workers still won strikes and indeed, won higher wages and benefits with each strike. The USWA and the New Deal helped create, even in the midst of the Cold War, something like a political democracy (admittedly less so for black workers, and not at all for radical ones) in what had long been a stronghold of industrial feudalism where the only votes that counted were those of coal barons and iron lords.

I have attempted to heed Jack Metzgar's call to indicate how workers won their victories, and to point out the difference that these victories made in workers' lives. But like other radical scholars, I analyze the limitations of unions or liberalism. Collective action can work; indeed, the history you are about to read shows that workers have won numerous victories when they have discovered ways to work together. But capitalists also learn from the past, and they have also discovered new tactics, in the workplace and in the realm of politics, that have allowed them to win at workers' expense. Until that lesson is learned, and incorporated into workers' political and union strategies, every victory will prove fleeting.

Chapter One

⁂

The Secret of Industrialization in Pittsburgh

"Here as nowhere else in America, the growth and development of the capitalistic system of mass production has prepared the way by precept and example . . . for the rapid and stalwart growth of the revolutionary proletariat. There is but one thing lacking, viz.: leaders."

Albert Parsons, 1886.[1]

OVERVIEW

Pittsburgh is well known as a labor town. The founding conventions of what would become the American Federation of Labor (1881) and the Congress of Industrial Organizations (1938) were held in the Steel City.[2] Yet in the 1920s, the labor movement in Pittsburgh and throughout the nation was weak and isolated from the commanding heights of the economy: coal, steel, electrical machinery, and railroads. However, beginning in the mid-1930s, unions began to organize factory workers, and by the late 1940s, most of heavy industry's workforce belonged to a labor organization. Strikes by coal, steel, or railroad workers threatened to bring the national economy to a standstill, and workers won gradual improvements to their rates of pay and working conditions. The last major strikes by Pittsburgh's industrial workers occurred in the 1980s and failed to affect the national economy. They ended in defeat. In the 1990s, less than 14 percent of American workers belonged to a union, less than half of comparable levels of organization in the 1950s. Today, trade unionists think twice before going

1

out on strike, and successful national strikes (such as the 1997 struggle at UPS) are rare events.

Nonetheless, the city's history of labor militance apparently continues to trouble corporate, media, and university elites who all regularly cite the specter of big labor as one of the chief causes for sluggish regional investment in the 1980s and 1990s.[3] Yet employers, not unions, shape the terms of the region's labor markets and most of the centers of Pittsburgh's post-industrial economy—health care, higher education, services, and corporate research—are nearly 100 percent non-union. As a result, rates of income inequality, once amongst the lowest in the Commonwealth, are now among the highest. Whether measured by access to jobs, housing, or heath care, Pittsburgh's racial inequality is also amongst the worst in the country. Job losses have been so severe and sustained that Pittsburgh boasts the largest geriatric population of any big city outside of Florida. Labor lacks the organizational strength or political understanding to reverse the levels of economic and racial polarization that have become as bad as conditions before the CIO was founded.[4]

Labor scholars, leaders, and members all agree that since the late 1970s, unions and workers have confronted tough times and that substantial legal, economic, and cultural barriers confront current organizing efforts. It is my contention that to begin to understand the decline of labor and its embattled and intimidated nature in the present, we have to investigate the real forces behind its rise in the 1930s. In this decade, industrial unions arose on a mass scale never seen before or since. It was a heady time when millions of workers joined strikes, organized unions, and altered the political priorities of the country towards the needs and aspirations of workers. At the center of those changes was the CIO, and to understand its influence on America and Pittsburgh, one must understand the answers to a series of questions. How did the CIO organize in the workplace? How did it carry out its political aims? How well did it overcome, or seek to overcome, various forms of racial, ethnic, and gender discrimination in the workplace? What kinds of responses did the CIO engender from big business? From government? In short, how did the CIO contest for power, how much did it win, and how well did it consolidate it?

The dominant account of the unionization of U.S. Steel in 1937 offers an excellent vantage point for understanding how the CIO changed the relationship between Western Pennsylvania's working and owning classes. This was one of the most important incidents in the history of modern labor, and consequently many of the facts of the story are well known to labor historians. The first ingredient in the unionization of steel was the resurgence of the United Mine Workers of America (UMWA) in the mid-1930s. The UMWA organized the coal industry on an industrial basis, that is all workers regardless of occupation, race, or ethnicity were eligible for membership. In 1933–34, miners, including tens of thousands around Pittsburgh, took advantage of New Deal legislation that afforded organizing workers protection from company retaliation. Union membership mushroomed. One major employer of miners refused to bargain: steel companies. As long as steel companies supplied their mills with non-union coal, the fate of the UMWA was precarious. So mineworkers' leader John L. Lewis went on the offensive by launching the CIO and a host of industrial unions in steel, auto, meatpacking, and other areas. The Steel Workers Organizing Committee (the SWOC) hired numerous communist organizers, who were especially important in signing up large numbers of immigrant, black, and Mexican workers around Pittsburgh. Meanwhile, in the winter of 1936–37 CIO auto workers engaged in a brilliant sit-down strike that resulted in victory against General Motors by February of 1937. The head of U.S. Steel, Myron Taylor, was a so-called enlightened capitalist who recognized the inevitability of unionization and sought out a pleasantly surprised Lewis to hammer out a deal. By early March, the two arrived at the basic framework. Steelworkers received five dollars a day for eight hours of work with some provision for seniority, vacations and union representation. The company signed a nationwide agreement with the SWOC, an agreement so unexpected and momentous that one SWOC top official later called it a "miracle."[5]

There are many reasons why this account of the founding of the SWOC has become the most popular narrative. It is dramatic, heroic, and mostly true. But there are a number of questions that the story does not answer. First and foremost, why didn't U.S. Steel call the SWOC's bluff? U.S. Steel had a long history as one of the most aggressively anti-union companies in America, and other large steel firms successfully resisted the union for several more years. Big steel had recently defeated an organizing drive by the AFL's Amalgamated Association of Iron, Steel and Tin Workers (the Amalgamated), and before that it had bested the Steel and Metal Workers Industrial Union, an organization connected to the Communist Party. "The Corporation" had huge reserves of money, an army of spies, and stacks of machine guns and tear gas in their mills. Of course, so had General Motors. But General Motors only agreed to recognize the union in those workplaces where the CIO could prove it had the majority of workers' support. By contrast, the SWOC gained a national contract despite its relatively weak shop-floor organization. In Pittsburgh, most of the workers who had joined the union paid no dues and were too scared to support the union openly. According to Philip Murray, the union's chief organizer, steelworkers were "shot through with fear."[6] Whether or not the steelworkers could have won a strike (and subsequent events suggest that a strike might have gone either way) U.S. Steel did not have to agree to a *national* contract. Important questions about why the SWOC triumphed remain unanswered by the dominant narrative.

The secret to U.S. Steel's "generosity" resulted from a profound shift in the political priorities of both the Pennsylvania and the federal governments. Indeed, I contend that a key factor behind U.S. Steel's recognition of the SWOC was military contracts. For decades, U.S. Steel had supplied enormous amounts of war materiel to the federal government and "the Corporation" benefited mightily from it. U.S. Steel's place in the military-industrial complex began in the 1880s when Andrew Carnegie (who later sold his company to U.S. Steel) sold armor plate to the U.S. Navy. Carnegie enjoyed extremely close relations with key naval officers who inspected his product and informed him of government policies and potential contracts.[7] With only two suppliers—later three—the Secretary of the Navy found that "their policy is to make the government pay much beyond a fair profit." One shipbuilder confessed that "if I could get the profit on armor plate, I would build a war ship at cost."[8] Andrew Carnegie's armor profits enabled him to pay cash for the Mesabi Iron Range, then the richest source of iron ore in the world. During World War I the price of armor plate skyrocketed to seven times its pre-war price before the government convinced the companies to accept 258 percent of the prewar price. Skyrocketing wartime prices allowed U.S. Steel in 1917 to garner a $600-million profit on a total investment of just $1,600 million. Close ties to the Commonwealth of Pennsylvania's monolithic Republican party machine, which lost only three statewide elections between the 1870s and 1934, protected steelmakers' lucrative public market from numerous attempts by Populist and Progressive legislators to build a government armor mill. U.S. Senator Boise Penrose (R-PA) admitted that public ownership would prevent "the money of the taxpayer [from pouring] out like water in a lavish and improvident way." But Penrose fought the government mill until his death in 1921 because the taxpayers' money poured into the pockets of his constituents. Only in 1921 was the government armory finally completed. For a brief time it operated efficiently and was quietly dismantled.[9] Little armor was rolled in the 1920s, and most of it by private firms.

In 1937, the Corporation's military contracts made it vulnerable to political pressure. The SWOC drive coincided with an enormous U.S. and British naval construction program on the eve of what promised to be a major European war. Furthermore, an investigating committee headed by Senator Gerald P. Nye (R-ND) looked into the close and profitable relationship between government officials and large military contractors. The outrage of progressive Congressmen was a familiar, if unwelcome, aspect of supplying armor to the navy. Yet the controversy refused to die, and labor reform legislation (notably the 1935 National Labor Relations Act) signaled the willingness of Congress to act. Furthermore, steel firms refused to abandon the forty-eight-hour week, thereby flouting the 1936 Walsh-Healy Act which required government contractors to employ workers for no more than forty hours a week. The Labor Department forced the navy to enforce a ban on granting contracts to corporate lawbreakers. Throughout the winter of 1936–37, construction on several ships ground to a halt for lack of twelve thousand tons of armor plate. In late February, members of the Cabinet mused that it might be necessary to restart the government's Charleston, West Virginia, armor plant. Rather than lose military orders, steel companies negotiated to bring their labor practices in line with federal policy. And the government only accepted new bids on naval contracts after the ink was dry on the contract between U.S. Steel and the SWOC.[10]

Thus, U.S. Steel's March 2, 1937, agreement on wages and hours was a concession to the government as much as to the SWOC.[11] Unsurprisingly, the union contract specified little more than the new minimum standards for government contractors of a forty-hour week and a five dollar day for workers. (Perhaps as a quid pro quo, the government later leased its armor mill in Charleston to U.S. Steel). The intervention of the federal government into industrial relations points to the importance of politics and the state to the rise of modern unionism. Whatever inducements were offered at the secret meetings between politicians, businessmen, and union officials should not obscure the fact that for the first time in decades, workers had a seat at the table of power politics.

CIO unions were unabashedly political and left a profound legacy for us in federal law and programs. The CIO and its predecessors pressured government to increase workers' social wage through reforms such as public

relief (beginning with the 1933 Federal Emergency Relief Act), unemployment insurance and social security (the 1935 Social Security Act), public
housing (1937 National Housing Act), and the minimum wage and the
forty-hour week (the 1938 Fair Labor Standards Act). These policies essentially allowed workers to win, through the political process, some of what
they lost through market forces. Such programs marked a profound change
in the relationship between American citizens and government. One
aspect of that shift was that state government was frequently eclipsed as an
arbitrator of relations between business and labor.[12] Equally important,
workers gained their "industrial citizenship," and government responded—
at least to a degree—to their interests.[13]

The fact that steel unionism (and one might argue the New Deal more
generally) flowed from the barrel of the gun remains an important irony
because for the previous seventy years, the secret of Pittsburgh's industrialization was the legal repression of labor. Government's extensive and
often brutal policing of labor, often joined by capital, profoundly shaped the
industrialization of the Pittsburgh region. Beginning in the 1850s, government consistently privileged capital and beggared labor. The state undermined workers' ability to organize or to shape labor markets. The state facilitated the control of a few industrialists over an ever-larger portion of the
region's resources, markets, and labor power. Pittsburgh's industrialization—
its transition from competitive capitalism in the middle of the nineteenth
century to monopoly capitalism by 1900, and the subsequent dominance of
a few large firms over the region—was thus a political process as much as an
economic one. For this reason, this chapter examines the efforts of business
and workers to shape the development of the political and manufacturing
process between the middle of the nineteenth century and 1937. Because of
the political and police hegemony of big business, the road to steelworkers'
victory in 1937 was a long one. To understand SWOC's victory (and its limitations) one must assess how its predecessors grappled with questions of
political and workplace organization in the face of an extremely heterogeneous working class and an extremely powerful and ruthless owning class
and government.

THE ECLIPSE OF COMPETITIVE CAPITALISM

In the decades after 1800, Pittsburgh developed into a manufacturing region
that supplied the rapidly growing western portions of the United States.

Until the 1850s, the region's abundant forests provided the fuel (generally in the form of charcoal) for the manufacture of iron and other energy-intensive industries such as railroads and glass making. The Ohio River provided industrial entrepreneurs with a ready route to supply the farmers, slaveowners, and merchants who colonized the vast river valleys of the Middle West and South. Manifest Destiny, in the form of the country's "Indian wars," conflicts with Britain, and the Mexican adventure of 1846–48, required vast amounts of weapons, uniforms, and other goods. Each war simultaneously expanded the American market and stimulated manufacturing in Pittsburgh. After the 1830s, industrialization accelerated when workers began to mine the region's rich seams of coal. By 1840, the Pittsburgh region shipped approximately 25,000 tons of coal down river a year. By 1860, nearly one-sixth of Allegheny County's 20,000 workers were coal miners, and the region sold well over 1 million tons of coal. Prodigious amounts of coal melted iron in blast and puddling furnaces and powered the growing number of rolling mills. As the 1860 *Manufacturing Census* observed, "the growth of Pittsburgh, which had coal at its very doors, is very much due to this cause."[14]

While Pittsburgh's rapid growth increased the size of its industries and the wealth of its industrialists, manufacturers lacked monopoly power over markets. No group of firms or banks dominated the production or prices of raw materials, labor, or manufactured goods. In coal, the legal and financial barriers to entry were so low that overproduction remained a chronic problem. Numerous transportation companies vied to haul goods on the rivers. The supply of capital remained scattered among numerous small banks, although two or three had already emerged whose capitalization was several times that of the average bank.

This is not to say that industrialists lacked power. The iron industry was relatively concentrated, and one-third of the mills sold two-thirds of Pittsburgh's metal.[15] Large companies such as Jones and Laughlin (J&L) formed when Benjamin Jones and James Laughlin merged their companies because "they decided they could make more money being partners than by being competitors."[16] The sheer size of a few firms and the "fear of the employers blacklist" allowed them to dominate workers and thereby labor markets. As one unionist later recalled, even skilled workers "had become accustomed, through years of hard practice, to accept the fiat of employers."[17] But even the largest iron makers bought their raw materials and sold their finished products in a relatively free marketplace.[18] Pittsburgh stood on the threshold of a new round of economic growth that would simultaneously increase the scale of industry and concentrate its ownership into fewer hands.

Two entities that propelled Pittsburgh towards monopoly capitalism at mid-century were the Commonwealth of Pennsylvania and the Pennsylvania Railroad. The state legislature exercised enormous economic power in part because of its right to grant or deny corporate charters. The corporate form, which limited the liability of managers and investors, greatly facilitated the accumulation of capital so necessary for large-scale industrial firms. But to prevent the formation of powerful monopolies, the state restricted corporations to specific sets of economic activity for a limited number of years. As early as the 1830s, in order to encourage industrialization, the Commonwealth began to ease its restrictions on corporations in capital-intensive areas such as railroads and iron.[19] Nonetheless, the legislature still individually wrote each charter, and the Pennsylvania Railroad became adept at manipulating the chartering process to enrich itself and confound its competitors. One notable instance of skullduggery occurred in 1847 when the Pennsylvania blocked the Baltimore and Ohio from completing its line through the state into Pittsburgh by convincing the state legislature to grant the Pennsylvania Railroad exclusive rights to statewide traffic.[20] Over the next several years, the Pennsylvania and other railroad firms convinced many municipalities and the state itself to finance connections to the main line. Ostensibly to ensure its competitive position vis-à-vis other cities, between 1849 and 1854, Pittsburgh purchased $1.8 million dollars worth of railroad stock. Most companies went bankrupt, and within a few years the city's investments were sold for a mere $7,000. The completion of the Pennsylvania's system merely changed the form and rationale of public subsidies. In 1857, the Commonwealth sold its statewide canal system and other rights of way to the Pennsylvania Railroad at a substantial discount. Such practices were so common that later that year voters amended the state constitution to ban the practice of publicly financing private companies.[21]

In the 1860s, the impetus of railroad expansion and wartime spending accelerated Pittsburgh's industrialization. The government with its "navy, vast workshops and other establishments during the late rebellion" absorbed the output of Pittsburgh's foundries, rolling mills, railroads, and coal mines. Pennsylvania supplied over half of the iron and 80 percent of the coal for the Union; war contracts rendered these trades "unusually prosperous."

Ten percent of all iron was rolled in Allegheny County alone. During the war, the average price of a ton of bar-iron increased by 50 percent, and the employment of capital and labor in the iron and steel industries in Allegheny County quadrupled during the 1860s. The value of its products increased sevenfold.[22] The hectic growth of railroads consumed about half of the metal and almost one-quarter of the coal produced in the Pittsburgh district.[23] The coking coal fields south of Pittsburgh fueled 80 percent of the country's iron furnaces, and one survey estimated that they were worth one thousand times more than all gold mined in California.[24] As a center of coal mining, iron making, and railroad manufacture, Pittsburgh supplied the building blocks of industrial expansion to the country. To its owners flowed a king's ransom.

Industrialization was accompanied by an expansion of the political influence of big business. During wartime the passage of special legislation dwarfed all other concerns. For instance, in April 1861, the legislature dropped the tonnage tax on the Pennsylvania Railroad, saving the corporation $700,000 in back taxes alone. Between 1866 and 1873, 95 percent of the laws passed by the legislature were special acts.[25] One railroad magnate boasted to a colleague that "I have taken money there [to Harrisburg] myself to corrupt the legislature."[26] Not surprisingly, "public" laws also served the interests of big business. In 1866, the Commonwealth permitted industrial corporations to employ uniformed and armed police, ostensibly to protect their property. In hundreds of coal camps and unincorporated mill towns, thousands of "Coal and Iron Police" possessed the monopoly of legal, if not completely legitimate, coercive power.[27] The *National Labor Tribune* labeled "the great Commonwealth of Pennsylvania . . . the catspaw of these combinations" which granted companies the power to "intimidate the work people and rule them with an iron rod."[28] By 1873, corporate influence over the legislature had become so pervasive that voters convened a Constitutional Convention that attempted to place meaningful distinctions between the legislature and the state's corporations. For instance, the General Assembly was forbidden to abrogate its powers of taxation over corporations. Under the new popular guidelines, railroads would function as "public highways" and common carriers.[29] The new laws barely interrupted the emerging public-private consensus between politicians and corporations.

Even as the Commonwealth did its utmost to smooth the path for corporate growth and profits, it impeded workers from combining to advance their interests. Courts and lawmakers considered unions de facto conspiracies whose chief aim was to monopolize labor markets. In 1815, some of Pittsburgh's first unionists were convicted of conspiracy for attempting to enforce a common wage scale with their employers.[30] Unlike businesses, unions were not allowed to incorporate, and their members and officers had few protections against personal liability for the actions of members of their organization. By 1842, the state courts grudgingly began to accept trade unions as legitimate organizations, although not until 1869 did the legislature pass a law that established the legal basis for unions. Yet the Commonwealth's labor law punished unionists who "hindered" those who sought work during strikes. Public pressure resulted in an 1872 law that limited sanctions to so-called violent hindering, but many miners and other unionists served up to four months in jail for encouraging workers not to cross picket lines. In one infamous case, mineworkers from Westmoreland County were severely fined for "hindering" strikebreakers with a brass band.[31] One trade unionist bitterly summed up labor's legal history: "the law and the judges are against workingmen. Whatever workingmen do to protect their wages is 'unreasonable and oppressive.'"[32] The right to organize, so freely provided to industrialists by the Commonwealth, was largely denied to workers.

The political influence and enormous size of railroads enabled them to transform the laws not just of Pennsylvania but of the marketplace itself. By the early 1870s, the Pennsylvania had grown larger than all other railroads in the Commonwealth combined; the line employed 200,000 men, making it the country's largest private employer.[33] Its capital requirements and ability to borrow exceeded that of the state whose name it assumed. Until the 1890s, there was no effective regulation other than corporate policy to determine the "market" price for shipping. No law barred railroads from establishing rate pools that raised the cost of shipping several times that of lines with effective competition. Strong firms sometimes joined forces with railroads. In the case of Standard Oil, which refined much of the crude oil produced in Western Pennsylvania, John D. Rockefeller convinced the railroads to pay Standard Oil a rebate from the shipping costs of other oil companies. Railroads thus accelerated the trend towards the centralization of oil refining and helped to ensure that its center would be Cleveland rather than Pittsburgh.[34] A well-known joke was that when the Pennsylvania Railroad had no further business, the state legislature could adjourn.

In 1877, Pennsylvania passed a law that made strikes against railroad companies all but illegal. Within weeks, a massive railroad strike convulsed the state and nation.[35] The immediate cause of the Great Strike of 1877 was a 10 percent wage cut, but it also represented a direct, if disorganized, protest of railroads' economic and political control. Pennsylvania was a strike center, and many members of Pittsburgh's working class enthusiastically joined the fray. One radicalized ironworker said that "I won't call employers despots, I won't call them tyrants, but the term 'capitalist' is sort of synonymous and will do as well." The local militia, itself recruited largely from Pittsburgh's working class, refused to discipline the strikers.[36] The Governor brought in regiments from Philadelphia, but after shooting at least twenty workers, including three children, the Guard was driven out of town by armed workers. According to an owner of an iron mill, "matters grew from bad to worse and the crowd swelled into proportions beyond all control made up of the worst element around the city."[37] A Pittsburgh newspaper observed that "there is no disguising the matter. The people of this city sympathize with the strikers. They are incensed beyond measure with the cold, corrupt legislation which has fostered the colder and more corrupt organization known as the Pennsylvania Railroad."[38] Before federal and state troops restored order and broke the strike, over one hundred died throughout the nation, half of them in Pennsylvania.[39]

The Great Strike stimulated strikes by ironworkers. The private secretary of one of the owners of J&L observed that the dramatic events of July "had a bad effect on the laboring classes" at the firm's American Iron Works. "After holding an excitable meeting, they have all (some 350 men) marched out of the mill saying they must have 25 cents per day added to their wages."[40] In part because the mill was well guarded and the military and vigilantes patrolled the streets the strikers failed in their "attempt to have the firemen and foundry hands join them." They "did not succeed, *used no force*." Laborers did, however, have the support of the puddlers, who had just forced Benjamin Jones, one of J&L's owners, to accept a one-year contract on June 12.[41] At mass meetings of strikers, such as that of the "unterrified," "speeches were made advising the holding out of the men."[42] Production at the mill slowed considerably. On August 13, Jones observed that the strikers were "still out. Foundry and machine shop worked all last week. Rest of the mill all out."[43] Managers failed to restart the mill, and the hands decided to return to work en masse. "The firm has made no concessions but will of its own accord" raise "some of the eighty cent men to $1 per day . . . Great rejoicing, so the strike is ended and we are all glad of it."[44]

Even after the riots were repressed and the strikes settled, the aftershocks of the Great Strike reverberated through the body politic. The Pennsylvania legislature attempted to compensate the Pennsylvania Railroad for property destroyed during the riot, but a bribery scandal prevented the passage of the $4 million bill. Instead, the courts forced Allegheny County to pay over $1.5 million in damages to the railroad on the basis that local government had not kept the peace. The refusal of the company to negotiate with its workers was ignored as a possible cause of the upheaval.[45]

In the wake of 1877, politicians colluded with railroad barons and other big businessmen as the latter sought to safeguard their interests by making the National Guard more effective for strike duty. Numerous units, particularly those from working-class districts, were disbanded. Professionals and businessmen now comprised nearly all of the Guard's officers. Oliver S. Hershman, editor and publisher of the *Pittsburgh Press*, was typical of the new bourgeois colonels whose activism in the Republican Party complemented his other civic duties. Hershman once owned the *Pittsburgh Evening Telegraph*, which the official historian of the Guard found was of "a conservative character that made it a great power for good in the community."[46] (By contrast, union men considered it to be "owned body, soul and breeches by the railway interests generally, and the Pennsylvania Railroad Company particularly."[47]) The legislature greatly expanded military expenditures to supply the state militia with better equipment and to compensate its members for time spent on duty. For its part, the Pennsylvania Railroad, in addition to its contributions of tents and other supplies, relayed a standing offer to transport the entire Guard to any point in the state within twenty-four hours.[48] Until the formation of the State Police in 1905, the National Guard was deployed dozens of times to police major industrial disputes.[49] One historian has characterized the changes in the social composition of the militia as the process whereby "the captains of industry became captains of the army."[50] Although the wealthiest industrialists preferred to call upon rather than participate in the Guard, the observation was essentially correct.

To contemporary observers, and some historians, the Great Strike was the American equivalent of the Paris Commune. This comparison overstates the political advance made by American workers, who unlike their Parisian counterparts had not seized state power nor run the factories independently of their owners. In Paris, thousands (and not dozens) of workers died at the hands of their government. In Paris and elsewhere in Europe, the specter of socialism, often in the corporeal form of Socialist Parties and radical unions, threatened to transform the economic organization of society. While the railroad strike reflected the widespread resentment to the economic and political power of industrial corporations, in Pittsburgh and throughout the United States, the chief challenge to the free market arose not from a radicalized working class (most unions decried the violence in 1877 as counterproductive) but from the ranks of businessmen who increasingly mimicked the Pennsylvania Railroad by monopolizing other sectors of the economy.[51]

THE RISE OF ANDREW CARNEGIE

Andrew Carnegie epitomized the ruthless spirit and organizational skills of those entrepreneurs whose very success under competitive capitalism provided them with the means to destroy it. Carnegie came to America an impoverished Scottish immigrant, and his meteoric rise to business titan was and is the stuff of legend. His skills as a telegraph operator brought him to the attention of Thomas Scott of the Pennsylvania Railroad. He quickly became a member of the "inner circle" of the Pennsylvania, arguably the world's largest, best run, and most politically influential corporation. By 1859, at the tender age of twenty-four, Carnegie became the superintendent for the Pittsburgh district of the Pennsylvania. His skill in selling railroad bonds, even in the midst of severe depressions, made him especially valuable to Scott. Backed by the capital, connections, and good name of Scott and other managers of the Pennsylvania, Carnegie made a number of shrewd investments in oil, telegraphs, railroad car, and railroad bridge companies that made him one of the wealthiest men in Pittsburgh by the time he was thirty-three. Carnegie became an iron maker when he purchased the Keystone Bridge Company, which manufactured iron railroad bridges. In his later career as an iron master, his intimate relationships with and understanding of railroads, ability to raise large amounts of capital, and killer instinct would eventually make him the richest man in the world.[52]

The impact of railroads on the iron and steel industries was profound. Railroads demanded prodigious amounts of iron rails for new track and especially to replace worn rails. Carnegie convinced railroads that rails made from the new Bessemer steel process were superior to iron rails. By the 1880s, railroads consumed almost 90 percent of Bessemer steel. In 1875, Carnegie named his first steel mill in Braddock, Pennsylvania, after the then-President of the Pennsylvania Railroad, J. Edgar Thomson. Flattery and low prices won him a long-term contract with the railroad. Railroads were also the chief means of supplying mills with raw materials and shipping steel to markets. And while the relative importance of railroads to steel makers halved over the next two decades, in terms of tonnage consumed, railroads remained a crucial market.

But the very importance of railroads made them an "economic narrows." To lessen his tribute to these latter-day corsairs, Carnegie situated his mill near the lines of both the Pennsylvania and the Baltimore and Ohio.[53] But in the face of rampant price-fixing, Carnegie struggled relentlessly in the coming years to reduce his shipping prices. In 1884, he attempted to break the Pennsylvania's stranglehold over his mills by allying himself with the Vanderbilt interests who sought to build a new route through Pennsylvania. But the Pennsylvania bought out the Vanderbilts, and the rates rose again. Carnegie attempted to defeat the Pennsylvania in its home ground of the state legislature. He failed. After years of wrangling, Carnegie won a secret rate rebate on steel shipped by his competitors. He also created his own railroad, the Union Railway. The railroad paid for itself simply by eliminating the charges paid to the Pennsylvania and B&O to move goods inside Carnegie's mills. With only 100 miles of track, it shipped more freight than the Union Pacific, Northern Pacific and the Missouri Pacific combined. Yet Carnegie felt the Pennsylvania was charging him more than other firms to ship coke and iron ore, and in 1899 he laid plans to extend the Union to Lake Erie and ally himself with Jay Gould to have untrammeled access to the Minnesota ore field.[54] Carnegie's tactics interfered with the machinations of other railroad and steel barons, notably J.P. Morgan. In 1901, Morgan paid Carnegie $492 million for his steel company, removing Carnegie from the railroad business. It was an astronomical sum. As we will see, it was worth every penny.

Despite Carnegie's antipathy to the railroads, they were his industrial mentors. What Carnegie learned from the railroads helped make his mills marvels of efficiency. Until the 1870s, melting iron and rolling it were done in different workshops. Carnegie reorganized the Edgar Thomson Works (ET) so that all aspects of iron making occurred in one complex. An internal system of railroads connected its workshops and minimized delays. The result was one of the world's first "integrated" steel mills; ET could produce as many rails "in a day as had been produced in all of Pittsburgh in a year in the 1830s." Opened in the midst of a depression, the ET nonetheless turned a profit. In 1889, fourteen years after it opened, ET produced 25 times more steel than it had in 1875 and at half the cost per ton. Carnegie methodically reduced production costs through the judicious use of proven technology, low wages, and incentives for his managerial staff. In order to increase their incentive to watch costs, junior partners were paid with company shares rather than in money, and by the 1890s, even a one-sixth of 1 percent share was worth $450,000. Carnegie incorporated the Pennsylvania Railroad's advanced system of accounting and tracked production costs in every department in his firm. His maxim was to "watch the costs and the profits will take care of themselves."[55]

Such efficiency placed relentless pressure on Carnegie's competitors. One biographer observed that Carnegie's tactics were to reach "out one hand to grasp the market," while "he constantly hammered at costs with the other."[56] In 1883, Carnegie bought the Homestead Works, an integrated steel mill downriver from Edgar Thomson. Homestead was originally a rail mill, but Carnegie recognized that the railroad boom could not last indefinitely and remade Homestead into a structural mill that supplied the building trade with beams and plate and the federal government with armor plate.[57] In 1886 Carnegie joined forces with Henry Clay Frick, thereby gaining control over half of the country's supply of coking coal. Carnegie's efficient mills, his alliance with Frick, and his access to the capital and prestige of the Pennsylvania Railroad made him a feared adversary.[58] He would enter pricing pools with other steel makers only to abandon them during depressions when he would relentlessly force prices further down. When marginal firms ran short of cash, Carnegie would buy their mills at a deep discount. By 1894, he had cornered one-quarter of the steel market. In the mid-1880s, competitors of Carnegie's built a highly modern mill in Duquesne, practically abutting both the Homestead and ET Works. Carnegie blocked this firm from joining the rail pool that supplied the Pennsylvania Railroad and other concerns, thereby depriving the mill of its natural market. On the edge of bankruptcy, the owners sold out, and the mill paid for itself six times over in the next five years.[59] In the 1890s, Frick prevailed upon Carnegie to buy half of the fantastically rich iron ore fields of the Mesabi Range in Minnesota. Carnegie leased the other half of the Mesabi range from John D. Rockefeller, and to prevent him from building a mill in Cleveland, Carnegie agreed to ship all his ore on Rockefeller's railroads.[60]

Carnegie dominated the market, largely on his own terms, and the results were profits that would have impressed Croesus.

Carnegie's enormous profits never dulled his desire for more. In 1888, his profits were $2 million; two years later his firm netted $5.4 million. Even in the midst of a depression, as in 1894, Carnegie's company made $4 million on a capitalization of just $25 million. The Spanish-American war of 1898 boosted profits to $11.5 million and in 1900, the firm earned an astounding $40 million.[61] Yet Carnegie often treated his partners little better than his competitors. Those he considered unproductive or untrust-worthy—or who simply rebelled against his avarice or his overbearing per-sonality—were pushed out through the use of an "iron clad" agreement that forced partners to sell their shares to Carnegie for their book rather than their market value.[62] Even Frick, whose coke and talents had done so much to develop the firm, was eventually driven out. In 1899, Carnegie sought to buy all its coking coal from Frick's company for $1.35 a ton while the market price was $3.50 a ton. Frick won a lawsuit against Carnegie, and the settlement brought Frick six times more than offered by the stock's book value. The lawsuit also exposed the enormous profits that accrued to Carnegie behind the walls of a tariff designed to protect "fledgling" indus-tries. Critics cried for the elimination of tariffs, but to no avail. Indeed, as early as 1876, Carnegie privately noted that "even if the tariff were off entirely, you couldn't send steel rails west of us."[63] Carnegie was simply ahead of the times as the Brookings Institute later found that "from about 1896 [until 1928] . . . the industry was independent of the tariff."[64] As his comment about the tariff suggests, Carnegie became a self-made man in part through the generosity of the public purse.

The chief way that steel's political capital reassumed its financial form was through the alchemy of armor contracts. In the late 1880s, Con-gress approved funding for a deep-water navy. Pennsylvania's Congressional delegation prevailed upon the navy to "buy American" from private com-panies. Carnegie Steel and Bethlehem Steel, both located in Pennsylvania, submitted identical bids of $600 a ton. With profit margins exceeding 60 percent, Carnegie privately confessed that "there is a good deal [of money] in the armor-making plants working in perfect unison." Later, he confessed to his managers qua lobbyists that he "must have that armor plate." Carnegie was caught selling armor plate to the Czar for a third of what he charged the U.S. Navy, and Congress capped prices at $350 a ton. But both Carnegie and Bethlehem refused to sell armor for less than $400 a ton, and prices soon crept back to $450. Even after a third competitor entered the field, profits remained at least $150-$200 a ton.[65] The navy's demand for armor plate steadily rose, from five thousand tons a year in the 1880s to six to seven times that in the early 1910s. A similar process in England caused Winston Churchill to remark that "the Admiralty had demanded six ships; the economists offered four; and we finally compromised on eight."[66]

The profits from military contracts facilitated the survival and expansion of Carnegie Steel and its successors. The profits from armor plate provided the $3 million in cash for Carnegie's purchase of Mesabi iron ore lands in 1896–97. Military contracts also saved Carnegie from his reckless habits. At the Homestead Works, the iron master had encouraged supervisors to run the mill flat out twice a year to set an almost impossibly high rate for "tonnage men." The result was chaos as completed orders disappeared under piles of "efficiently" produced steel, and other orders went unfinished. But, as one supervisor noted, the government "bought practically all the duplicate plates at high prices, thus cleaning up the whole mess." The government also footed the bill for the mill's subsequent modernizations.[67]

In the decades after the Civil War, industrialists like Carnegie transformed Pittsburgh into the undisputed center of American steel production. Companies such as Jones and Laughlin, National Tube, American Bridge, and Crucible took advantage of the region's coal fields, transportation network, and tough anti-union climate and crowded the Steel City's narrow flood plains with a nearly unbroken chain of mills and foundries.[68] A host of smaller firms supplied specialty markets, but they were eclipsed by the emerging monopoly corporations who divided up the market amongst themselves.[69] The sooty ash and acrid fumes of steel produced the unmistakably sweet smell of money. In 1899, Carnegie wrote to a friend that he was "ashamed to tell you the profits these days."[70] The precondition for Carnegie's "shameful" state of mind was the organization of the market on his terms, a process that necessitated disorganizing the industrial workforce. As one trade unionist observed, "consolidation, centralization of wealth is all the rage, and a very bad rage it is . . . to meet it is a simple problem in theory: Workmen must concentrate more closely in union."[71] Why such a simple theory remained so difficult in practice is the subject of the next section.

THE ORGANIZATIONS OF IRON AND STEELWORKERS

From the 1860s through the 1890s, ironworkers built some of the strongest craft unions in America. Largely denied legal protections, workers found that their skill formed the basis for their strength. Certain jobs such as puddling (refining high-quality iron) or rolling were crucial to any iron or steel mill and took years to learn. Puddlers formed the Sons of Vulcan in 1858, but employers' blacklists destroyed the organization of these "aristocrats of labor."[72] Puddlers rebuilt their organization in the 1860s, when "the war of rebellion finally evolved the opportunity." Even during the war boom, trade unionists "organized in secret" and then forced employers to improve wages. Ultimately wages rose or fell on a "sliding scale" that was indexed according to the market price of iron.[73] By 1873, three thousand five hundred puddlers had joined the Sons of Vulcan.[74] Other skilled craftsmen, such as iron rollers, formed separate organizations.[75] The sliding scale accounted for market fluctuations in iron prices but took wages out of competition, thereby stabilizing the lives of ironworkers (who made up 20 percent of Allegheny County's wage laborers) and the playing field for employers.[76]

Once unionized, skilled ironworkers enjoyed relative autonomy. The men who had mastered the secrets of iron making demanded and received a large measure of respect. One indication of this was that in the iron industry, the pay of rollers, heaters, and melters sometimes exceeded the pay of managers.[77] Skilled workers' tastes dominated the social and cultural landscape in what Francis Couvares described as a "craftsmen's empire."[78] Until the 1880s, skilled ironworkers resembled subcontractors who were paid so much per ton of metal that they produced. Furthermore, these craft workers had the power to hire and fire members of their crew. Their union regulated wages, working conditions, and access to the craft.[79]

During the depression of 1873, however, iron prices fell below the bottom levels of the scale, and employers slashed wages and attempted to destroy the union. The Sons of Vulcan was nearly destroyed during the bitter lockout of 1874–75. The Pittsburgh Bolt Company bought new equipment that was run by non-union puddlers from Virginia who received less than the sliding scale. The unionized rollers continued to honor their separate contract, a common occurrence at the time. Even after the rollers were convinced to join the strike, the non-union puddlers, "black in both color and principle," continued to work. According to one white trade unionist, "the firm [is] very anxious to get only one 'nigger' killed so they can call it a riot and call in the militia, and arrest a few puddlers, to demor-alize the rest." Several private police protected the strikebreakers, and the union skirted disaster. But strike support flowed into Pittsburgh, production lagged, and the puddlers soon forced companies to return to the sliding scale. The puddlers lost their national sliding scale, but maintained regional ones in a "dearly bought victory of labor over avarice." Yet the problems of new technology, limited solidarity, and the use of police to break strikes continued to bedevil unionists in the iron industry.[80]

Unionists responded by building broader organizations. In 1876, pud-dlers, rollers, and other crafts joined together in the Amalgamated Associa-tion of Iron and Steel Workers. The Amalgamated created greater possibil-ities for inter-craft solidarity, especially in Pittsburgh, its stronghold. In 1878, J&L refused to sign a contract with the "boilers" or puddlers because B.F. Jones "thinks owing to the great depression in business (particularly iron) that the 'sliding scale' should be a little lower." Jones was "surprised by a committee, or rather all the heaters coming to the office this after-noon and refusing to work longer than tomorrow unless the 'boilers' agree-ment' was signed." The next year, a joint committee of boilers, heaters, and rolling mill hands sought to convince Jones to extend the contract for another year. He locked them out and refused arbitration. But within a week, the manufacturers decided "under existing conditions it is inexpedi-ent to further resist the unjust demands of the boilers."[81]

Yet solidarity had its limits. Not until 1881 did the Amalgamated allow blacks to join Jim Crow lodges. Not until 1889 could lodges (or locals of the Amalgamated) admit common laborers. Their inclusion tempered but did not dissolve the tension between craft workers and their subordi-nates. Finally, craft rivalries plagued the Amalgamated.[82] Although the Amalgamated evolved towards greater solidarity, it only partially overcame the hierarchies of the workplace.

An even broader form of union arose in the 1870s: the Knights of Labor. The Knights sought to organize all workers into one union regard-less of occupation, sex, or race.[83] In 1875–76, coal miners and laborers joined the Knights in impressive numbers. One worker observed "such was the excitement in the Pittsburgh district . . . that a man must have been dull indeed not to know that some kind of secret organization was being organized, and very rapidly too."[84] At many iron mills, unskilled workers joined the Knights. Cooperation with the Amalgamated was somewhat strained. The Knights had a more inclusive organization and favored creating worker-owned cooperatives to replace private factories. They also advocated shortening the workday to eight hours. Not only was the Amalgamated more politically conservative, but skilled workers opposed giving unskilled workers an equal voice in the union. Furthermore, because Amalgamated members were paid on the number of tons they produced in a day (the tonnage system), they did not seek a workday shorter than ten hours or the time it took to make five "heats" of iron.[85] Although one of the largest assemblies in the country, Pittsburgh's Knights failed to match the organizational power of their employers. Although thousands of coal miners and steelworkers joined striking railroad workers in 1877, even ardent solidarity faltered in the face of bayonets. The Knights' boldest gamble, and largest failure, came later that year when they sought to organize workers into a new party.[86]

The increasing diversity of the workforce also challenged unions. Despite the constant mechanization of iron and steel making, the number of iron and steelworkers increased dramatically, and employers increasingly sought workers from a wider variety of backgrounds. One of Carnegie's managers explained that the most tractable workforce was a "judiciously mixed" group of "Germans and Irish, Swedes and what I denominate 'Buckwheats' (young American country boys)."[87] But the increasingly heterogeneous workforce favored by employers threatened the social cohesion of the Amalgamated where native-born and Northern European rollers and puddlers had built up a union tradition based on their technical skills and a cultural solidarity based on white manliness.[88] From the perspective of many unionists, native-born common laborers possessed neither the requisite technical skill nor the proper social identity to join the craft unions. As more immigrants were hired from Southern and particularly Eastern Europe, the social distance between skilled and unskilled widened still further. The President of the Amalgamated saw cultural differences as a direct threat to union scales, arguing that Slavic workers did not know "the difference between light work and heavy work or between good wages and bad wages . . . these people can live where I think decent men would die; they can live on almost any kind of food, food that other men would not touch, and in houses that other men would not live in at all."[89] Yet despite the ethnic chauvinism of many in the Amalgamated, craft workers in Homestead developed a culture of solidarity so strong that immigrant workers joined their picket lines and barricades in 1892.[90]

By contrast, the union failed to convince white workers to extend solidarity to black workers. Before the ban on black membership was lifted in 1881, the few black ironworkers who entered Pittsburgh's mills did so as non-union men. After black strikebreakers helped employers win "several rounds," whites feared that employers were engaged in a "systematic effort to replace white with negro labor." In response, the Amalgamated opened its membership to black workers.[91] Inter-racial solidarity initially held. During 1881–82, when "the colored puddlers at the Black Diamond steel works" went on strike, they secured work at another union shop. The *National Labor Tribune* exulted that "the [white] members of the A.A. [Amalgamated] are getting their eyes opened to the fact that the color line is being used against them, and the objection to working alongside a colored man is fast fading away." However, racial prejudice remained strong. One black steelworker recalled that during one 1889 strike, "the company had to put police to guard the colored workers [strikebreakers] so they would not run away." When black workers tried to join the Amalgamated, they were rebuffed.[92] In 1890, four hundred white unionists walked off the job to protest the hiring of black workers who now represented between 2 and 3 percent of all iron and steelworkers in Pennsylvania. By the 1892 Homestead conflict, some African Americans supported the union but more crossed the picket line. Carnegie and a few other employers hired skilled black workers whose mere presence reminded whites that with a "systematic effort" they could be replaced.[93] Racial tensions would remain a stumbling block to the unity of steelworkers for years to come.

Struggles over technology represented another means by which employers sought to divide and conquer unionists. The Bessemer furnace promised employers a means to make larger amounts of metal without puddlers. Whereas puddlers could make no more than six hundred pounds of iron per batch, Bessemers could produce five times that much steel. In other countries, such as England, employers simply renegotiated the tonnage scale with unionists. In Pittsburgh, however, industrialists used new technology to weaken craft unions, lower costs, and raise productivity. In 1877, Carnegie shut down the Edgar Thomson mill to install Bessemers. Afterwards, men could only return to work if they renounced the union. Renounce they did, and although they later rebuilt their union, wages of puddlers fell by about 40 percent and by the 1890s, Bessemers were outproducing puddling furnaces by a factor of ten to one.[94] In the 1880s, most of the Amalgamated's strikes failed, and by 1885 the union had just five thousand members. The union recovered and entered the 1890s with twenty thousand members but had to confront ever-larger and stronger companies.[95]

In and of themselves, Bessemers or the host of other technologies were not enough to destroy unionism. Bessemer workers may have lacked puddlers' highly developed manual skills, but they occupied a strategic place in the production process. Because the batch of a Bessemer was several times as large as that of an iron puddler, a botched heat was several times more costly, and it imperiled the timely rolling of iron. Carnegie sought to circumvent unionists at ET by hiring entirely green men with no experience in iron making—or iron unionism. He also resorted to threats. Recognizing that if these men quit en masse, production would suffer, he promised that if ten or more Bessemer workers quit at the same time he would prosecute them for criminal conspiracy. This might have provided an opening for savvy union men, but the opportunity was missed.[96]

At Homestead, Amalgamated activists had successfully incorporated Bessemer workers at the Pittsburgh Bessemer Steel Company into the union. In 1882, despite the presence of the National Guard, armed scabs, private police, and deputy sheriffs, unionists' organization and solidarity held solid. Strikebreakers unfamiliar with the mill's unique equipment produced shoddy goods and cost the company to lose orders. Unionists' threat to extend the strike to other mills owned by the company forced the company to sign a contract.[97] A year later, the company sold the mill to Carnegie. For the next ten years, Carnegie sparred, skirmished, and battled with the members of the Amalgamated for complete control over the pace of production. The stakes were enormous; between 1891 and 1892, tonnage at Homestead's various departments increased between 17.5 percent and 52 percent.[98]

In 1892, Carnegie finally found the means to destroy the Amalgamated in Homestead. Technology alone had proven insufficient to break the union, although disputes between unionists and management over labor's share of the benefits from new technology and improved productivity fueled the conflict. Amalgamated activists had proven themselves flexible enough to incorporate Bessemer workers into the union. Management had hired a far more diverse workforce, but prejudice did not cripple Homestead's unionists. They had successfully extended a culture of solidarity towards Slavic immigrants, although not to African Americans. Carnegie finally resorted to a combination of private and public armies that defeated labor with brute force. Carnegie's road to triumph was paved in the 1870s when Pittsburgh's labor movement was outmaneuvered by a pro-business political "machine."

THE ORGANIZATION OF POLITICS

In the 1870s, trade unionists developed broader and stronger workplace organizations but failed to develop effective political organizations. In the elections of 1877–78, the Knights and some Amalgamated activists threw their support behind the Greenback-Labor Party, the most successful attempt by unionists to transcend the limits of the two-party system. Among other reforms, the GLP sought to limit the power of banks by forcing the federal government to reissue paper money, "greenbacks," as it had during the Civil War. The GLP would have also eliminated the practice of many companies, particularly coal companies, of paying workers in scrip redeemable only at company stores. The GLP also promised to outlaw blacklisting. In 1877, the GLP won 10 percent of the statewide vote, and far more in Allegheny County. Even without a secret ballot, the GLP polled more votes for statewide office than any working-class party before or since. Yet most labor activists were disappointed and drifted back to the major parties.[99] Workers' failure to extend their organizational gains from the workplace into the political realm would cost them dearly in the years ahead.

Politics in Pittsburgh evolved into a pro-business enterprise. By 1879, the dominant force in the city's elections was an organization that was, in the phrase attributed to its leader, Christopher Magee, "as safe as a bank." This political monopolist, like his industrial counterpart, Andrew Carnegie, rose quickly through the ranks. In 1874, while just twenty-five, Magee exploited family connections to become chairman of the Allegheny County Republican Party and Treasurer of Pittsburgh. The rebate system that Rockefeller and the Pennsylvania established on the railroads was duplicated in Magee's city contracts. Those seeking construction contracts or to bank the city's moneys paid "rebates" to Magee, ensuring his control over the Republican Party organization and making Magee and his partner, William Flinn, into millionaires. In one nine-year period, the city let $3 million in paving contracts; less than 1 percent failed to go into the hands of the firm of Booth and Flinn (the lowest "responsible" bidder). The railroads, particularly the Pennsylvania, paid Magee handsomely for his aid in procuring rights of way through the region. Throughout the country, graft helped to fuel political machines, and few ran more smoothly than Pittsburgh's. In Pittsburgh, graft was perfected to such an extent that one observer argued that New York's Tammany Hall "was a plaything by comparison."[100]

Patronage provided the machine with an indispensable means to woo working-class voters. The state Republican organization controlled over six thousand federal jobs and comparable numbers of state, county and municipal positions.[101] In Allegheny County, Magee and Flinn adroitly co-opted labor's opposition with jobs. If workers were Democrats, Magee did not demand them to change parties, but he did demand loyalty to the machine. So in the 1880s, almost one-quarter of Pittsburgh's patronage jobs went to registered Democrats. These machine Democrats proved invaluable to Magee; in case a reform Republican won that party's primary, the machine would support a machine Democrat.[102] Thus a politician of either party who was "too closely affiliated with the labor interests . . . was slain without compunction, while apparently in the house of his friends."[103] Flinn and Magee brought numerous labor activists onto the payroll of a political organization that was also backed by the state's most powerful corporations. According to historian Paul Krause, Magee "learned how to present the cause of his machine to Pittsburgh's workers as the cause of Pittsburgh's workers." Even high-ranking labor leaders were not immune to the reach of the machine. For instance, in 1866, labor activists elected William C. McCarthy as Pittsburgh's mayor. In 1874, McCarthy was again elected mayor, but his allegiance had switched to Magee. In 1881, Magee backed another mayor with solid pro-labor credentials.[104] Loyalty to the Republican Party ensured that many trade union leaders ended their careers in comfortable patronage jobs.[105] In later years, a leading Republican "machinist" urged that "if you have to choose between losing an election and losing control of the organization, lose the election."[106] Pittsburgh's workers did just the reverse; they occasionally won elections but never developed control over their own political organization. Labor's political weakness, particularly acute at the state level, allowed industrialists to amass the necessary force to emasculate unions. For this reason, advocates of independent labor politics decried those "white slaves" of the political parties who "forge[d the] chains at their feet," but such rhetoric had little practical effect.[107]

The ascendancy of big business relied on close relations with Pennsylvania's hegemonic Republican Party. The Commonwealth's politicians maintained a pro-business climate out of ideological conviction and mercenary self-interest. Matthew Quay, the boss of the 1870s, 1880s, and early

1890s termed corporations his "revenue producers." One Standard Oil representative wrote to John D. Rockefeller that "Mr. Quay might be of great use to us in the state, but he is fearfully expensive."[108] One such "great use" that the machine provided manufacturers was the 1889 law that exempted all manufacturing capital from tax.[109] Quay's successor, Boise Penrose (U.S. Senator from 1897–1921), financed his organization through the "squeeze." "He would have his lieutenants introduce measures in the Pennsylvania legislature aimed at wealthy industries, such as railroads, public utilities, and banks. Then for a large campaign contribution, Penrose would ensure that the bill never became law."[110] Because so many politicians "found their politics in their pay envelopes" intra-party factionalism was intense, but kingmakers such as Quay or Penrose maintained discipline on the party. And the costs to business, as high as they were, were generally worth it. One wag quipped that the only thing that corporations such as Standard Oil hadn't done with the Pennsylvania Legislature was to refine it.[111]

The rewards were not simply financial. When industry required muscle, the state was there. Most infamously, the backing of the Commonwealth allowed Carnegie to mobilize enough police power to destroy the Amalgamated. In 1888 and 1889, hundreds of armed Pinkertons escorted scabs into Carnegie's mills in Braddock and Homestead. Carnegie succeeded in breaking the union at Braddock where the Knights of Labor had won the eight-hour day the year before. The union was vanquished, the twelve-hour day returned.[112] Yet at Homestead, the guards were simply disarmed by armed workmen and escorted out of town. Crushing the Homestead local had to wait three years. In 1892, enough Amalgamated members served in local government that Homestead deputized strikers to keep the peace. Carnegie and Frick's reliance on three hundred armed Pinkerton "detectives" testified to their inability to recruit local police to break one of the last major strongholds of the Amalgamated in the Pittsburgh region. When the Pinkertons attempted to land on the shore of the Monongahela River, they were repulsed by hundreds of armed workers, including many immigrant laborers, several of whom died on the barricades. After several Pinkertons were killed, the "detectives" surrendered to local police, but angry citizens attacked the toughs, which precipitated the Democratic Governor's decision to send in the entire state militia.[113] The union's leaders were tried for treason, although they had resisted private guards and not public police. The case failed, but strikers could only regain their jobs if they renounced the union. Within a few years, the national membership of the Amalgamated plunged from twenty-four thousand to ten thousand. The union was finished in steel.[114]

THE DISORGANIZATION OF SOLIDARITY

After 1892, American employers enjoyed almost complete freedom to remake the iron and steel industry. Their first priority was to consolidate their monopoly power and to disorganize their employees. The Amalgamated presented little challenge to the reorganization of the workplace or the implementation of new technology. If the wages of most workers remained virtually unchanged, the pay of highly skilled workers (the "tonnage men") fell dramatically. At Homestead, the pay of heaters fell 50 percent.[115] Even those rolling mills that relied on puddlers, the rates of pay mirrored Homestead.[116] At Jones and Laughlin's Southside mill, wages increased through 1896 as Bessemers and other new technology expanded output. Yet until 1897, J&L was the last major mill in which the Amalgamated held a contract. The new techniques provided by university-trained engineers, scientists, and chemists further increased managers' knowledge and control over the workplace. Every worker became replaceable. By the early 1900s, employers boasted that with eight weeks of training, a green hand could replace even the most highly skilled worker in the mill.[117] The steel industry redesigned its workplaces to maximize production and minimize workers' control.

The modernization of the workplace accelerated as companies installed electric overhead cranes, mechanized rollers, and other marvels of the machine age. The introduction of labor-saving devices accompanied a dramatic increase in the workday of steelworkers. By 1900, the average steelworker labored seventy-two to eighty-four hours a week or twelve hours a day, six or seven days a week. Every other week, workers' "turn" alternated from days to nights or nights to days. Thus every other Sunday, the switch from day to night turn required two back-to-back turns. The dreaded "long turn" made men so tired that Thomas Bell wrote in his semi-autobiographical novel *Out of This Furnace* that "at three o'clock in the morning of a long turn, a man could die without knowing it."[118] In 1911, the Corporation eliminated the seven-day week, but the fact remained that the twelve-hour day simply wore men out.[119] Even as production boomed, wages inched upwards at the rate of roughly 1 percent a year.[120] In technical terms, the industry modernized; in social terms, steel became increasingly barbaric.

Steel mills were extremely unsafe. In 1907, one investigator found that 526 industrial workers were killed in Allegheny County, and over one-third of them were steelworkers. Over half of those killed were immigrants.[121] The dangers were so pervasive that workers became inured to them. One observer was astounded that a steelworker referred to such "trifles" as the times that a burn from molten metal laid him up for six weeks or the accident that nearly cost him an eye.[122] As employers became liable for accidents, employers began to address the problem.[123] By 1916, the first year that the Commonwealth kept systematic records, just 808 factory workers and 1,065 coal miners were killed throughout Pennsylvania. These numbers declined as employers such as U.S. Steel (with its "safety first" program) provided safety goggles, work shoes, and guards on machinery. One scholar found that "in 1907 about 250 out of every 1,000 men who worked a full (3,000 hour) year were injured . . . by 1939, U.S. Steel had cut this rate to about 3."[124] Yet the modernization of safety standards coexisted with systems of social control that many termed industrial feudalism.

Industrialists relied on an extensive spy system to identify and punish activists. In 1895, 1899, and 1901, workers attempted to rebuild the union at Homestead. In response, "the company let the newly made union men know that it was cognizant of every move that had been made." Some leaders were invited to spy on their comrades; if they refused, they were fired. Hundreds were fired. Once out of a job, even highly skilled workers frequently found it impossible to find work in the same firm or the industry. In many towns, workers knew that "if you want to talk . . . you talk to yourself." One Homestead worker put it this way: "they own us body and soul; our bread and butter depends on our silence." Given the pervasive company presence, John Fitch asked "is it any wonder, therefore, that [steelworkers] suspect each other and guard their tongues?" The effects of the spy system reached far beyond the mill gate. In 1906, steelworkers at Jones and Laughlin called a public meeting to protest Sunday work, but "a foreman, with several mill policeman, stationed themselves where they could see every man who went into the hall. As a result, no one attempted to go to the meeting." The blacklist bled the workplace of its natural leaders and deterred other would-be unionists.[125]

In the post-union workplace, workers were allowed advancement without security. As John Fitch observed, "in every department of mill work there is a more or less rigid line of promotion. Every man is in training for the position above. If all the rollers at the Homestead plant were to strike tomorrow, the work would go on . . . There would simply be a step up along the line; the tablemen would take the rolls, the hooker would manipulate the tables . . . In this way the companies develop and train their own men. They seldom hire a stranger for a position as roller or heater. Thus the working force is pyramided and is held together by the ambition of the men lower down; even a serious break in the ranks adjust itself automatically."[126] As workers competed for resources, they helped to maintain, sometimes unwittingly and sometimes consciously, a social division of labor that stabilized industrialists' power.

Companies adroitly manipulated "identity politics" to reinforce the "pyramided" system of workplace hierarchies. Employers increasingly recruited Eastern and Southern Europeans into the ranks of unskilled labor. In 1890, just 10 percent of steelworkers in the United States were from Southern and Eastern Europe. Twenty years later, more than half of Pittsburgh's steelworkers were immigrants, the vast majority from Southern and Eastern Europe.[127] Most foremen "say that they prefer Americans, yet, as far as I could learn, they make no effort to secure American labor. Even those men who hire their own men directly, employ Slavs."[128] One observer opined that employers greatly preferred Eastern European immigrants "because of their docility, their habit of silent submission, and their willingness to work long hours and overtime without a murmur."[129] By 1907, less than one-quarter of Carnegie's workforce remained American-born whites. The tide of immigration lifted many white Americans and Northern and Western European immigrants into the ranks of foremen and skilled workers. Frustrations and resentments trickled downwards. One Scotch-Irish boss referred to the "hunky" immigrants on his crew: "they don't seem like men to me hardly." Just before an accident killed one Slavic laborer, he complained to his foreman about the danger. "But the foreman insisted, telling him with a rough laugh that it did not matter whether he was killed or not. He went, afraid to lose his job." Not surprisingly, the oral histories of immigrant steelworkers are filled with recollections such as "at that time, discrimination was practiced, particularly against the Slavs."[130]

The tide of European immigration swept black Americans into an occupational eddy. Amidst massive job growth, the numbers of black iron and steelworkers in Western Pennsylvania remained about 1–2 percent of the total. At some firms, no blacks were hired and at a few others, African Americans made up about one-tenth of the workforce. Many black workers were skilled, their presence an implicit threat to whites not to take their relative privileges for granted.[131] Racial prejudice among white workers remained strong, fueled by an implicit sense that whites and blacks shared a common experience of "wage slavery." When one white worker complained about conditions in the mill, he remarked that "it's slavery, the mill, slavery worse than what the niggers had before the Civil War."[132] The remark reveals the mix of bitterness, frustrated republicanism, and racial supremacy of many white American steelworkers at the turn of the century. The daily jockeying for jobs, often rooted in the ethnic and racial realpolitik of the mills directed anger to the branches of oppression rather than its roots.[133]

Industrialists' desire for a heterogeneous and cheap labor force and the aspirations of immigrants from Europe and the countryside of the United States combined to make the Pittsburgh region one of the most ethnically and racially diverse in the country. Allegheny County grew from 262,204 people in 1870 to 1,018,463 in 1910 and to 1,374,410 in 1930. Foreign-born whites from Eastern and Southern Europe comprised the bulk of the region's industrial workers, and as late as 1930, after the cutoff of European immigration, they made up 16 percent of the population. Between 1890 and 1930, the children of immigrants comprised slightly more than a third of the region's population. African Americans comprised a relatively modest 3 percent of the region's population in 1890, and by 1930 made up 6.1 percent of Allegheny County. The task of creating unity amidst such ethnic and racial heterogeneity was a goal that eluded unionists for a generation.

The devastatingly effective coercive tactics of corporations remained perfectly legal. In 1897, the Pennsylvania legislature passed a weak anti-blacklisting law. However, the courts maintained that even blacklists shared by all employers in an industry were reasonable defenses of property rights against the greater danger of labor conspiracy. Courts also upheld the "iron-clad" oath, which allowed employers to first require employees to swear not to join a union or fire them for breach of contract if they did. Only after the passage of the federal Norris-La Guardia Act and a comparable state law in the early 1930s would the law enjoin employers from firing employees because they had joined unions.[134] Judicial rulings invariably found pro-labor laws unconstitutional. In 1895, state courts struck down a law that would have prevented employers from paying workers in company scrip. Three years later, the courts overturned a state law that would have protected coal miners from being short-weighed on the amount of coal they had mined. While labor did occasionally elect or influence local judges, state courts overruled them in order to uphold the interests of large corporations. For instance, when local police and magistrates attempted to prevent strikebreakers from carrying concealed weapons, state courts ordered local law officers to cease and desist.[135] The success of the courts in striking down pro-labor legislation helped to convince many unionists that politics was a waste of effort and drove them towards "pure and simple" unionism.[136]

It is worth considering how a different legal status for unions might have affected the course of history in steel. In England, the struggle to establish unions in the iron industry began in the 1830s. Although British ironworkers lacked as wide a franchise as their American counterparts enjoyed, English unions were put on firm legal ground much earlier than in the United States. British politicians feared the labor vote more than their American counterparts; consequently, they paid much more attention to workers' issues.[137] After 1875, lawmakers and the courts viewed unions as legitimate organizations, and British unionists were spared court injunctions or threats of conspiracy or hindering charges. While English companies resisted unions, after 1869, British steel companies accepted government-run arbitration boards and avoided major strikes. By the 1890s, industrial councils set standard wage and tonnage rates, and most disputes were resolved locally or through arbitration. (In 1893, Pennsylvania established arbitration boards, but without effective enforcement, employers rarely submitted to them).[138] When British employers implemented Bessemer technology and began steel production on a large scale, it did not displace the numerous craft unions. British iron and steel unions were notoriously conservative, and the only national strike from 1869 until 1982 occurred when they reluctantly joined the 1926 general strike. As a result, only seven British workers in all industries were killed on picket lines between 1872 and 1914, a level of mayhem several hundred times less than that in the United States.[139] Ironically, a constitutional monarchy afforded workers far greater legal protection to form unions than did the largest republic in the world. As late as the 1920s, American unions were hamstrung by court rulings based on English common law that British lawmakers and courts had long abandoned as outdated.[140]

THE CORPORATION AND PITTSBURGH

Over the course of the late nineteenth century, monopoly eclipsed competition in many sectors of the economy. Companies such as the Pennsylvania

Railroad, Standard Oil, American Telephone and Telegraph, and United States Steel dominated vital sectors of the economy. By 1909, 80 percent of Pennsylvania's economic activity was controlled by 20 percent of its firms whose power became increasingly concentrated.[141] Horizontally integrated firms controlled a large enough part of one stage of production or distribution to set prices without fear of competition. Vertically integrated monopolies did not have to buy their raw materials on an open market where prices and supplies fluctuated. Instead, they supplied their own workshops with raw materials purchased within their own internal market. Within vast factories, corporations often developed vast "internal labor markets" that offered workers steady work and opportunities for upward advancement within the company. These new companies and workplaces bedeviled craft unions that proved unable to cope with the new technologies and spy networks. Public policy also played a part in weakening unions and protecting trusts. Laws designed to limit monopolies, such as the federal Sherman antitrust law, were instead turned against unions as "labor trusts."[142]

The formation of U.S. Steel in 1901 signaled the consolidation of monopoly capitalism in the Pittsburgh district. Overnight, "the Corporation" became the world's largest firm, with dozens of mines, hundreds of miles of railroad, and over two hundred production plants. Its sheer size, almost two-thirds of national steel production, enabled it to set prices for the industry.[143] Just prior to the formation of U.S. Steel, Carnegie calculated that "the merger of companies proposed ensures ten dollars per ton profit *at least*. . . . Steel is king."[144] With real assets of perhaps $682 million, J.P. Morgan sold $1.4 billion worth of U.S. Steel stocks and bonds.[145] U.S. Steel later argued this discrepancy resulted from "intangibles" such as the "good will or earning power . . . versus tangible assets." Carnegie had driven prices down during recessions; by contrast, U.S. Steel maintained high and stable prices, adjusting them downwards only during severe economic downturns. U.S. Steel's production was concentrated in Pittsburgh to such an extent that from 1907 to 1921, steel bought throughout the country was figured on a "Pittsburgh Plus" basis. That is, steel's consumers paid the production price charged by Pittsburgh's mills plus freight costs. Even if buyers in Chicago bought steel made in Chicago, they paid fictitious freight charges as if the steel had been rolled in the Mon Valley. The system caused few complaints among steel producers. Until the 1920s, when other basing points were added, the Pittsburgh Plus system minimized the disadvantages of Pittsburgh's distance from growing markets in the Midwest and West.[146] Even *Fortune* remarked that "no Soviet planner ever designed a more flagrantly artificial system."[147] Morgan kept the peace with competitors and sought to avoid antitrust regulation by allowing U.S. Steel's share of ingot production to slip from 65 percent in 1902 to 46 percent in 1920.[148] Until the 1920s, profits (measured against assets) averaged over 12 percent a year. Considering that half of the assets of the company were fictitious, real profits (not including the initial windfall) topped 20 percent.[149] While the control and profitability of the steel trust ultimately followed its diminishing market share, by that point, the Corporation had paid for itself several times over.

The formation of U.S. Steel affected the dynamics of competition in the industry in peculiar ways. By 1902, powerful financiers headed by the Mellon family assembled an integrated steel firm in the heart of U.S. Steel's Mon Valley. The Union-Sharon firm mostly existed on paper, although it did own a few mines and mills. Its chief asset was the deep pockets of the Mellons, who threatened to build a modern mill. According to a government inquiry, "there remained one solution . . . the Corporation decided to pay." U.S. Steel paid premium prices, totalling $75 million to eliminate the *possibility* of a competitor. Mines purchased by Union-Sharon for $150,000 were sold to form U.S. Steel for $4 million. Yet not all competitors bested the Corporation. Crucible Steel's effort to build a $10 million mill in Clairton ended in disaster. In 1904, it was caught in a credit crunch and was forced to sell to the Corporation for ten cents on the dollar. Andrew Mellon, one of Crucible's directors, had extended the firm the loans that eventually sunk it. A similar cycle brought two large coal firms, each underwritten by Mellon's banks, into the U.S. Steel fold at a substantial profit to the Mellons and the steel trust. One cynic (correctly) observed that the Mellons prospered in both boom and bust. "Each period of prosperity brought its harvest of added millions . . . in each succeeding depression he wielded energetically the broom of foreclosure."[150]

While the Mellons and U.S. Steel reached an amicable accommodation, no such policy was possible between the Corporation and its workforce. U.S. Steel offered no quarter to unions. At its formation, the Corporation acquired several rolling mills with contracts with the Amalgamated. Against the advice of other unionists, the Amalgamated's leaders led a strike against the Corporation before it could consolidate its position and eliminate the union. In 1901, the Amalgamated called a strike with the goal of unionizing all of the company's hoop, sheet, and tin mills. Workers at non-union mills, such as the Duquesne Works and National Tube in McKeesport, who answered the Amalgamated's call and joined the thirty-five thousand strikers were blacklisted. The Amalgamated offered no support; years later, one worker recalled that he had never abandoned the union but that "the union left us."[151] Racial bigotry compounded incompetence. When black strikers from the Lafayette Lodge sought temporary work at another union mill, a standard practice for union men, white unionists refused to work alongside them.[152] In 1909, another steel strike eliminated the last Amalgamated lodges at U.S. Steel, and the company announced its adherence to the principles of the open shop. Despite calls for unity among white workers ("forget you are English, Irish, Welsh, Slavish"), the Amalgamated remained hostile to black workers. One skilled union man briefly worked in a non-union mill, but quit because "no self-respecting American" could work alongside the "great, dirty crowd of Negroes and Syrians. . . . It is no place for a man with a white man's heart to be."[153] In the coming years, unions in the coal fields, on the Corporation's ships, and even those members of the building trades who erected the Corporation's skyscrapers were wiped out. The Amalgamated retreated to the wrought iron industry, where puddlers' skills were still indispensable. The puddlers revolted against the Amalgamated and reestablished the Sons of Vulcan on a lily-white basis. In 1910, Amalgamated members scabbed on one of their strikes. The Amalgamated "won" this contest, but the union was a hollow shell, with no resources, strategy, or will to organize steel.[154]

Steelworkers did not always wait for the Amalgamated to organize them; sometimes they acted on their own. In 1909, the Pressed Steel Car company in McKees Rocks unilaterally reduced workers' wages. The largely immigrant workforce convinced American workers to go on strike, but the company soon encouraged native-born skilled workers to cross picket lines. Ethnicity was also the alibi for repression: when "American" workers had claimed that intimidation from immigrant strikers had prevented them from going to work, the company called upon the State Police. Troopers rode their horses into armed pickets, a riot broke out, and about a dozen strikers and two troopers were killed. More State Police arrived, and they conducted house-to-house searches for weapons, but only in immigrant neighborhoods. Even the staid Amalgamated observed that "there is no stronger proof that the power of government is allied against the working men in their effort to resist the despotism of capitalists than the existence of the state constabulary."[155] The company helped to organize a company union, and the disarmed strikers were unable to prevent the subsequent back-to-work movement led by newly "unionized" Americans.

Faced with these tactics, the immigrants called upon organizers from the radical Industrial Workers of the World. The IWW—or Wobblies—promised to kill a trooper for every striker killed, and the union was as good as its word. The Wobblies did not shy away from violence, but understood that workers could not win their strike with guns. But workers' solidarity soon forced the company to rehire all the strikers. Back in the plant, the antagonism between the immigrant and American unions remained fierce. In 1910, the American union went out on strike and called up the IWW to support it. The IWW offered this bitter reply: "What for? Do you want us to take the Hunkies up on the hill again, make us do the picketing and offer ourselves as targets for the Cossacks . . . and then you will take your flag and march back to work as you have done before? . . . Nothing Doing!" With a base at Pressed Steel Car, the Wobblies spread their organization to nearby plants. By 1912, the IWW had led several partially successful strikes in the region and claimed four thousand members.[156] Nonetheless, within a few years, just a handful of die-hard Wobblies remained as dues-paying members. While internal disputes and the IWW's refusal to sign contracts with employers weakened the union, the Wobblies complained that steel's spy system "made the Russian police look like amateurs."[157]

Police repression also destroyed the first industrial union of electrical workers. In the 1910s, the IWW and the Socialist Party developed a strong following in the milltowns surrounding the Westinghouse complex. In 1912, Eugene Debs won between a quarter of the vote in most steel towns, and 40 percent of the vote in the "electrical valley" mill towns. In 1914, radical electrical workers led a successful strike and established an industrial union with thousands of members that survived for two years. On May 1, 1916, electrical workers convinced over thirty thousand workers from nearby plants (according to historian David Montgomery "an angry and joyous tide of humanity") to join a general strike for the eight-hour day. When they marched to the gates of Edgar Thomson, hundreds of private police fired into the "mob." Dozens were injured; at least three died. The National Guard was called in and crushed the strike. Several leaders were jailed, thus destroying the union. Many electrical workers remained true to unionism and radicalism, but until the 1920s, such concerns became a private matter to be discussed only amongst trusted friends.[158]

The case of the IWW at Pressed Steel Car and the independent union of Westinghouse workers reveals that numerous industrial workers desired their own workplace organizations and were willing to fight and suffer for them. The demise of both unions reveals that the problems of organizing workers did not result simply from the failure of will or ideology on the part of unions. The IWW was a tenacious union, unafraid of struggle and willing to organize all workers regardless of race or ethnicity. In the face of widespread anti-immigrant bigotry on the part of native-born workers, the IWW's willingness to organize all workers limited its membership as much as its revolutionary agenda. Nonetheless, the most crucial reasons for the destruction of the Wobblies or the independent union at Westinghouse were the sustained and ferocious corporate attacks. Government did little to restrain corporate spies and company police; more often, they stepped in to finish the job.

In steel, the dynamics of World War I transformed the relationship between government and employers. The Allied war effort required vast amounts of goods, and especially steel for ships, arms, shells, and barbed wire. Production boomed, and prices skyrocketed. Between 1914 and July 1917, the prices of most goods had doubled. But coking coal had risen to five times its pre-war price and the price of armor plate rose sevenfold. When the United States entered the war, it convinced steel firms to set prices at just two to three times their pre-war levels. One government report estimated that such voluntary price fixing saved the government $3 billion and was "considered a great achievement and a wonderful monument to the patriotism of steel manufacturers." Despite their sacrifices, steel firms managed to profit from the war. In 1913, U.S. Steel enjoyed profits of $131 million. By 1917, the flood of war orders (even at controlled prices) raised the declared profits to $585 million or 36 percent of total capitalization. Other steel firms earned up to ten times that rate of return. By one estimate, the total profits of steel companies exceeded the wages paid out to all American soldiers who fought in France.[159]

The war wrought substantial changes in the composition of the workforce and its relationship to government. The war halted European immigration, and companies recruited Southern blacks and white women in unprecedented numbers. Several thousand black men entered the steel mills as unskilled laborers, a historic shift in employment patterns. In the Pittsburgh region, several hundred white women became clerical workers, and some labored in the mills. A small number of African American women were also hired for the duration of the war.[160] In order to boost production and promote wartime loyalty, the government convinced employers to bargain with unions through the War Production Board in exchange for a no-strike pledge.

Americanization programs begun during the war to ensure the loyalty of immigrant male workers—still the bulk of laborers—boomeranged on employers when these workers became interested in their own version of industrial democracy and flocked to the Amalgamated.[161] The "legitimacy" of AFL unionists did not prevent unprecedented levels of government surveillance, harassment, and jailing of labor radicals and anti-war activists. At the forefront of the public spy system was the Commonwealth's State Police, which established one of the country's first Bureaus of Criminal Identification and Information which tracked radicals and criminals. Federal military and organizations demanded the services of Pennsylvania's highly trained troopers. For instance, Superintendent Groome of the State Police headed up the new U.S. Military Intelligence.[162] Public spies effectively sapped radicals' strength. By the war's end, the secretary of the IWW in Pittsburgh was an agent for the Justice Department's Bureau of Investigation (renamed the Federal Bureau of Investigation in 1924).[163] Unfortunately for workers, the state's surveillance of labor proved more durable than its aid.

The federal government's faltering interest in workers' rights contributed to the fierce conflict between capital and labor. Once the Armistice was signed, government pressure on employers to negotiate with unions vanished. By 1919, the growing militance of unskilled immigrant steelworkers forced the leadership of the Amalgamated to call a general strike. The leadership of William Z. Foster, a former IWW member, led to charges that strikers were radicals bent on revolution. The State Police justified its role in the strike on the basis that "this appeared to be an industrial war in which the leaders were radical, social and industrial revolutionaries while their followers . . . were . . . chiefly of the foreign element, steeped in the doctrines of class struggle." Employers once again relied on thousands of their "Cossacks," the Coal and Iron Police, deputy sheriffs (five thousand in Allegheny County alone) and state troopers.[164] One union organizer grimly observed that "Pennsylvania today, the fourth day of the great steel strike, presents all the aspects of war, with the exception that only one side is equipped to fight it." Machine guns were mounted in front of some mills.[165] One organizer caustically observed that "steel towns have laws all their own." In Donora, the Mayor disarmed strikebreakers, but most resembled the "czar-like attitude" of Duquesne's Mayor who told unionists that "Jesus Christ himself can't hold a meeting."[166] Throughout the region, mounted troopers or private police disrupted workers' gatherings and even dispersed wedding guests. In McKeesport, "state troopers on horses with clubs about three feet long" broke up meetings.[167] Pittsburgh's Mayor prohibited "large crowds congregating in the strike zones," and the courts upheld the decree.[168] After the strike, a state trooper defended his methods to a group of U.S. Senators: "I would not say I hurt any of them, I just clubbed a few of them."[169]

Workers' inability to overcome potent ethnic and racial divisions bolstered management's hand during the strike. Numerous native-born workers believed that the 1919 strike was a mere "hunky strike." In the Pittsburgh district, the Amalgamated failed to even try to organize black workers into the union. One Amalgamated activist later recalled that "Negroes were never a question . . . you never even heard it mentioned."[170] Thus numerous American workers, black and white, crossed the picket lines in Pittsburgh. (There were exceptions: in Cleveland, black workers strongly supported the union.) In Duquesne, skilled whites joined supervisors as deputy sheriffs; in other areas, black workers were deputized.[171] Some white Americans struck one mill only to scab in another town. Other white Americans remained true until the union called off the strike. As in the past, blacks' labor solidarity was no guarantee that unions would respond in kind: "At Youngstown, for example, one lone [black] machinist striker, who struck to the end, was never admitted to the striking machinists' local."[172]

The racial and ethnic dimensions of the strike set the tone for the "100% Americanism" of the 1920s.[173] The crucial role that skilled whites played in defeating the strike has been largely forgotten, in part because many employers argued that their victory was because "the niggers did it."[174] The racial animus was so strong by the end of the strike that some employers fired or downgraded black workers in order to regain the loyalty of white strikers who were rehired.[175] But most employers hired even more black workers in the 1920s because they viewed the black worker as "more individualistic, does not like to group and does not follow a leader as readily as some foreigners do."[176] Industrialists believed that "the Negro . . . shows little susceptibility to radical doctrine."[177] Indeed, at least one black worker, a strikebreaker in 1919, took out his frustrations on immigrant workers in the 1920s. "The foreigners are worse than the true Americans," he said, in part because a gang of them had opposed his promotion to foreman. He bided his time until "it was my job to weed the men out"; the leader of the immigrants "was the first to go." As in the past, managers stoked the fires of hatred, fear, and resentment in order to smother class organization.[178]

Once again, the Amalgamated and the AFL had let steelworkers down. The twenty-four craft unions that formed the "National Committee for Organizing Iron and Steel Workers" failed to provide the necessary funds or leadership. Much of the money came from left-wing (and non-AFL) unions in textile and the needle trades. While the Amalgamated took the dues money of strikers, it later claimed that it only represented men in lodges with contracts. During the strike, it sent some union men back to work to protect the "sanctity" of its contracts! Similarly, some railroad workers offered to strike, but their union urged them to honor their contracts. One worker bitterly observed that "if the railwaymen in the steel plant yards had struck, this strike would have been won." The unions "made them strike-breakers." Although 100,000 strikers stayed out, the Amalgamated's leaders called off the strike. Much of the strike fund donated by other unions remained unspent, as did much of the dues collected from immigrants. Whether the Amalgamated spent the money on investments in real estate or a lackluster organizing drive in 1923 was immaterial. The Amalgamated and the AFL had utterly failed to provide leadership to steelworkers.[179] It would be another decade before steelworkers attempted to unionize again.

FROM GENERAL STRIKE TO GREAT DEPRESSION

Steelmakers emerged victorious against the Amalgamated; nonetheless, industrialists' social control over Western Pennsylvania began to slip in the 1920s. The death of several major Republican kingmakers, including Boise Penrose, allowed reform Republicans to win control of the party. The support of the mineworkers, brutalized during strikes, allowed Gifford Pinchot, who opposed the Coal and Iron Police, to win the office of Governor in 1922.[180] And in 1923, a year after he took office, Pinchot ordered the State Police to review the Coal and Iron Police commissions issued by the Commonwealth; he then revoked four thousand of them. However, the Republican machine was far from dead. The legislature blocked further reforms, such as attempts to prohibit companies from paying the wages of deputy sheriffs. In 1926, Pinchot ran for the Senate but was beaten by

Philadelphia's boss, William Vare. (Vare outspent Pinchot five to one and stuffed so many ballot boxes that the U.S. Senate refused to recognize the election.) Alas, Pinchot's successor as Pennsylvania's chief executive was a "machinist." Under the guise of reform, he actually increased the powers of industrial police. Furthermore, Governor John Fisher refused to prevent the "coal and irons" from brutalizing UMWA strikers.[181]

Beneath the quiet surface, resentment smoldered. While industrial unions were destroyed, the increasing number of immigrant and working-class voters slowly changed the political calculus. In many mill towns and coal patches, immigrants and their children gained access to party positions and patronage jobs. In Homestead, the WASP leader of the Republicans reported that "he didn't want the Hunky vote. So he didn't get the Hunky vote and Mr. [Jack] Cavanaugh [an Irish American] won out." Cavanaugh continued to repress unionists, although he prevented police harassment of immigrant parties and clubs and increased the representation from Slovak and other ethnic groups on the city and county payroll. Even in company coal towns, party leaders conceded contracts and jobs to immigrant politicians.[182] The loyalty of ethnic voters to the Republican party withered as a result of its support for Prohibition and the Catholic baiting of Democratic Presidential candidate Al Smith in 1928. Another sign of change was that immigrant voters elected a few reformers, like Pittsburgh's Michael A. Musmanno, to the state House.[183] Musmanno opposed the Coal and Iron Police and publicized the 1929 death of John Barkoski, an immigrant coal miner, at their hands. Barkoski's killing sparked a wider movement to restrict the powers of private police. In 1930, Gifford Pinchot once again became Governor of Pennsylvania and further undermined the police powers of industrialists.

The weakening grip of Pennsylvania's political oligarchy ran parallel to the declining economic fortunes of U.S. Steel. The advent of peace and naval disarmament in the early 1920s reduced the company's lucrative military contracts. Even the Navy League, sponsored by the steel and munitions trusts, proved unable to stimulate a new round of military spending.[184] Because of its "gentlemen's agreement" to respect the territories of its competitors, the Corporation did not build a mill in Detroit to supply the burgeoning auto market. Disgusted with fixed prices, Henry Ford built his own steel mill.[185] U.S. Steel relied on hand-rolling mills and lost 60 percent of its share of the rapidly expanding sheet steel market to mechanized mills.[186] Even in its traditional strongholds of structural shapes, rails, and steel pipe, the Corporation lost ground to companies like Bethlehem that now rolled beams instead of welding them from three separate pieces of metal. Other companies developed seamless tubes, effectively marginalizing U.S. Steel in the booming pipeline construction trade. Only its deep pockets allowed the Corporation to buy new technology and stabilize its share of national ingot production at around 30 percent.[187] Harvey O'Connor, one of U.S. Steel's harshest critics, observed that "every great advance in the industry . . . was forced on the Corporation by men on the outside." A more sympathetic business historian, Thomas Misa, found that "the real price" of U.S. Steel's stable and fixed prices for steel "was the stifling of technological innovation" and an indifference to the needs of customers. For example, while the Corporation had scattered research and testing laboratories, it did not build a central facility until 1928.[188] The fate of U.S. Steel held special meaning for Pittsburgh as the hardening of the Corporation's arteries slowed the pulse of Western Pennsylvania itself.

Pittsburgh had become a "mature" industrial region. Its mines, railroads, and mills were relatively old. The newest mills in the Pittsburgh district were J&L's Aliquippa Works, finished in 1909, and Crucible Steel's Midland Works, constructed in 1911.[189] In the 1920s the fastest growing markets were in "light" steel products such as sheets for automobiles, household appliances, and tin plate for cans, but most of the steel produced in Pittsburgh was "heavy" steel—that is, structural shapes for bridges and buildings, and bars and plates for railroads and industry.[190] The proportion of steel rolled in the Pittsburgh region fell from 40 percent of the national total to about 25 percent in the 1930s.[191] The region continued to employ around 20 percent of the nation's steel workforce and 10 percent of its coal miners and electrical workers. But as the Great Depression deepened, few skyscrapers were erected, and railroads made do with old cars; companies required fewer electrical machines and less fuel.[192] As a result, an official of a major steel company announced that "we have no intention of ever building another mill in the Pittsburgh district."[193] Pittsburgh's relative decline to other manufacturing centers had begun.

Most steelworkers had enjoyed only a small portion of the famed prosperity of the 1920s. Yet work remained steady, and in 1923, most companies began to abandon the twelve-hour day in the face of substantial public pressure.[194] A rise in the hourly rate did not make up for the loss of hours, however, and U.S. Steel effectively cut the wages of laborers 20 percent or to $4 a day.[195] And while workplaces were becoming safer, injured workers received scant protection from company policies and state laws. In 1927, Matt Shamich, a former coal miner who had worked at a small rolling mill, developed the "hot-mill cramps" (severe dehydration). Complaining throughout the day, he returned home and died. On the basis of the company doctor's report, the Workmen's Compensation Board found that Shamich did not suffer an injury at work. He left a wife and two children.[196] While U.S. Steel offered workers a modest pension plan as part of its "welfare capitalist" package, few workers could afford to stop working in old age. In the early 1920s, the National Tube Works employed over 6,000 men, but just 160 (less than 3 percent) were on pension.[197] Nationally, U.S. Steel allocated $1,448,000 for pensions and $108,500,000 for profits.[198] In 1929, the annual income of Duquesne's steelworkers hovered around $1,350. Over the next few years, falling wages and limited hours reduced that figure to around $300. In the heart of the Depression, Harvey O'Connor observed that "now many homes are bare of the furnishings for which the workers sacrificed so much. Vans have pulled up in front of the squalid homes and taken away living room and bedroom furniture that represented the savings of a decade."[199] The loss of steady work wrought havoc on the lives of steelworkers; in time, it would devastate the system of industrial policing that had kept workers in place for almost fifty years.

THE DEPRESSION

The Depression devastated Pittsburgh's working class. By 1931, the steel industry ran at just half of its capacity; two years later, production was just one-third of capacity.[200] By 1933, U.S. Steel did not employ a single full-time employee anywhere in the country; all the Corporation's workers worked part time.[201] The next year, U.S. Steel's Mon Valley mills were operating at just 30 percent of capacity and only a third of its workforce worked full time.[202] Every worker feared for his or her job. Phil McGuigan, a McKeesport steelworker, remembered that "you'd go and stand in a line and the foreman would come and say, 'you, you and you . . . that's all today.' Everybody else would turn around and go back home. You didn't get one penny for that. Nothing. If you would get two or three days pay in two weeks, you were happy."[203] Low wages were compounded by kickbacks to foremen. Many workers complained that they had to pay supervisors to keep their jobs. At

J&L, one pipe mill foreman confessed to stealing ten thousand dollars over the years. A judge fined him three hundred dollars and sentenced him to one year in the county workhouse.[204]

Exacerbating unemployment was the fact that steel firms continued to manipulate ethnic and racial antagonisms in order to control their work-force. One researcher found that personnel directors "never permit a gang of workers to be all of one nationality or of one color 'because under these conditions they stick together too much.'"[205] McGuigan recalled that before you got a job with U.S. Steel in the 1930s, the personnel office "would ask: nationality?" That irked him, because "we're all Americans here, and that's all we should have to say."[206] Ashton Allen, a black steel-worker at Homestead, remembered that "the color question at Homestead was quite rigid . . . the mill was structured so that certain people of central European extraction" operated machines and maintained equipment. "At a higher level, they were given to the Irish. Then you had your top super-intendents that were mostly Germans or English, and on top of that sits your Scotch, which was Andrew Carnegie's gift to the Scotch."[207]

The vast majority of blacks were laborers. While some managers argued that this was because blacks in the 1910s and 1920s had simply "flocked to common labor," others admitted that "it is hard to get a white man to do [the] type of work" required on "black jobs."[208] In mills that refused to hire black workers, Eastern Europeans occupied the bottom rung of the occupational ladder. According to one white worker, the best jobs were held by "all the WASPs. As for a Slovak, or a Polish, or a Hungarian, or an Italian, it was absolutely no."[209] According to one black worker, in the coke ovens, blast furnaces, and open hearths, these European immi-grants "were treated almost like blacks, to a certain degree."[210] The degree of difference was critical. Among steelworkers, poverty had long been com-pounded by fear, and the temptation to grasp at whatever privileges that ethnicity, race, or gender offered was an old one.

Blacks and "foreigners" both bore the weight of discrimination, but in the case of blacks the Depression increased their burdens. John Hovanec, who ended up as a gang leader and boilermaker, recalled that at the Homestead Works "a lot of the people were making break-throughs in the 1920s and early 1930s." A few, like John Mornack, rose to the level of superintendent of the open hearth.[211] Such limited advancements hinted at the gains Catholic workers would make after the union grew in strength. The intensity of the Great Depression led many steel firms to conclude they needed no ethnic hedge against unionization, and black workers were disproportionally laid off.[212] Steel managers informed one researcher that they were "forced in self-protection to reduce employment to large numbers of demoralized former Negro employees . . . who have become radicals and malingers since long exposure to the subversive influences of slums and the relief set ups."[213] Anger at discrimination fed the determination of industrial workers for a change.

Not even U.S. Steel could have prevented the Depression, but steel companies' welfare policies engendered enormous ill will. For instance, the Corporation promised that any employee who received county or city welfare payments would be fired. Instead, the company distributed food baskets of dubious quality, and the cost of the food was deducted from future paychecks. J&L imposed a similar system. Tony Riccitelli was fired because he refused to caddie for a manager in exchange for a basket of government surplus food.[214] Marches and rallies led by different radical groups became a new feature of political life in mill towns. Just how far workers were willing to go was carefully explored by radicals, journalists, politicians, and military intelligence. (One army officer reported in 1932 that "the attitude of the unemployed in general continues to be patient. Very little radical tendency. That radical forces are actively engaged in the fertile field of unemployment is apparent.")[215] Reformers such as Governor Gifford Pinchot and Franklin Delano Roosevelt promised to expand and modernize the system of public relief.[216]

As Pittsburgh entered the 1930s, its industries were strangely quiet, and blue skies were visible for the first time since 1919. It was the calm before the storm. Without adequate numbers of jobs or relief, unemployment became hunger, and the growl of stomachs grew into the mutterings of angry men. From those men emerged political forces that would unravel the systems of social control that industrialists had carefully maintained for decades. Over the course of the Depression, private police, labor spies, and blacklists were outlawed. Private charity was eclipsed by an expanded system of public relief and unemployment insurance. New state and federal laws were enacted to protect the rights of workers to organize unions.

Once the state no longer openly sided with employers, workers built powerful industrial unions that consolidated the political realignment in Pennsylvania and throughout the country. In steel, coal, and electrical machinery, unions were forged that upheld an egalitarian vision of solidarity.

Yet the basis of workers' solidarity remained fragile, and it was uncertain whether they would be able to overcome the inequalities that lay at the heart of industrialists' power over Pittsburgh.

The reforms of Pinchot slowly undermined companies' authority in the Commonwealth's little Siberias. Pinchot embraced the expansion of government relief, in part as a means to bolster the number of patronage jobs he could control. But public relief provided many workers with an alternative to the company's food baskets. Equally important for trade unionists was Pinchot's extension of civil liberties to pro-union workers. In part as a response to the agitation of radicals and liberals, Pinchot revoked all the commissions of private police on June 30, 1931. Companies still retained numerous armed guards and spies and—assuming a friendly sheriff—as many deputy sheriffs as they could afford. Trade unionists complained that "every mill had more police than a penitentiary" but hoped that the days of industrial feudalism were numbered.[217] Journalists discovered that J&L and Aliquippa officials had railroaded George Issoski, an Amalgamated activist, to the state insane asylum. Pinchot ordered him released, but Beaver County Republicans balked. One claimed that "Issoski was crazy, the victim of a persecution complex, the same as Pinchot. I'd like to see a commission appointed to examine the Governor." In the end, Issoski went free.[218] Pinchot won other reforms, such as the abolition of the poll tax and the iron clad contract (whereby joining a union was a violation of contract), but many of his reforms faltered in the Senate.[219] The final blows to the spy system would come after 1934, when Democrat George Earle was elected Governor and Democrats controlled the legislature.

PREMATURE INDUSTRIAL UNIONISTS: COMMUNISTS, MINERS, AND THE RANK-AND-FILE

The Depression stimulated political reforms, but it was unclear how far politicians' support for workers would extend. Certainly Roosevelt's New Deal offered as much aid to big business as to workers. After he took office in 1933, FDR expanded the amount of federal support for public relief. But Roosevelt also bolstered business through the National Industry Recovery Act (NRA).[220] The NRA was supposed to balance the needs of capital and labor by allowing prices and wages to rise. In some sectors of the economy, notably garment and coal mining, unions were able to use the NRA to build independent unions and improve wages and working conditions.

However, steel firms embraced NRA's provisions that allowed them to set prices but ignored Provision 7A that encouraged independent unions. One steelmaker said "we have found that the [NRA] code does for steel what steel has wanted to have done for it since the start of the century."[221] In some cases, wages of steelworkers fell to bring them into compliance with NRA codes.[222] Government spending boosted corporate revenues; by one account, almost half of the steel rails bought by companies derived from federal funds.[223] Nonetheless, many businessmen viewed the expansion of government macro-economic planning as an improper expansion of governmental authority and applauded the 1935 Supreme Court ruling that the NRA was unconstitutional. While the constitutional dramas of these years suggested that a historic shift in government was under way, this phase of the New Deal had done little to shift the balance of power between workers and corporations in steel.

Despite the conservative tendencies of the New Deal, some workers pushed for fundamental reforms. During the early 1930s, activists in the National Miners Union, the Steel and Metal Workers Industrial Union, and the rank-and-file movement of the Amalgamated struggled to build industrial unions. The NMU and the SMWIU espoused a radical critique of the alliance between capitalists and government while the Amalgamated retained more faith in reformers. These efforts failed, although they laid the groundwork for the emergence of CIO unions in the coal, steel, and electrical industries.

Communists naturally viewed the Pittsburgh region—one of the most industrialized regions in the world—as a logical base for their movement. Victories won here would leverage revolutionary gains in other regions. In coal, steel, and the metal trades, wages and working conditions remained poor, particularly for the large numbers of European immigrants and African Americans concentrated in the mines, mills, and factories of the region. Revolutionary unionists included numerous black and immigrant cadres whose organizing was nominally overseen by William Z. Foster, an experienced trade unionist best known for his leading role in the 1919 steel strike. Communists first sought to organize coal miners whose wages had plummeted and whose union was devastated since the late 1920s. Many miners were angry with UMWA President John L. Lewis for his harsh centralization of decision making, an arguably stolen national election in 1926, lost strikes, and the "sellout" of miners to the coal operators. Before being thrown out of the union, dissidents, radicals, and communists developed a formidable opposition to the UMWA's machine. Communists then launched the National Miners Union, but soon discovered that Lewis, to say nothing of coal operators, was a formidable opponent.[224]

The NMU tried to build a union without the support of either the state or federal government and failed. The party's implacable opposition to "social fascists" meant that when the NMU led Pennsylvania miners on strike in 1931, reform Governor Pinchot provided little assistance. Pinchot had proven himself willing to protect UMWA pickets from company attacks, but the NMU had to go it alone. The twenty thousand or more miners who joined the NMU strike were brutally attacked by deputy sheriffs, the Coal and Iron Police, and at times, the UMWA itself. According to one observer, the only thing in ready supply amongst hungry miners was angry and radical rhetoric. NMU members labeled mine operators, their gun thugs and UMWA leaders such as Lewis, Pat Fagan, or Philip Murray with the same epithet: "Mussolini."[225] The CP sent Foster and twenty-five organizers into the Pittsburgh district, but sheer militancy failed to win the strike. The union lacked sufficient strike funds or political leverage to force owners to capitulate. Indeed, employers signed contracts with the UMWA, and the strike collapsed. Several hundred miners joined the party, but three-quarters of them soon left the organization.[226] By December 1933, the NMU was a hollow shell, and most party members in the region were "composed almost exclusively of the blacklisted, foreign-born miners."[227] By 1934, left-wing miners had returned to the UMWA where they hoped to rebuild internal opposition to the Lewis machine.[228] In their eagerness to prove their fighting credentials, communists overestimated their strength and destroyed their union.

After the collapse of the NMU, the UMWA enjoyed explosive growth. The NRA was tailor-made for the UMWA. UMWA organizers assured workers that the NRA promised government protection from company reprisals. Employing the classic slogan that "the President wants you to join the UMWA" (whether Roosevelt or Lewis they did not specify), organizers often had simply to collect completed application cards. In one especially good period, 300,000 miners joined in ninety days.

The union had had a long history of organizing the thousands of small coal operators into regional price-setting agreements in which all companies voluntarily agreed to pay the union scale. Under the NRA, the UMWA reorganized the employees of commercial coal companies from Illinois to Pennsylvania whose agreements were given the backing of the federal government. Yet the union failed to organize the so-called captive mines. Steel companies, such as U.S. Steel's H.C. Frick Coke Company, employed thousands of miners who supplied the mills and coke ovens with coking coal. In 1933, a resurgent UMWA tried to force steel companies to bargain with the union.[229] Tens of thousands of miners answered the UMWA's call and struck the captive mines in the Connellsville fields south of Pittsburgh. Sheriffs and the Coal and Iron Police injured dozens; a few miners were killed. After several weeks, U.S. Steel eventually agreed to the wages and working conditions of the NRA coal code. However, U.S. Steel would not agree to bargain directly with the UMWA. Workers responded by spreading the strike throughout Pennsylvania, affecting three-quarters of all coal production.[230]

At this point, left-wing miners attempted to gain control of the strike and led a mass picket of the biggest consumer of their coal: the U.S. Steel Clairton Works. Clairton supplied the fuel for all of U.S. Steel's mills in the Mon Valley, and a successful strike here would have effectively shut down the Corporation. Although the strike had been called by the UMWA, or at least its left wing, many rank-and-file Amalgamated members like Francis DiCola answered its call for solidarity: "If everybody would have come out, they would have got the union." At a mass meeting in Clairton, three thousand Amalgamated members voted to strike. But half of those "union men" ended up crossing the picket lines of the miners, and most of those steelworkers who struck were blacklisted. "I knew a lot of cranemen . . . they never got their jobs back." Years later, many steelworkers claimed that the company organized the strike in order to fire Clairton's activists. More likely, trade unionists were embarrassed that they had not joined these "premature industrial unionists."[231]

Pinchot intervened to help the UMWA salvage the strike of the seventy thousand captive miners. Pinchot ordered the State Police and the National Guard into the coal fields; under the guise of preventing violence, they also helped to prevent strikebreaking. Several months later, in January 1934, U.S. Steel signed an agreement that bound them to bargain with whomever their employees elected to represent them. The company insisted that this agreement preserved the "liberty" of their employees to bargain on their own behalf. Most miners chose the UMWA. Harvey O'Connor observed that when the miners returned to work "there was no jubilation. As a final gesture of defiance they marched in columns, headed by the American flag, and marched, sullen, silent but united back into industrial feudalism."[232] Nonetheless, the miners had breached the ramparts of the steel trust.

That fall, the miners' offensive took a political form. The UMWA and other industrial workers provided the margin of victory for Pennsylvania's first Democratic chief executive since 1890. George Earle's alliance with labor was so close that his Lieutenant Governor, Thomas Kennedy, was also the Secretary-Treasurer of the UMWA.[233] Democrats also elected a U.S. Senator, Joseph Guffey, who sponsored legislation in 1935 to replace the NRA that the Supreme Court had just deemed unconstitutional. The Guffey-Snyder act was the brainchild of John L. Lewis, who engineered support from miners and many coal operators; it established price boards for coal operators and provided government protections for unions. The resurgence of Pennsylvania's Democrats and the New Deal provided coal miners with the rare opportunity to use government to achieve their ends.[234]

In time, the UMWA would once again lay siege to steel, but first the day belonged to the communists. As in coal, communists' capacity for uncompromising struggle with employers and the state helped lay the groundwork for Lewis and his CIO. The communists had been slowly preparing for their offensive in steel. In the late 1920s, they had virtually no members in the metal trades. In 1927, the Pittsburgh District of the Communist Party could claim just one shop paper, that in the Westinghouse electrical complex. Over the next two years, party cadres built four more. The party claimed roughly eight hundred members, but most were unemployed. (In 1931, one cadre lamented that Pittsburgh's party possessed only five employed steelworkers.) Mobilization of the unemployed played a central role in party work; jobless steelworkers, for instance, were used to bolster NMU picket lines. But since communists lacked large numbers of employed steelworker members, the development of a shop-floor presence in steel was slow.[235] Shop papers such as the one at Crucible Steel attacked the danger, intense heat, inadequate sanitation, low wages, and speedups. Politicians, including those from the Socialist Party, were denounced as tools of the bosses.[236] By November 1929, the Communist Party had established a headquarters in Pittsburgh and had hired several organizers, including three African Americans.[237]

During the Depression, increasingly desperate men adopted desperate measures, and the influence of the communists grew. By 1934, the organization that came to be known as the Steel and Metal Workers Industrial

Union (SMWIU) had peaked in strength. Membership was modest. The Pittsburgh district had nine SMWIU branches, several in Ambridge, one in McKees Rocks, and another in McKeesport. One local in Greensburg claimed nine hundred members. The SMWIU was strongest in smaller shops, although nuclei existed at J&L's Aliquippa and Southside Works and at the Homestead Works of U.S. Steel. One organizer claimed between three thousand and four thousand members in the Pittsburgh region with two to four times that number throughout the country. Its appeal was strongest amongst immigrant and black laborers, the most vulnerable workers in the industry. Most native-born white workers joined company unions, the Amalgamated or nothing at all.[238]

The union and its members often fell short of the Communist Party's expectations. Unlike the CP itself, the organization of the union stressed "rank-and-file control" that in practice allowed union locals a high degree of autonomy. Communists dominated the national leadership of the union, although most union members were not party members. Some communists lamented that there were not even party units in some union locals. In contrast to the party's view that the global Depression had deeply radicalized industrial workers, just a dozen unionists joined the party from the SMWIU. In the wake of one SMWIU strike in which several thousand workers participated, one journalist found most unionists were completely unaware of any connection to communism. In the workers' view, the SMWIU was "just a union, our union. Just because Eagan [a leader of the SMWIU] was a communist didn't matter. Never talked communism around Ambridge. They all seem to stress the importance of legal frummery. The charter, for example, was a 'legal charter.'"[239] Some CP officials blamed the slow pace of recruitment, in both the union and the party, on SMWIU cadres who put union work ahead of party work. Communist steelworkers often refused to sell the *Daily Worker* or to campaign openly on behalf of the party. Rather than acknowledging the real limits that the spy system imposed on activists in steel towns, party officials preferred to view cautious communists as "party comrades . . . capitulating before the red scare."[240] In numerical terms, the results were meager; one leader of the SMWIU later admitted that it was a "skeleton organization."[241] A contemporary assessment of the SMWIU concluded that it had "no organizational integration, no funds, and suffered from a lack of competent personnel; but these inadequacies were more than compensated by the tremendous courage and energy of the union's leaders."[242]

Yet the SMWIU was nothing if not militant. The Communist Party's view that conditions were ripe for a revolutionary upsurge among workers led the SMWIU into numerous strikes; in some instances they were pulled along by events.[243] A few strikes were successful; others less so. In 1933, the SMWIU succeeded in leading 500 workers off the job at the Pressed Steel Car plant in McKees Rocks and getting dozens of union members rehired.[244] A harsh fate awaited most workers who ventured onto the picket line. Organizers were run out of many towns, and members were frequently blacklisted.[245] For instance, a month after 1,100 SMWIU members in Greensburg struck the Walworth Company, 300 of them were blacklisted.[246] A terse report from Coroapolis laid out the difficulties that industrial unionists confronted: "The SMWIU was going along fine until the bosses shot and clubbed the workers."[247]

The 1933 Ambridge strike was indicative of the strengths and weaknesses of the SMWIU. A handful of members led thousands of workers from mill to mill in a march reminiscent of the May 1, 1916, Westinghouse workers strike. In 1934, strikers arrived at the gates of the Spang-Chalfant company, where events took a familiar and bloody turn. The town's burgess, a former union man, told organizers that "whether you call off the pickets or not, they're coming off." Two hundred deputy sheriffs (many from the Coal and Iron Police in nearby Aliquippa) used "four tear gas guns, twenty buckshot guns, two machine guns, revolvers and riot sticks" to drive strikers away from the plant gates and then "fired unnecessarily at the fleeing men." Although not a target of the strike, U.S. Steel's nearby American Bridge Company donated almost six thousand dollars to pay for this incident of industrial policing.[248] One bystander was killed, and several pickets were wounded.[249]

The unwillingness of Governor Pinchot to safeguard the SMWIU pickets, as he had done with the UMWA at Clairton, left steelworkers vulnerable and exposed. Pinchot supported reformist unions, but not radical ones as they faced the full power of the "industrial police." In Ambridge, the sheriff bragged that "we've broken this strike" and that in the event of another, his "men have been given instructions to have no mercy."[250] Harvey O'Connor found that after the strike, the "whole town [was] pretty well terrorized" and thus steelworkers were spared from confronting truly "merciless" riot control.[251] Years later, a black steelworker recalled simply that "they beat 'em up. They *beat them up*."[252] The failure of the state to guarantee steelworkers the right to picket, a right Governor Pinchot ensured that members of anti-communist unions such as the UMWA enjoyed, doomed the SMWIU and the Ambridge workers to defeat.

But the internal weaknesses of the SMWIU and the CP-USA compounded the weaknesses engendered by the antipathy of the state and employers to the union. After the Ambridge strike, communists in the SMWIU reassessed their tactics. Some argued that members' eagerness to call strikes, while consistent with the ultra-radical line of the party, in practice precluded the development of the necessary levels of organization in the workplace that would ensure the survival of the union. John Meldon, the national Secretary-Treasurer, admitted that fifteen members in Ambridge recruited three thousand members solely through advocating a "mass organization and strike." Yet in the rapid movement to strike, cadres ignored the "detail work so necessary in the building of an industrial union." There was no shop steward system, secondary leadership, or strike support. The result was a failed strike and the collapse of the union.[253] Meldon's approach would have required slowing down workers and the party in order to build a durable, rank-and-file union. The party rejected Meldon's assessment as overly pessimistic; in their view, Meldon misread the revolutionary character of the times.[254]

Instead, the Communist Party decided that its only tactical error had been to try to lead strikes in small shops or where communists did not control the union. In the future, it would concentrate party membership in the largest workplaces. Party leaders envisioned a strike like that at Ambridge, but led by communists and conducted on a larger scale. While James Eagan admitted that most union members to date worked in small machine shops, he opined that "without solid basis for our union in the steel industry the organization in the metal industry will not be a stable and powerful union." A single strike would prove easier to coordinate than sending organizers "hither and thither to reach these smaller mills."[255]

Confronting the largest, strongest employers proved to be the undoing of the SMWIU. As in Ambridge, big steel companies possessed the full cooperation of elected officials, whose ire against reds was especially strong. One journalist reported that "no communist meeting can be held in Homestead—or in any steel borough for that matter. 'We just won't tolerate it and there's no use arguing. That's final and absolute,' announced Homestead's police chief." Duquesne's police "maintain[ed] an absolute checkup on every available meeting space" in order to prevent communists from gaining a foothold.[256] In December of 1933, Homestead's SMWIU members reported to the union newspaper, the *Steel and Metal Worker*, that their mill's managers urged workers to join the Amalgamated instead of the SMWIU. Whether that report was true or not, it revealed the union's weakness in the larger mills.[257] By February 1934, SMWIU activists were reduced to selling a few copies of the *Daily Worker* at the plant gates, and they soon shut down its Homestead office.[258] The campaign to capture the large mills for the SMWIU had failed. Communists now shifted their focus to building a united front with the "rank-and-file" members of the Amalgamated.[259]

In the wake of the SMWIU's failed drive and the passage of the NRA, the Amalgamated attracted numerous members. With little or no encouragement from the national leadership of the Amalgamated, steelworkers joined its locals. National membership surged from about five thousand to at least eighty thousand. Steelworker William Theis recalled that "the Amalgamated made some effort to organize steel, but [it was] a rather feeble effort." Some employers viewed the Amalgamated as a lesser evil than the SMWIU, but more important was the different attitude that government took toward the Amalgamated.[260] John Fitch, a long-time observer of the steelworkers, noted that U.S. Steel executives, who admitted that "a few years ago we would have fired" unionists "like that," now feared the repercussions from government if they penalized unionists.[261] On October 14, 1934, Aliquippa workers met in a hall in Ambridge (where the SMWIU pickets had been brutally assaulted) and enjoyed their first mass union meeting. The explanation of Ambridge's transformation bore witness to the political support enjoyed by the Amalgamated: "everything went along peacefully due to the protection of the State Police."[262] In addition to Pinchot's protection, Amalgamated members counted on support from the Democratic administration in Washington. Workers delighted especially in one highly publicized sign of the company's waning power over government. In 1934 Secretary of Labor Frances Perkins met with steel unionists in Homestead over the strenuous objections of local Republican politicians. Perkins' reported assessment of Homestead's Mayor Cavanaugh ("he's a very nervous man") suggested the strain the spy system and its agents were under.[263]

Yet steel companies had not dismantled the spy system. Radical journalists discovered that U.S. Steel retained a firm that kept extensive files on its employees, activists, and those employees who signed union cards. These reports were shared with the press and the FBI. Arthur Young, Vice President of U.S. Steel, claimed that "the Corporation does not spy upon its men, although it is forced to follow to some extent the activities of certain outsiders." Private detective agencies, however, contradicted this claim. J&L's officials openly admitted that their spy system was "excellent."[264] In expectation of a strike, "the J&L police force was strengthened and equipped equal to a well-equipped army."[265] Even so, government support embold-ened many workers to join the Amalgamated.

Despite the prejudices of its national leadership, many rank-and-file activists in the Amalgamated saw inter-racial unity as the precondition for success. The President of Duquesne's local, William Sprang, was particu-larly concerned about racism: "My sole idea in going into the movement," he said, "was to get white and colored people together whom capitalists have tried to keep apart."[266] In the Fort Dukane lodge (Duquesne), blacks were elected to numerous offices.[267] One worker described Fletcher William-son, Fort Dukane's black Vice President, as "always ready to die for his fel-lowmen in order that they should have a better day's work and better wages."[268] Black workers responded enthusiastically in Duquesne and Rankin, but in Homestead and Clairton, where blacks had been elected only to minor offices, African Americans remained skeptical.[269] Unionists willing to recruit black workers apparently proved more successful in organ-izing all kinds of workers. By one estimate, Fort Dukane had organized 90 percent of the workers while the "Spirit of 1892" local in Homestead had signed up perhaps 30 percent of the mill.[270]

Managers attempted to frustrate solidarity with appeals to racial and ethnic prejudice. In Duquesne, an anonymous leaflet from a "citizens' committee" charged that unionists were led by "a Bunch of Hoodlums, Hunkies and a few Negroes banded together by their own greed." Vigi-lantes threatened to lynch unionists of both races. In Rankin, a supervisor told a black unionist, "don't let them fool you. Remember 1919. They [the white unionists] . . . will go back and leave you out." Given the historic animosity between white unionists and black workers, it is a credit to the efforts of Amalgamated activists that U.S. Steel had to work hard to con-vince black workers *not* to join the union. The extent of inter-racial organ-izing was all the more remarkable because the national leadership of the Amalgamated remained indifferent to black workers. Horace Cayton and George Mitchell argued that "seldom in the history of the American labor movement has there been a more genuine and straightforward attempt by white workers to join hands with Negroes in spite of the supineness of their national officers."[271] Support for the Amalgamated amongst blacks was strongly correlated to skill levels. Black laborers supported the Amalgamated as strongly as immigrant whites, while the hostility of skilled blacks matched that of their white counterparts.[272]

By 1934, many "rank-and-filers" in the Amalgamated dreamed of a large strike that would shatter the power of steel companies. While this was also the ambition of the SMWIU, most leaders in the Amalgamated rejected open collaboration with the SMWIU because they would have "been smeared immediately as Communists."[273] Instead, rank-and-filers lobbied for federal intervention. But Roosevelt dreaded a replay of the earlier coal strike, and New Deal administrators did little more than stall unionists with promises of investigations and legislation. The experience helped the NRA to earn the epithet "National Run Around" among radical workers. Without political support, few were willing to carry out their threat to strike in June of 1934. (Few rank-and-filers believed that the willingness of the SMWIU to support their strike outweighed the antipathy of their own union and Roosevelt to the strike.) The Amalgamated's national leadership remained as timid and inept as it had been in 1919; however, excelling in political infighting, it expelled many rank-and-file locals. Membership in the union plunged.[274] At this point, communists were ordered by the party to abandon the SMWIU for the Amalgamated. Small in number but highly disciplined, communists played a key role in maintaining an Amalgamated presence in the mills and consolidating the rank-and-file's opposition to the leadership of the Amalgamated.[275]

The final constituency in the union movement consisted of the company unionists. After the passage of the NRA, U.S. Steel established the Employee Representative Plans that "bargained" over inconsequential items like the quality of the bathrooms—anything but wages and working conditions. At National Tube, the manager promoted the ERP as "a friendly medium of direct contact between men and management," adding that "this condition would not be possible under outside union domination."[276] The ERP at Jones and Laughlin was set up without an election of its "members." At Duquesne, the ERP held few meetings and collected no dues; instead, the company paid all expenses. The President of Duquesne's ERP, Charlie Erickson, argued that the union could strike if its members voted to do so. But when asked "who would pay your strike benefits?" he had no answer.[277] Some workers saw in the ERPs a safe means to organize, and some minor issues were resolved. Indeed, after the collapse of the Amalgamated, these organizations were increasingly taken over by activist employees. For instance, in May 1935, the ERP at Edgar Thomson demanded a 10 percent wage increase, and by January 1936, at least nine of the larger U.S. Steel ERPs were coordinating their demands. While there were many "company men" in the ERPs, unionist-minded ERP officials from Braddock, Clairton, Duquesne, and throughout the country were demanding a grievance procedure, a forty-hour week, and higher wages.[278] While U.S. Steel made numerous small concessions, it was a matter of too little, too late; by 1937, many ERP men were openly working with the CIO to establish an independent union.[279]

THE STEEL WORKERS ORGANIZING COMMITTEE

Formed in 1936, the Steel Workers Organizing Committee (SWOC) absorbed the Amalgamated (communists and rank-and-filers) and the ERPs, but the chief influence on the new union was the UMWA. The UMWA provided the SWOC with much-needed financial support, organizers, and political muscle. Its pledge of $500,000 proved to be just a down payment on what it would cost to organize steel. Desperate for organizers, John L. Lewis (who, as the President of the UMWA and largest donor to the SWOC, determined all of its key policies) turned to old enemies from the UMWA, such as progressive John Brophy, to help fill the SWOC's two hundred staff jobs. Lewis also hired sixty communists to organize immigrant, black, and Mexican workers.[280] The union's leadership reflected different priorities from its organizing staff. SWOC's leaders, Philip Murray, David McDonald, and Van Bittner, were chosen as much for their loyalty to Lewis as anything else. They made sure that each communist hired was "a marked man, closely watched at all times and dispensed with as soon as possible." After having spent years in bloody fratricide to centralize the UMWA, Lewis made sure that most of SWOC's authority was in the hands of its national officers from the outset. Thus, although local elections were held after 1937, the UMWA appointed all of SWOC's national officials, and no national elections were held until 1942. By this point, SWOC was renamed the United Steel Workers of America (USWA). According to Len De Caux, the CIO's chief publicist, the SWOC was a "well-oiled union machine" from the beginning.[281]

The SWOC benefited from the fact that New Deal Democrats had already begun to dismantle the legal supports for the spy system. Like his predecessor, Gifford Pinchot, Governor George Earle refused to grant charters for private police, and on June 15, 1935, he signed legislation that abolished the Coal and Iron Police.[282] After the passage of the Wagner

Act in 1935, the federal government committed itself to protecting workers
from company intimidation. One of the first expressions of this commitment was the La Follette committee. Throughout 1936, U.S. Senator Robert
La Follette and the Committee on Education and Labor investigated the
extensive networks of spies, agents provocateurs, and hired gunmen maintained by corporations. The La Follette committee's hearings documented
that steel firms were not only monitoring CIO activists throughout the
region, but were stockpiling machine guns and tear gas in mills at locations
such as Homestead and Duquesne. The La Follette hearings and the resultant press releases coincided perfectly with SWOC's organizing drive.
Additional assistance came from Pennsylvania Democrats. In July 1936,
Lieutenant Governor Kennedy proclaimed to two thousand steelworkers
and coal miners in Homestead that the state would protect their civil liberties and provide them with relief if they were fired for union activity.[283]

The SWOC placed enormous importance on the election of New
Deal Democrats to state and national office. During the 1936 elections,
the CIO donated $600,000 to the Democrats, but money was just the tip
of the iceberg. At Lewis' urging, the Pennsylvania Federation of Labor abandoned its traditional "non-partisanship" (and rhetorical support for building a Labor Party) in favor of endorsing Roosevelt through a vehicle called
Labor's Non-Partisan League (LNPL). The LNPL operated as labor's organization within the Democratic Party. The LNPL signed up 150,000 members
and through them distributed over 7 million pieces of campaign literature.[284]
Union organizers sought out pro-labor candidates, offered them opportunities to speak before union audiences in Roosevelt's cause, and that of organized labor. The CIO then got out the vote. The SWOC emphasized the
plank of the Democratic platform that promised "organization without interference from employers."[285] The result was a "smashing victory" for Roosevelt.
In Aliquippa, Homestead, Duquesne, and McKeesport, Roosevelt won by a
two-to-one margin. Numerous old-guard Republican state senators were
swept out of office.[286] The political investment soon paid dividends. Steel
companies unilaterally raised wages and seven thousand new members joined
the union in the ten days following the election.[287] During 1937, Pennsylvania passed the "little Wagner Act" which prohibited the use of privately
paid deputy sheriffs, labor spies, company unions, and blacklists.[288]

Political victories removed many obstacles to unionization, but fear
lingered. Steelworkers had been twice bitten by the Amalgamated, and
they proved thrice shy with the SWOC. Even though organizers assured

workers that there would be no strike and provided three months of free dues, the SWOC found it rough going. Philip Murray "found the men in the steel mills shot through with fear—fear of the boss, fear of the job."[289] Charles Bollinger recalled that in 1936 "it was a slow hard struggle getting them to sign up. We used to hit the gates and they used to rush past us." Few believed that there would be no reprisals for joining the union. As Bollinger remembered, workers "thought that if you'd even dreamt about a union last night, you didn't have a job" the next day. Freeman Patton, a black worker at the Clairton Works, recalled that "I got enough slobber on my arm to float a canoe. You try to hand him a card to sign him up and give him three months free dues" and black or white "he'd spit on your hand."[290] After a year of effort, the SWOC had 1,100 members at the Homestead Works, about 10 percent of the total.[291]

Yet the SWOC's timing was inspired, and its political connections allowed it to attract many workers to its banner. At the beginning of the SWOC drive, the Homestead Works was operating at 70 percent of capacity; by May of 1937, Homestead was operating at nearly 90 percent of capacity, and it employed twice as many workers as had been working there just a few months before.[292] The SWOC's threatened strike of coal miners and steelworkers at U.S. Steel, set to begin on April 1, 1937, went untested. Political events favored the SWOC. Steel companies were harassed by Senate investigations into corporate abuses of workers' freedom of speech and assembly (the La Follette committee) and war profiteering (the Nye committee). In this context, the refusal of the federal government to release military contracts proved decisive. On March 2, 1937, U.S. Steel signed a national agreement with the SWOC.[293]

In the coming months, the SWOC built its strength as much through legal and political maneuvering as through on-the-ground organizing. Its first major victory came as the courts upheld the constitutionality of the Wagner Act. The April 12, 1937, decision of the Supreme Court declared company unions illegal, thereby preventing U.S. Steel from attempting to bargain with both the SWOC and the ERPs. The National Labor Relations Board demanded that unionists who had been fired for organizing, a particularly severe problem at the "little steel" firms of J&L and Republic, had to be rehired. (For months, *Steel Labor*, the newspaper of the SWOC, carried stories and photos of union men who got back their jobs and collected thousands of dollars of back pay.)[294] While the more hard-line steel firms maintained the spy system, they were unusually circumspect about it.

Early in 1937, a SWOC activist was interviewed by Captain Mauk, the head of J&L's security, for a job as a spy. The unionist claimed he saw the magazines for machine guns in Mauk's office, but most of what Mauk related indicated a new caution in the spy system. Mauk told the union man that while spies had formerly been paid directly by the company police, new laws meant that spies were now put on the general payroll and given easy jobs. Mauk admitted that openly employing spies would result "in a lot of federal men snooping around."[295] (Only in January 1938 would the NLRB would rule that the Wagner Act prohibited employers from employing spies to intimidate or restrain their employees from joining a union of their choice.)[296]

In contrast to U.S. Steel, J&L was bracing itself for a confrontation that was not long in coming. Yet support from workers and politicians enabled the SWOC to best J&L. When the SWOC ordered a strike against J&L on May 12, 1937, Governor Earle ordered state troopers to prevent picket-line violence. J&L never had a chance to attempt to break through the mass pickets in front of its Pittsburgh and Aliquippa mills. The walk-out remained solid among blacks, immigrants, and native-born whites.[297] Steelworkers were well aware of Earle's aid; when the Governor and his wife (whom steelworkers termed the "Joan of Arc of Labor") appeared on the streets of Aliquippa, strikers cheered.[298] The playing field thus leveled, the strike fever spread to Pittsburgh Steel Company on May 14.[299] With most of their production concentrated in the Pittsburgh region, both employers quickly agreed to allow an election to determine whether SWOC should represent their employees. Workers overwhelmingly chose the union, and for the first time in almost fifty years, unionists emerged victorious from a major steel strike.[300] Not a life had been lost. "There is real solidarity now," remarked one observer, "and certainly no fear. In fact, workers go out of their way to thumb their noses at company police by whom they have been cowed for years."[301]

Victories won against these "little steel" firms, however, could not be extended beyond the limits of SWOC's organizational and political support. On May 20, 1937, Republic Steel stole a march on SWOC and locked out several SWOC locals in Ohio. The union called a strike at all mills owned by Republic, Inland, and Youngstown Sheet and Tube. The centers of strike action were in Ohio and Illinois, and there companies massed sufficient force to overpower workers. Outside the Republic mill in Chicago, the Chicago police shot and killed several workers, many as they attempted to flee. Roosevelt saw his strategy of economic recovery being bogged down by SWOC's strikes. He equated the violence of companies with the irresponsibility of unions and called for a "plague on both your houses." It was an eloquent symbol of the limits of the New Deal. John L. Lewis retorted that "it ill behooves one who has supped at labor's table and who has been sheltered in labor's house to curse with equal fervor and fine impartiality both labor and its adversaries when they become locked in deadly embrace."[302]

Seeking to salvage something from the debacle, the SWOC struck Bethlehem's Johnstown, Pennsylvania, mill on June 12. The strike began promisingly. After some picket line violence, Earle called state troopers into Johnstown to prevent bloodshed. Once again, the effect was to use troopers to protect pickets from harassment. But the strike was collapsing in the face of the company's determined "back to work" movement. The UMWA called upon thousands of coal miners to march in Johnstown to stiffen steelworkers' resolve. Neither coal miners nor the declaration of martial law by Earle could stem the tide moving against the SWOC. In the face of widespread public outcry, Earle was forced to rescind martial law.[303] The strike was over, the union beaten.

LABOR'S FAILED BID FOR POLITICAL HEGEMONY

Yet the CIO still maintained considerable momentum. After their victory at the hustings in November 1936, some in the Democratic Party claimed that "labor did not make the Democratic Party, the Democratic Party made labor." Thus, the next year, members from the SWOC set out to prove that labor was the driving force of the Democratic Party. In local elections in November 1937, "CIO Democrats" were swept into office in sixteen steel towns.[304] The LNPL mobilized to support its slate of candidates in the Democratic Party's primaries and then again in November. The CIO's triumph came after the split of CIO unions from the AFL, which barely affected the forward motion of Pennsylvania's trade unionists. When the AFL ordered Pittsburgh's Central Labor Union to expel members of the CIO, shortly before the 1937 elections, the CLU complied, but with enormous reluctance. After all, the UMWA, the SWOC, and other CIO unions were now sizeable, powerful unions on their way to political victory.[305] Indeed, in politics, for once, the unions gained the upper hand. In some areas, these were the first Democrats ever elected, and in instances such as that of Elmer Maloy in Duquesne, the new mayors were members of the SWOC.[306] Some officials were simply career Republicans who switched tickets, as, indeed, Governor Earle had been.[307]

The LNPL represented labor's most important effort in fifty years to build an organization and not just win an election. The LNPL was not an independent political party, and thus did not face the obstacles of gaining ballot status and developing a statewide administrative apparatus. Instead, it functioned as a highly organized caucus within the Democratic Party. Its victories in the mill towns were significant, but relatively easy because trade union membership was concentrated in these towns, and the police and taxation powers of local government were limited. In larger cities, such as Pittsburgh, the LNPL proved unable to field a trade unionist, supporting instead a Democrat who turned on the LNPL within a year. Through Governor Earle, the LNPL gained indirect control over state government and its police, but this stirred the Republican Party (and much of the Democratic machine) into action. The politics of policing proved a two-edged sword. While troopers had been called into industrial disputes for years, ostensibly to prevent violence, Lynn Adams, the Commissioner of the State Police, resigned over Earle's "partisan" use of troopers in the Johnstown strike. Adams then became the principal detective who investigated the Earle Administration for graft. While only three officials were convicted, these scandals were unduly publicized by the state's anti-labor media and helped to turn the Democrats out of office in 1938.[308]

The 1938 elections should have been labor's finest moment. Unions had more members than ever before; the UMWA and SWOC alone had hundreds of thousands of members in Pennsylvania. The CIO and the LNPL backed Lieutenant Governor Thomas Kennedy for Governor, while the AFL endorsed the candidate of the Democratic machine, an unknown Pittsburgh lawyer. Rumors circulated that FDR himself opposed Kennedy and the LNPL in order to check the growing strength of John L. Lewis. Furthermore, the LNPL spent less on the 1938 primaries than on the 1936 general elections.[309] Whatever the cause, the CIO proved unable to overcome the opposition of the AFL and the mayors of Pittsburgh and Philadelphia in the primaries. One leader of the AFL's carpenters union urged his fellows to "Stop Lewis! Stop Kennedy! Stop the CIO!"[310] While the LNPL swung its support back to the Democrats, the Democrats lost the general election. Republicans retained control of the seat in the U.S. Senate and regained most of the State Legislature. The defeat prevented any expansion of the New Deal and slowed the growth of the CIO in the Commonwealth.[311] The house of labor stood divided against itself. The AFL and CIO fought it out in the 1938 Democratic primary and ultimately defeated each other. Labor's fratricidal conflicts, within and between the two union federations, would deepen over the next two years.

The spy system condemned by the SWOC and investigated by the La Follette committee was dying, but a new one spearheaded by the government had already begun to take its place. Even as steelworkers signed their first contracts, the Justice Department circulated a list of communists on the SWOC's payroll to other AFL unionists and the press.[312] A veteran anti-communist, Philip Murray carefully weeded reds from the union's payroll.[313] But between 1936 and 1939, communists in the locals diligently worked within the SWOC and the Democratic Party as part of their tactic of building a "popular front." But in 1940, when the Communist Party sought to develop its political independence by getting its party on the ballot, all hell broke loose in Pittsburgh. The newspapers printed the names of voters who had signed petitions to put the CP on the ballot. Citizens were invited to inform the committee headed by Congressman Dies or the FBI if their signature had been forged. On the strength of these affidavits, twenty-eight communists (some of them SWOC members) were convicted of ballot fraud.[314] Anti-communists in the SWOC sought to expel members of the CP. At J&L's Pittsburgh Works, local unionists took "the initiative in eliminating Communists, Nazis and other un-American subversives from [their] . . . fold."[315] David McDonald, a leading anti-communist at the top of the SWOC, told steelworkers to "reject communism in the same breath with which they reject fascism or Nazism."[316]

The federalization of labor surveillance would accelerate during World War II. All defense workers, including tens of thousands of steelworkers, were required to register with the FBI. As in World War I, the FBI harassed radicals. The State Police continued to monitor those 120,000 criminals or "persons with communistic and radical tendencies," coordinating their efforts with "Federal, State and Local Governmental Authorities."[317] In one high-profile case at Duquesne, a left-wing worker was investigated by the State Police in 1942. In 1943, both the State Police and the War Department investigated him and then in 1944, the FBI also checked up on him.[318] While some union officials "were damn sick and tired of the FBI nosing around" their districts telling them "that this guy in our outfit is a Communist," others bragged about their relationship with the FBI. One District Director prided himself on the "very official" data that allowed him to ferret out radicals in the union locals. "Only certain people . . . on the right track" could receive such information.[319] Thus while the destruction of private police and the creation of labor law was the precondition for the unionization of steelworkers, the federalization of labor policing helped to discipline unionists as to the limits of the possible.

CONCLUSION: THE INEVITABILITY OF CONSERVATIVE UNIONISM IN STEEL?

From the late nineteenth century until the 1930s, Pennsylvania's employers and government frustrated the organization of industrial workers. Labor parties were destroyed by pro-business "machines," labor politicians were co-opted, and labor legislation was overturned by the courts. Private police, spies, the militia, and the state police battered unions. Industrialists compounded the disorganization of workers by structuring job markets along racial and ethnic lines. By contrast, industrial corporations enjoyed enormous economic power that was maintained by their privileged legal status, widespread political influence, and extensive police powers. Publicized efforts at "trust-busting" notwithstanding, government accelerated the concentration of wealth of monopolists through its policies of industrial policing and the generous military contracts granted to a few firms. As a result, before steelworkers could build a union, they needed some measure of political power to offset that of steel companies.

Thus, rebuilding labor in the 1920s and 1930s was a decidedly political process. Communist attempts to organize coal miners and steelworkers failed, although they facilitated the consolidation of other groups such as the Amalgamated and the UMWA. The challenge of the left spurred the efforts of pro-labor reformers in the Republican and then the Democratic Parties to undermine the police powers and spy systems of industrialists. Eventually, workers in mill towns enjoyed a widened range of civil liberties. As importantly, politicians extended crucial support to certain unions such as the UMWA, the Amalgamated, and the SWOC. Workers began to develop levels of class organization and solidarity that transcended race and ethnicity.

The SWOC succeeded where so many others had failed. Unlike the SMWIU or the Amalgamated, the SWOC had enormous resources, able leaders, and the unswerving loyalty of hundreds of thousands of workers. The dictatorial power of John L. Lewis over the UMWA—and to a large extent over the SWOC—allowed him to mobilize pressure on the New Deal governments in Harrisburg and Washington. The resultant political support was crucial to labor's victories. The cutoff of naval contracts to steel firms in 1936 and 1937 helped to bring U.S. Steel to the bargaining table. When steelworkers struck J&L, state troopers guarded their pickets and federal administrators oversaw workers' union election. The resulting victory for industrial unionism was rooted in shop-floor and political organization.

The SWOC was organized on an industrial basis, meaning that any steelworker, regardless of skill, race, or national origin, could join. Gone were the days of craft unionism in the face of industrial feudalism. But what kind of union was the SWOC? In comparison to other industrial unions, the SWOC was conservative in outlook and top-down in style. Unlike the United Automobile Workers, whose local leadership and organization proved crucial to its early successes, the SWOC was more dependent on its national leaders and staff. The CIO union in meatpacking was far more responsive to the interests of black workers than the SWOC. The United Electrical, Radio, and Machine Workers of America (UE) tried to have an elected steward for every foreman so that workers' grievances were resolved on the shop floor. By comparison, the SWOC possessed fewer stewards, and shop-floor organization was less important than shrewd legal strategies and high-level political deals.[320] As we will see in the next chapter, the union proved far less willing and able to counter the disorganization of the workforce, particularly with regard to black workers.

Historians of steel's unionization have argued about whether events could have turned out otherwise. In the 1970s, Staughton Lynd asserted the "possibility of radicalism in steel" in the early 1930s, arguing that had the communists and the rank-and-file Amalgamated activists joined forces before the abortive 1934 general strike, steelworkers might have built their own union from the grass roots. According to Lynd, such a union would have been far more democratic and far less centralized and conservative than the SWOC. On the other side, James Rose has argued that the sheer power of steel companies and the deep divisions among steelworkers precluded any union in steel except a tightly controlled, top-down organization that was national in scope: "The alternative to SWOC unionism in Duquesne was not an alternative, community-based, radical union. Instead it was no union at all."[321] In light of this controversy, it is worth reconsidering the post-1934 history of the SMWIU. Vanquished in steel, the left-led union proved enormously successful among other metalworkers. In 1934, the SMWIU merged briefly with the International Association of Machinists and in 1936 split from the IAM and joined forces with independent unions of electrical and radio workers and formed the UE. The UE became the third largest union in the CIO.[322]

With respect to unionization, metal workers possessed several advantages over steelworkers. Employers in machine-tool shops were generally smaller than big steel companies. Many machine plants were not located in company towns, or at least not towns dominated by machine-tool companies. As a result, skilled machinists were less intimidated and offered younger unionists the benefits of their experience. Organizers still confronted spies and gunmen, particularly in the big electrical and radio plants. According to James Matles, who joined the SMWIU and later became the first Organizing Director of the UE, "for that reason the Metal Workers adopted for the most part the strategy of organizing cautiously and secretly." While the "Metal Workers" led numerous strikes in small shops, in the large plants the emphasis was on building networks of activists who might be active in either the SMWIU or AFL unions. The SMWIU's emphasis on rank-and-file control of the union facilitated impressive member-led organizing. The UE was formed with just thirteen thousand paid members. Within a year, fifty-eight thousand workers joined the UE, a feat accomplished with just four paid organizers. Politics was always hotly debated in the UE, and while the union generally supported the positions of the CP, there was surprising tolerance of political diversity because of the union's culture of rank-and-file control. Still, it took the UE several years to gain what the SWOC won in 1937: a national contract with the dominant employer in the industry.[323]

In 1938, the different political visions and styles of the UE and of SWOC were compatible in the same union federation: the CIO. Both unions supported the Democratic Party and its New Deal. To different degrees, both would support the coming war effort. During the war, the coercive powers of business faded, and battles over the interpretation and enforcement of labor law replaced the naked power struggles of the past. Ironically, the next time labor confronted a spy system, the federal government would run it.

Chapter Two

&

From Great Depression to Great Fear: The "Warfare State" in Steel

"War is Pittsburgh's fairy godmother. The darker the pall that shrouds the battlefield, the blacker the cloud over the city of Iron and Steel. Raging fires leap through a thousand furnaces; great engines beat and hammer the ruddy steel into munitions for Mars; the masters of the mills wring their hands in glee as gold drips from the smoke and gas which are vomited into the leaden skies."

Harvey O'Connor, 1933.[1]

OVERVIEW

In the late 1930s, war, Pittsburgh's grisly "fairy godmother," restarted heavy industry and reshaped the relationships between the steel industry, steel-workers, and government. To some extent, World War II facilitated the extension of the progressive features of the New Deal. Private companies were reluctant to develop war materiel, so government invested billions of dollars in industrial facilities and housing stock. Some wartime agencies minimized the ability of industrialists to reap windfall profits, while others minimized industrial unrest and encouraged unionization. As in World War I, the federal government sought to mobilize a maximum of labor power by dampening the existing patterns of racial and gender discrimination and discouraging labor radicalism.

Within the context of global war and industrial peace, steelworkers consolidated and defined the organizational and political character of their union. The wartime boom favored the union. While the armed services absorbed tens of thousands of unionists, full employment bolstered the will-ingness of workers to participate in the union. Steelworkers surrendered their right to strike as a contribution to the war effort, in exchange for which government agencies and courts defended workers' ability to bargain with employers. Managerial resistance to the union provoked numerous illegal and unauthorized strikes as workers felt their oats. Nonetheless, most struggles between workers and bosses were channeled into wartime agen-cies and publicly monitored in-plant "court systems" that helped to central-ize decision making in the union. While bureaucratic, the system was a welcome relief from the unilateral decision making of foremen or personnel directors. The outcome of policy battles and shopfloor struggles continued to discipline and shape what became the USWA (United Steel Workers of America) into a powerful and highly centralized union.

The growing power of the union caused substantial changes in the relations between workers and managers in the workplace. Struggles over the division of labor, particularly over the implementation of the seniority system, reveal the accumulation of power and solidarity of workers. Senior-ity greatly reduced the arbitrary power of companies over workers and held enormous potential to eradicate discrimination. It was a tremendous vic-tory for workers, who anticipated a future where ethnicity or race (and per-haps even gender) would not dictate what jobs they held. For that reason, employers struggled to maintain long-standing systems of racial, ethnic, and gender discrimination. While steelworkers realized substantial gains in implementing seniority, their effectiveness was initially hampered by the fragility of the union, the determined opposition of employers, and by work-ers' often weak commitment to principles of solidarity. As we shall see, the organizational gains of steelworkers in government and the workplace out-stripped their political development.

THE EFFECTS OF WORLD WAR II ON STEEL

The war revived the steel industry. Between 1936 and 1939, steel firms earned $250 million in profits on sales of $3.3 billion. By 1941, sales had doubled and profits quadrupled.[2] War orders boosted steel production from 50 percent of capacity in 1939 to almost 100 percent two years later.[3] From 1940 until 1944, U.S. Steel alone filled nearly $2 billion worth of war orders, making it the sixteenth largest military contractor in the country.[4] Lobbying by companies and military agencies in the fall of 1940 convinced

Congress to abandon legislation that limited the profits of government contractors to less than 12 percent.[5] Still, strict price controls and progressive taxation prevented steel firms from reaping the windfall profits they had enjoyed during World War I. Nonetheless steel companies' profits during 1940–45 remained well above the amounts earned during 1936–39, and the war afforded them the opportunity to benefit from government-sponsored modernization.[6]

The federal government assumed most of the costs of wartime plant expansion. After the seven lean years of the Depression, industrialists had shown reluctance to invest substantial amounts of their capital on the eve of war. Instead, government financed over half of the expansion during World War II and provided generous tax depreciations for most of the rest.[7] Federal agencies spent about $16 billion on new industrial facilities, ultimately resulting in public ownership of roughly a fifth of the nation's industrial capacity.[8] The navy and the Defense Production Corporation (DPC) invested about $550 million in facilities that were managed by, and later sold to, U.S. Steel. Only General Motors, DuPont, and Alcoa received more public funds than the Corporation. In one of the biggest projects of this kind, the navy invested almost $100 million to build the fifth set of open hearth furnaces at the Homestead Works. This round of modernization proved critical to Homestead's subsequent production; OH 5 remained in operation until the mill was closed in the early 1980s.[9] The navy also leased its Charleston, West Virginia, armor mill to U.S. Steel so that plates forged in Homestead could be rolled in either facility.[10] Wartime modernization reversed the pattern of the 1920s and 1930s which had favored the Midwest over Pittsburgh and lighter products over plates, rails, and structurals. Pittsburgh's fairy godmother, in its New Deal form, provided the basis for postwar prosperity.

THE POLITICAL ORGANIZATION OF STEELWORKERS, 1939–42

Steelworkers' responses to World War II were conditioned by their faltering independent political strength in the years following 1937. The failure of the CIO and Labor's Non-Partisan League (LNPL) to win Pennsylvania's 1938 general election confirmed the growth of opposition from the AFL, employers, and the Republican Party. Roosevelt further weakened the SWOC by refusing to deny military contracts to other companies violating labor law as he had done with U.S. Steel in 1936–37. Despite Bethlehem

Steel's numerous violations of labor law, the company continued to enjoy lucrative military contracts and federal modernization funds. Part of the reason that steel firms escaped punishment, according to the official history of the Bureau of Ordnance, was the aid of "Naval officers turned diplomats" who lobbied against any interruption to war production.[11] The unwillingness of an ostensibly pro-worker President to enforce labor law led John L. Lewis to wonder "is the law just for the weak and the lowly, or is the law to be enforced against the powerful and the strong?"[12]

Frustration that Roosevelt preferred to prepare for a possible war in Europe rather than aid workers in their ongoing battles with employers prompted Lewis' notorious showdown with Roosevelt in 1940. Lewis opposed Roosevelt's bid for a third term, partly because of the National Labor Relations Board's (NLRB) increasingly anti-CIO policies. Lewis also believed that the CIO's alliance with the Democratic Party would ultimately result in extending government's control over unions. And he also feared that FDR's efforts to aid Great Britain all but guaranteed American involvement in a world war. (Lewis' stance garnered the support of left-wing CIO unions who at this point opposed the coming war.) After considering launching an independent Labor Party, Lewis instead endorsed the Republican candidate for President. Lewis promised to resign as CIO President if workers supported Roosevelt. Workers, even mineworkers, overwhelmingly voted for FDR.[13] Lewis, who had engineered the alliance between labor and the Democratic Party, proved powerless to shatter it.

At one level, the 1940 elections underscored labor's ability to get out the vote. The Republican Party spent at least $3 million in Pennsylvania, six times that of the Democrats, but still lost the state by a wide margin. Much of the Democrats' success was due to the enthusiastic support of most of Pennsylvania's CIO unions and the LNPL (over the objections of Lewis). The LNPL argued that "enough members can be elected to the General Assembly to save what few crumbs yet remain of liberal and social legislation" and prevent "disaster at Washington" should reactionaries win control of the White House. While Pennsylvania's Democrats returned U.S. Senator Guffey, they failed to retain their once-formidable majorities in the state assembly or the Congressional delegations.[14] The CIO maintained considerable political influence but failed to extend it.

The 1940 election helped set in motion a set of dynamics that badly splintered the CIO. Following Roosevelt's victory, Lewis kept his promise to resign as President of the CIO. He chose Philip Murray of the SWOC (who also retained his office of Vice President of the UMWA) as his successor. As the President of both the SWOC and the CIO, Murray pursued still closer relations between labor and the Democrats. Lewis maintained a confrontational relationship with Roosevelt, leading his mineworkers into a major strike on the eve of America's formal entry into the war in December 1941. Murray provided unambiguous support for the war effort and agreed to give up the right to strike for the duration. (Lewis led another strike in April 1943, one that helped crystallize anti-labor sentiment in Congress.) By 1942, relations between the SWOC and the UMWA chilled, and then froze. In 1942, Lewis withdrew from the CIO and stripped Murray of his office in the UMWA, claiming that it was improper for him to hold two salaried positions. Forced to choose, most of the UMWA officials on loan to the SWOC abandoned Lewis. Lewis attempted to force the CIO to repay the millions of dollars the UMWA had spent on CIO organizing drives. The federation refused. Although the USWA repaid its legal obligations to the UMWA, the steelworkers owed their existence to the miners, a more substantial—if not financial—debt that would never be discharged in full.[15]

The split between Murray and Lewis shattered any possibilities for cooperation between the UMWA and the SWOC. While miners and steelworkers continued to work for and battle the same companies, little substantive cooperation or solidarity on either the political or industrial front occurred in the coming years. Indeed, without the enormous financial and organizational support of the UMWA for the LNPL, that organization seemed unable to generate political momentum. In 1941, Pennsylvania's LNPL won few electoral victories. In 1942, it failed to carry the primary for its candidate for the Democratic nomination for Governor. Although the USWA funded half of the cost of the LNPL, its meager budget, just eight thousand dollars, precluded any major political breakthroughs.[16] By 1944, Republicans amended Pennsylvania's election law (via the Farell Act), which sharply restricted the amount of money that unions could contribute to candidates or organizations such as the LNPL.[17] Federal legislation also prohibited unions from spending their funds for electoral activities for the duration of the war.[18] For the previous fifty years, the "Coal and Irons" and the spy system effectively disenfranchised most workers; within a decade of labor's political reorganization, new laws prevented unions from political organizing. The LNPL had lost its potential to function as the political vehicle for the working class. Labor's precariousness led Murray to conclude that labor's only choice was an ever-closer relationship with the Democratic Party and government. Thus, World War II represented an opportunity for Murray to stabilize the SWOC and bolster its power without developing an electoral organization within the Democratic Party or independent of it.

THE EFFECTS OF THE WAR ON THE USWA

The war boom eradicated two of the USWA's major preoccupations, the reality of unemployment and the threat of "technological unemployment." In the 1920s and 1930s, mechanized hot strip mills had eliminated forty thousand hand rolling workers in the sheet, bar, and plate industry.[19] In U.S. Steel's Irvin Works (completed in 1938) four thousand men rolled as much steel as sixteen thousand displaced workers.[20] The SWOC feared that one in six steel jobs would disappear into other "big morgues" populated with massive machines and a handful of workers.[21] Union President Philip Murray embraced automation as "progress" but argued that the enormous social disruptions of technological unemployment required greater public control over investment decisions.[22] Murray envisioned a system of national industrial planning by government, business, and labor that would address the needs of each. New technology would be jointly planned, its social consequences anticipated, and its economic benefits shared.[23] By 1939, a flood of war orders caused the mills to run full out, and workers' fears eased. Newly established war planning boards failed to provide labor with the kind of influence over investment decisions that Murray had initially envisioned, but they provided the union with important avenues of information and legitimacy.[24]

The leaders of the steelworkers viewed their participation on these boards as a major opportunity. The War Production Board (WPB) brought together representatives of business, government, and labor in order to maximize the production of war materiel. Likewise, the War Labor Board (WLB) sought to prevent industrial conflict so that production would not be affected by strikes, lockouts, or low productivity. Harold Ruttenberg, the USWA's man on the WPB, observed that "realistically, the situation amounts to this: first, we are given an opportunity to get on the inside, and on the inside we have to battle away, and the question of being victorious on this question or that question will depend on our ability to make our weight felt, which is . . . primarily a question of organization."[25] Lee Pressman, who represented the union on the WLB, described the new agency as "just a horrible mess."

Nonetheless, Pressman admitted that "we are getting some results . . . the other unions are getting nothing." In particular, Pressman got the "little steel" pay scale applied to all companies so that each appeal for a pay rise did not have to grind through the administrative chaos of the WLB.[26] Another USWA representative to the WLB, Van Bittner, estimated that the USWA won 325 out of 350 cases brought to the board. Bittner admitted that "we have had our headaches and our heartaches on the Board, but we had our heartaches and our headaches in 1937 before we had the WLB."[27] Although the union faced setbacks on the political front and problems in the corridors of power, the union mustered enough power to force management to slowly surrender ground in the mills. It was there that most workers experienced—and shaped—the changes and gains won by the union.

STEELWORKERS' STRUGGLE FOR SECURITY AND SENIORITY

Steelworkers had long endured job insecurity and favoritism; unionists well understood the significance of establishing seniority as the basis for layoffs and promotions. Freeman Patton, a black steelworker, recalled that prior to SWOC "there wasn't too much moving to be done . . . when a fellow was hired, he just worked on that job until he got fired, quit or died."[28] John Warady described the system of hiring and promotion in McKeesport thusly: "before the union came in, it was a sure thing" that the foreman "sent his friend up on that job to make more money." The white worker went on to observe that "the foreign people, the colored people hardly had a chance."[29] One worker recalled that after the union won a contract he told his fellows that "gentlemen . . . they aren't going to call us 'hunky' anymore."[30] At one of the first meetings of SWOC at Homestead, workers attempted to settle the "controversy . . . [over] what is meant by seniority rights." Unionists decided that seniority meant "the oldest man got the promotion" while managers viewed "ability as the primary factor."[31]

Forcing managers to abandon "ability," the criterion of which in practice was often pure favoritism or discrimination, required a long and difficult struggle. Charles Bollinger recalled that H.G. McIlvried, Homestead's new general superintendent, was "one of the best organizers SWOC ever had." Bollinger's sardonic comment about McIlvried's ability to unwittingly drive steelworkers into the union resulted from his 1940 decision to fire more than a hundred older workers. Some of the men had forty-five years with U.S. Steel.[32] McIlvried planned to close the paint, tin, and carpentry shops and lay off the workers in those shops. The callous disregard for these men's lifetimes of service to the company resulted in "a rush to the union hall to sign membership cards . . . the union collected over $10,000 in one day." Ten years later, unionists at Homestead were still talking about the incident, and probably still chuckling over their victory.[33] Because of workers' determination, seniority eventually replaced "ability" as the determining factor in promotions and layoffs. As Leon Dassi, a steelworker at Homestead, recalled, "my first nine or ten years in the mill, I stood where I was, 'till the union came in—then I moved." Eventually, because of his seniority, Dassi became known as "top dog Dassi."[34] Before workers could enjoy seniority, still a very fluid and contested concept, they first had to make the union strong enough to enforce its will.

Many of SWOC's early struggles revolved around building itself into a self-financed membership organization. As early as 1937, Lewis reduced SWOC's funding, forcing the union to raise its own revenue from its own membership. The union's membership drive was also designed to "show the company that we had a big majority of the men working in the mill."[35] Until 1940, the union would not have survived without substantial support from the UMWA. In addition to cash loans and grants, many SWOC organizers remained on the UMWA payroll. SWOC members collected dues from other steelworkers, but when they sought permission to collect them at work, "the answer [from U.S. Steel] was in the negative."[36] Consequently, soliciting dues remained a time-consuming and often unsuccessful process. As a result, one worker explained, "the first couple of years there was the union, it didn't mean a thing." The union "did not have enough membership, and they didn't have enough money, and without that you ain't strong in any respect."[37] While that condition was soon to change, another recalled that at National Tube "our union was very weak because we were nothing but a bunch of laborers and cranemen."[38]

Enrolling most production and maintenance workers into the union proved a daunting task. Many workers, particularly those furthest down on the economic and social hierarchies of the steel industry, supported the union, but most did not pay dues. The stalwarts of the union remained the lower-paid immigrants and blacks while "native born Americans were the last to come into the union."[39] Even some blacks and foreigners were frustrated with the union's performance, but most supporters did not understand why they should pay dues while most workers did not. Therefore, the union offered incentives to activists, allowing members who signed up recruits to keep one-quarter of their initiation fees.[40] By August 1939, unionists won the right to collect dues in U.S. Steel facilities. Nonetheless, only three hundred workers at Homestead paid dues in 1940.[41] And managers still watched SWOC activists closely. In the summer of 1940, managers at Duquesne complained that the union's financial secretary was "foxy enough to obey plant rules and job requirements enough to get by, and still create trouble."[42] As a result of such "troublemaking," the union was stronger at Duquesne, but between 1939 and 1940 membership fluctuated from the low hundreds to two thousand out of a potential membership of five thousand.[43] SWOC faced a serious financial shortfall and a crisis of credibility. How could it negotiate with steel companies if steelworkers did not support the union financially?[44]

SWOC members grew increasingly tough about collecting dues. After 1938, the union turned to "dues pickets," preventing non-union men from entering the mill. In the past, the union had discouraged such "hard boiled tactics" but now sent out roving pickets from plant to plant.[45] Fights inevitably broke out, and in Duquesne, the city's Mayor (a SWOC member) called out the fire department who turned hoses on workers—particularly those who had not paid their dues.[46] Shop stewards debated how to "spread the gospel of trade unionism amongst the men," particularly the native-born and "big money men."[47] The campaign to build and hold the membership slowly succeeded, with workers fighting in the mills and steel towns, and their officials bargaining with management.[48] On June 18, 1942, as a result of the union's negotiations with management, the NLRB held an election to determine support for having dues deducted from paychecks (dues check off). The Homestead Works was one of the closest elections, and there the SWOC won by a ratio of ten to one.[49] From that day, people who joined the union and failed to keep current with their dues could be fired. As one contemporary observer wryly noted, "this clause has the effect of stabilizing the membership of the union."[50] By late June, the union had won the dues check off for 238,000 workers.[51] By the fall of 1942, the union's financial situation had improved to the point where it was able to purchase a substantial headquarters opposite the White House. In a clear indication of its new power, the union paid for the building in cash.[52]

The union's financial stability and political influence were two indications of its power, but developing a strong seniority system proved harder to achieve. Workers' seniority succeeded in weakening workplace discrimination, particularly against white "ethnic" workers. John Hovanec, a second-generation Slovak worker at Homestead, recalled that before the union "if you were Polish-Catholic you'd never make it."[53] According to Frank Takach, Catholic workers "couldn't get a high job in the mill if you were foreign until the union came in. Now they got Hunkies doing all the jobs."[54] In jobs not covered by seniority, such as managerial positions, ethnic favoritism remained strong. Otis King, a black worker at Homestead, recalled that while there were many Irish foremen, management "wouldn't let a Catholic be a boss."[55] Black workers also benefited from seniority. Junius Brown, a black tin plate worker from McKeesport recalled that "the colored didn't have no real good jobs, they just had any job that the white just didn't want . . . the union made 100 percent difference."[56] Another man simply praised the union as the "boon, if not the salvation" of African American steelworkers.[57] But ironically, seniority also institutionalized discrimination. During the early 1930s, in mills like Clairton, steel managers had replaced black workers with whites. In some mills, seniority hampered veteran black steelworkers from regaining their old jobs. Because promotions and "bumping" occurred on a departmental basis, seniority hampered black workers from escaping foundries, blast furnaces, and coke ovens.[58] While immigrant white workers realized the benefits of seniority relatively quickly, extending workplace opportunities to black workers proved more difficult.

The weight of decades of racialized discrimination, and its ongoing practice, often overwhelmed the union's fragile interracial activism. In the formation of the union, numerous blacks provided strong and early support for the union. Amongst many others, Nathaniel Sallie in Clairton and Fletcher Williamson in Duquesne were founding members of Amalgamated Lodges.[59] Junius Brown was Vice President of his McKeesport local.[60] One scholarly account of the union movement found that "during the SWOC campaign (by and large) Negroes held office in a greater proportion than their numbers warranted." One black steward reported that "as long as the Negro goes to meetings, speaks when he is right, and shows intelligence, the whites are for you 100%." But the union recognized that many black workers, particularly those with highly paid jobs or who carried the scars of the 1919 strike when the union barred them from membership, refused to join.[61]

Many white unionists failed to overcome the racial prejudice that pervaded American society. Despite the interracial rhetoric of the union's leadership, many white unionists continued to bar blacks from restrooms, shanties, and (where possible) the better jobs in the mill.[62] Rocky Doratio recalled an incident when a black worker approached the union President at National Tube for help in obtaining relief, a common request of the union in those days. The official turned him away because he did not belong to the union. Doratio said, "when the black man left, I walked up to him and said, 'you lousy bastard! Is that the way to build the union? . . . Why don't you sign him up; maybe he'll belong to the union afterwards. The money isn't coming out of your pocket."[63] As late as 1940, unionists at Homestead remained uncertain about "the best way to organize the colored workers in the mill."[64] Black workers joined the union, although many remained frustrated with the shallowness of white workers' commitments to inter-racial unionism.[65] A black unionist at J&L caustically criticized white motives: "you know as well as I do that the union didn't bring us in because they wanted us. They needed us to protect themselves."[66]

In this context, steel companies continued openly to discriminate against black workers and particularly against active unionists. Junius Brown observed that racism was "one problem we continued to have. After the tin mill was sold out [in 1940], I went down to the National Tube, and they weren't hiring. Well I couldn't *make* them hire. Then I went to Homestead. They gave out application blanks over my shoulder. I went to J&L in Pittsburgh and it looked like the man seen us coming through the door. When we got there, he was standing in the doorway saying, 'we're not hiring.' What are you going to do?"[67] The *Pittsburgh Courier* reported that although the Clairton Works hired numerous whites, blacks could only get jobs if they received a "letter of introduction" vouching for their anti-union credentials.[68] Union or no, companies hired whomever they wanted and placed them into whatever department they wanted. Leroy McChestes recalled that "a colored man couldn't get a job . . . at least not a good job . . . . [T]here was no room for advancement."[69]

The dynamics of wartime provided trade unionists with an excellent opportunity to eradicate racial discrimination in industry. As unemployment receded after 1939, the United States mobilized Americans to wage war against fascist regimes that promoted racial superiority. Yet white supremacy remained entrenched in the Jim Crow South and throughout American industry. When A. Philip Randolph and other black unionists threatened to march on Washington to highlight this hypocrisy, Roosevelt created the Fair Employment Practices Committee or FEPC. The FEPC was empowered to investigate companies with government contracts and

to urge compliance with Roosevelt's Executive Order that forbade government contractors from discriminating against minorities, but the under-
funded agency lacked the remedy of denying contracts to violators. Fearing a
political backlash, black trade unionists did not press Roosevelt to improve
upon the FEPC's mandate. And racial discrimination simply did not loom
that large in the calculations of the national leaders of the CIO or the
SWOC. When pressed by black workers, Murray hired a single black "troubleshooter" for the international USWA, who accomplished little more
than serving as window dressing. USWA officials admitted that unlike the
UE, Murray failed to recommend any African Americans to serve on government boards or to force all districts with appreciable numbers of black
members to hire a black representative.[70] Black steelworkers praised the
FEPC and the union for their aid in helping them gain access to better
jobs.[71] Likewise, the FEPC praised the CIO's non-discrimination policies for
their "great leavening influence" on the region.[72] But the records of the
FEPC offer evidence of missed opportunities as well as progress.

Many factors limited the pace of steel's desegregation. First and foremost, companies upheld discriminatory hiring and promotion practices.
Black workers at J&L's Hazelwood coke ovens protested that the company's interpretation of the seniority system barred them from becoming
pushers or temporary foremen. Milo Manly, the FEPC investigator, reported
that after considerable argument with J&L managers "it became more and
more evident that Management's proposal [to change this department's
system of seniority and promotion] would use up every white employee in
the entire plant before a single non-white could become a pusher."[73] Black
advancement into "white jobs" was occasionally greeted by white "hate
strikes." On November 19, 1943, seven white grinders at Duquesne refused
to train three African American "learners." But the union upheld its inter-
racial principles and refused to back the action, and the black men quickly
assumed the job.[74] In another incident, white crane men refused to train
black workers on the job. The workers acknowledged that the no-strike
pledge bound them to work, but "human nature and principles will still
rebel at times." While the union refused to support the strike, the black
workers "did not report for work"—while they were probably intimidated,
the precise reason went unrecorded—and the matter ended there.[75] Hate
strikes remained isolated, exceptional events, but this was due to the slow
pace of change as much as to the union's principles.[76] Moreover, the slow
pace of black advancement in steel resulted in numerous instances of

black-led strikes. These protests led Manly to observe that in terms of racial conflict, Pittsburgh was the "touchiest and most tense" city in America.[77]

Black wildcat strikes bore witness to both frustration with the limits of trade unionism and the tactics and discipline absorbed from it. In 1942, Cornelius Culpepper and Amos Champ attempted to lead a gang of black laborers off Duquesne's OH 1 to protest the fact that "white boys with less service were given preference over them." Even the men who refused to back them explained that "Champ was right, but he didn't handle the problem the right way."[78] In some instances of black protest, white unionists extended solidarity, such as the case of a black furnaceman who refused to move bricks on his furnace because workers considered it a laborer's job.[79] But the largest strikes were those led by frustrated black workers who protested an inadequately enforced seniority system. For instance, on February 25, 1944, fifty-three black workers at the Clairton Works refused to maintain the equipment that generated fuel for the furnaces, claiming they "were being steadily barred from any of the higher jobs they had once held." Because Clairton supplied the fuel to every U.S. Steel mill in the region, the shutdown threatened to cripple production, particularly if unattended machines burned up. In this case, workers bypassed the union, bringing the FEPC and navy into the equation. In the end, "the men felt they had accomplished their purpose by striking, by getting into the picture four government bureaus that could help them work out an improvement of their condition." The men returned to work having received management's promise that seniority would guide future promotions. The fact that other black steelworkers at Clairton (and elsewhere) continued to resort to wildcat strikes suggests both the foot dragging by management and the limits of whites' conversion to the principles of seniority.[80]

The politics of solidarity, or lack thereof, helped determine the shape of seniority in practice. During the war, workers had "job seniority," but lines of promotion and demotion within each department remained generally on an ad hoc basis.[81] In 1945, the national contract between the USWA and U.S. Steel stipulated that workers and local managers negotiate more formal seniority agreements. From management's perspective, the most pressing issue was "whether the unit of operation [for seniority] shall be plant, department, division, or job." Companies expressed a clear preference for job and departmental seniority units, in part because they caused the least disruption to production.[82] But such narrow definitions of seniority provided workers with the least amount of flexibility in improving or protecting their jobs. The union won a more uniform and codified system, a major advance, but management retained the practice of job and departmental seniority. Large mills, such as Homestead and Clairton, adopted separate job seniority for 108 different job lines in each mill. Such a narrow definition of seniority helped to reinforce the racial division of labor, as workers surrendered all their job or departmental seniority if they simply entered a new job line even within the same department.[83] The system locked black workers out of many good jobs, as managers retained sole control over hiring, and since at Duquesne, as in many other mills, there were "no promotional sequences leading into trade or craft jobs."[84] Consequently, blacks from other departments could not apply their seniority in order to get those jobs. Yet in Duquesne's blast furnace, workers had won the right to bid on new jobs in different job lines, albeit only within their departments.[85] While such flexibility was the exception rather than the rule, it was nonetheless sacrificed in the name of progress.

As the union forced the companies to adopt clear and open standards, workers did enjoy progress. During the war, the union sought across-the-board wage increases, "rather than percentage hikes. Thus, hour wage rates rose 50 percent during the war for the lowest pay grades and only 20 percent for the highest."[86] Within a few years, the union forced management to reclassify every job in every mill to ensure that workers throughout the country received the same rates of pay for the same work. Prior to this, steel companies paid Southern workers less than Northern ones, and thousands of black workers, as well as white ones, suffered from the infamous "Southern differential." Furthermore, even up North, each mill, and often foremen, determined the workload and pay scale for workers, and the result was a crazy quilt of tens of thousands of different pay scales. The union required that managers define each job and its duties, and pay uniform rates of pay throughout the country. When in doubt, the companies had to pay workers the higher rates of pay.[87] But if the union was a rising tide that lifted all workers' boats, black and white, a few workers remained trapped on islands of caprice and discrimination.

WOMEN WAR WORKERS

The interaction between prejudice and occupational competition also affected another minority group of steelworkers: women. Prior to the war, female steelworkers had been restricted to a handful of job classifications.

Steel companies hired female industrial sojourners in lieu of their traditionally male sources of "second-class" workers. The war afforded women,
particularly white women, access to a wide variety of jobs but only on a
temporary basis. As the vastly different experiences of black and white
women reveal, the workplace and seniority status of white women proved
as much a function of race as gender.

Prior to World War II, industrialists relied on men to do the hot, heavy,
and dangerous work of making steel. In 1940, female steelworkers made up
only about 3 percent of Pittsburgh's steelworkers, and more than half of
them held "light" jobs in tinning mills or small fabrication shops. Like most
of its counterparts, *U.S. Steel News* explained this situation with an allusion
to nature: "there are few operations" in a mill "to which the gentler sex is
adapted."[88] The classic female job niche were "tin floppers" who inspected
tin sheets for defects. U.S. Steel ventured that "it's hard to explain, but,
somehow, women have a capacity for observation that makes them superior
to men."[89] Few women found jobs in large integrated mills owned by U.S.
Steel. In June 1942, Duquesne employed ninety-three women, and the vast
majority were clerical workers.[90] About two-thirds of Pittsburgh's 5,544
female steelworkers held jobs as clerks.[91] Clairton employed just twelve
female production workers.[92] Wartime labor shortages pushed industrialists
to expand their ideas of what jobs women could handle.[93]

Women entered the steel workforce about halfway through the war.
By January 1943, the War Manpower Commission anticipated widespread
shortages of laborers for the mills.[94] Later that year, the WPB found that
women made up over 35 percent of the non-agricultural workforce, although
the figure was far lower in steel.[95] In 1943, a U.S. Women's Bureau survey
showed that women comprised 12,073 of the 119,000 workers in the
Pittsburgh-Youngstown area.[96] Women were first hired at the Homestead
Works on March 8, 1943, as "clean-up" and brick laborers in the Carrie
Furnace. By the end of that year, 1,100 women worked in the Homestead
Works; another 1,000 toiled at Duquesne. By 1945, the number of women
at Homestead had nearly doubled to 2,000. Women made up the entire
crew of one furnace in the 100-inch mill.[97] Women operated cranes, ran
machines, labored in gangs, and a few even became gang leaders of men
and women. Some, like Miss Alda Mae Hilliard and Mrs. Margaret Ruth
Davies, became machine-tool operators in the Number 1 Machine Shops.
In 1944, U.S. Steel employed 40,000 women throughout the country, 25,000
of them in production jobs, and championed their prowess.[98]

The relaxation of steel's gender roles barely benefited black women. Prior to the war, steel companies hired only a handful of black women. In 1940, steel companies in the city of Pittsburgh employed just seven black women as laborers and janitors. Another seven had similar experience but were unemployed.[99] Beginning in 1941, A. Philip Randolph, the Urban League, and the NAACP pressured industrialists throughout the country to employ more black women. But black women entered the mills far later than their white counterparts.[100] In May 1945, ET began to hire black women only after the president of the steel local, Leo Blotzer, criticized the hiring practices of U.S. Steel. Blotzer wrote that the employment office "to forestall any outward sign of discrimination on their part will take the application of a colored woman. Then curtly advise her she will be called. Which to date has not happened." As a result of Blotzer's criticisms of management, a dozen women were hired.[101] But the union's actions came too late in the war to alter the intense discrimination faced by black women.

While white women gained access to a wide variety of jobs, most black women remained laborers. Many white women were initially placed in heavy jobs and then moved after a few days onto lighter auxiliary jobs. Few black women were permitted to advance.[102] While "ethnic" women at U.S. Steel's National Tube mill in McKeesport were more likely to work heavy production jobs than their "American" counterparts, in general, white women enjoyed a far wider range of less physically demanding, better-paid jobs than black females.[103] An observer from the Women's Bureau found black female laborers in the sinter plants that prepared iron ore for melting in the blast furnaces. Amidst the dust, noise, and heat "they . . . were reported as moving as much dirt and material as men."[104] Black women like Lillie Mae Jenkins and Elizabeth Ferguson labored in the masonry gangs at Homestead or alongside black men in the open hearths of the Duquesne, Homestead, and Clairton Works.[105] The Women's Bureau also found many white female laborers, but few who were sent into the furnaces, into the masonry gangs, or onto repairing railroad track like black women.[106] This group of industrial sojourners suffered from the classic "double burden" of gender and race.

White women benefited from and unwittingly helped to preserve the pervasive racism of the steel industry. Whereas the Homestead Works had barred black men from the machine shop, cranes, and clerical jobs, white women moved quickly into those positions. White women's rapid advancement resulted from management's desire to keep those departments reserved for white workers. White women entered the Homestead Works in 1943 after "the available manpower in the Homestead area has been scraped clean" by the armed forces and other mills.[107] When whites worried about "reports that a mass migration of 1,000 colored workers were to be brought in to work in the local mills," U.S. Steel publicly assured all concerned that white women and not blacks would receive preference in the recently constructed departments of the Homestead Works.[108] Black men resented having newly hired white women placed over their heads onto decent paying jobs.[109] One man admitted that "I got a little bitter for a while. When you see women move in on jobs that you thought you would have a chance to get, and they would actually put [women] on better jobs than the [black] men that had been there for years. It was discrimination . . . but nobody would stick their neck out."[110] CIO activists confronted similar patterns in other mills. One unionist explained, "I am not prejudiced against women but in many cases they are placing women on men's jobs where they should be putting skilled Negroes who are available. They [managers] haven't used 10 percent of skilled Negro labor."[111] Apparently, supervisors calculated that white women could be convinced to abandon jobs when veterans returned but that black men would prove harder to dislodge.

Trade unionists' response to female workers was motivated by a complex mixture of principle and self-interest. At the national and local levels, trade unionists defended the principle of equal pay for equal work, partly to prevent steel firms from lowering wage rates of men at the war's end.[112] While steel firms agreed to pay women the same rate as men, in practice, managers sought to reclassify jobs into less skilled categories. For instance, at Duquesne, managers sought to pay female crane operators two cents less an hour than male trade unionists since state law barred them from completing certain aspects of the job.[113] Management apparently ignored regulations from the Labor, Navy, and War Departments that required contractors "to pay equal rates for women for comparable work."[114] Managers felt justified in paying women less because many believed that women were inherently slower, smaller, and less apt to learn than men, although once trained they remained "well adapted to highly repetitive tasks."[115] As with seniority, enforcing the promises of steel firms was delegated to local unions. In Duquesne, unionists staunchly fought for equal pay for women in categories as diverse as laborers, crane operators, and clerical workers.[116] When supervisors reduced the pay along with the amount of maintenance work that women crane operators would have to do, Duquesne's unionists offered to let male workers on the "opposing shifts" do the work rather than pay them less money.[117] The union generally defended the skill and pay levels of union jobs, but most unionists awaited the day when men would return to the mill.

Many male steelworkers resented the presence of women in the mill. One told Helen Schalko that he would not help her learn his job because "I know I am going to war and I'm going to be killed." She recalled that "I never thought of it, that these boys are going to war and some of them don't want to go. After that, I never asked him to do anything for me." Most men gradually accepted the participation of women, but most made it clear that their participation was accepted only "for the duration."[118] As a result, the union was less than eager to protect women against harassment by male unionists. Local 1256 protested when one of its male members was suspended without pay because he allegedly abused a female worker. The union representative, a communist, argued that management's discipline was a form of fascism "right here" in the Mon Valley.[119] Thus, resentment against women was shared by even the most class-conscious unionists.

During the war, women had proved that they could act as bona fide trade unionists. In 1943, 800 USWA members from the Mon Valley, the vast majority of them men, elected a female war worker as their representative to the state CIO convention. When the question of female war workers arose, she told the other union delegates that "women don't want special power. We want the opportunity to sit at your tables, to have you tell us your problems and have us assist in the problems."[120] Women war workers not only held down "men's jobs," but they went on strike like men. When 2 women were suspended at the Irvin Works on April 9, 1945, 157 workers—mostly women—walked off the job. Located in the vital tin-plating department, this wildcat idled 509 other employees. The union, management, and army conciliators all tried to get the strikers to go back to work and to work through the grievance procedure. But only after two days did the strikers vote to return to work.[121] Later that month, Irvin Works' managers suspended four sorting room "girls" for engaging in a "deliberate slowdown." These workers had protested a War Labor Board delay in putting through a one dollar a day raise. The next day, 87 sorters, "mostly women" and 25 wire strappers walked off the job. The day after that, another 28 workers vowed not to return to work until the suspensions had expired. True to their word, the workers returned only when the three-day suspensions were over.[122] These strikes underscore how quickly and easily women made the transition to the role of mill worker.

THE POLITICS OF PEACETIME CONVERSION, 1945–1947:
AN OVERVIEW

By the spring of 1945, the leaders of the USWA grew increasingly concerned about what would happen when the war ended. During a top-level meeting of trade unionists in May 1945, Philip Murray began a discussion on "perhaps the one which transcends in importance any other question," which was the "problems which are bound to grow out of the ending of the European phase of the war." Clint Golden, another top leader, observed that the older men could "remember pretty vividly how an organization that had been built up through considerable fortunes during the war [World War I] evaporated pretty quickly after the war." Trade unionists worried that steel companies were preparing for a post-war bloodbath, as in 1919.[123]

In the next year, enormous changes confronted steelworkers. In the summer and fall of 1945, many military contracts were canceled. Steelworkers returned to a forty-hour week, and without premium pay on overtime, paychecks shrank by 20 to 30 percent. In real terms, steelworkers earned less than before the war.[124] By August, the FEPC expired and the "golden years" of black industrial workers came to a close. By the close of 1945, more than half of female war workers had either quit or been fired. In early 1946, steelworkers hit the bricks in the first national steel strike in almost thirty years. Rather than a reprise of the past, the 1946 strike indicated that the union would be a permanent institution in the post-war world.

The 1946 strike was the first national steel strike since 1919; the two are a study in contrasts. Of necessity, the 1919 strike committee had addressed steelworkers in a wide variety of languages. During the 1946 steel strike, a speech in Polish drew protests from steelworkers, including many of Polish descent: "We don't know that language. We're Americans and we want an American speaker."[125] In 1919, steelworkers had been brutalized by private and public police. In 1946, the strike was peaceful, and pickets were joined by mayors and congressmen.[126] As in 1937, the union succeeded in attracting the attention of the U.S. President, but this time he urged steel companies to settle the strike as quickly as possible. Philip Murray concluded that "we are fortunate. . . in that our union is again supporting the government and supporting the President. That is of tremendous significance."[127] While the CIO unions organized only minimal coordination between the strikes, the steelworkers, autoworkers, and electrical workers led one of the largest "strike waves" in history, and wage gains helped offset wartime inflation and the end of overtime. However, in steel and auto and other leading sectors of the economy, workers' pay raises came alongside even larger price increases by industrialists. Furthermore, labor's victories spurred employers and anti-labor politicians who mobilized against "big labor."

Throughout 1946, labor lost political ground. In August, the government sold its mills to steel companies for less than half of their original cost.[128] By that point, the federal government had dropped wartime price controls. Lee Pressman, the USWA's general counsel, warned that "the political arena is where the attack will come . . . [Steel companies] can't meet our organization on an economic front . . . so they have shifted, they have gone to an arena where admittedly we are weak."[129] David McDonald, head of the CIO-PAC, confided to the union's top leadership that "the financial condition of the CIO-PAC is to say the least, very, very, very bad." Only about 1 percent of the CIO's 6 million members had contributed to the fund, and that ratio was even lower in the USWA. He pleaded with the district directors: "We have got to elect some friendly Congressmen, and we just have to do it, it is our protection."[130] But the union proved unable to mobilize enough of its members to offset the militants of the middle classes, and after the 1946 elections, Congress passed Taft-Hartley, the so-called slave labor bill.

The 1947 Taft-Hartley Act amended the Wagner Act and laid the groundwork for labor relations during the upcoming Cold War. In fact, Taft-Hartley was in many regards the opening volley in this Cold War. The law maintained unions as legal institutions but severely restricted their activities. Secondary strikes and boycotts were outlawed, and unions' ability to spend money on political activity were further restricted. The President could intervene and impose eighty-day "cooling off" periods on either strikes or lockouts. Employers gained far more flexibility in fighting workers' organizing drives, and states were allowed to pass "right to work" laws. Finally, in order for unions to receive the protections of the law, the organization had to pass a political litmus test. Union officials were required to sign affidavits swearing that they were not members of the Communist Party.[131]

The USWA's experiences with Taft-Hartley underscored the extent to which labor law, or anti-labor law, defined the parameters of trade union practice. The USWA had decided in 1946 to purge the union of its remaining communists, but like many CIO unions refused to sign the anti-communist affidavits as a protest against the new law. As a result, the USWA was denied access to the NLRB. Organizing drives fizzled because the government refused to allow the union to appear on workers' ballots. Each contract expiration threatened to provoke a "decertification" campaign. The union soon decided it could not survive without even the severely restricted Wagner Act and signed the affidavits.

The USWA enthusiastically attacked communists in steel and throughout the CIO.[132] Philip Murray made it a point of honor to try to eliminate the UE, viewing this as "patriotic assistance" as the quid pro quo for support of President Harry S. Truman. The USWA's anti-communism arguably bolstered the union in that it gained numerous members from the UE in Philadelphia and elsewhere. But anti-communism failed to revive the political fortunes of the CIO. After 1947, the USWA signed more of its members up for the CIO-PAC, about 20 percent throughout the country. (The rates in the Pittsburgh region, now a stronghold of the Democratic Party and labor liberalism, were far lower.)[133] By 1951, the rank-and-file of the CIO was completely demoralized. In Pennsylvania, only a third of the members of the CIO were registered to vote, a fact that made it "pretty rough going" when organized labor contemplated changing the composition of Congress. Philip Murray remarked that "there just isn't any question about . . . the ghastliness of the national picture . . . the onslaught of those forces which are evidently hell-bent upon . . . the destruction of the labor movement in America. So the answer is to be found in the work that must be done to strengthen the CIO-PAC."[134]

THE EROSION OF DIRECT ACTION AND WORKERS' POWER

But the CIO-PAC was not significantly improved, and the only factor off-setting the union's declining political influence was its growing strength in the mills. Wartime full employment had emboldened many workers and encouraged many to resist. Francis McNary, a worker at J&L, recalled that "anytime a foreman became overbearing, we just quit."[135] Another black worker recalled that strikes and collective action were widespread, or as he put it, "people stuck together" during the war.[136] At Duquesne in 1942, maintenance workers and machinists struck in order to remove time-study engineers as they "did not want anyone standing over them while they were working."[137] Although the USWA's leaders opposed wildcat strikes, they also indicated workers' power, and they helped push management to accept the grievance procedure as a lesser evil.[138] Its slow, legalistic procedures encouraged managers' practice of "reducing wages and telling the Union they are ready to take up a grievance . . . where the men go on strike they won't deal with the men until they go back to work."[139] Workers (and even local unionists) enjoyed little direct control over grievances. Even after the war, managers refused to settle grievances with local unionists (steps one through three) and most grievances were settled late, months after they were filed in meetings between district officials from the union and management (step four). Workers who protested against the combination of their jobs, seniority, or working conditions often found that they filed a grievance, which languished and then died.[140] The union favored the in-plant court system, as victories won in one mill through arbitration could be extended to other mills throughout the country. The grievance system also facilitated centralized decision making, which the union clearly preferred.[141] In any case, the union pressured workers not to strike during the war as it would interrupt vital defense production.

The end of the war freed workers from any inhibitions against strikes. At the Duquesne Works, workers acted on long-standing grievances. For instance, stripper cranemen (the men who moved ingots from the molds to the soaking pits) protested that new work had been added to their jobs. They now had to label, sort, and move test ingots. They filed a grievance, but in April of 1944 it became stalled, and management forced them to do the extra work. Shortly after V.J. day (Victory over Japan), the stripper cranemen simply stopped doing the extra work as (according to management) "they did not have to be patriotic . . . any longer." As a result, the test ingots were no longer labeled or sorted. Management unwittingly jumbled up different batches of steel. This total lack of quality control went unnoticed for almost three months, until November 5, and ultimately customers began to complain. The fact that the slowdown had gone unnoticed by managers for so long allowed the rebellion to build up steam. Although management could have theoretically fired all the workers engaged in this slowdown, managers feared that this would spark a wildcat. Instead, a supervisor ordered one craneman to move the test ingots. The craneman demanded: "you are putting me on the spot; what are the other boys going to do?" Although refusing a foreman's command was grounds for dismissal, the unionist held firm, and management did not press the point. Instead, managers convinced a grievance man to try to convince the craneman to file a new grievance. But again, the craneman refused to move the ingots. Only after the intervention of a fellow craneman did both agree to the union's proposal. The workers received a promise of twenty cents more an hour, and "the ingots have been moved okay since."[142]

The constant turmoil of strikes and slowdowns aggravated management. In October of 1945, the General Superintendent of the Duquesne Works cast about for ways to dampen the "union attitude" and "put them on the defensive for a change." Supervisors considered filing grievances protesting wildcat strikes and the use of company time for union politics. However, managers thought that if they began filing grievances, it would erode their authority and force them to arbitrate disputes in the future. Instead, the company pressured the union to uphold the no-strike clause and stop "condoning strikes and slow downs."[143]

The USWA brought considerable pressure to bear on local unionists who led wildcats and disciplined strike-prone locals. In 1945 and 1947, the USWA suspended the leaders of Local 1407 in Glassport because they had led eleven hundred members on a twenty-day strike over the arbitrary downgrading of forty-five workers.[144] The union argued that local strikes fractured unity and exposed the union to lawsuits and negative publicity. As part of its preparation for the 1946 general strike against the steel industry, the union promoted the slogan of "let's have no unauthorized strikes."[145] So when eight workers struck over long-standing grievances at the Clairton Works in March, 1946 U.S. Steel Vice President John Stephens urged Philip Murray to "take the proper steps" to punish the men. Murray sternly warned workers to resolve their disputes through the grievance procedure.[146] Management clearly valued the union's role in helping to moderate slowdowns and workplace rebellions. It became U.S. Steel's policy to try first to solve the problem, then to give the union one or two days to try its hand.[147] As a result, elected leaders rarely led local strikes, which themselves became generally smaller and more isolated affairs.

In this context, once unionists decided to go beyond the grievance procedure, their only hope was that their fellow workers would back them up. Without any contractual protection to strike over local issues, solidarity was not always forthcoming. On a hot August night in 1946, George Kordich, a union official at the Duquesne Works, refused to work overtime and tried to lead the shear and stripping crews out with him at quitting time. The crews' foreman convinced them to stay behind. Kordich ended up with egg on his face and a five-day suspension.[148]

The cancellation of military contracts left many workers "fearful for . . . their jobs and cut into their willingness to strike."[149] In 1944, there were 12,662 workers employed at Homestead; by 1946, that figure had fallen to 8,981.[150] Milton Macintyre, a black worker at the Duquesne Works, recalled that in a period of unemployment, "naturally people had to look out for their jobs and people didn't stick together as much."[151] U.S. Steel even threatened to close some mills, such as the Duquesne Works.[152] Taft-Hartley further demoralized workers: as Francis McNary recalled, after Taft-Hartley, "you walk off the job, you didn't have no job."[153] Equally important, as we will see, was that a disproportionate amount of the pain of layoffs was born by female steelworkers.

THE RECONVERSION OF FEMALE STEELWORKERS

Women steelworkers had done their part to ensure wartime production. With the advent of peace, many residents of "victory valley" eagerly looked forward to the return of "normalcy"—that is, male breadwinners and female dependents. One Homestead reporter worried that working women lacked the appropriate sensibilities to appreciate their country's victory over fascism. He observed two women workers who brawled, in pants, on the street outside the mill taunting each other with "you hate to see the war end" and "now you'll be laid off." Daniels contrasted their unpatriotic and unladylike behavior with that of an elderly mother at St. Mary's church who "knelt in reverence. In her hands, fondled ever so gently, I could make out the picture of a soldier. She would kiss the picture over and over. Here was Victory, she knew the war was over."[154] In case women missed the meaning of such literary appeals, local newspapers echoed the Corporation's call for women to vacate the mill as "vets [will] want jobs at mill on [their] return."[155] Most women left their jobs "apparently without any bitterness," in deference to the sacrifices of veterans and the hegemony of conservative family values in the region.[156] But while many women war workers gladly gave up their jobs, a few did not, and their inability to exercise their rights to seniority boded ill for other groups of workers who fell afoul of the agendas of steel companies and the USWA.

Women war workers who left steel did so quickly. The USWA estimated that in the second quarter of 1945, women comprised just over one-quarter of all basic steelworkers in the United States. Three months later, that figure was 12.1 percent, and it stabilized at around 11 percent by the end of the year. Black women, the last hired, were the first fired. Comprising just 2 percent of all steelworkers in mid-1945, by the end of the year their numbers had been reduced by 75 percent.[157] Many female laborers, such as those at Homestead, were given dismissal slips with their pay. Before the war, the union had won the right of servicemen to maintain their seniority in the mill; indeed, military service counted as "super seniority" when they returned. Unlike regular seniority, military service applied to every job and could never be lost through transfers or layoffs. (Super seniority was gradually phased out.)[158] Nonetheless, by late August, "the return of men from the fighting fronts" found five hundred jobs at the Irvin Works formerly held by women.[159]

Steel companies led the fight against female employees. According to management, women had been hired "temporarily during the war emergency because of the manpower shortage." Now, the company said that "it is necessary to replace these women with men to get full efficiency."[160] When pressed by the union to retain women production workers whose seniority entitled them to their jobs, U.S. Steel replied that the Pennsylvania Department of Labor and Industry barred women from jobs that required them to work "turns." Because steel mills rotated the shifts or turns of most workers every two weeks from days to afternoons to nights, management had a convenient excuse to rid the plants of women.[161] Under the guise of "reconverting" its employment policies towards women, managers further *restricted* women's employment opportunities. After June 28, 1946, married women were barred from all Carnegie-Illinois mills unless they were wives or widows of disabled mill employees or veterans. By July 1949, there were only ninety-eight women in the Duquesne Works; of those, only thirty-four were married. The twenty-six women whose husbands were either "employed or employable" faced considerable social pressure to quit.[162]

By and large, male unionists complied with the drive to fire women. The union supported Pennsylvania's protective legislation that barred women from most mill work.[163] Most unionists only went through the motions of filing the grievances of those women who refused to leave the mills quietly. Five black female bricklayers' helpers at the Duquesne Works demanded their seniority rights when they discovered that they had been laid off for minor boys with less seniority than themselves and not veterans. The grievance committeechair was "no more anxious to return the women to work than was the company"; indeed, he had previously agreed to the layoff. Adding insult to injury, the head of industrial relations supplied a "detailed job description" for their position which asserted that women could not "climb ladders to work on hot patch work" or handle other heavy labor. As the industrial relations expert noted, "periodic sickness further reduces the usefulness of women on *all* jobs." He provided no support for his argument, nor apparently felt any need to account for the fact that the women had already been doing the work that he claimed they could not handle.[164]

Managers' arguments that women were inherently unsuited to mill work were based on social logic and not technological necessity. Even if many laborers' jobs in the mills required a great deal of upper body strength, some women had that strength and wanted those jobs. Furthermore, many jobs did not require brute strength at all. John Scott observed that in Soviet mills, whose work process was less technically developed than in the United States, "in many jobs, such as crane operating, mill operating and so forth, where reliability, dexterity, and consistency were required rather than physical strength, women largely replaced men." There, a woman could become a master of the blooming mills, controlling the operation of the mill from a pulpit.[165] Scott's observations of the Russian steel mills underscore a point made by women activists in the 1970s: men did not make steel, machines did, and women could run machines as well or better than men.

However, in the mid-1940s, feminist arguments were seldom made, and in any case they carried little weight with male unionists anxious to avoid a return to the male unemployment of the Great Depression. Few questioned shifting the burden of unemployment onto women.[166] At least some of male workers' antipathy towards married women working in the mill was directed against steelworker couples who were widely viewed as "money grabbers."[167] The chair of the Grievance Committee at the Duquesne Works promised that he would cooperate in getting married women to give up their "seniority rights" to single men and women. In fact, he promised to fight "his top union people" if it came to that.[168] It is unclear whether his bravado was necessary; no record of the USWA's response survives. At any rate, the vast majority of women who remained employed at Duquesne or Homestead were single, worked in clerical or service jobs, and had been hired during World War II. Those women production workers, such as Elizabeth Jarsulic who worked as a tin-plate inspector at the Irvin Works, remained employed in a traditional female job niche.[169]

Unionists were sometimes even more eager than management for an all-male workplace. On August 21, 1945, Duquesne's unionists made it clear to management that they wanted women out of the mill as soon as the war was over. In the view of the leadership of Local 1256, women had been hired "on a temporary basis," and *any* male should be given preference over them in allocating work. In fact, management replied, "they could understand the feeling of the union representatives on this point," but for a while longer "we will have to use women as needed."[170] The national office of the USWA would have been little help to women seeking to keep their jobs. The USWA rarely intervened in local affairs, and the union took little interest in the special problems faced by women or African American men who had been hired during the war.[171] (Let us be clear that women's "special problem" was their inability to exercise their "normal" rights, such as seniority.)

The USWA was not alone in the problem of "female reconversion." The question of how seriously to take the job rights of female war workers confronted numerous CIO unions. Many provided female workers, especially those with enough seniority to remain on their jobs, with better protections than the USWA. Women represented a far more sizable part of the electrical workforce, (one-third before the war and half during it), and out of principle and self-protection the UE vigorously fought for equal pay and job status for women.[172] Similarly, the United Auto Workers forced companies to honor women's seniority regardless of marital status. Indeed, the UAW established a Women's Bureau in 1944 to recommend policies to aid the special needs of female workers.[173] When Ford management fired female employees after the war, women UAW members surrounded Detroit plants with mass pickets, arguing "the hand that rocks the cradle can build tractors too."[174]

Unlike their counterparts in Detroit's auto industry, women in Pittsburgh did not protest their firings by mass pickets. This probably reflected women's knowledge of the conservatism of the steel companies and the USWA, as much as or more than their own willingness to leave the mills. However, women steelworkers did walk at least one picket line. During the 1946 strike, small bands of black and white women picketed in front of both the Duquesne and Homestead mills. They advocated the goals of the USWA, not a women's agenda.[175] Organized by their local unions, they carried signs that read: "We Support Our Husbands," "Feed the Kids," and "We Wives and Members Need and Demand 18 1/2 Cents."[176] While substantial gender and racial discrimination remained, such solidarity indicated the extent to which workers of all genders and race supported the union.

THE STRUGGLE OF BLACK WORKERS WITHIN THE USWA

Black steelworkers emerged from the war with substantial experience in using the union and the federal government to fight the unfair promotion practices of steel companies. Black union activists knew that they had made substantial gains into skilled and semi-skilled positions and looked forward to further gains. Unfortunately for militants, full employment and the FEPC ended more or less at the same time. In August 1945, the government canceled war contracts as well as the budget for the FEPC.[177] Later that month, an estimated ten thousand black workers in the Pittsburgh region, three thousand two hundred of them USWA members, lost their jobs.[178] After a brief recession, the mills recalled most workers, but blacks' chances for upward mobility continued to deteriorate. Some industrial firms, formerly constrained by FEPC guidelines, began advertising for "white only" or "Christian only" positions, and even highly skilled black workers, such as machinists, complained that in the midst of a hiring boom, they could not find jobs.[179] The chances for college educated workers was even bleaker. The 1946 Fisk Race Relations Survey found that 40 percent of all industrial firms in the region hired no African Americans. About 16 percent of these firms were iron and steel plants, mostly small shops. Most large mills hired blacks for the coke ovens, furnaces, and foundries.[180] Black steelworkers knew that as bad as steel was, it offered the best opportunities for occupational progress in the region.

The major issue confronting black steelworkers was how to enforce their seniority rights. Supervisors often manipulated the system of job and departmental seniority in order to prevent blacks from advancing into decent jobs. Some managers transferred blacks from department to department, keeping them from acquiring enough seniority to advance.[181] Edward McNary, a shop steward at J&L's Southside Works, complained of the "lily-white policies" of many managers, observing that "there are many of these jobs on which the 'line' is frozen . . . and no one can do anything about it but the union itself. . . . Someone has to put pressure on them to relieve the situation."[182] In the months after the war, black workers' ability to exert that pressure dissipated.

The case of J&L's Hazelwood mill exemplifies the erosion of the power of black workers. Blacks on the coke ovens watched with anger as whites advanced into departments that were "not hiring" when blacks asked about jobs. The few highly skilled jobs on the coke ovens, such as heaters, were classified in a separate job line from heater helpers, who did the hot, dirty, and gassy work under these men. The nastier jobs on the ovens gave many men cancer, so it was particularly infuriating to watch only native-born whites move into the few decent jobs in this department.[183] (A medical study later found that "mortality from respiratory cancer" for black coke oven workers was three times that of steelworkers as a whole).[184] One black Pittsburgher observed, "they've taken those jobs out and given 'em to white men. That's the way they're doin' all the time."[185] Furthermore, there were no black foremen, engineers, or clerks.[186] In August 1946, 250 black and a few white steelworkers staged a sit-down strike over racist hiring and promotion policies at J&L's coke ovens, the fifth wildcat since 1941. The leaders of the strike were two brothers, Charles and Harold Winbush, who compared the "slow strangulation of Negroes on the job in Pennsylvania to [a recent] lynching in Georgia." The strike was indicative of both the possibilities of inter-racial unity and the limited effectiveness of wildcat strikes in the post-war order.

Pittsburgh's Mayor, David Lawrence, fearing a race riot, personally appealed to the President of J&L to meet with the strikers. They demanded that Boyd Wilson, the USWA's only black official, attend the meetings. When told by their District Director that Wilson was out of town, the strikers said that they (and by extension the entire mill) would wait until he returned. He was quickly produced. The Winbush brothers complained that after ten and eleven years in the mill, they had never seen a black foreman, although they had personally trained several whites for that job. When offered a foreman's job by H.E. Lewis, the President of J&L, Harold Winbush told him that "I can't be bought." Winbush promised that his promotion would only give him a platform to agitate for more black advancement. For its part, the USWA promised it would grieve any case in which workers refused to work under an African American foreman, but the union's promise was never tested because of the dearth of black foremen. The men returned to work in return for a promise for a "full-scale investigation."[187] In the end, the 1946 wildcat led nowhere. Their grievance failed and many workers were disgusted because, as one striker put it, "the whole thing in a nutshell is that our local union and local grievance man put up no fight at all."[188]

In 1947, another wildcat broke out. This time, J&L fired twenty black workers; the USWA, citing its no-strike pledge, refused to aid them in recovering their jobs.[189] One reporter for the *Pittsburgh Courier* observed that without adequate support from the union or government, the black employees of J&L were "snugly behind the same old eight-ball."[190] And there they remained; disputes over discrimination in the administration of J&L's seniority system remained a problem for decades.[191]

The failure of the J&L wildcat was indicative of the wider barriers to black advancement into so-called white jobs. In 1946, Roger Thornhill, a first helper in Homestead, reported that blacks had been denied transfers to new departments since 1941. "No new men have been put on Open Hearths Two, Three, Four, and Five." The highly skilled worker observed that "older men who have good records and who I know can do the job have not advanced . . . . White workers have been upgraded ahead of them." When men grieved the issue, the union gave them "promises and excuses." Blacks could only become foremen of black crews, and even then it was a rare event. In 1946, James Madison was a first helper in an open hearth at the Homestead Works and led the record-breaking crew that produced 365,261 ingot tons in January of 1947. Madison was an exemplary worker, but he knew he could never become a foreman. William O. Washington observed that although most labor gangs were mixed, there was only one black supervisor in the entire Homestead Works.[192]

Some African American unionists believed that the USWA's indifference resulted from the fact that relatively few black workers were active members of the union. Although no hard data is available, the numbers of African Americans in local union posts appears to have peaked in the mid-1940s and fallen throughout the post-war period.[193] Of course the election of blacks to leadership positions was an imperfect measure of African-American activism, but veteran unionists frequently complained that black unionists did not attend local union meetings. Joe Shepherd, a former SWOC organizer and recording secretary of Local 1531, complained that although half of his local was black, 98 percent of the members at union meetings were white.[194] Harold Winbush, the leader of the 1946 wildcat strike at J&L, echoed Davis' complaint. Although District 16 had six thousand blacks, there were no Negro members of the USWA district staff, the result of the fact that too many blacks "seem to be too well satisfied with their present condition." As evidence he noted that he and his brother were the only two blacks at the January meeting of his local union.[195] Edward McNary, a shop steward in Local 1272, bemoaned the fact that while one thousand five hundred blacks worked in J&L's Southside Works, only ten to twenty-five regularly attended meetings, and only eight were actively involved in the union.[196] Nathaniel Sallie worried that blacks only got involved when "'something' is coming up." During World War II there had once been seven black union officials in his local, but now "I'm by my lonesome." He mused that maybe the working conditions had become "too good."[197]

Whatever the reason, the evidence shows that African Americans were more alienated from the union than were whites. Thomas Augustine, a University of Pittsburgh graduate student, analyzed union participation, and found that in 1947, attendance at large locals averaged from 1 to 5 percent of the total membership. While white attendance was low, black turnout was even lower. Radical white unionists often argued that the bureaucratization of the USWA alienated it from its members. The President of one local advanced the "rank-and-file" critique in its starkest form: "In the early days it was united, one for all. . . . Now it's different. We're tied up by a contract. . . . And the International are getting the monthly dues regularly, what do they care?" However, Augustine found that blacks' attendance at union meetings had to do with the quality of local, not international, leadership. Blacks attended meetings if they felt the local's leadership was sympathetic to their needs. But if the President and other local unionists were prejudiced, most blacks stopped attending meetings. White unionists even acknowledged the limits of inter-racial solidarity at the local level: "There was some danger in being regarded . . . as too friendly to the Negro members."[198] Finally, Augustine's observations about his experience as a researcher revealed that even talking about race could be a problem for white unionists. He found that some USWA members and staff "who were cordial and open" about the union in general "gave close-lipped responses to questions about the racial policies of the union." One USWA staffer helped to explain: race talk had become identified with the left. Augustine's questions about black steelworkers tagged him as "a goddamned communist." That put an end to all discussion.[199]

CRUSHING THE LEFT

At the end of World War II, the Communist Party (CP) retained scattered but significant working-class support in Pittsburgh. The CP first opposed the war as an imperialist struggle over colonies, but when Germany invaded the Soviet Union, the party abruptly changed its position, convincing many that the party was indeed controlled by Moscow. Nonetheless, the CP remained the largest organized anti-capitalist presence in Pittsburgh, and even its bitterest radical foes tended to organize, or suffer disorganization, at roughly the same rate. Steve Nelson, the CP's District Organizer for Western Pennsylvania estimated that in 1948 "there were perhaps three hundred Party members in and around Pittsburgh, with the largest concentrations amongst steel and electrical workers and their wives and husbands."[200] But while the membership of the UE frequently elected left-wingers to local and national offices, the USWA's leadership actively rooted out left-wing staff members of any party and worked to isolate local radical officers or members.[201] The leaders of the USWA viewed the purge of communists as a form of union hygiene. The Director of District 19, the North Side, revealed the connection between communism and disease in his remarks made before the union's International Executive Board (IEB) in 1946. His region, he remarked, "has for some period been infested with these babies [various factions of communists], and we jointly with the Local Union officers, staff representatives and myself, we have cleaned them up. We don't have them any more." When one worker passed out party cards at the Pressed Steel Car Company, "we made up our minds to get him out of there." He was fired, and "his wife is not working at National Supply any more."[202]

Such rigorous anti-communism (compounded by the Party's self-inflicted wounds) was perhaps, strictly speaking, unnecessary in the late 1940s when Pittsburgh's CP's membership had declined to a third of the peak reached in the 1930s. Even before the Cold War, the party was smaller and more embattled than in cities such as Philadelphia. The Soviet Union's policies towards Eastern Europe cost the CP much support among many ethnic workers. Nonetheless, this relatively small group of left-wing unionists retained the power to influence thousands of industrial workers, which is why the CP, the USWA, and the FBI placed enormous emphasis on them.[203] Throughout the period of the Cold War, Pittsburgh's anti-communist establishment mobilized enormous resources to guard against the possibility that the CP would gain in popular influence.

In the main, the agenda of the pre- and post-war CP might be described as social democratic: left-wing trade unionists generally sought to extend and deepen the progressive features of the New Deal. In 1945, Elmer Kish, Vice President of Homestead's Local 1397, joined other steelworkers in Washington in lobbying for improved unemployment insurance and a permanent FEPC.[204] In Duquesne, Anthony Salopek, Financial Secretary of Local 1256, joined attacks on segregated swimming pools and appealed for a citywide FEPC.[205] Communists also sought to increase workers' solidarity by vigorously opposing discrimination in the workplace. Black communists such as Joseph "Sonny" Robinson credited left-wingers in Local 1276 with ensuring that blacks advanced to skilled positions at Crucible Steel. By 1947, Robinson had been elected grievance committeeman by his mostly white co-workers.[206] Communists sharply differed from the USWA's leadership in that communists placed enormous emphasis on the need for greater interracial unity in the workplace and the community.

Communists possessed the only rank-and-file organization of steelworkers with the potential, or the inclination, to challenge the leadership of the USWA throughout the region. According to the records of the USWA Director for the lower Mon Valley, only eleven communists were members of the union, but "quite frankly, I am fortunate if I can take care of the ones in my District."[207] Communists' support for the Soviet Union angered the leadership of the USWA; Philip Murray said that he had "no sympathy for any American who yields greater loyalty to another country than he does to his own, no sympathy whatever."[208] But what really concerned the District Director from the North Side was that there were hundreds of other communists in Pittsburgh who mobilized workers and raised money "so that the party could place responsible and capable men in positions to fight for the rights of the Steelworkers. I have a mistaken belief that we were all elected to do that job."[209] Another observed that "it is getting to the point where they are pretty well organized, and you can't overlook that fact, and this thing we call democracy in this country, if we are not careful, is going to lick us with our own instrument."[210] Murray signaled that the period of "tolerance" for the left had ended and instructed the officials of the USWA to "see to it that the Communist Party does not elect delegates to the coming Steelworkers convention."[211]

Immediately following the 1946 strike, the USWA's leadership led a concerted attack on communists. "We are now ready to do a job," reported one Director. A member of the USWA staff looked forward to the fight with confidence: "hell, I think one white man can whip a dozen damn communists anywhere you meet him."[212] In the months to come, the USWA did "do a job" on radicals. The balance of forces was more like twelve "white men" to each communist, but the crudely racialized rhetoric suggested the imbrication of anti-communism and "all American" racism. From early in 1946 onward, it was open season on the left.

Before the 1946 USWA convention, the word had already gone out to the members, and numerous locals passed resolutions against communism and maintained a "cordon sanitaire" against radical ethnic organizations.[213] At the 1946 USWA convention, Murray warned communists not to "meddle" in his union's affairs.[214] Locals similarly channeled the spirit of the era. A typical resolution passed in McKeesport read that "persons who advocate and or support totalitarian forms of government such as Nazism, Fascism, or Communism, members of the Ku Klux Klan or other un-American hate disseminating institutions shall not be eligible to hold office in Local 1000."[215] While the ban on communists holding office was rigorously maintained, the bar against the KKK was seldom, if ever, upheld.[216]

Thus before the infamous 1948 USWA convention, at which communists were banned from holding office, most left-wingers had already been driven from office.[217] Communists, along with steelworkers who simply valued traditional First Amendment rights, resisted the onslaught in vain. Despite warnings from their District Director, Grievanceman "Sonny" Robinson and President Zigmunt Paszkowski of Local 1276 refused to sever ties with the CP. After a union trial, both lost their positions.[218] Later, in an attempt to "live in harmony with all my fellow workers and union brothers of Local 1276," Paszkowski penned a "confession" to Pittsburgh's high priest of anti-communism, Father Charles Owen Rice, in which he explained "I thought it [the CP] was just a progressive organization that would help the workers, the foreign born and the Negroes." In an attempt to clear his name, the trade unionist claimed that communists were "poison" and that "Communism . . . [is] harmful to the working class of America and the world." But Rice and the USWA refused Paszkowski a clean bill of health.[219] Paszkowski was barred from holding office or attending meetings. He appealed to the USWA IEB but missed his "court date" because "he ha[d] not been working regularly and he had a chance to pick up a day's work." The IEB noted with satisfaction that Paszkowski's ally, Robinson, had been driven from the industry entirely and thus was no longer eligible for membership or leadership in the USWA. The matter closed, the

USWA's IEB was satisfied that "Mr. Paszkowski and Mr. Robinson are still silenced."[220]

An important factor fueling anti-communism in the USWA was the left wing's challenge to the Democratic Party. In 1944, most of the CIO had favored Henry Wallace over Truman as the Democratic Party's nominee for Vice President. In 1946, Philip Murray admitted that "quite frankly I do not believe too deeply in the roots of the present day Democratic or so-called Republican politics."[221] And in 1948, many steelworkers, including Murray, remained hostile to Harry Truman because of his record of breaking strikes. In 1948, however, Murray strongly opposed Wallace's candidacy for President on the ticket of the newly formed Progressive Party, an organization Murray viewed as a communist plot whose only purpose was to advance Soviet foreign policy by opposing the Marshall Plan. According to a somewhat feverish Murray, the Progressive Party was "a well planned, ill conceived piece of trickery that is now underway. We are going to have trouble with it, of course, in the CIO. . . . [M]any good people will no doubt believe" that they should support it.[222] The USWA feared that Wallace would rob votes from Truman, or as the minutes of Local 1256 put it, "the only thing the third party will do is to help elect Dewey [the Republican candidate] as President."[223] The fact that the Progressive Party received the strong, if unofficial, support from the UE and other left-wing unions only confirmed the USWA in its view that the Progressive Party was the Communist Party in disguise. Those on staff of the Steelworkers who supported Wallace, such as Lee Pressman, the USWA's chief counsel, jumped before they could be pushed.[224] We have already seen that members of the Western Pennsylvania Steelworkers for Henry Wallace Committee, such as Salopek and Robinson, were targeted by the USWA leadership, allegedly for accusing Murray of "selling out" steelworkers to the steel companies.[225]

The Wallace campaign encouraged President Truman to run a populist "Give 'em Hell, Harry" campaign that blamed the dismantling of the New Deal on the Republican Congress. And the mobilization of the USWA and other conservative CIO unions helped to ensure a poor showing for the Progressive Party in the 1948 election. Nationally, Wallace polled just over 1 million votes, a third of the result he had hoped to achieve. In Pennsylvania, the campaign was disjointed and poorly funded and met with extreme hostility from the CIO unions.[226] In Allegheny County, Progressives barely edged out the moribund Socialist Party. As James Matles of the UE recalled, "there was no question that the Communist Party contributed towards narrowing the base of the Progressive Party . . . but on the other hand, neither is there any question that there were many elements both in the labor movement and in the liberal communities that were in support of Wallace on the issues."[227] Whether the failure of the Progressive Party resulted from the left's lack of support or the alliance between the conservatives in the CIO and the Democrats, the election removed the last obstacles in the path of the anti-communist juggernaut.

The barrage by the media and the USWA against left-wing steelworkers began in the fall elections and continued long afterwards. In September of 1948, the *Pittsburgh Post Gazette* publicized the case of Elmer Kish, a "comred" who had "wormed his way into a vice presidency in the local."[228] Union guidelines prohibited officials from being communists, or even "fellow travelers," so Kish was declared ineligible to hold any union office. His wife later recalled the union "simply ran scared" in the face of vigorous red-baiting.[229]

Even where individuals were defended by their local union, communists were banned from office. Antony Salopek was a good case. The leadership of Local 1256 censured Salopek for circulating leaflets defending Nick Migas, a communist steelworker who had been ejected from the 1946 national convention of the USWA. (Supporting Migas was considered by USWA officials as proof of membership in the CP.) As Salopek observed, "Philip Murray is not Christ and they [members] had a right to criticize him."[230] When the issue came to trial in the local, Salopek was charged with attempting to "gain control of the Unions for the Communist Party." In his defense, Salopek "proceeded to disrobe . . . to show the members that he is wearing a brace from an injury he received in the mill and that the company would be only too glad to discharge him now." Members voted to reprimand him, but not bar him from office, at which point "[b]edlam broke loose."[231] In January of 1949, Salopek was nominated to become a grievanceman for the rolling mills, but that nomination was ruled invalid by the executive committee because Salopek was a "fellow traveler." At the next membership meeting, Salopek questioned "whether the membership has a voice in the union," but his ban stuck. Appalled by the level of sympathy for Salopek, district officials, and then international officials, enforced the bar against him. As the District Director observed, "Salopek is a constant source of trouble."[232] As with Paszkowski, Robinson, and Kish, Salopek was effectively silenced, although he did retain his job.

The USWA also sought to eviscerate left-wing unionism outside the USWA. The UE, the largest progressive union in Western Pennsylvania, had always been a thorn in the side of the USWA. The Cold War made it more so. The UE refused to simply endorse the U.S. government's policies abroad or at home. After 1946, when Murray signaled that the period of "tolerance" for communists had ended, the conservative CIO unions joined the AFL unions in trying to destroy the UE altogether. In 1947–48, CIO unions raided UE shops, and the UE's appeals to the CIO for unity failed; in disgust, the UE left the federation in 1948. Raids accelerated after the passage of the Taft-Hartley Act. Unions that refused to sign anti-communist affidavits lost their standing with the NLRB. When a "real" union challenged the UE's right to represent workers at a workplace through decertification elections, the UE could not appear on the ballot. In a Kafkaesque twist, the UE's supporters had to vote "no union" in order to retain the status quo. And in a ghostly echo of John L. Lewis' support of the SWOC, the USWA provided enormous financial support to the CIO's new electrical workers' union: the IUE. While the UE retained a few strongholds, the union lost roughly half of its membership to the new union supported by an unholy alliance of the CIO, networks of anti-communist Catholic priests, electrical manufacturers, and the FBI. But there was no honor among thieves, and the IUE's raids on the UE's shops were joined by AFL unions, the UAW, and the USWA. Under the banner of anti-communism, electrical companies launched their own decertification elections but then fought reunionization by even "patriotric" unions; many former UE shops remained non-union or were moved to Southern states which had passed "right to work" laws, made possible by Taft-Hartley. Over the next decade, fewer electrical workers were organized, and those that were were represented by several different unions. Not surprisingly, the wages and working conditions of electrical workers deteriorated, especially in comparison to steel or auto workers.[233]

The USWA's anti-communism would have merely been union politics as usual if it had not joined the government and big business in its offensive against dissent. At U.S. Steel's Duquesne Works, departmental supervisors were urged to keep a "watchful eye" on those unionists that had defended Salopek's right to remain active in the union.[234] It had long been U.S. Steel's policy to avoid hiring known communists, although this problem was less "forceful" than it had been in the 1930s.[235] Nonetheless,

U.S. Steel extended its blacklist to supporters of the Progressive Party. Voters who signed petitions to put Wallace on the ballot were forwarded to the personnel office in order to prevent their employment.[236] Foremen and supervisors were routinely asked to monitor those workers suspected of communist sympathies as possible security risks.[237] In some cases, such as that of Elmer Kish, supervisors balked at cooperating fully with the FBI. Kish's supervisor held the position that whatever Kish did outside of work was his own affair. But if Kish retained his job, anti-communism still completed its work: "free" to pursue his political interests, Kish nonetheless resigned from political causes because any organization or cause that he supported got red-baited.[238]

Other left-wing steelworkers, like Mike Filewich, were not so lucky. This member of the left was driven from the union and fired by his employer. When he appealed to be reinstated to the USWA, he explained, "I had to move to Detroit last December as I was unable to obtain any job in Pittsburgh and am now trying to make a living in Detroit. I am still hoping that the decision in my case will be reversed so that I can get a job either back in Pittsburgh or here in Detroit. Practically my whole life's work has been in steel and unless I am reinstated as a member of the Union, I am afraid that I will never be able to find any good work again."[239] The union turned him down.

CONCLUSION

In the months after the end of World War II, progressive public policy faded. Federal ownership of heavy industry barely survived the war, although military spending remained one of the most important factors shaping the direction and profitability of American industry. In 1945, the government abandoned those policies that had provided some protections for minority workers, and, predictably, the situation of black and female steelworkers deteriorated. By 1946, in exchange for modest wage gains for some workers, the federal government abandoned price controls. Taft-Hartley greatly restricted workers' ability to strike or to organize in the industrial or political realms. By 1948, it was becoming clear that the period of peacetime reconversion had ended as the country mobilized for yet another global conflict, this time against communism. As in World War II, this war reshaped the lives of workers, affecting in particular the ways and the means of self-organization.

The USWA participated in the new war effort as eagerly as it had entered World War II. But the Cold War demanded greater sacrifices from labor; now many of the CIO's own principles and members became the enemy. Radicals in the unions were attacked as dangerous subversives by government and big business. The USWA did its part to root out "traitors." Militance against racial and gender discrimination, never a hallmark of the USWA, nearly vanished altogether as the struggle against racism and sexism became equated with communism. Thus, one of the first victims of the Cold War was the fight against racism in the workplace.

Taft-Hartley, combined with an increasingly aggressive FBI to ferret out and punish labor radicals, signaled the imposition of a new regime of legal repression. Workers confronted the irony of a federal government that simultaneously protected their right to organize unions while maintaining an aggressive spy system and blacklist. In time, the institutional arrangements of the Cold War might raise steelworkers' standards of living; it also eroded their political understanding and limited their power.

⊗

Chapter Three

Cold War Pittsburgh: 1949–1959

INTRODUCTION

In the 1950s, the USWA formed one of America's largest, strongest, and most militant unions. With over 1 million members and hundreds of full-time staff throughout the country, one-quarter of them in Pennsylvania, the Steelworkers dominated the trade union movement in Pittsburgh and transformed the lives of steelworkers. Steelworkers shut down their industry in 1946, 1949, 1952, 1955, 1956, and 1959. Each cutoff of the country's basic metal threatened widespread economic dislocation and prompted the President to intervene. Steelworkers had come a long way from the non-union era, and one measure of that distance was that by the standards of the early twentieth century, the steel strikes of the 1940s and 1950s were peaceful. Pickets did not battle Pinkertons, deputy sheriffs, or state troopers. Big steel firms never attempted a "back to work" movement, a telling change from past tests of strength; companies respected the solidarity and power of steelworkers. Fierce struggles ensued over the content of the national contract, but not over whether companies would negotiate with their union. The union's political power and strength in the workplace ensured that companies remained within the boundaries of labor law.

Steelworkers' wages and benefits improved until they could almost enjoy a middle-class standard of living, and the union's successes seemed to justify its staunchly patriotic and (by the standards of the CIO) conservative political perspective. Despite several lengthy, bitter strikes—including one lasting 116 days in 1959—the union consistently maintained that class struggle was a thing of the past. The labor militancy of the USWA never threatened to evolve into labor radicalism. In its day-to-day relationship with steel companies, the union consistently directed workers into routinized forms of struggle such as grievances and arbitration meetings and opposed slowdowns or local strikes. In politics, the union urged its members to support Democrats, and while it won many workers to a kind of economic populism, the USWA consistently opposed any policies that seemed to verge on socialism. In fact, one USWA President later (in the mid-1970s) complained that the union never got the credit it deserved as a "responsible force" for working within the two-party system and capitalism.[1]

Rhetoric to the contrary notwithstanding, the USWA's embrace of the Cold War ideology that America was a "classless society" did not end the class struggle in Pittsburgh. The union could and did force companies to raise the wages of its members, almost 3 percent a year over and above inflation, no mean feat. But steel firms still retained the power to lay off employees or to close mills. No matter how much the union defended the profit motive, each pay raise the steelworkers negotiated cut into the profits of steel companies. No matter how much steel companies praised their "partners in production," rising productivity invariably resulted in lost jobs. Indeed, over the course of the 1950s, U.S. Steel discharged a quarter of its workforce while raising its production, productivity, and prices. While steel firms remained profitable, profits were not as high as companies thought they should be, which helps explain the bitter struggles that rocked the steel industry in this decade at the "end of ideology."[2] In between national strikes, intense struggles took place in the mills over crew levels, production quotas, and how new equipment would be implemented. That more jobs were not lost was a testimony to workers' power and determination. Despite the best efforts of the USWA, local unionists did lead wildcat strikes, and workers did engage in slowdowns. Whether measured by national strikes or day-to-day conflict in the workplace, class struggle remained a feature of life in Cold War America, and in this decade, workers often gave as good as they got. But rank-and-file resistance did not evolve into labor radicalism, in large part because workers, their union, and the class struggle it disavowed were all deeply affected by the ideology and legal-political institutions of the Cold War, which constrained both workers and capital.

The USWA embraced the Cold War "consensus." In both politics and production, there were important areas of cooperation among unionists, government, and business. The USWA enthusiastically joined with government agencies and large companies in attacking communists and radicals in the labor movement and throughout Pittsburgh. The union's support for American foreign policy—and the ever-increasing amounts of military spending—never wavered. Towards steel companies, union officials negotiated over the terms of modernization, won incredible wage gains, and defended many workplace gains. But union officials also respected the prerogatives of managers to determine the pace and direction of new investment. While the USWA relied heavily on its Democratic political allies to pressure companies to settle strikes, many Democrats joined Republicans and bolstered the profitability of steel companies through federal legislation. Closer to home, Democrats cooperated extensively with local industrialists to transform downtown Pittsburgh into a city suitable for corporate headquarters and taxed workers, not big business, to pay for these programs. While this "Pittsburgh Renaissance" arguably slowed the rate of regional decline, it did little to address endemic problems of unemployment and poverty that remained particularly acute for African Americans. On questions of race and gender in the workplace, the USWA sometimes embraced a "middle ground" with management, often acquiescing in workplace segregation in spite of the union's principles of non-discrimination. However, the union won important gains on this front, both by raising the wages of black and female workers and by helping to win federal legislation, such as the dramatic increases in the amount and coverage of the minimum wage.

On the margins of this political consensus, disaffected workers fomented a modest degree of activism, seeking to bring the Cold War order into line with their ideals and interests. Some workers sought to reinvigorate the union by arguing for a more aggressive civil rights struggle against employers. Others sought to build a more democratic union or to develop a more confrontational stance against plant modernization. These struggles were sometimes explosive, as in the challenge to the presidency of the USWA, but often remained local, decentralized, and episodic. But all of these forms of protest pushed against the limitations of the Cold War consensus, albeit sometimes in contradictory directions. Government, companies, and the unions pushed back against these "outlaw" movements and organizations and succeeded in dampening this aspect of the class struggle, ensuring that opposition remained scattered and disorganized. In short, the first decade of the Cold War improved steelworkers' lives—dramatically so in economic terms—but steel unionism proved both an aid and a hindrance to overcoming the forces that had long disorganized workers in Pittsburgh.

THE POLITICAL CONTEXT FOR BUSINESS AS USUAL

Like many labor leaders of his generation, Philip Murray dreamed of a tri-
partite system of national economic planning among corporations, labor,
and government. Such a system never came to pass in the United States.
Yet after World War II, most industrial democracies did establish some
form of institutionalized power sharing. In West Germany and Scandi-
navia, representatives of unions routinely sat on the boards of directors of
their employers, which moderated the demands of both labor and capital.
Throughout Europe and Japan, workers' political parties prompted the creation of extensive social programs, including publicly financed health
insurance, pensions, and education. In the United Kingdom, unions realized their long-standing goal of the nationalization of the steel industry,
and several other sectors of the economy. Much of the steel industry in
Western Europe operated as de facto nationalized concerns. In the United
States, the federal government stimulated the economy through a unique
combination of military expenditures and social spending. At the behest
of the CIO unions, governments expanded the social safety net and regulated relations between unions and companies. But U.S. corporations resolutely rejected any formal collaborative role with labor or government,
which ultimately limited the range of labor's influence over public policy.
But in the 1950s, the informal collaboration, itself wracked by intense
class conflict, helped to raise the standards of living of American industrial
workers to the highest in the world.[3] Although the American government
forced employers to respect the limits of labor law, which helped protect
unions and their gains, it also rendered substantial support and largesse to
manufacturers. In the future, the contradictions of this system would come
asunder, protecting neither workers nor their industry.

The lion's share of public stimulation to the economy resulted from
high levels of military spending, a process that some scholars have termed
"military Keynesianism." Strategically vital industries, particularly aerospace, computers, and electronics (the so-called ACE industries), benefited from enormous amounts of federal spending and expanded rapidly. In
the case of aerospace, up to 87 percent of its research moneys derived from
the military which also bought most of its products. The results were rates
of profit of 20 to 30 percent, far higher than those of most lines of manufacturing. Certain regions, notably parts of California and the South, benefited from the expansion of ACE industries or the growth of military bases.

In the 1950s, the Southern share of defense spending doubled, and California's increased from 13 percent to over 21 percent of the national total.[4] The rise of the industrial "gunbelt" in the South and the West resulted from New Deal policies and came at the expense of already industrialized parts of the country, such as Pennsylvania.

Big steel companies, historically the beneficiaries of military spending, suffered from their declining importance to the armed forces. The government still required vast amounts of steel and armor for its shells, bombs, and armored vehicles, but the technological center of the naval vessel was now its electronics and not its armor or guns. The Korean War witnessed the final major naval bombardments of ground troops; from the 1960s onward, battleships would become platforms for the "electronic battlefield." As a result, steel companies attracted just a fraction of federal research moneys (or procurement dollars) that subsidized the ACE industries. Unsurprisingly, the dramatic growth of the ACE industries bypassed steel.[5] In the early 1950s, however, steel enjoyed lucrative military contracts as the "police conflict" on the Korean peninsula kept Pittsburgh's mills humming at "100 percent of capacity or better."[6] At the Homestead Works, forgings for the navy, such as armor plate or rudders for ships, made up less than one percent of the mill's tonnage, but produced almost one-quarter of the mill's profits. While the mill could produce forgings for the commercial sector, one management study reported that U.S. Steel "found the market highly competitive" and abandoned it.[7] As the military gradually abandoned steel, the industry found itself in unfamiliar territory: the free market.

In the early 1950s, military Keynesianism granted steel one final infusion of public capital. Following World War II, the rates of private investment in steel remained sluggish, causing widespread shortages and "gray markets." By 1949, in the midst of a booming economy, steel companies added just 2.2 million tons to their annual capacity.[8] On the eve of the Korean conflict, policy makers worried that shortages of steel would hamper either the war effort or national economic growth. Manufacturers rejected any attempts to return to federally owned production facilities as in World War II. So in 1950, the government accelerated the tax amortization schedule in war-related industries from twenty years to five. The government generously defined "wartime" tax write-offs and approved 98.8 percent of all applications. For instance, although J&L had begun its modernization of its Pittsburgh facilities *before* the Korean War began, the company qualified for hundreds of millions of dollars of tax subsidies. More tax moneys were spent in a few months on such "wartime" expansion than in all of World War II. In what even *Fortune* called a "rapid and lavish fashion," the largest steel firms added 13 million tons of new annual capacity. By 1956, steel's share of the "five year gravy" totaled $5 billion, or half of the capital it "invested" in this decade.[9] This proved steel's last hurrah with the warfare state.

Unrelated to military Keynesianism, but consistent with the pro-business bias of the federal government, was policy makers' indifference to steel's monopolistic pricing structures. Except for a brief return to price controls during the Korean War, President Truman's (and later Eisenhower's) only reaction to virtually identical price rises by the major steel companies was to "jawbone" them. Jawboning was the process of bringing "highly publicized pressures to bear on important economic interests in an effort to have them voluntarily reduce their demands." The practice proved remarkably, if predictably, ineffective. Between 1940 and 1960, the average price of steel increased more than a third above the Consumer Price Index.[10] But without tariff protection or another infusion of free capital, companies argued that their profitability hovered between 6 percent and 9 percent.[11] The Bureau of Labor Statistics found that steel's profitability (as a percentage of sales) did range between 6 percent and 9 percent but that this was higher than the average for manufacturing. Compared to steel's massive capital requirements (stockholder's equity), steel's after-tax profits were generally under the average for manufacturing.[12] According to U.S. Steel's Roger Blough, "price increases since WWII have not been enough to widen profit margins."[13]

Whether companies' concern over their declining profits was largely bluster (and it largely was) steel companies remained tough and powerful concerns; consequently, President Harry S. Truman remained central in the calculations of the USWA. Murray had no illusions about Truman, whose price control boards proved ineffectual. Furthermore, Truman's FEPC (Fair Employment Practices Board) was even weaker and shorter-lived than its counterpart during World War II.[14] In other unions' strikes, Truman had used his Taft-Hartley powers to order workers back to work. Nonetheless, the USWA's leadership relied on Truman as its trump card during negotiations with steel companies. In 1949, Truman sponsored a strategically timed fact-finding mission that bolstered steelworkers' case for improved pensions.[15] However, Truman's assistance did not spare steelworkers from several weeks of walking picket lines before steel companies agreed to guarantee pensioners with more than twenty-five years of service a minimum of $100 a month.[16] Truman's intervention in the 1952 strike was more problematic. In addition to other issues, the union sought an 18.5 cent raise.[17] Steel companies refused, and Truman convinced both sides to submit their case to the wartime Wage Stabilization Board. Management eventually agreed to an increase of 13.7 cents, but only if it could increase the price of steel far beyond what the Office of Price Stabilization recommended. On April 8, Truman "seized" the mills to prevent a walkout and pressured the steel companies to settle. The Supreme Court subsequently ruled Truman's action unconstitutional, and workers struck for fifty-three days before they won their demand for a modified union shop. Steel companies got their price increase, but workers received only a 12.5 cent an hour raise, less money than was on the table before Truman intervened. It was mute testimony to the problems of allowing the President of the United States to help negotiate alongside the President of the USWA.[18] Despite his often pro-business policies, Truman's interventions on behalf of the USWA earned him the enmity of steel owners.

Steel companies hoped to hobble the USWA by electing a Republican President.[19] In 1952, Dwight D. Eisenhower became the first Republican to be elected chief executive in twenty years. His policies, while more favorable to big business than Truman's, nonetheless disappointed steel companies. At the end of the Korean War, Eisenhower abandoned price controls, which did please big business. Eisenhower also replaced the FEPC with the Office of Contract Compliance, which simply required defense contractors to periodically submit paperwork that monitored their hiring and promotion patterns. But the Republican President failed to accomplish what steel firms really desired: a change in the federal tax depreciation schedule to encourage investment in steel. Furthermore, Eisenhower helped to settle the 1955 and 1956 steel strikes on terms that granted considerable wage gains. L. Conrad Cooper, the chief negotiator for U.S. Steel, explained what he thought of Eisenhower's "help:" "the government, which is supposed to be the referee, comes in and kicks us in the nuts."[20]

Amongst themselves, the leaders of the USWA freely admitted their political shortcomings. In 1953, the union sought to lay the groundwork in order to elect "a new liberal Congress" the next year, but it failed to energize its members.[21] In 1954, the union investigated its Political Action Committee (PAC) and found that 87 percent of USWA members "received no union political literature and political problems were not a topic of conversation." While most steel towns had become Democratic Party bastions, Secretary-Treasurer I.W. Abel admitted, "We have been talking political action and have supposedly been in political action, but when we analyze our past we have done a lot of talking, and that's about the sum and substance of it."[22] Nonetheless, the unions retained considerable political power in the 1950s, and won some legislative gains. In 1956, an election year, Congress and President Eisenhower raised the minimum wage to $1 an hour at the urging of trade unions; the wage stood at approximately 60 percent of the average wage of manufacturing workers, or almost $7 an hour in adjusted 2000 dollars. Ironically, labor's political victories coincided with remarkably low contributions to the union's political action fund. In the fall of 1957, the USWA was less than one-third of the way towards its quota to the AFL-CIO's PAC. One district in the Pittsburgh region had collected no money from its fifty thousand members, and another had gathered $161.[23] Over the next year, however, the union convinced workers to contribute at three times their normal levels, and the USWA amassed $200,000 to spend on that year's elections.[24] Thus the union slowly reversed the political tide of the 1950s, and remained a credible force in the political calculations of major politicians, particularly presidential candidates.

In 1959, steel firms prevailed upon the President to stay out of negotiations; even so, steel companies failed to cripple the union.[25] Even after 116 days on strike, steelworkers refused to accept management's proposals that would have made redundant tens of thousands of workers. Eisenhower remained amenable to steel companies' demand that he invoke Taft-Hartley; the President ordered USWA members back to work for 80 days. (The "cooling off" period allowed steel companies to replenish their customers' stockpiles.) Even then, the USWA refused to surrender. When it became clear that workers supported going back out on strike, Eisenhower went abroad and ordered Vice President Richard Nixon to help negotiate a settlement in which the workers retained their work rules and won major wage gains.[26] It was a crushing defeat for steel companies, whose enormous economic and political power failed to weaken workers' resolve.

During Eisenhower's administration, steelmakers failed to secure the public policies that might have restored the rates of profit they enjoyed prior to the 1930s. Big steel's sizeable profits, plus the USWA's political clout, led even Republican Presidents to urge steel companies to make concessions to their employees. But labor costs were simply one part of big steel's political problems. The government refused to raise its historically low tariffs. (As we will see, steel companies began to urge higher tariffs from the late 1950s onwards). Indeed, the government pursued progressively lower global trade barriers in order to encourage the internationalization of American corporations and promote more vigorous trade. Towards the latter end, both Truman and Eisenhower strengthened industrialists in allied countries through loans and grants. Between 1947 and 1956, the United States subsidized $866 million worth of steel mill construction and iron ore development around the world. By 1960, that figure had grown to $1.4 billion, $200 million to Japan alone. By the mid-1950s, imported steel began to cut into the market share and began to affect the profits of domestic firms. Nonetheless, Eisenhower continued Truman's policies of reinforcing international political alliances by keeping the American market open to steel imports.[27] By the end of the decade, America had ceased to be a net exporter of steel. During the 1959 strike, many manufacturers turned to lower-cost foreign steel suppliers whose "new and modernized plants," according to U.S. Steel's Benjamin Fairless, "now compares favorably to our own."[28] Throughout the early 1960s domestic steelmakers struggled to recover those markets, and their previous levels of profitability, with only limited success.[29]

Despite its vitality, big steel had problems it refused to acknowledge, because they were not the industry's favored scapegoats of high wages, union featherbedding, and imports. Most importantly, steel inherited its own history of reluctance to invest in its own mills. True, little protection was offered to steel from a government whose loyalty was first to capitalism on a global scale and only secondarily to steel or other domestic industries. The U.S. government reduced tariffs on all industries, but some firms and sectors received lucrative military contracts and support for their research and development costs. (This was in sharp contrast to most industrialized countries that subsidized steel production but generally encouraged companies to maximize employment.) But as we will see in the next section, even when steel companies received what amounted to publicly financed capital, they eschewed pioneering technologies that might have forced them to change ossified corporate practices. Instead, steel firms invested moderately and chose to boost production out of existing facilities with fewer workers. While steel's conservative course of modernization failed to prevent foreign producers from entering the U.S. market, the American steel industry dramatically increased productivity.

From workers' perspective, there was no easy answer to the question of productivity and efficiency. Workers could lose their jobs in the short run to new technology and work rules or lose their jobs in the long run if their mill became hopelessly noncompetitive. The USWA opposed job losses, but part of its grand strategy of improving wage gains and benefits was justified by arguments that workers deserved "the fruits of the productivity gains to which [they] contribute."[30] Thus a contradictory investment in both efficiency and their own security lay at the heart of workers' struggles.

THE MODERNIZATION OF STEEL AND ITS DISCONTENTS

Steel companies' investment strategies avoided the substantial costs of innovation. One former steel executive, recalling management's approach to planning, said that "the definition of intelligence or ability" was to do things the company way. And that way was "the way we always did it in the past."[31] Thus steel firms remained indifferent to research and development, spending about a third as much on R&D as most manufacturers.[32] Instead, European and Japanese steelmakers bore the costs of innovation and developed the new technologies that would ultimately transform steelmaking, notably the basic oxygen process (BOP) and the continuous caster. BOPs were able to produce a heat of steel in thirty minutes instead of the several hours required with open hearth technology.[33] Continuous casters could pour steel directly into blooms, eliminating the need for a blooming mill and thereby reducing both energy costs and jobs. (Ironically, one of the first continuous casters in the world had been planned in 1948 in Beaver Falls, Pennsylvania, in a joint venture with Babcock and Wilcox and Republic Steel.)[34] Robert Tyson, U.S. Steel's finance committee chairman, knew that the BOP was "the furnace of the future, but that doesn't mean you can toss out what you have."[35] Some critics observed that steel firms required a return of "20 percent before taxes" before they would commit capital.[36] Even when enormous government subsidies were available to them in the early to mid-1950s, steel firms failed to pursue an aggressive modernization strategy.

Instead, American steelmakers modernized piecemeal. With billions invested in open hearth furnaces alone, steel companies retained proven moneymakers and "rounded out" existing facilities, adding new departments or modernizing existing ones. (Companies believed that rounding out cost one-quarter as much as building an entirely new facility.) Rounding out accounted for most of the industry's 55 million tons of new capacity added in this decade.[37] Because the center of steel markets continued to shift away from the Mon Valley, rounding out proved the most efficient course for U.S. Steel, allowing it to boost production in Pittsburgh by roughly 10 percent or 1,268,000 tons per year.[38] For instance, in 1954, the corporation added 200,000 more tons a year by improving Duquesne's OH 2. Two years later, modernizing and enlarging the existing furnaces at Homestead's OH 5 increased output there by 30 percent.[39] Rounding out not only provided low-cost modernization, but it helped moderate labor costs by reducing employment levels.

Piece by piece, steel companies also remade their workforces. In 1947, the mills in Allegheny County employed eighty thousand workers who were paid $227 million and produced $410 million value added. (Value added is one way of measuring wealth produced and is calculated by the amount of the final product minus the costs of raw materials and labor; the resultant figure is the value added by manufacturing.) In 1954, Allegheny County steel producers employed only sixty thousand workers who were paid $260 million in wages and produced $580 million worth of value added. In less than a decade, production had gone up by a third, the number of employees had decreased by a quarter, and wages had increased by about a fifth. This feat was accomplished with relatively little new capital, averaging just $29 million in 1947 and $40 million in 1954.[40] Post-war modernization eliminated numerous unskilled jobs and engendered resistance by many trade unionists.

But managers also enlisted workers to boost productivity and eliminate jobs through incentive programs.[41] In 1946, the union had agreed to U.S. Steel's proposal to embrace a "fair day's work" for a "fair day's pay." Managers initiated incentive schemes that paid workers more than their base pay, but only if they exceeded production targets. A third of the incentives offered no returns, another third offered about 15 percent above the base pay, and keeping track of the criteria was so complicated that by 1951 the union turned the problem over to the locals. The criteria were often so complicated that, according to Philip Murray, "even the fellow who wrote the book doesn't fully understand what that book means. . . . It is knavery, it is trickery, it is designed to deceive the fellow on the job."[42] But deceptive or no, extra income opened Pandora's box and inevitably resulted in layoffs.[43] For instance, an incentive plan at Duquesne caused tonnage to increase by 250 percent and resulted in eighteen men losing their jobs. But one manager observed that "as the earnings of a few fellows increased . . . others increased their efforts in an effort to increase their earnings and opposition to the plan soon dissolved."[44] John Hughey recalled how workers at the Carrie Furnace got a 25 percent bonus, but only after production shot up several times its previous level. In the beginning there were three crews of workers producing submarine ladles; in the end, there was only one. As Hughey explained, a worker "wants to take home as much as he can. He don't care about the other man."[45] At the Homestead Works, the union had to remind its members that "a good union member will refuse to put a man out of work for the sake of a few cents an hour."[46]

Incentive programs promoted the interest of the individual over any collective solidarity and succeeded in raising the tempo of work. John Hoerr worked at the National Tube Works in the summers before he became a labor journalist and later recalled the often leisurely pace of many workers. Hoerr, himself a white-collar worker, claimed that he worked perhaps two hours out of an eight-hour turn and was fascinated by a worker on incentive who tended "two machines and work[ed] on four blanks at a time, he moved back and forth between the machines in a near blur of motion."[47] Philip Bonosky, a writer from the Steel Valley, described how incentives increased the pace of Duquesne's conditioning workers in his novel *The Magic Fern*. When a steelworker was given a tour of his new job, he saw that when a scarfer "finished the set of beds he was working on, he didn't stop, throw back his helmet and take a breath of air. Instead he dropped his torch where he was, and started on a trot across the yard. . . . [A] new set of beds had already been prepared for him and the other scarfers. . . . They used to have spells in between when they broke out with a smoke or went to the John, horsed around, joked, told stories. . . . [T]he only reason for that must be, Leo thought, a fiercely competitive tonnage rate. It made them meaner than usual, and scarfers were known for their meanness."[48]

Low-cost "labor economies" formed the bedrock of steel's modernization strategies. Management reorganized the work process and eliminated jobs often with little or no new technology. For instance, in May 1950, the Supervisor of Industrial Relations at the Duquesne Works proposed a comprehensive modernization plan which would cut 391 jobs and save the company over a million dollars a year at a cost of only sixty thousand dollars. In a typical case, the duties of janitor and laborer were combined. In other cases, managers installed a minor piece of equipment such as a telephone or mobile radio to justify eliminating a helper.[49] Workers, resentful that managers had added new duties to jobs that had "already [been] described and classified," promised to "take matters into their own hands" before they would wait for their case to work its way to an arbitration meeting. The limitations of the grievance procedure were clear: members did not want another "useless" meeting with managers as they "had one interpretation and the Company another."[50] Union officials warned that job combinations would result in a "work to rule" movement as "feeling in the plant was running rather high."[51] Having probed their union's defenses, management withdrew; but over the course of the next year, managers quietly phased in most of the plan.[52]

In some shops, workers offered stiff resistance to labor economies. On April 21, 1950, Local 1397 led a wildcat designed to force the management at the Homestead Works to fire outside contractors in order to allow the mill's 2,500 maintenance workers a five-day week. After seven hours, the strike ended when the International USWA pressured the local executive board to lead the back-to-work movement. The local executive board reluctantly complied.[53] (The USWA, whose attitude was that "wild-cat strikes must stop," allowed its locals far less latitude in leading local strikes than the United Auto Workers or United Packinghouse Workers.)[54] After the modernization of the Duquesne Works Electric Furnace, its crew size was reduced prompting the longest illegal strike at that mill in the post-war period. In August 1950, 150 men struck for three weeks, but the crew was not punished since management believed "positively that the men are being kept from working by the top union people."[55] In February 1951, 169 members of the Duquesne Works' Bar Mill struck for two turns over a reduction in the size of the workforce.[56] In February 1952, workers in Duquesne's OH 2 had begun a slowdown because "employees in No. 1 Open Hearth have been receiving higher incentive earnings." Managers, fearing that the walkout would spread, dared not discipline workers.[57] It was mute testimony to the power of workers' solidarity. Following an unsuccessful strike in March 1953, fifty-one swing frame grinders began a slowdown in May over an inferior incentive plan than that covering grinders in another department. Twelve days of negotiations with the union failed to stop the slowdown; management then shut down the department. After five days, the crew was called back.[58] The best that workers could expect from stiff resistance was a stalemate: status quo ante.

Managers often calculated that workers' resistance would weaken. From February 1951 to May 1952, management eliminated 104 jobs (3 percent of the total) at the Duquesne Works. Management estimated that this round of job eliminations engendered only one large-scale strike at the Number 5

Rolling Mill. Expecting further resistance, management held off from the lion's share of its job cuts.[59] In April and May, 1952, management carefully planned eight incentive plans and twelve force reductions and braced itself for trouble.[60] To its delight, in only one or two instances was even a grievance filed.[61] In nineteen separate incidences involving crew reductions, the union filed only five grievances, and only one of those made it to arbitration where it was decided in favor of the company. Management laid off workers by seniority, but still eliminated numerous jobs.[62] Management could afford to wait out grievances that only slowed the pace of job cuts; in a war of attrition, time was often on management's side.

Managers also knew that some incentive programs and job combinations went unopposed. In June of 1951, the Industrial Relations Department at the Duquesne Works proposed cutting 136 workers from the payroll. While new technology made some jobs redundant, the lion's share involved the reorganization of the work process. In one instance, the oxygen for the Electric Furnace would now be supplied via new piping from the Merchant Mills, eliminating a full-time Air Compressor Operator. Another worker would be required one day a week to check on the equipment. Laborers in the Blast Furnace Department were given an "increased work load." Managers estimated that they could eliminate eight out of the fifty-eight laborers. Rather than risk a confrontation with workers by firing the eight redundant men, managers decided to simply let any new vacancies go unfilled.[63] The power of workers was such that the eight men could not be fired outright, but the limits of workers' power were clear enough.

The end of the Korean War boom brought another major round of layoffs. In 1954, "with the heat off the defense program," steel companies dropped from 100 percent of capacity to 75 percent.[64] By July 1954, over 200,000 steelworkers were laid off, and I.W. Abel observed that "there has been no upward trend, no bright spots . . . in fact we are still going downhill."[65] Employment at the Homestead Works sagged from over 12,000 in 1953 to about 8,000 in 1955, reaching the lowest point since 1940.[66] The newspaper of the local at Homestead grimly observed that "none of us need be reminded of the startling events and incidents that have reduced the Homestead Works from a production giant to a shadow of itself."[67] At Duquesne, employment of production and maintenance workers fell from 7,600 in 1953 to 3,850 two years later.[68] Local unions were in a bind. Without modernization, mills could be closed, yet new facilities cost jobs. For instance, a new primary mill at Duquesne reduced employment from 325 to 110.[69] John McManigal, a prominent unionist at Homestead, correctly warned that job losses due to automation "are only . . . beginning."[70]

The return of prosperity in 1956 stabilized the number of workers who had remained in the mills during the slump but only brought some of them back.[71] David McDonald observed that companies "prevailed upon the frailties of human nature and the [hunger] pangs [of] the men by telling them their departments" would be restarted, but only if the crew sizes were smaller.[72] And management continued to eliminate jobs through incentive schemes and contracting out maintenance and building projects. Even the relatively conservative local at the Homestead Works had had enough. Of the six wildcat strikes at Homestead in the post-war period, four occurred in May 1956 over incentive programs.[73] The General Superintendent let it be known that anyone who joined such a strike would be fired[74] (Such rhetoric begs the question of why he had not fired workers in the past for such actions). Indeed, workers protested that they had wildcatted in the past without punishment, but with so many workers unemployed, management clearly held the stronger position and made it clear.[75] By the end of the decade, large local strikes were relatively rare, and most wildcats occurred amongst one gang or a section of a department.[76] Wildcats in steel, except during wartime, had lost most of their strategic value, such as that enjoyed by auto workers during the preparation of new models.[77]

Local strikes stiffened the resolve of the USWA to deal with unemployment. The national strikes in 1955 and 1956 sought wage increases and relief from high unemployment. After a sixteen-hour strike in 1955, workers won a substantial pay raise and important contract language regarding layoffs. Departmental seniority could be modified to allow laid-off workers to "back down through their promotional lines until they reach their respective department or Division Labor Pools." Labor pools provided additional security "for older service employees," because with enough plant seniority they kept their job even if their department was shut down. During mild layoffs, affected workers with five years or more entered the labor pool, but later in the decade, workers needed ten or twenty years to enter the pool.[78] However, workers in the labor pool were prevented from acquiring departmental seniority in a new department.[79]

Some locals supported widening company seniority so that laid-off workers could bid on new jobs at other mills owned by their company. In this scenario, never adequately implemented, a worker could move from Clairton to Homestead without "losing his rights to seniority status of his home plant or department unless he transfers on his own request." This proposal was put forward by a black trade unionist, but as we will see below, labor pools (the most significant modification to the seniority system) were often set up in ways that harmed black laborers.[80] After another brief strike in 1956, workers won higher wages, a cost of living clause, and better health benefits. The USWA also won SUB (Supplemental Unemployment Benefits), a company-paid unemployment scheme that augmented workers' unemployment insurance.[81] SUB payment helped take some of the sting out of layoffs. In 1958–59, when two to three thousand workers were laid off at the Homestead Works and most others worked a four-day week, SUB pay enabled workers to avoid depleting their savings. Even in cases of mill closures, such as the Donora zinc mill, SUB pay applied to workers looking for a new job. However, in times of severe, widespread unemployment, the SUB fund ran dry.[82] While workers never welcomed unemployment, it was far more tolerable as a result of the gains won through the USWA.

Throughout the decade, Pittsburgh's steel industry experienced sharp booms and busts, and job levels swung accordingly, but most mills slowly bled jobs. New projects such as Duquesne's "Dorothy Six" blast furnaces and old-fashioned labor economies allowed management to trim the number of steelworkers in Allegheny County by 20 percent between 1954 and 1958. Production rose by 17 percent and wages by just 11 percent. Job losses would have undoubtedly been higher without workers' determination to preserve as many jobs as possible. At Homestead, at the beginning of a deep recession in 1958, workers held almost as many jobs as several years before, but up to half of them were working short shifts.[83] The burdens of unemployment fell hardest on those with low seniority, but the pressure of modernization even began to pinch skilled workers, who led numerous wildcats in the late 1950s. Managers began to worry that USWA President McDonald "will not do much, if anything, to help in settling" wildcats.[84] Layoffs also placed enormous pressure on seniority, and management's violations of those provisions prompted a few stay-aways, such as in 1958 when the entire Irvin Works honored the picket line of ten men who felt they had been unfairly laid off. The local union's leadership disclaimed the strike and convinced the men to return to work.[85] Nonetheless, the strike was indicative of the growing determination of steelworkers to hold the line on the issue of jobs.

THE ROAD TO THE 1959 STRIKE:
THE BATTLE OVER WORK RULES

Workers' struggles for greater job security and better pay increasingly collided with steel companies' desires for higher profits. The result was an intensification of shop-floor struggles that culminated in the longest strike in the union's history. By the end of the decade, incentives, modernization, and a deep recession that hit heavy industry particularly hard had decimated the ranks of steelworkers. By February 22, 1958, only 3,307 workers remained "active" at the Duquesne Works, and just 1,228 worked five days a week.[86] On March, 8, 1958, Homestead shut down its OH 4, and by January, 1959, over 2,200 workers were laid off at that mill.[87] The resulting unemployment caused one unionist to observe that "bars do not a prison make . . . thousands of Homestead steelworkers who have been laid off would like to go behind these bars of the locked 'hole in the wall' gate" to the mill.[88] A brief and paradoxical respite came in 1959 as manufacturers stockpiled steel to weather a threatened strike. The mills ran at 96 percent of capacity, and quarterly company profits soared to their highest levels in decades.[89] Homestead restarted OH 4, but the union suspected that this facility would never be modernized and would only be used during rare periods of peak production.[90] Steel companies argued they needed relief on work rules and many workers resolved to hold the line against further layoffs.

In the midst of a severe recession, emboldened managers accelerated their campaign of labor economies. At Duquesne, managers often violated union work rules by ordering production workers to carry out routine maintenance ordinarily done by craftsmen.[91] David McDonald opined that companies believed that "by God, if [workers] are going to take it we'll rub their noses in it."[92] On May 23, 1959, hundreds of Duquesne's craftsmen who had "lost faith" in the grievance procedure walked out of the mill. To get them back in, management agreed to a meeting. Management admitted that they had assigned work outside of workers' job descriptions but argued that current conditions made that necessary. Most craftsmen were building the Dorothy Six Blast Furnace, construction work was generally contracted out, and an upsurge of orders had caught management short-handed. Supervisors held that modernization would eliminate layoffs by eliminating the "extreme up-and-down swings in operations."[93]

But events confirmed fears that in a more modern mill, fewer craftsmen would be required.

The skirmish resolved little and produced nothing but new warnings and a few punishments. If workers did not show some "restraint" and work within the grievance procedure, management promised that all future capital projects would be contracted out.[94] All strikers were suspended for a day and three leaders for five days. The union did not challenge this discipline; in fact, union officials expected harsher punishment.[95] After another walkout of pipefitters, one grievanceman frantically tried to distance himself from the wildcat. His department superintendent related, with some relish, that the panicked unionist said that "he was sure that someone was going to be fired over this [wildcat] and he did not intend it to be himself." He "did not underestimate Duquesne Works Management" and would tell them who started the walkout rather than lose his job.[96]

Testy battles in a "war of position" over modernization and work rules formed the background for the bitter strike in 1959. Foreign steel and alternative materials such as aluminum and plastics had nibbled at steel companies' market share, and management pushed for substantial concessions from the union.[97] Steel companies attacked work rules, such as Section 2-B in the contract, as needless featherbedding. (More on the history of Section 2-B below.) Management entered negotiations determined to force the union to agree to more job cuts.[98] Most industry "experts" predicted a short strike. The relations between the President of the USWA, David McDonald (who succeeded Murray after he died in 1952), and the President of U.S. Steel remained cordial. *U.S. News* polled steelworkers before the strike, and found that most did not want to hit the bricks.[99] Harold Ruttenberg, once a member of the USWA's staff, now the head of a steel company, pointed to the huge inventories that suppliers had built up and concluded that the union would not risk a major strike.[100] Managers apparently thought they could force workers out on strike, break their will to fight, and then negotiate a new contract from a position of strength.[101]

But workers surprised everyone but themselves. One worker in Braddock put it this way: "management's been spoiling for a fight for a year and they're sure as hell going to get it."[102] Managers blundered by making work rules and "featherbedding" the central issue of the strike. John McManigal, a union stalwart at Homestead, spoke for many workers when he observed that "In twenty years in the mill I have yet to see any 'feather-bedding.' Not unless the companies mean the college boys, the sons, cousins and nephews of 'big wheels' who are hired during the summer . . . with a pre-determined position in the higher echelon of management."[103] Steel companies were surprised by the tenaciousness of the rank-and-file who fought to preserve their union and to end any further job losses. Steel companies maintained that steelworkers did not really support their union and maintained that fiction over the next four months. After a decade of strikes, steelworkers hunkered down, and their determination and culture of solidarity deepened. The son of a steelworker recalled that what the strike "required of us was persistence, endurance, and loyalty to the union. So long as those were there, we could bend the will of giant corporations, stand up to the dictates of Congress and the Supreme Court and eventually persuade the president of the free world to enlist himself in our cause."[104] When the companies gave in, at the urging of the President of the United States, they failed to win any ground; indeed, workers forced them to pay a high cost for peace. Workers retained their work rules and won a substantial wage increase. Back in the mill, workers returned to a grinding war of attrition.[105]

THE FIGHT OVER SECTION 2-B

In truth, Section 2-B provided workers with scant legal protection against modernization, although it afforded them far more protection than most workers. Since Section 2-B had been introduced into the national contract in 1947, its effects had been relatively modest on overall productivity. In 1947, the USWA believed it had won firm protection of crew sizes while steel firms believed that Section 2-B protected "management rights."[106] Ultimately, arbitrators ruled that past practices, which had formerly been used by both union and management to resolve disputes, could only be used in the workers' favor. By 1953, arbitrators ruled that this section could be applied to crew sizes, seniority, discipline and discharge, layoffs, and work rules. U.S. Steel understood that the USWA could use 2-B to "restrain management from acting alone, or without negotiations with the union . . . in changing the 'status quo' of the plant" with regard to crew sizes, etc.[107] If the union proved a past practice existed, management could not simply reduce a crew's size or job duties on the basis of cost efficiency; indeed, it had to negotiate the issue with local trade unionists and possibly submit to the ruling of an arbitrator. As a result, workers enjoyed an important protection against arbitrary changes in work assignments and work loads. But if managers changed the underlying conditions that caused the past practice to emerge, it was a different story. If the "underlying conditions" which had given rise to the past practice had changed as a result of new technology or incentive programs, then arbitrators generally ruled that the past practice was null and void. One popular management story about Section 2-B revealed how companies misunderstood the issue. According to one story popular with managers, the union won a relief man for a crane that worked over a furnace. Even after the crane was air-conditioned, the union demanded that the relief operator spell the cranemen. It was a great example of featherbedding; the only problem was that it was pure fiction. One top manager explained, "dammit, we looked all around the industry for that example [hoping to use it in press releases during the 1959 strike] and we couldn't find it. What we did find was that the supervisors who had been doing all the complaining kept no records."[108]

In the context of a constant managerial offensive to boost productivity, past practices often imposed on managers the responsibility to negotiate with workers. The union had a Sisyphean task proving that past practices existed. Workers won fewer than 20 percent of 2-B grievances that made it to arbitration, although those that did applied to all mills throughout the country. One early case revealed the limitations of 2-B. Prior to 1947, two workers had tended the Duquesne Works' 40 Inch Mill's "hot beds" or conveyor belts. Over the next three years, management removed one of the beds, mechanized the unloading of the metal, and then combined two jobs. The hot bed operators protested that the loss of one man from their crew violated their past practice rights, but the arbitrator ruled that management had changed the underlying conditions. Section 2-B did, however, provide unionists with the opportunity to negotiate over the workplace, its modernization, and how to moderate job losses.[109] If workers only won a fraction of past practice grievances, it was a sizeable fraction, and when arbitrators handed down their rulings, they decided questions of crew sizes and work rules. That threat was enough to force managers to negotiate. And that process of negotiation was key to preserving workers' dignity on the job.[110]

Managerial reports suggest that union work rules deflected the full impact of automation. In preparation for the 1959 strike, U.S. Steel compiled the costs of "restrictive work practices." According to this survey, the annual costs at some of its Mon Valley facilities were $164,708 at the Duquesne Works, $525,510 at Homestead, and $161,088 at ET. By this account, managers calculated that workers had preserved perhaps as many as one hundred jobs per mill. For instance, at Duquesne, larrymen helpers in the blast furnace would only clean spillage on their car track, and when ore or coke spilled elsewhere, managers were forced to borrow laborers from other departments resulting in an annual cost of $5,000. The head of Industrial Relations cautioned that if they attempted to eliminate the practice the "repercussions" from the union would outweigh any benefits, which is why they had attacked only 20 percent of the existing past practices. After the strike, U.S. Steel required each mill to resubmit its reports so that the joint management-union Human Relations Commission could evaluate and resolve them on a case-by-case basis. Inexplicably, the new head of Industrial Relations at the Duquesne Works reported to the city office that "none of the restrictive work practices contained in our 1958 survey are applicable at this time." A new primary mill, mechanization throughout the plant, and "changes in operating conditions and production requirements" had ostensibly eliminated any past practices. In reality, the main cause of the "improved" situation was office politics. Industry observer John Strohmeyer found that local management preferred to hide men on the payrolls in anticipation of peak production periods. Indeed, before sending the 1958 survey to the city office, Duquesne managers unilaterally reduced their estimate of restrictive work by almost two-thirds. Strohmeyer's argument fit the case at Duquesne as several inefficiencies reported as eliminated in 1960 had magically resurfaced in a survey several years later.[111] Workers had apparently intimidated managers, but local managers also had their own reasons to promote or hide instances of past practices from their supervisors.

In most instances, management negotiated with local union leaders on how to implement modernization with a minimum of disturbance. For instance, in 1958, industrial engineers at the Duquesne Works pointed out to the Blast Furnace Superintendent that the $775,000 spent on new submarine ladles, which transported the molten metal to the open hearths, could allow them to cut one person from a five-man crew. Management's last attempt to reduce the Cast House and Stock House crews nearly resulted in a strike, and a job cut now seemed "certain to cause labor trouble." After weeks of debate within management and with union officials on how to proceed, management cut the crew, and the grievance man reported that he "doesn't expect trouble, but anticipates filing a grievance."[112] In that telling phrase, the black unionist revealed the dilemmas posed by steel's modernization and the faith of the union in the grievance procedure, sometimes more so than in its own members.

SENIORITY

For steelworkers, seniority was more than a contractual obligation: it represented an institutionalized expression of workers' solidarity. Seniority blunted the pervasive favoritism of the non-union era, making it one of the union's most profound accomplishments. Workers could anticipate promotion or layoffs without having to curry favor with the bosss. Yet discrimination remained, and the ways that workers and managers responded to inequalities in the workplace tell us much about how seniority, and by extension solidarity, was practiced and undermined. In the face of pervasive racism and other forms of discrimination, steelworkers were often complacent or disorganized. Tragically, workers' leaders consistently failed to help them enforce the principles of industrial unionism against their employers.

Seniority determined the order in which workers could advance or were laid off and consequently was a crucial factor in the lives of steelworkers. One Homestead unionist observed that "steelworkers only talk about sex and seniority."[113] Managers knew that seniority disputes remained a "majority source of complaint," and steelworkers filed more grievances over seniority than any other issue, one-quarter of the total.[114] One management survey from the mid-1950s found that a third of steelworkers held less than five years' seniority, another third between six and thirteen years, and another third between fourteen and fifty years.[115] But workers accrued seniority in only one of a mill's several departments. For instance, if a worker with twenty years in the blast furnace transferred to the rolling mill, he would be the "youngest" man in the department. Furthermore, workers advanced or were bumped downwards on a job ladder, or a Line of Progression (LOP). Despite most workers' preference for broad interpretations of seniority (e.g., departmental seniority over narrow LOP seniority), twenty years of seniority in one job line might not apply to another LOP in the same department—and not at all in a LOP in a different department.[116] For instance, Bethlehem's Johnstown mill had 130 job lines in eighteen different departments, and the "employees have rights within their respective departments but have no rights in any other department."[117] Departments had several LOPs—for instance, just one section of Duquesne's blast furnace had eight job lines. Furthermore, all LOPs were not created equal;

some had more positions and led to good jobs, and others led workers into dead-end jobs. In case of a layoff, an LOP with plenty of jobs in it offered more security than a short LOP. (LOPs could be revised as the result of negotiations between local unions and management, and later we will see that this opened the door for both solidarity and favoritism.) Seniority helped to ensure that skilled jobs were generally held by the most senior men, but the vagaries of chance, layoffs, and seniority itself meant that "older men" might be laborers rather than highly paid operators.[118] Thus, to which departments and LOPs the company assigned workers on their first day shaped the rest of their working lives. There were many factors that undermined seniority. Race proved one of the most potent and shows us the limits of working-class solidarity.

Steel companies like U.S. Steel adamantly maintained that they were "color blind" employers, and if discrimination could be gauged solely through numbers of persons hired, steel firms were good employers.[119] U.S. Steel and J&L were the region's largest employers of African Americans. Seven to 8 percent of the regional workforce was black, roughly the same proportion as the population of the region.[120] African American employment varied from mill to mill. Numerous blacks worked at U.S. Steel's Clairton, Homestead, and Duquesne Works, but very few found jobs at nearby facilities owned by the same company such as National Tube or the Irvin Works.[121] Because many jobs outside of heavy industry were barred to African Americans, blacks relied more heavily on steel than did whites. Almost 30 percent of adult black men worked in steel, compared to about 22 percent of white men.[122] The problem was not that steel companies did not hire blacks, but that steel firms did not *promote* their black employees. African American men languished at the bottom of the occupational ladder at a rate twice that of white men. Conversely, blacks rarely rose to skilled positions. In the 1940s, blacks were five times less likely to be skilled than their white counterparts. The 1950s witnessed slow but steady gains. Nonetheless, by the end of the decade, blacks were only half as likely as whites to hold a skilled job.[123] One reason for the pace of occupational desegregation was the seniority system.

Segregation began as soon as companies assigned workers their jobs. Employment offices routinely sent blacks to the hottest and dirtiest departments: the blast furnace, open hearth, masonry, transportation, sanitation, and conditioning. Blacks were far less likely to be sent to relatively clean or better-paid jobs in such departments as maintenance (crafts), rolling mills, or the machine shop. In the blast furnace where John Hughey worked, race affected the careers of even the men hired on the same day. Blacks were assigned as laborers on the furnace, but "when you got to daylight, the Caucasian you were hired with would have a bell on saying that he was a millwright . . . [and he] automatically learned on the job, with on the job pay."[124] One internal report for managers at the Duquesne Works concluded that "by far the majority of our colored employees" worked in the Blast Furnace and Open Hearth Departments while only a handful worked in the Blooming Mills.[125] The situation was similar at Homestead where 80 percent of its black employees worked in four of its eleven departments.[126] Departmental seniority served to reinforce occupational segregation as those who transferred to a different part of the mill lost their original departmental seniority. Thus many workers pursued conservative job strategies, investing years in a single LOP, waiting for a good job to open up. George Henderson, a skilled black worker, advised the men under him to "stay in one place and protect the job you got."[127] That advice was followed by many workers, both black and white.

Seniority was only as good as the men involved in administering it. National contracts between the USWA and steel firms allowed enormous latitude to local unionists to negotiate and administer the seniority system.[128] As Hughey recalled, seniority should have meant that "if ability was equal and physical fitness was equal, if it was a church mouse, he should have been promoted."[129] But given the complexity of LOP lists (one manager admitted that there were "generally as many different opinions as there were different people . . . in the meetings" between the company and the union), it was entirely possible for unionists and managers to enforce separate LOPs for blacks and whites, such as the ones that sparked the 1945 and 1946 wildcats at J&L.[130] Alex Powell recalled that in Duquesne's Open Hearth Department, it was tough to escape the labor gang because managers "moved around us . . . they would deal around you in the promotional sequence."[131] Another black trade unionist argued that his grievance man "fixes it so white boys can move up and colored can stick with pick and shovel."[132] If members were not actively involved in their union, there was little that could be done to prevent corrupt union officials from manipulating plum jobs into their own LOP. Nat King, a black worker at Homestead, related how one union trustee got his job reclassified to a higher pay grade. When he was fired twenty years later for stealing lumber, the black worker who moved into that position found that it had been recently re-reclassified, this time downwards.[133] Seniority represented one of workers' most important lines of defense, but betrayal remained a constant danger.

Companies' racism dovetailed with their long-standing histories of paternalism. While steel had long spied on its employees and violently repressed union drives, companies like U.S. Steel promoted the practice of hiring the sons of trusted workers as a form of social control.[134] Between one and two thousand men at Homestead had one or more sons working in the mill, many of them in the same department. U.S. Steel proudly publicized the fact that the McKinney family had eight brothers working at Homestead—more brothers working together than at any other mill.[135] The company enforced discipline on fathers through sons, and vice versa. Some, particularly those who moved into skilled jobs, were philosophical about this benign "family division of labor."[136] (Family connections, preferably with management, could also get women jobs, although their range of jobs was far narrower.)[137] Otis King, who had been denied a promotion because he was black, simply noted that "nepotism ran wild in the mill."[138] While both black and white men could get their sons jobs in their departments, this "equal access" paradoxically helped to reinforce steel's racial division of labor.

Some black fathers gave their sons the most important gift they could by steering them away from the worst departments. Most fathers wanted their sons to work with them, but Milton Macintyre recalled that his father *ordered* him not to get a job in the blast furnace. Armed with that knowledge, he struggled to get into the Conditioning Department at Duquesne.[139] Lee Robinson's father, who worked on the coke ovens (and eventually died of cancer) in the Clairton Works effectively blackballed his own son from getting a job there by telling his foreman "I'd rather see him shot than see him come to the coke works."[140] One returning World War II veteran knew enough to refuse his old job in Duquesne's Masonry Department. When he returned home with a "pin" or badge for the blast furnace, his father told him "nope, you don't want that. So I brought it back and I got sent to the bar mills."[141] The reputation of the father often carried over onto the son. Donald Woodington became a second helper on a blast furnace at Duquesne in the early 1950s in large part because his father had a reputation as a hard worker: "Everybody said he was one of the best."[142] Jesse Larrington was assigned to the furnace because "my father was a good furnaceman. So right there they tagged me as a *good* furnaceman." Larrington "hated it with a passion" but had to endure the job for thirty years before being able to transfer to a better department.[143] In short, the pervasive power of steel firms may have been experienced as racism or paternalism, but both corroded the promise of seniority.

HOW MODERNIZATION UNDERMINED SENIORITY: THE CASE OF DUQUESNE

When confronted with major layoffs, steelworkers' ideals about seniority were put to the test. In 1949, one-quarter of Duquesne's 8,038 employees were unemployed, and unionists rallied to defend seniority and the jobs of older men.[144] Local unionists questioned why layoffs were "more drastic than at any other plant in the Country" and wondered why after they had broken "all production records" and made "huge profits for the Corporation, the Corporation ha[d] turned them out into the street."[145] In turn, the company warned that the plant's antiquated equipment might cause a permanent shutdown.[146] Management laid off men primarily on the basis of their estimate of a worker's skill and physical ability. As one supervisor put it, "the majority of our plant is not covered by any written [seniority] agreement . . . naturally . . . a number of problems arose."[147] Thus in the Conditioning Department, managers laid off men with up to thirty-five years of service, arguing that they could not be demoted to physically demanding jobs such as scarfers. Instantly, affected sections of the mill became "hot spots," and the company was forced to compromise by allowing older men to use their company rather than their departmental or LOP seniority to bump younger men.[148] (A new round of investment and the Korean War boom ultimately prevented a closure, but in the interregnum, the union fought to save older men from losing their jobs.)[149] Similar problems confronted Homestead's Local 1397 in 1949 when U.S. Steel closed OH 2. In that case, the union convinced management to allow workers to transfer into newer open hearth departments.[150] In the cases of both Duquesne and Homestead, security for older workers was achieved by allowing them to apply their long-term plantwide seniority to jobs outside their home department. In select cases, both union and management departed from departmental seniority in order to achieve the desired effect. As we will see, such flexibility rarely worked to the advantage of women or African Americans.

Departmental seniority invariably produced anomalies. Because some departments such as the blast furnace could only be run full out or shut down completely, layoffs hit some departments harder than others. In some departments "younger" men (with relatively low plant seniority) kept working while workers in another department with more seniority were put out on the street. For instance, open hearth workers were almost twice as likely to be laid off as workers elsewhere, and the highly skilled "roll shop" experienced no layoffs at all.[151] In the open hearth, five years' seniority was enough to protect your job, but considerably more was required in conditioning. Race played little role in the layoffs, as "black departments," such as the blast furnace, experienced no layoffs.[152]

When confronted with mass unemployment, layoffs inevitably dominated local unions' agendas. One U.S. Steel report found that most of the serious grievances at Duquesne protested various aspects of the company's layoff procedures.[153] Workers generally fought management, but the scramble for jobs also caused workers to squabble amongst themselves. In March and April 1950, workers at Duquesne maneuvered to become swing-frame grinders after it became clear that layoffs would bypass those jobs. Twenty-one men bid on these jobs within the allotted thirty days, but local management had already met with their grievanceman to allow "older men" to fill the jobs. In exchange, the grievanceman agreed to tell the twelve men who failed in their bid why they were being laid off and to try to head off their grievances.[154] Historian Robert Ruck concluded that management gladly turned "over to the union the headache of policing the system."[155]

The end of the Korean War launched another round of layoffs and once again strained the seniority system. On December 24, 1953, managers at the Duquesne Works closed the fifty-four-year-old OH 1, and 1,145 workers lost their jobs. Open hearth workers had earlier won the right to transfer between OH 1 and OH 2.[156] Consequently, more than one-half (641 workers) immediately transferred to other departments, and a few either retired or were transferred to other plants. About half of the 500 laid-off men qualified for severance pay, and eventually all were given the option of returning to the mill, though not at the same rate of pay.[157] "Eventually" could be a long time. Henderson Thomas, a black worker, waited almost two years before being recalled and had almost lost his recall rights. His return to the mill was brief; within weeks, he was laid off again.[158]

As in the past, the union expressed concern about employees with lengthy plant service who suffered layoffs due to departmental seniority. The company agreed that in the future it would try to ensure that employees with fifteen or more years' service would never lose their call-back rights.[159]

Part of what allowed such "generosity" to older men was the fact that the seniority rights of other workers were ignored, particularly those of women hired during the Korean War. It is to their case that we now turn.

"TEMPORARY SENIORITY": THE CASE OF WOMEN STEELWORKERS

In the late 1940s and 1950s, there were slightly more than 7,000 women steelworkers in Pittsburgh, about half of the peak levels of employment during World War II.[160] The numbers of black female steelworkers were far more modest: just 135 in 1950, and half that number would remain ten years later. Despite their small numbers, women often became ardent trade unionists. Alice Massey, an African American worker at the Rankin Steel Wire Works, represented her local at the Steel City Labor Council in the early 1950s. The only black woman at her mill, she strongly supported the union's fights for better wages and working conditions.[161] How the union interpreted its end of the bargain was another matter.

During the Korean War, industrialists once again turned to women to alleviate labor shortages, and many women were granted a second-class version of seniority rights to prevent them from keeping their jobs once the war was over. Before the war began, managers at the Duquesne Works suggested hiring women into dead-end jobs or simply refusing them seniority, but trade unionists rejected those proposals.[162] Philip Murray advised locals that "women are entitled to all of the protections that go to every member of the organization, and they cannot be denied either their constitutional or contractual rights," but other officials, including the union's chief counsel, Arthur Goldberg, defended the constitutionality of temporary seniority.[163] In the case of Duquesne, trade unionists ignored Murray, and management agreed to the proposition that "all women hired" in both the clerical and production unions "shall be considered to hold their positions on a temporary basis and that their continuous service with the Company shall not be applied . . . in preference to men." Most of the women hired during that "police action" were placed in clerical jobs, such as stenographer or typist.[164] With the return of peacetime, most were fired. By 1954, only twenty-seven women remained of all those hired after January 1, 1951.[165] The net effect of temporary seniority and a strong bias against married women working was to deny women in general the opportunity to pursue full-time employment in steel.

The male bias of most trade unionists and managers ensured that women enjoyed little protection against layoffs. During a force reduction at the Duquesne Works in 1954, one woman's grievanceman argued that management should lay her off rather than put the rest of the union members in the Engineering Department on a four-day week. The union official reasoned that she was the youngest in her LOP, and, more importantly, she was a married woman. Management refused to accept the grievanceman's reasoning, not because they supported the woman, but because the grievanceman's method of scheduling would force management to lay off several draftsmen at the Homestead Works. Only when it became clear that both she and the man above her in the LOP would be laid off did the grievanceman promise to pursue the grievance.[166] Unlike in other industrial unions, notably meatpacking or the UE, women remained a low-status minority in the union and enjoyed few of the protections of seniority.[167]

The cumulative effect of managerial paternalism and discrimination—and trade unionists' failure to extend solidarity to women—was to worsen their occupational segregation. Women were increasingly shunted into clerical positions and away from production jobs. In 1940, women had made up just 18.6 percent of all clerical workers in the steel industry. By 1950, that figure had increased to 33 percent, and by the end of the decade had crept up to 37 percent.[168] By contrast, women production workers lost ground. In 1940, 2.2 percent of all operatives were women, and that figure sagged to 1.5 percent by the end of the 1950s. By 1959, U.S. Steel's large mills employed a handful of women on the evening or night turns: one at Donora and Johnstown, five at Clairton, eight at Duquesne, nineteen at ET, thirty-three at Homestead, and forty-seven at Irvin.[169] Women found it almost impossible to advance into skilled or supervisory positions. In 1940, just 0.3 percent of all foremen or skilled workers were female. While that figure doubled to 0.6 percent in 1950, undoubtedly as a result of women hired during World War II, it fell back to 0.4 percent by the end of the 1950s.

If the steel industry was a difficult place for women, it was doubly difficult for African American women. In the 1940s, black women made up less than 0.1 percent of female steelworkers in Pittsburgh. While the number of women employed by steel firms remained constant in the 1950s, the number of black women *fell* by 50 percent.[170] Only a handful of black women were fortunate enough to remain steelworkers where they earned more than any other sector of Pittsburgh's female blue-collar labor markets.

THE PATTERNS OF BLACK MALE ADVANCEMENT

The experiences of black men also show the persistence of racial discrimination, although seniority proved far more effective in protecting their rights and incomes that it did with black women. Nonetheless, disputes within the union over seniority, often racialized or gendered, could become "cutthroat affairs" able to "tear apart a local" as the "dispute is always between union men." A long-time President of one local remembered that the only defeat of his career came when he tried to institute "plant service" [seniority] to accommodate laid-off workers from the closed-down Bessemer Furnace, a department with large numbers of black workers: "I called a meeting and the whole plant turned out to see these guys weren't going to get their jobs."[171] At Duquesne, unionists disputed how to best implement labor pools, and one member filed charges with the NLRB against other workers, a fact that contributed to the slow implementation of a labor pool.[172] At ET, managers attributed the conflicts over labor pools to "a few assistant grievance committeemen and minority employee groups to accept the principles established in the new agreement."[173] By definition, seniority meant that a person could only "go down the way he came up"; thus it provided those relatively privileged workers with incentives to defend the inequalities that been built into the ways that companies hired workers.[174]

De facto segregation often occurred between what should have been the same jobs. Almost all workers began their time as laborers, and *advanced into more skilled or at least better-paid positions after a few weeks or months*. By contrast, black laborers often languished for years in those jobs.[175] Many blacks worked in masonry departments, which frequently involved hot or dusty work, particularly when a furnace required relining. However, very few blacks ever became masons. As one black worker in Homestead's Masonry Department put it: "the only training I got was learning the side of bricks."[176] The best jobs for a black laborer in that department were low-level semi-skilled positions, such as helper or mixer.[177] Although grinding and scarfing steel was a dead-end semi-skilled job in the Conditioning Department, workers in those positions could increase their pay through incentive schemes. White workers periodically tried to keep blacks working on "back-breaking steel" while they worked the softer "money steel."[178] Thus many of the normal paths of upward mobility were barred to blacks, who therefore pursued different strategies of advancement.

Most African Americans found the opportunities for skilled work in "black departments." For instance, many transportation departments had large numbers of black workers on the labor gangs, but a few transferred their departmental seniority and became locomotive engineers. At the Duquesne Works, many of the engineers and about half of the switchmen were African American.[179] After years of working as an engineer on a diesel locomotive in the Homestead Works, in 1948, Albert Reid became gang-leader yardmaster of OH 3. Reid noted that he had been working so long that "no one could put anything over on me."[180] Yet active resistance by white workers sometimes blocked some black men from skilled positions in transportation. In one case, a black worker had worked as a temporary engineer for years without incident. He believed, however, when he became a full-time engineer, white co-workers sabotaged his engine and caused it to burn up. He was demoted to switchman (though after twenty years of filing grievances to no avail, he finally won his case).[181]

Black advancement in the blast furnaces and open hearth departments was also highly uneven. Most African Americans remained laborers, although a few rose to highly paid production jobs. Blacks made up about 8 percent of the skilled furnacemen in the region, although in some mills that rate was far higher.[182] A 1953 study by the Urban League estimated that half of the Duquesne Works' keepers, a responsible and well-paid job on the blast furnaces, were black. One of that mill's most respected first helpers was African American.[183] Thomas Walker explained that the reason there were many black furnace workers was because "you in heat all the time. You dead at it. You at the *hole* man, at the metal." So while skilled furnacemen were well paid, they also had "the most dangerous job around." Walker had risen to his position during the labor shortages of World War II only after his foreman compelled the incumbent foreign-born hot blastman to train Walker. When Walker's crew challenged his authority, again his foreman supported him.[184] But such support was unusual. Otis Bryant recalled that he was sent off his job as a second helper on the open hearth; as he walked back, he heard the supervisor announce over the speaker system that he "wanted a white boy" for that job.[185] Such attitudes explain why many black workers believed that in general it took far longer for blacks to rise to skilled production jobs than for whites.[186]

Black workers confronted still higher barriers to employment in the skilled trades. Jobs such as carpenters, plumbers, pipefitters, electricians, painters, or motor inspectors were off limits in invariably lily-white maintenance departments. In the Homestead Works, no blacks worked in the Maintenance Department, the Boiler Shop, the Machine Shop, or the Electrical Shop. There were a handful of black laborers in the Carpentry or Masonry Shops.[187] John Hughey, a black union official in the Carrie Furnace, knew that management "wouldn't even allow blacks to sweep the floor in maintenance" because they would then accrue departmental seniority there.[188] In 1950, there were 3,266 millwrights and 10,774 machinists in all of Pittsburgh's industries, and of these, only 12 millwrights and 83 machinists were black.[189] Ten years later, the situation was practically unchanged.[190]

Companies claimed that the compression of blacks in unskilled positions resulted from a dearth of skilled men to hire, but big steel firms consistently denied blacks access to their in-house apprentice programs. One worker recalled that managers at the Clairton Works refused him a masonry apprenticeship but placed an Italian immigrant who spoke no English in that job.[191] In 1950, black apprentices made up less than 0.5 percent of the total number of apprentices in the region.[192] At Homestead, one white supervisor reportedly confessed that "eighty-five percent of the Negroes in general labor have [enough] education enough to hold down a skilled craft job." Meanwhile, whites with sixth-grade educations moved into these positions.[193] Attempts by the Pittsburgh Urban League (PUL) to open up U.S. Steel's apprenticeship programs resulted in one or two isolated successes, each met with great fanfare.[194] But the general picture gave little to celebrate as virtually no progress resulted after ten years.[195]

Even blacks who trained themselves often could not enter the skilled trades. In the late 1950s, Otis King went to vocational school to become a mason at the Homestead Works. He was told several times that he had failed the qualifying test, although he had passed it at his training center. Finally, his supervisor told him "you know they'll never let you have that job."[196] Booker Kidd recalled that William Taff was a licensed electrician outside the mill, but in the mill he was just an electrician's helper.[197] Breaking into white jobs or white departments required perseverance, luck, or political pressure. One black electrician at the Duquesne Works received a craft job because he had passed his exams and had an Irish name, unlike Otis King, so they did not recognize his name and fake his results.[198] Despite the fact that John Turner had passed the qualifying exam in 1956, he was turned down for an electrician's job in the Homestead Works. When U.S. Steel featured him in one of its public relations ads as an electrician who volunteered his skills to Pittsburgh's public television station, the hypocrisy so angered Turner that he led a series of protests against the local union; afterwards, he became the first black in the crafts at Homestead. Another unionist noted wryly that they advanced him to shut him up, but Turner later filed a class action lawsuit against U.S. Steel and Local 1397.[199]

Because whites often refused to train black men for even semi-skilled production jobs, blacks often resorted to clandestine measures. Workers whose seniority qualified them for a new job were entitled to thirty days' on-the-job training in the new position. However, blacks were frequently denied that right. When Edmond Holmes tried to become a shearman, the man who cuts steel blooms in a blooming mill, his foreman gave him only three days to learn the job. "It's yours," his foreman explained, "but if you can't handle it, give it up." A white friend of Holmes who was retiring had already taught him how to handle the equipment, but he warned Holmes not to reveal to anyone who had taught him the job.[200] Another would-be shearman at the Duquesne Works surreptitiously watched the incumbent worker for more than a year. When the foreman brought in "a white dude from shipping" for the job, he complained and they allowed him to try his hand, though not before warning him that if he could not do the work, he would be fired.[201]

White foremen and workers often tried their utmost to block African Americans from strategic jobs. In many LOPs, a craneman's position was located just below skilled jobs or was a bridge into better LOPs. Normally, all mill men sought these jobs. But managers and unionists devised elaborate schemes to keep blacks out of these positions. Black workers at the Homestead Works observed that U.S. Steel brought in "inspectors and cranemen from the streets and [hired] them right over our heads. Although we [had] been in the mill a long time, we can't even get these jobs."[202] John Hughey recalled how the first African American became a craneman at the Carrie Furnace in the 1950s: "The test that Ralph Johnson had to go through, he'd should a been driving a rocketship. Because they put a little bucket down there, a little tea pot there. Put him up on the crane and give him one try to come down with the boom and put it in the bucket. One try. But Ralph was lucky. He came down the first time and didn't that damn thing go in the bucket. Right in the bucket it went and they almost dropped over."[203] Through such extraordinary efforts, combined with some luck, the number of African American cranemen in all industries rose from 2 percent to 3 percent of the total.[204]

The highest hurdle blacks faced was into management itself. Although most front-line foremen began as laborers and had moved up the ladder, few blacks received this opportunity. Some blacks became "pushers" or temporary leaders of a crew or gang, but very few black men were offered the chance to direct other workers on a full-time basis. Those who did generally only supervised black workers. For instance, in the early 1950s J&L had just three black foremen. One was in the Sanitation Department, and two were in the largely black Nail Department. In 1956, U.S. Steel had only two black foremen throughout the Pittsburgh region, and one was in charge of a Sanitation Department.[205] It was a hard fight to get these jobs. In 1959, one black steelworker became a foreman only after he took his case directly to the downtown headquarters. After seventeen years in the mill, he remained in the lowest grade and was the only black foreman. There were no African Americans among the 100 inspectors at his plant.[206] Seniority was never an issue in the hiring of foremen, as companies retained complete control over who directed workers. Had companies been truly color-blind employers, certainly there would have been more black foremen.

Similarly, black technical and white-collar workers were also extraordinarily rare. Throughout the 1950s, the Pittsburgh Urban League met with little success in convincing U.S. Steel and other steel firms to hire qualified African Americans into these positions.[207] "Breakthroughs" came at a painfully slow rate. In October 1955, the PUL succeeded in helping place a black Chemical Research Assistant at U.S. Steel's Monroeville center. (Each job was dutifully heralded in the region's black newspaper, the *Pittsburgh Courier*.)[208] Blacks who advanced were often overqualified for the positions they held. One of the first blacks promoted to a clerical position at J&L had a college degree from the Carnegie Institute of Technology.[209] But a degree was no guarantor of success. In Homestead's open hearths, several black men with degrees from the University of Pittsburgh remained laborers while whites with high-school educations became observers and clerks.[210] In 1958, James A. Jordan, the Chair of the NAACP's Labor and Industry Committee noted that "only recently have we begun to make headway in industry. Negroes are now employed as chemists, engineers, foremen, stenographers, accountants and also in management positions."[211] Yet the extremely low numbers of black foremen, supervisors, and technicians suggest that white managers and not white unionists were the most vehemently opposed to the upward mobility of African Americans.

Given all of the barriers to the advancement of black men in the steel industry, why did they remain in the mills? Because alternative sources of employment were invariably worse. Non-union mills either barred blacks outright or paid far less than steel. In the 1950s, blacks made up about 2 percent of steel's skilled jobs, but this was far more than blacks' share of skilled positions in the building trades or professional jobs in the city's major corporations. For instance, in the late 1950s, Alcoa employed seventy African Americans in its downtown headquarters: sixty-two were janitors, and the rest were in menial positions. Two of the janitors had college degrees.[212] And as bad as the USWA was on this issue, it was far better than the vast majority of unions. For instance, the USWA ensured that black steelworkers enjoyed some chance of moving into skilled railroad jobs inside the mill. Once outside the mill's gates, few black engineers were found because the railroad unions were notoriously nativist and racist. In fact, when the Railroad Brotherhoods proposed to represent the workers on railroad lines inside the mills, black and foreign-born workers strongly protested.[213] Given that steelworkers' wages were far higher than the other jobs available to black workers and most professionals, many black men chose not to risk what they had.[214]

THE POLITICS OF CIVIL RIGHTS IN THE USWA

In 1948, after years of pressure from black steelworkers, the union established a Civil Rights Committee (CRC). Certainly the scale of discrimination in the plants warranted one, as did the charter of the union which promised equal protection to all its members regardless of race, ethnicity, or national origin. Despite pressure from its members to enforce its own stated commitment, the USWA ensured that the CRC lacked the authority, personnel, and resources to mount a serious challenge to racial bias in the union or the industry.[215] (The civil rights of female steelworkers were simply ignored during these years.) The committee was entirely white and headed up by Thomas and Francis Shane as the chair and executive director. The CRC promoted social reform and civil rights legislation.[216] The union paid the Shanes to work on civil rights full time, but they lacked a staff to investigate the conditions in their own industry. Instead, the Shanes drew together a few union officials four times a year to make recommendations to the USWA President.[217] When periodically confronted with a recalcitrant company or union local, the Shanes could rely only on moral suasion.[218] In terms of confronting racism in steel, the CRC was designed to fail. Years later, even committed black unionists referred to the committee as a "farce" or a "laugh."[219]

The CRC revealed its character at its first civil rights conference in 1950. Problems in the mill or union were ignored, while the CRC urged the five hundred delegates, mostly local union leaders from Pennsylvania and adjacent states, to circulate petitions to pressure Congress to pass a national FEPC.[220] Even the most bigoted local leaders could tolerate high-minded resolutions that changed nothing and challenged no one. One white union official remarked that the widespread practice of racial discrimination combined with near-universal support for civil rights constituted a "personal schizophrenia" on the part of trade unionists.[221]

Yet the CRC was not a manifestation of collective mental illness, but an example of Cold War liberalism in action. The CRC took as one of its main goals the global fight against the "communist menace."[222] According to Philip Murray, socialism "would bring about the enslavement of all men—regardless of race or color or creed." Therefore, a permanent FEPC would not only be of value at home, but "worth two or three army divisions . . . in our worldwide struggle against communism."[223] When *Steel Labor* argued that "communism thrives on dissension—management against labor—Christian against Jew—White against Negro," it suggested that the problem of civil rights was a lack of harmony, or an excess of dissent, rather than too little justice.[224]

In the USWA's civil rights crusade, anti-communism took precedence over all other concerns. Black unionists who tried to mobilize the union to fight company racism were labeled reds. When one black steelworker asked a staff representative "why a man with 12 years service should get a job promotion over a Negro worker with 22 years service," the official told him he was "slurring the union." The white worker got the promotion, and the black worker learned to hold his tongue.[225] According to an informal survey by the *Pittsburgh Courier*, many black workers kept quiet in their unions for fear of being labeled as communists.[226] Even inter-racial socializing was so tightly associated with left-wing ideas that one white communist from a steel town near Pittsburgh sardonically recalled that the FBI identified white communists by watching black steelworkers' homes. Any white person who visited a black person was a communist.[227] In 1949, the *Courier* observed that "growing in intensity, the all-too-obvious retreat of labor leaders from the 'touchy' problems of civil rights and fair employ-

ment practices has finally grown into proportions of a stampede."[228] Harold
Keith, the Courier's labor reporter, lambasted the USWA for expelling
communists as opponents of democracy while allowing white supremacists
in Alabama and elsewhere to remain in the union.[229] Harry Hamilton
Doty, a black recording secretary from a steel local in Donora complained
that Murray "preaches democracy, but I don't see where he fully practices
it. . . . On the surface the Steelworkers' program is liberal and fair to all,
but is it being carried out to the letter? No!" Doty also complained that
the union failed to confront the company's pattern of discriminatory
hiring and promotions and that those who spoke out on this issue were
red-baited.[230]

Boyd Wilson, the USWA's "racial troubleshooter," dismissed claims
like Doty's, asserting that the "machinery of the Steelworkers union . . .
grinds out justice for all."[231] But the CRC never pushed USWA locals to
confront discrimination in steel. In 1950, Thomas Shane rejected proposals that "every local" should have "a special committee . . . to do all the
fighting for civil rights." Shane maintained that civil rights remained the
responsibility of the union as a whole.[232] A year later, the union directed
local unions to establish CRCs but carefully instructed that these committees only mobilize support for legislation. Even this limited program was
"too hot" for most local unions. For instance, five years after Homestead
should have set up a CRC, in June 1956, black members petitioned for an
"FEPC." (The proposed name for the committee was instructive as many
members desired an organization to fight shop-floor problems rather than
a CRC.)[233] The first head of the committee was Al Everett, a fiery black
assistant grievanceman, but within three months his committeeman, John
Duch, fired him from his union post.[234] In January 1957, blacks failed in
their attempts to put Everett back onto the CRC and to remove Duch
from his post.[235] One member disgustedly observed that Homestead's CRC
"has never functioned . . . and is still not functioning."[236]

Two years later, black steelworkers at Homestead had regained control over the CRC, only to discover it was totally powerless. Homestead's
CRC wanted to monitor how grievances were processed, as many black
steelworkers believed that back-room deals between racist foremen and
grievancemen maintained job segregation.[237] Company supervisors rebuffed
the CRC's request to sit in on grievance meetings: "such matters as had
arisen had been satisfactorily handled between higher levels of both management and the Union."[238] Homestead's CRC remained a paper tiger. Yet

Homestead was better off than most locals, the majority of which had not even set up a committee almost ten years after they were required to do so.[239] The national CRC was little better. Black unionists at the Homestead Works, J&L's Southside mill, and several southern mills notified the national CRC several times that management had violated their seniority rights with the approval of their locals, but Shane did little more than wring his hands.[240] The International Executive Board of the USWA rarely discussed racial discrimination and never pushed for anything other than a weak and inactive set of Civil Rights Committees.[241]

Unable to challenge the content of the CRC's program, black steelworkers focused on the composition of its membership. For years, demands to appoint blacks to union offices had been opposed by the USWA leadership, including Thomas Shane, as a form of "reverse" Jim Crowism. At national conventions, African-American loyalists stepped up to the microphones to back up Shane and this line of reasoning.[242] However, activists lobbied Murray directly, and in 1952, he "caved in" and appointed one African American and one Mexican American to the CRC.[243] Murray's appointment of Joe Neal, an African American from Baltimore, was viewed by many black workers as rank tokenism. Many believed Neal was "not as militant . . . as he should be for such a job . . . particularly when he is *hand-picked*."[244] Moreover, the Shanes continued as the CRCs only paid staff.[245] The campaign for more black faces in high places continued unabated.

The CRC did support steelworkers' efforts to pass municipal and statewide legislation. In Clairton, steelworkers from Local 1557 and the local NAACP helped to pass a local FEPC in 1953. A similar coalition in Pittsburgh resulted in the passage of an FEPC that same year and one in Duquesne the following year.[246] A black official from Duquesne's Local 1256, Carl Dickerson, was one of the first members of that city's FEPC.[247] The CRC supported the decade-long drive for Pennsylvania's Fair Employment Practices Commission that was created on January 30, 1956, and consistently supported state bills promoting fair housing.[248] Municipal FEPCs had virtually no authority to affect the hiring and promotion policies of the steel companies within their boundaries. Even the state's fair housing and employment measures lacked the capacity for effective enforcement or punishment of lawbreakers. While black unionists complained that the union's civil rights program had "hypocritical aspects," the USWA had already won the praise of civil rights organizations content to win symbolic "political" victories.[249] When black steelworkers attempted to lead a fight against racism in steel, they would do so on their own.

"FAIR SHARE" ACTIVISTS

There was little room in the USWA for civil rights activism that fell outside the parameters laid down by the CRC. Nonetheless, frustrated black unionists protested conditions in the industry by leading or threatening wildcat strikes, agitating in union locals, and forming protest groups. Their efforts heralded the more aggressive civil rights movement of the 1960s, but inconstant black unity and persistent white hostility prevented the development of any durable, powerful grassroots organizations within the USWA. Consequently, black workers had little success in moving the union to confront the steel industry on questions of racial discrimination.

Black-led wildcats became more uncommon, but they continued to represent an important form of collective response. Curly McCloughlin recalled short strikes at ET's Open Hearths in the late 1940s. Until then, managers "would always send us up to the furnaces to clean out that hot burning soot and stuff, no respirators or nothing." Older black men told them that they were "crazy if you [all] keep doing it and don't put up a squawk." A new superintendent convinced the strikers to go back to work and then there were "some changes made . . . things start[ed] coming our way." The older men were able to earn higher incentive pay, and the younger men were able to bid on jobs such as bulldozer operator and crane-man.[250] Dennis Dickerson reported that blacks at Clairton led a wildcat in the early 1950s when a black man was denied his promotion to become a pusher or vicing foreman.[251] Compared to the strikes led by steelworkers over seniority, contracting out and layoffs, or even black-led wildcats during World War II, this form of black protest remained at best a specter haunting the steel industry. The lower levels of organizational capacity, self-confidence, and leadership can be partly explained by the fact that the full employment of the 1940s had been replaced by periodic and severe layoffs in the 1950s. Compounding these problems was the hostility of the USWA, companies, and the FBI to "subversive" activism among black workers.

Despite their infrequency, managers apparently took seriously the threat of black-led wildcats. In 1956, black church leaders, in protest of the suppression of the civil rights struggle in Alabama, declared that March 28 was "National Deliverance Day" and called for a national work stoppage between 2:00 and 3:00 P.M. Managers at the Duquesne Works became concerned that black workers would heed the call. In a meeting with managers, a black Duquesne unionist said he had heard a "small amount of talk" but could not judge its seriousness. The unionist claimed that he did not support this proposed strike, but thought some activists might "cause trouble." The USWA also disowned this strike, and indeed nothing happened.[252]

But civil rights did periodically affect union politics. In 1957, long-simmering resentment against discrimination burst into the open at the Homestead Works. Led by Albert "Sweet Lucy" Everett, and supported by members of the black protest organization Fair Share, these men charged that the local union aided and abetted the company's discrimination. The battle began over the case of Everett (Local 1397's first black assistant grievance-man), who had been appointed and then fired from this position by John Duch. When blacks packed a meeting of the local union to defend Everett, in part because his situation had been publicized by the *Pittsburgh Courier*, Pete Jackson, a black USWA representative, urged Everett to "exhaust your union remedies" before taking his case to the press. Everett and Jackson traded insults; Jackson labeled Everett a liar while Everett charged that Jackson was "one of the fellows that has been holding us back."[253] Although one hundred blacks packed another union meeting, they were balanced by an equal number of whites.[254] Similarly, between four hundred and five hundred men, half of them black, attended the "trial meeting" of Duch, where he was found not guilty. Fair Share activists accused the union leadership of intimidation, because union leaders had Munhall police check the union cards of members before they could enter the union hall. One activist noted "it might have worked ten or twenty years ago" but that it would not work now.[255] Appeals to the USWA's IEB proved fruitless.[256]

Despite the extensive problems of discrimination at the Homestead Works, the protest died out. Within a couple of weeks of the Duch "trial," rank-and-file blacks from Homestead were denying any ties to Fair Share or its related organization, the "Committee for Solid Unionism."[257] Much of the reason was that Fair Share was routinely subjected to intense intimidation. The national CRC explicitly discussed how to "eliminate" organizations like Fair Share that formed as "special interest groups."[258] More important were the house visits by agents of the FBI, who investigated alleged communist involvement in Fair Share.[259] Although Fair Share members such as John Hughey claimed that they had "never seen a communist," the red-baiting seemed to have intimidated many black workers.[260]

Mass support for Fair Share crumbled. Fair Share activists reminded black unionists that a few weeks before they had been "kicked around, lied to, and treated like second-class workers. You weren't even receiving crumbs from the table. You still need us as much as we need you." But by then, many black workers were too intimidated.[261] By March, when the local voted on the question of Duch's racism, only eighteen blacks attended the meeting, and were voted down by twenty-five whites, (the majority of whites were especially angry at the four whites who voted with black unionists to convict Duch). Leroy Lewis decried the laxity of black unionists, noting that "three quarters of the fight" was getting members to meetings.[262] By 1960, a Fair Share sympathizer tersely observed that the organization had "collapsed some time ago."[263] However, Fair Share did result in minor gains. In August, Homestead Local 1397 elected George Backer, its first black officer. The local president had openly backed another candidate, so this was an especially sweet victory for black workers.[264] A black was moved into the machine shop, another from OH 5 was taken on as a millwright helper, and blacks were tested for cranemen's jobs.[265] But in terms of an organized caucus, blacks remained almost as scattered as before.

Civil rights activists failed to build a viable alternative organization within the USWA. Union officials generally opposed organizations such as Fair Share, and efforts by the few black officials on this score proved decisive. Situations in local unions varied, hampering inter-mill networks around issues. Homestead was one of the worst; some black members called it the most Jim Crowed local outside of the South. The local at the Carrie Furnace in Rankin, Pennsylvania, was perhaps the most progressive in the Pittsburgh region. This local had many black members, as few whites wanted to work in the heat and dust of a blast furnace. Given the variation of local conditions, and the real risks that activists took, most workers did not participate in the "Fair Share" strategy. As we will see below, African American steelworkers developed other strategies to help them negotiate some upward mobility in steel. Though often informed by other forms of collective action, these were largely individualistic and defensive strategies.

THE SHOP-FLOOR STRATEGIES OF BLACK MEN

The oral histories of black steelworkers suggest that black unionists were well aware of the limitations and benefits of the USWA. A few felt that the union "was just as prejudiced as the company was." Another recalled that the "union was segregated too, to some extent."[266] However, most workers believed that "without the union, things would've been worse."[267] Without a union "your voice don't go, you know. You ain't gonna be heard no place."[268]

Yet despite their arguably greater need for a collective voice, to an even greater extent than white steelworkers, most black USWA members remained passive in their union.[269] Lee Robinson, a Duquesne Works employee, noted, "I went to a few meetings, that's about all."[270] Another worker recalled that "I was a union member and that was it . . . union was the clique, if you was in the right clique, you was in. If you weren't, forget it. That's the way the union was. . . . If your clique was in, you was in the union." Another worker remained a union man although one union official tried to get him fired. Edmond Holmes held a job as a stamper in the Duquesne rolling mills, and like many workers, he stored good dies in his locker so he could identify his steel. The union official tipped off a foreman of this "theft" of company property; but a friend tipped off Holmes so that all the foreman and the union official found was Holmes' angry note.[271] Another worker recalled that white incumbent unionists simply "bought the votes" of black unionists with food and beer.[272] Good-old-boy unionism hampered black involvement. Other workers were pro-union, but temperamentally unsuited for the activist role. Henderson Thomas spoke for many black steelworkers. He "praised the union . . . but I'm a sideman. I never got on the front lines." Like many men, Thomas was not an activist but remained deeply "concerned about jobs [and discrimination]. Always."[273] Such "inactivity" resulted in some of the changes in the workplace.

A persistent complaint of black unionists was the low number of elected and appointed officials in the USWA.[274] In 1946, Carl Dickerson sat on the influential Wage Policy Committee. It would be fifteen years before another black man from the Mon Valley was elected to this committee and then only over the "strenuous objection" of his local President.[275] Attempts by black workers to use District elections to gain more positions went nowhere. In 1948 there were two black staffmen in the three USWA Districts in the region: James McCoy in District 16 (Pittsburgh) and Milford

"Pete" Jackson in District 15 (Homestead).[276] As the Cold War deepened, the prospects of increasing the number of black officials dimmed. The 1949 race for Director of Pittsburgh-area District 17 (Lawrenceville) was instructive. The incumbent red-baited his opponent, an activist in the virulently anti-communist Association of Catholic Trade Unionists, in part because he had promised to hire a black staff man if he was elected. In order to shore up his base, the incumbent later matched this pledge. The incumbent won, and for the first time blacks provided the margin of victory in a district election.[277] A year and a half later, Harold Keith reminded black workers that "you don't even have one heater in your entire district. Hello, suckers!"[278] In 1953, Carl Dickerson complained to David McDonald that "dozens of staffmen have been added. . . . However, no Negroes are among them. The majority of the districts do not have even one colored staffman. One seems to be the quota."[279] The refusal of most local unions to hire even black secretarial staff further alienated black steelworkers.[280] Outnumbered by whites, increasingly alienated from the union, and in a Cold War atmosphere that linked civil rights activism to communism, few blacks rose to positions of authority in the union.

A few black steelworkers immersed themselves in union politics. Most locals had one or two blacks elected to a marginal office such as trustee.[281] Yet active unionists persisted. In the Duquesne Works, Carl Dickerson, Vernon Sidberry, and Roger Payne were all active, influential black unionists. One worker recalled that Eugene Dirl did such a capable job representing workers in the blast furnace of the ET Works that management "respected him like we respected the bosses."[282] In the Carrie Furnace, several blacks occupied union office. John Hughey, for many years the Chair of the Grievance Committee, recalled that blacks in his local participated in the union "because they wanted to move up."[283] However, just across the river in the Homestead Works, few if any blacks had ever been elected. In 1956, at the Homestead Works, Albert Reid ran for Vice President of Local 1397 on the slate of Norman Butterfield, a white worker. Reid failed, although Butterfield was elected.[284] As Reid recalled, "people didn't attend the meetings. What can you do with no backup?"[285]

The higher one went in the union, the wider grew the gap between rhetoric and action. The ascension of the "liberal" David McDonald to the USWA presidency made no difference to the appointment of blacks to offices or battling shopfloor discrimination. Eugene Dirl, an assistant grievanceman at Edgar Thomson complained that if McDonald was such a "liberally inspired leader" then "why aren't there more black faces in our downtown headquarters?"[286] McCoy and Jackson would remain the only black staff representatives in Pittsburgh throughout the 1950s. And the appointment of blacks to office was no solution. Although Boyd Wilson regularly met delegations of angry black steelworkers, his role as "troubleshooter" made little difference in the direction of policy. His influence was limited to his powers of persuasion. As one colleague recalled, "his authority? Well he didn't have any."[287]

Largely frustrated in the realm of union politics and in the workplace, black steelworkers could not rely on normal avenues of job placement, promotion, or transfer. As a result, African Americans developed different job strategies from white workers. Frequently the only way blacks could advance into better-paying jobs, LOPs, or departments was through their own persistence and determination. As one black worker observed, "I got to the top of the ladder. I fought for it mostly by *myself*. Not through the union."[288]

Extremes of individual effort were frequently necessary to advance into jobs such as cranemen. In the late 1940s, Henderson Thomas had worked a few years in the Duquesne Works and was "really interested in the crane. Two or three cranes would unload the boxcars [in the stockyard of the blast furnace] and swing it back and load the charging boxes. It was a team effort and that fascinated me. . . . I pursued that daily. I used to go to work an hour early in order to see what they did." For the next year or more, Thomas carefully watched new hires. Finally, he got a chance to try for the job. Although the union contract specified he was to be given training, he was given none. "But I went and got on the general crane. Only thing that helped me, was by going each and every day. I knew they did their hand for this. . . . I guess within two or three weeks, by eating, sleeping, *crane* I got as good as anybody. Seriously, I was determined." His determination was necessary to keep his job in the mill. "I used to work *every* day. Went in early if they called me, stayed over late if they called me." Over the next few years, Thomas worked on many different cranes in Duquesne, and trained between twenty and forty white cranemen. But Thomas was on the "traveling crane"; he never got departmental seniority in the maintenance department. When layoffs came in 1953 and 1954, "I was the first man out in the streets." Interestingly, he noted that "that's when I felt discrimination. Someone putting all your effort out." He was laid off for just under two years. He got one day's work in the mills, which let him keep his seniority; he was eventually rehired. He was recalled to the bar mills, and on his first day his foreman looked at him and said, "he'll be good on the gang, because he's a big strong man." He recalled, "I said, no sir, they sent me down here to be a craneman. . . . If I'd shut up, that'd be the end, as far as cranes was concerned."[289]

Those black workers who advanced up the job ladder recalled their rise as a struggle of an individual against an unjust system. Yet particularly for such "individualists," bypassing the grievance procedure was not an act of individualism but a more realistic form of political struggle. Moreover, such "individualistic" shop-floor strategies had important consequences for the struggle of African Americans as a group. Individualists advanced by drawing upon personal contacts with white managers or workers, exploiting or fighting others if necessary. Often individualists were not as confrontational as trade union militants. Although he fought hard to break into the craneman's position, Thomas claimed he had only talked back to a foreman once. Yet when convinced they were right, these "individualists" were willing to do more than file a grievance and wait to hear how it turned out. They confronted foremen, department heads, or even superintendents. When Edmond Holmes got into a dispute with his foremen, he refused to simply file a grievance. Instead, he went himself to the U.S. Steel headquarters in downtown Pittsburgh. Human relations people in the corporate headquarters backed Holmes and ordered his supervisor to make sure that he was treated properly. As Holmes recalled, "I had established myself in Pittsburgh . . . [but] I wasn't the most popular guy in my department."[290] In occupational terms, individualists were among the most successful black workers in the steel industry.

White workers often became crucial allies. After Otis King's white friend successfully transferred into the Homestead Works' Machine Shop, King was able to force the foreman to accept his transfer as well.[291] Alfred Macon, who became one of the first black rollers in the Valley, noted that "there was some people who cared just a little bit to give me a helping hand."[292] George Suber became one of the few black draftsmen in the 1950s. He recalled with appreciation a white friend who had shown him several important tricks of the trade.[293] The white cranemen who helped Henderson Thomas learn the ropes on the ladle crane could have been fired if a foreman had discovered him. However, not all friends proved true. Henderson Thomas recalled with pain that another white friend "never got around" to showing him how to operate a certain machine.[294]

In many cases, there was little contradiction between pursuing "individualistic" strategies and upholding the union. Furthermore, many "individualists" saw their advancement as part of a strategy to aid other black workers. George Henderson remembered the men in his crew: "they'd a quit long time ago if it wasn't for me. I made 'em stay. . . . See you can't run from place to place hunting jobs. You stay in one place and protect the job you got. That's all you got to do. So they all got to sticking."[295] After another African American at Duquesne became a skilled worker, he gathered together an all-black crew. In his view, getting a skilled position was the first step into to allowing other blacks to move ahead. Once he got his job, "we been moving pretty good."[296] By teaching workers how to defend their jobs or advance into previously all-white positions, skilled "individualists" played an important subsidiary role in breaking down institutionalized racism.

Yet the individualism of black workers often frustrated those who favored collective action. In 1957, a black worker in the Homestead Works captured the relationship between job protection and timidity in a letter to the editor of Pittsburgh's black paper. When a pusher or boss called them "son" or "boy" black steelworkers "merely smile[d], (a big one showing teeth) . . . and then grumbled among themselves . . . as they [were] afraid of losing their jobs." The writer was himself afraid for his job and requested that the *Courier* withhold his name from the public.[297] Edmond A. Holmes, a Duquesne worker, remembered that many blacks were "too chicken. They even told me, you better shut your mouth, because these people don't like what you're doing. . . . They were either content or afraid." In fact, many whites told him "you don't act Negro." When he asked them what they meant, they said, "Well, you know." Holmes replied, "No, I don't know."[298] Another recalled "the opportunities were there. But a lot of 'em [black workers] were scared, because of the pressure."[299] The individualism and conservatism of African American steelworkers frustrated militant workers who wanted them to take an active stand in the mill.

In the 1950s, most black workers stayed in the departments they were hired into unless they were laid off or convinced their foremen to transfer them. John Hughey, a black unionist at the Carrie Furnaces, observed that "Room service [department seniority] meant that if you lived to be as old as Methuselah, you never got out of the room."[300] Once outside of the "room" where a worker had built up seniority, he was vulnerable to being laid off. Despite the danger, black workers occasionally risked their departmental seniority. One black man left nearly twenty-six years of seniority in the Blooming Mills of the Duquesne Works to transfer to the Masonry Department in February 1948. He explained to his perplexed foreman that he desperately needed extra income to support his five dependents and he could work six days a week in masonry.[301] More common was the situation of Jesse Larrington. In 1955, Larrington wanted to transfer to the Carrie Furnace's Power and Fuel Division. His foreman would have approved him for it, but it would have cost him his three years of seniority. Fearing a layoff, he stayed put.[302] The dire consequences of switching jobs kept most black workers "safe" in black departments.

Another non-confrontational strategy for black workers was to be exemplary workers. Bob Morgan recalled that his father had a reputation as an extremely diligent worker because he held down one job in the mill and another for the city of Duquesne. When Morgan was about eighteen, his father told him, "Go down there and act like you want a job." So Morgan applied at the Duquesne Works and "instead of leaving, I just sat" in the employment office. "They went out for lunch, came back, and I was still there." A manager hired him because "he wants to go to work."[303] Robert Rivers, who ended up as a foreman in Homestead's OH 3, recalled that he had to "walk real straight."[304] George Henderson advised that in order for black workers to get ahead, they had to be honest, hard workers and build a close relationship with management.[305] By becoming exemplary workers, some blacks were able to blunt the impact of institutionalized racism.

But conservative job strategies did not mean that blacks were content "in their place." One worker worked forty-three years in the Masonry Department of the Duquesne Works, most of that time as a laborer, and recalled that he had no problems regarding seniority. In 1952, he had major surgery and preferred to stay where he knew the work and had ten years' seniority. Twenty years later, he surprised everyone he worked with by taking advantage of the 1974 Consent Decree and moving to a higher-paying job.[306]

THE COLLECTIVE STRATEGIES OF WHITE WORKERS

Though white workers often joined forces to thwart the civil rights agenda of blacks, the dynamics of discrimination that undercut African Americans failed to empower white steelworkers as a group. Indeed, there were broad similarities between the workplace and union strategies of black and white steelworkers, suggesting that shared workplace experiences and class oppression led workers of different hues to draw the same conclusions (or to internalize the limits of the time in similar ways). Most whites were also passive members of their union. Even in overwhelmingly white locals, participation was low except for the periods around contracts. In the larger locals, a turnout of 3 percent of the membership to a meeting was exceptional. (Of course this does not count participation in shop-floor activities, or strikes, which were often rock solid.) Most white steelworkers pursued conservative job strategies in response to the ups and downs of the industry and the peculiarities of job and departmental seniority.[307] Of course, the USWA remained unwilling to lead a serious fight against discrimination, and most white steelworkers remained uninterested in civil rights or opposed to it. Some whites benefited from intra-mill discrimination, but most did not, and indeed could not to a significant degree, as women and blacks never made up more than 20 percent of the workforce. Demographics imposed material limits on the rewards that white or male supremacy could offer white male steelworkers as a group. Of course many whites *expected* to benefit from discrimination, and such expectations, as much as the reality of the "wages of whiteness," help explain the union's position towards civil rights. Certainly white working-class cynicism towards discrimination and racial prejudice exacerbated the disorganization of black workers, but it left whites no stronger against their employers. Nor did black disarray translate into white empowerment within the union. When organizations of mostly white trade unionists mobilized to advance what they saw as their interests in the USWA, they too were crushed.

The left was the only force in the region, independent of the CIO unions, that argued that greater levels of inter-racial solidarity were necessary in order to challenge the power of employers. But the left offered no substantive challenge to the leadership of the USWA. Located in what David Caute termed "the violent epicenter of the anti-Communist eruption in postwar America," the Communist Party and other left-wing groups in Pittsburgh were shattered. In 1953, after a widely publicized trial of the leadership of the Western Pennsylvania CP, the Commonwealth outlawed the party. By 1956, roughly two-thirds of Pennsylvania's communists had left the party, even before Nikita Khrushchev's revelations about the extent of Stalin's horrendous crimes against the people of the USSR.[308]

Demonized in the press, hounded by the government, blacklisted by employers, red-baited by the USWA, communist steelworkers had little influence in their union. Any officer suspected of communist ties was tried by his local union and if found guilty, was removed from office. After the late 1940s, the USWA found little occasion to expel communists because only on rare occasions was a "red" elected to office. However, when discovered, the "commie" was quickly purged from the union.[309] Furthermore, the USWA rejected any policy that would protect workers who simply took the Fifth Amendment in front of the House Un-American Activities Committee or workers who had simply taken out insurance policies with the International Workers Order, a beneficial society linked to the CP. District Directors reasoned that when they were "a little short on being able to put the finger on" a worker, taking the Fifth was "pretty much the clinching argument."[310] Any possibilities for progressive political action led by left trade unions such as the UE were rendered impossible. Attacked by the FBI, electrical companies, the Catholic Church, the CIO, and the USWA, the UE struggled simply to survive. In Pittsburgh, the union lost over half of its membership.[311] The destruction of the CP and the UE ensured the steady rightward march of working-class politics. When rank-and-file opposition to the union's leadership emerged in the late 1950s, it was a loose and unstable network of populists, conservatives, and radicals.

Union dissidents confronted a deeply entrenched administrative machine. Members were eligible to hold local office only if they attended half of all local meetings. With regular attendance largely consisting of union officials, and a few would-be officers, the union's potential leadership even in large locals was whittled down to a handful of men.[312] Although most elections were clean, ballot stuffing was a common problem in some locals. One steelworker recalled that "if you don't have the power to count the votes, you don't have the power to win."[313] The spoils of office seduced some unionists. In large locals, officers were often paid for "lost time" on union business, and for many this was incentive enough to avoid returning to the shop floor. Control over dues was held by the national USWA. Local officers handled grievances up to the third step of a five-step process when they were turned over to district staff members. Sixty percent of grievances were settled at the third or fourth step, and the discretion of the district staff in handling grievances checked the power of locals.[314] Local trade unionists enjoyed prestige and power, but not the power of the purse, and their independent power was limited by their district officials and staff. Information was tightly controlled; until 1952, local unions were discouraged from publishing newspapers.[315] Debates and decisions at the biennial constitutional convention were regimented affairs, in large part because of the many union staff in attendance who remained loyal to the leaders that had hired them.[316]

Workers directly elected the directors of USWA districts, but they were able to mobilize vast resources to ensure their own victory. Very few incumbents lost. Between 1945 and 1961, only 40 of the 199 elections for district director were contested and just 8 challengers won office. Incumbents' power to appoint staff ensured that directors controlled the only network of people with contacts in every USWA local union in the region.[317] Candidates for district director had to receive several nominations from local unions, and staffmen often invalidated nominations for challengers as a result of "technicalities." Periodically, angry steelworkers from one district or another appealed to the USWA International Executive Board (IEB) with evidence that their district director had in fact stolen their own election. In one such case, a worker from Western Pennsylvania told the IEB that "you men don't know the conditions going on in that district or the feelings of the men. If you did, you would say it was time for a change." Another district director defended the practice of stealing elections by arguing that this represented a "higher form" of democracy; every member of the IEB "is going to use every damned trick he possibly can and exercise his democracy to the fullest, the kind of democracy . . . to save this union." Of course, what the director meant was that every official would do what was necessary to save his own job: "Let us not kid ourselves, there is not a man on this board, and I don't care who he is, who don't know what the hell is going on in the field." (This director knew what he was talking about—David McDonald later explained that he stole 4 elections for him.) In this case, as in virtually all others, the appeal for the right to contest the district election was turned down.[318]

Although the top officers of the USWA had been directly elected since 1942, no national election was contested until 1955.[319] Discontent crystallized in opposition to President David McDonald, Philip Murray's successor. McDonald had only a passing acquaintance with the steel industry, but he was the consummate insider. McDonald's rise to power was launched in Murray's office, where McDonald was his personal secretary. He later became a loyal officer whose chief distinguishing feature had been strident anti-communism. To foster McDonald's credibility amongst steelworkers (he was more at home in country clubs or among movie stars than foundry workers), the union published his biography, *Man of Steel*, which portrayed the suave careerist as a gritty, no-nonsense unionist. The book was so embarrassingly hyperbolic (in one incident, the young McDonald pulled a metal burr from a co-worker's eye as if he were Androcles pulling a splinter from a lion's paw) that the "biography" had to be withdrawn. As one unionist wryly observed, "there was a big expensive book burning."[320] Many steelworkers accepted that their President needed considerable power to negotiate with enormous, tough-nosed companies.[321] But many union members wondered if McDonald understood their concerns about rising unemployment and ongoing battles over "labor economies" when he rode to work in a limousine and wore tailor-made suits. Amongst the leadership, McDonald's arrogance and heavy drinking forced some to conclude a change was necessary. In 1955, McDonald's hand-picked replacement for the deceased incumbent vice president was challenged by District Director Joe Malony who advocated (as would every subsequent challenger to national office) greater rank-and-file control over the union.[322] Although Malony was defeated, several district directors were "reasonably sure" that McDonald's man had actually lost.[323] At the 1956 convention, McDonald won an increase in monthly dues and a salary raise for the union's leadership, but at the cost to his waning popularity. The next year, a network of dues protesters took on the "tuxedo unionist" and ran Donald C. Rarick, a grievanceman at the Irvin Works, for president of the union.[324]

The Rarick-McDonald contest was widely viewed as a referendum on the direction of the union. Rarick did little more than promise to reverse the dues increase, lower the pay of staff, and eliminate "dictatorships in local unions where they now exist."[325] Running scared, McDonald red-baited the Dues Protest Committee (DPC), claiming that he recognized clear evidence of the "Communist Party line" in some speeches.[326] Yet Rarick and many dues protesters were better described as conservative populists whose chief critique focused on clean elections. Red-baited or not, they retained strong support in the large locals in Pennsylvania and Ohio. While McDonald beat Rarick by an almost two to one margin, the fact that an unknown local official won 250,000 votes in the face of a well-organized machine suggested the depths of discontent in the union.[327] Support for the dues protesters was strong enough to preclude an all-out campaign by McDonald to oust the "bedbugs" and "traitors" such as Rarick and Nick Mamula (Aliquippa) from their local union offices.

Rebellion simmered, but the DPC failed to make significant headway. The opposition proved unable to reach the majority of the members of the

USWA who worked in small shops and were more dependent upon the organizational and financial support of the USWA leadership.[328] Even in District 15 (Homestead), the center of discontent, the rebels were outmaneuvered. In 1957, rebels elected "their man," Paul Hilbert, as district director. Hilbert soon realized that the price of power was loyalty to McDonald, and Hilbert "did a number on him [Rarick], what should have been done several months back."[329] In the next district-wide election, rebels sought to punish Hilbert as a turncoat, but he won re-election.[330] In no small part, Hilbert's victory depended on keeping opponents off the ballot by means fair and foul. When the DPC appealed to the IEB, the union's leadership upheld Hilbert's interests.[331] As they had so many times in the past, steelworkers won an election, but lost control of the organization. Despite the dues protest upheaval, control within the union remained as centralized as ever, and steelworkers as divided against the administration's machine.

RETREAT INTO THE FAMILY? STEELWORKERS' RISING STANDARD OF LIVING

Despite the USWA's problems and relative weaknesses, steelworkers were still better situated than other industrial workers. In the 1950s, steelworkers became the best-paid members of Pittsburgh's working class. Judged in constant dollars, steelworkers' average income rose over 50 percent over the course of the 1950s. The fact that real wages increased, by such a substantial amount, amidst rising unemployment in the industry, was a tribute to the efficacy of the New Deal and the power of the USWA. Certainly steelworkers had never enjoyed such massive and across-the-board wage gains in the non-union era. By the end of the 1950s, steelworkers earned twice as much as those in the service sector and significantly more than most other industrial workers. In this decade, white steelworkers earned about 90 percent that of the median income for all households.[332] Because white female steelworkers were concentrated in the industry's lowest-paid jobs, they earned just 75 percent of the income of male steelworkers. Nonetheless, their income put them far above that of women in the service sector.[333] Even male laborers, who enjoyed the lowest pay and were the most threatened by unemployment and automation, enjoyed better wages and steadier employment than laborers outside of the industry. Although the average income of black steelworkers was roughly 20 percent lower than that of whites, black steelworkers earned approximately 110 percent of the median income for black heads of households. Steelworkers had begun to enjoy the fruits of their labor, ascending into a standard of living that historian Mark McColloch has described as "modest but adequate."[334]

As the best-paid and most secure members of the industrial workforce, steelworkers have sometimes been viewed as members of America's middle class. Indeed, some steelworkers, such as Ed Gorman, described "going to work" for a steel company as "going into the middle class."[335] Compared to the lean years of the 1930s (or indeed, the 1980s), steelworkers in the 1950s certainly enjoyed a degree of economic stability and comfort. When asked what he would do if there was a strike in 1955, one steelworker said "Man, if we strike, I'm just going to fish and fish and fish!" This relative privilege was not lost on his interlocutor: "[O]thers discussed their various projects should the 'unpaid vacation' occur: a garage to be built, part of the yard to be landscaped, a house to be painted."[336] Steelworkers' rates of homeownership were high, but by the standards of the professional middle class, their homes were modest and close to the soot and smoke of the mill. Indeed, many younger steelworkers continued to build their own houses, living in the basements until they saved enough money to complete the rest.[337] Only in the 1960s did steelworkers move in large numbers into the blue-collar suburbs surrounding the mills. Periodic layoffs and strikes depleted the savings of many steelworkers, and the threat of automation or mill closings darkened the horizon of all workers. But steelworkers judged their gains not so much against the salaries of lawyers or doctors, but against their parents' wages, and by that measure, they knew they were doing very well.

USWA members won a range of important benefits that guaranteed a measure of security. One of the most important was company-paid pensions. Before 1949, U.S. Steel subtracted Social Security payments from workers' pension payments, arguing that it had paid into both schemes. After Social Security payments were deducted, some low-paid workers, including many African Americans and immigrants, received less than a dollar a month.[338] For instance, James Clark put in thirty-nine years at the Homestead Works, but after deducting his Social Security payment, his pension from U.S. Steel was just sixty-one cents a month.[339] Henry Mikula, a tractor operator at Homestead, spoke for many workers when he observed, "when a man gives thirty or fifty years of life to a job, he should be able to retire in comfort—a little comfort anyway."[340] The 1949 strike resulted in workers' right to enjoy both a company pension and social security benefits. Retired steelworkers made a slow climb out of poverty. According to a study conducted by the USWA and the University of Pittsburgh in 1953, most retirees quickly exhausted their savings and worked another job, lived with their families, or became dependent upon relief.[341] Steelworkers took another step forward in 1954 when companies doubled the amount they paid into the pension plans. In 1956–57, workers won automatic cost-of-living adjustments to wages and SUB pay. As Tony Vrabel, a worker at the Homestead Works, explained, "workers who are laid off temporarily get SUB in addition to unemployment benefits from the state, so that for a whole year if necessary, the steelworker who is laid off gets about 65 percent of his regular wages."[342] In the late 1950s, workers forced companies to pay half of their health insurance premiums, and after 1960, the company paid all of them, even if a worker was laid off for up to six months.[343] Through such measures, steelworkers took steps towards the modest goals that Henry Mikula outlined in 1949.

The USWA consistently linked its demands for economic security to a vision of family life in which women played a dependent role. By the early 1950s, the USWA represented women of steel almost exclusively as dutiful wives and mothers. In October 1951, *Steel Labor* featured these "Women of Steel" on its front page. These were not the welders who graced publications during World War II but rather white housewives shown shopping, canning, or baking pies for grateful children.[344] Although forty thousand women remained members of the USWA, the union did not challenge the bias against married women working. In 1951, *Steel Labor* featured a female President of a USWA local in a fabricating plant in the Western Pennsylvania town of Canonsburg. Asking rhetorically, "Who Says It's a Man's World?" the President was shown as a hard worker, a good unionist, and a very single *Miss* Margaret Cornel. Thus, even depictions of women as industrial workers and unionists carefully emphasized the constraints placed on their participation in the worlds of production and working-class activism.[345] Arguing for higher wages in the 1954 contract, the USWA argued on the front page of *Steel Labor* that "The Families' Needs Are the Real Issues at the Bargaining Table."[346] And to underscore the supremacy of the family, the USWA superimposed its update on recent contractual gains over a drawing of a wife in the kitchen.[347] The specter of a pensionless old age was posed in terms both paternalistic and patriarchal: "Is Your Wife Going to Work When You Retire?"[348] The question did have real bite, though not what its author intended: even with gains to the pension plans, the wives of steelworkers remained vulnerable to poverty. Not until 1969 would steelworkers' widows win rights to 50 percent of their husbands' pensions.[349]

The union's insistence on keeping women out of high-wage industrial ("their") labor markets reflected the middle-class aspirations of steelworkers as much as their conservative values and newfound prosperity. Many of the female war workers of World War II and Korea worked throughout their adult lives. For instance, one woman who left the Homestead Works to get married and have children also worked for twenty-five years in the mill's cafeteria.[350] Other war workers returned to low-paid service or factory work elsewhere.[351] Rates of women's labor market participation were far lower in the Steel Valley than the Pittsburgh area, which were already relatively low compared to the rest of Pennsylvania; whether this reflected the lack of "women's jobs" in mill towns or the desires of steelworkers and their families remains to be seen. But married women in "steel families" did work.[352] But the overall effect of the union's efforts on developing a "family wage" did help steelworkers and their families obtain a measure of prosperity and security.

THE EFFECT OF STEEL ON THE "RENAISSANCE REGION"

The outcome of steel's class struggles strongly influenced the rest of Pittsburgh. As steel was the largest employer and engine of the local economy, as wages in heavy industry rose, employers elsewhere were forced to increase their rates of pay. However, beginning in 1953, the steady erosion of jobs from steel triggered a profound regional economic decline compounded by a severe national recession in the later part of the decade. Until 1953, the military buildup of the early Cold War and Korean War prevented any substantial job loss, and the steel industry employed 160,000 people throughout the Pittsburgh area. Other sectors employed 688,000.[353] Job losses mounted after the mid-1950s due to declining military contracts, automation, and the closure of older departments and mills. By 1959, steel firms employed 119,000 workers while Pittsburgh's non-steel economy had shrunk to 645,000 employees.[354] Pittsburgh's sluggish economy attracted few migrants. The region's black community grew at less than half the rate of other Northern industrial cities, and migrants from Latin America, the Caribbean, and Asia bypassed Pittsburgh.[355] Not until 1968 would Pittsburgh regain the number of jobs it had held in 1953. As jobs drained from the region, people followed, and the greater Pittsburgh region began a secular loss of population that has yet to end.

Anticipating the decline of heavy industry by ten years, government and corporate decision makers had already laid ambitious plans for a postindustrial regional economy. As in steel, the costs of this new economy were shifted as much as possible upon government and especially workers. Similarly, economic and political elites opposed efforts by civil rights activists to desegregate the region's facilities, housing, and job markets. Within the Cold War "consensus," workers' economic victories failed to expand their organizational or political capacity. Whatever its other effects, steelworkers' rising standard of living bolstered the union's defense of the "American way of life" against communism. But the union's political perspective left it unguarded against the predations of Pittsburgh's owning class and the union's own political "allies" in the Democratic Party.

The regional elite sought to stimulate a post-industrial economy through an ambitiously titled Pittsburgh "Renaissance." The Renaissance was coordinated by the Allegheny Conference on Community Development (ACCD), the body through which the major corporations penetrated the political process. Headed by Richard King Mellon, the heir to the Mellon financial interests and the kingmaker of the Republican Party, the ACCD was a who's who of Pittsburgh's owning class: steel, electrical, rail, coal, real estate, and chemical barons formed what was the de facto "executive committee of the bourgeoisie" in Western Pennsylvania.[356] Elites calculated that the region needed to expand its white-collar job base if it was to survive, and a necessary precondition for that was overcoming the effects of decades of unchecked industrialization. (Threats to relocate corporate headquarters out of Pittsburgh in the late 1940s due to its intense toxicity stimulated elite reform efforts.) Ironically, these were barriers that business itself had largely created—from decades of unrestrained heavy industry and a weak and impoverished public sector—but could not now undo without the aid of government. But before a new regime of corporate profitability could be developed, the physical, ecological, and institutional barriers of the past had to be overcome.

At the heart of the ACCD lay the "public-private partnership" between the arch-Republican Mellon and David Lawrence, Mayor and boss of Pittsburgh's Democratic Party. It was a much-blessed marriage of convenience. Since 1937, the voting blocs of white ethnic and African American workers had turned Pittsburgh and its industrial suburbs into unassailable

Democratic strongholds.[357] Only David Lawrence possessed the influence to deliver the city, county, and state legislation to ensure the flood control, smoke abatement, traffic control, and generous public subsidies that the ACCD desired to renovate downtown Pittsburgh. With Lawrence on board for the Renaissance, Pittsburgh secured itself from the threat of flooding after the Corps of Engineers built dams upstream of the city. Smoke abatement eased the city's notorious acid rain problem, and trees returned to the hills and riverbanks for the first time in decades. Stories about office workers needing to change shirts at midday faded into folklore. Traffic congestion eased as the trolleys were removed from downtown, and a few freeways were constructed. More parking was added to downtown Pittsburgh. The cultural district flourished under the patronage of generous taxpayers and philanthropists. In exchange, Mellon rode herd on city landowners who shifted their industrial plants, railroads, and warehouses out of downtown to make room for the development of corporate headquarters in the so-called Golden Triangle. The ACCD's first success was to prevent the threatened relocation of corporate headquarters while the Mellons expanded their already substantial holdings in downtown real estate.

THE CLASS AND RACIAL POLITICS
OF THE RENAISSANCE CITY

Though scholars and Pittsburghers alike have judged the Renaissance was a success, and Lawrence enjoys a solid reputation as Pittsburgh's "civic statesman," the record is more checkered. Though Pittsburgh, like all cities, requires public planning, it is not clear that Renaissance Pittsburgh was planned with the public in mind. Individuals and taxpayers carried much of the burden for the greening of Pittsburgh. Pittsburgh's smoke abatement placed little burden on industry; instead, homes were no longer allowed to burn coal for heating or cooking. The mills added new scrubbers, although they still produced prodigious amounts of industrial pollution. Moreover, the Renaissance diverted public funds from developing better schools, low-cost housing, or other projects targeted at the city's working-class residents. Roy Lubove, perhaps the most trenchant critic of the Renaissance, judged the experiment "a welfare state in reverse."[358]

The terms of the Pittsburgh Renaissance suggest that despite the consolidation of the Democratic Party within local and county government, real power remained in the hands of industrialists and financiers who sat on the ACCD. Although the Renaissance helped to diversify the econ-omy, this did not compensate for the rapid erosion of high-wage industrial employment. With the exception of public-sector jobs, most of the jobs created during phase one of the Renaissance were and remained non-union, in keeping with the virulent anti-union sentiments of the Mellons and other industrialists. Nor did "public-private" partnership mean that pri-vate employers would address workers' most pressing public problems such as poverty, poor-quality housing, and racial discrimination. These "quality of life" issues were simply ignored by the ACCD, a high council which sim-ply did not include any trade unionists or civil rights activists.

The ACCD, of course, was only exhibiting organized and disciplined class solidarity. That is more than can be said for the organizations that purportedly represented workers' interests, the Democratic Party, civil rights organizations, and unions, that all failed, at least in some key respects, to meet the needs and aspirations of white or black workers. In economic terms, the USWA was a roaring success, but as a vehicle that organized and empowered steelworkers, it was more problematic. Although unions such as the Steelworkers abided by democratic norms, at the national and dis-trict levels, they remained resolutely hierarchical. Workers had little influ-ence on "their" party, which in addition to its pro-business bias was also substantially corrupt. Civil rights organizations proved too weak and too co-opted to take on either the Democrats or big business. Though a variety of popular struggles forced elites to yield resources and reforms to workers (notably industrial workers), in organizational terms, workers gained little ground in "the golden age of labor."

The monopoly tactics of Pittsburgh's corporations were mimicked by its political counterpart, the Democratic Party. The Democrats thoroughly dominated county government and the municipal governments in Pitts-burgh and its industrial suburbs. U.S. Steel could chisel consumers by raising prices; local politicians accepted "donations" from a variety of sources. While unions were a major constituency inside the Democrats, the "party of labor" also included local businessmen and the vice industry. For instance, numbers racketeers also supported the Democratic politicians who ensured that the police turned a blind eye to gambling.[359] Most of the jobs on the police force went to individuals with political connections. Indeed, a job on the borough or county payroll was the poor man's equivalent of a trust fund except that "brokerage fees" were paid to local politicians.[360] Police corruption was so pervasive that small-time numbers runners complained that payoffs to cops cut deeply into their profits.[361] Pittsburgh's handful of black cops indicated there was no honor among thieves, complaining that they did not receive a fair share of the payoffs due to the departmental color line.[362]

Due to its corruption, the Democratic machine was a relatively poor provider of services. Although the colorful tales of the beneficent graft of big city machines have charmed many social scientists, pervasive graft meant that corporations were not required to pay their fair share of taxes, that workers had to pay to get jobs, and that housing and health inspectors did not perform their duties.[363] Indeed, corruption instantiated the Democratic Party's class bias. Throughout the 1950s, the largely Democratic local governments provided ten thousand additional jobs, raising the total to sixty thousand by the end of the decade, yet new services were largely paid for through regressive taxation.[364] The political culture of the Democrats was pro-labor, but the basis for its taxation was not. In 1954, Pittsburgh instituted a wage tax (as distinct from an income tax) which exempted income from rents or stocks (e.g., from the Mellon family), leaving workers to shoulder most of the financial burden. Even the most resolutely Democratic mill towns were unable to overcome the history of gerrymandered municipal boundaries, and as a result, industrial property continued to be lightly taxed. Furthermore, local governments generally lacked the means to assess the industrial properties of large companies and relied on their estimates. On the issues of substandard housing, racial discrimination, or education, the Democratic Party's inactivity confirmed Michael Weber's judgment that "action on the social front occurred only when other matters dictated it."[365]

The Democratic Party's failure to live up to its liberal and pro-worker reputation was particularly pronounced in the African American community. Blacks had become loyal Democratic voters during the New Deal, though their share of the spoils was hard to claim.[366] Blacks comprised about 12 percent of Pittsburgh's population in the 1950s, although they never held more than 7 percent of the jobs in local government.[367] And according to the *Pittsburgh Courier*, about 75 percent of the city's African-American municipal employees were garbage men, although sixteen of their seventeen foremen were white. Most other municipal workers were hospital orderlies.[368] Although Pittsburgh employed a few black firemen and policemen, their numbers remained virtually unchanged throughout the 1950s, and only a handful held high rank.[369] Similarly, the vast majority of craft unions holding contracts with Pittsburgh and Allegheny County had never had a black member.[370] After a decade of struggle on the part of

African Americans, they enjoyed somewhat better access to municipal jobs. For instance, in 1959, only 40 percent of municipal black employees were refuse workers.[371] But progress under Democratic governance came at a painfully slow rate, and required considerable conflict.

Given the endemic poverty and unemployment in the African American community, gaining access to decent jobs was one of the top priorities of the civil rights movement. The chief barrier was the informal Jim Crow policies of big business. In 1947, the black community participated in mass picketing of downtown department stores to protest the stores' refusal to hire African Americans for a wide number of jobs, including salespeople. After mass pickets led by the Pittsburgh Urban League (PUL), NAACP, black churches, and the Negro Elks, the Retail Merchants Association, which included Kaufmann's and Horne's, agreed to hire a few blacks.[372] As soon as the ink had dried on the agreements, however, businessmen shut off donations to the PUL to pressure them to halt further protests. One store-owner articulated the intersection of class interests and philanthropy thusly: "Is this the reason we finance the Urban League, so you can send young people downtown and embarrass us?"[373] The demonstrations ended, and it would be a generation before comparable levels of protests transpired in Pittsburgh. Until the 1960s, the PUL negotiated with companies to place "pilot" employees in technical and professional positions. Indeed, in this decade, the proportion of salaried black professionals actually declined.[374]

Lacking adequate leadership, the mass protests stopped. Occupational segregation was challenged by informal groups, such as the ambitiously named Greater Pittsburgh Improvement League (GPIL). Formed in 1949, the GPIL sought to "gain employment for Negroes where it never existed" and led community boycotts and set up picket lines on companies that refused to hire blacks. While the GPIL could claim some successes, it was never more than a small network of friends operating out of a barber shop.[375] The organizational disarray of the civil rights movement was no match for Pittsburgh's powerful and conservative corporations and public employers. African American movement into "white jobs" occurred at rates that earned Pittsburgh its nickname, the "Birmingham of the North."

CONCLUSION

In the Cold War era, as American military and industrial might was deployed in the worldwide battle against communism, America's democratic traditions and institutions assumed a new ideological importance. According to politicians, America was the freest and richest nation in the world because its state guaranteed its citizens the rights to both private property and civil liberties. In the catechism of the American economy, free enterprise encouraged technical innovation and material progress. The state provided modest correctives to the free market, but the rule of law prevented abuses of power by individuals, companies, or government itself. American workers lived better, freer lives than workers abroad because they were middle-class owners of automobiles, homes, and appliances. And in this post-war utopia, class consciousness and class warfare were absent, although workers could organize themselves in unions or undertake strikes if they so desired. Both corporations and unions were free to compete in the marketplace of ideas, through which they competed for the political loyalty of the "people," who in their role as electorate determined the policies of government.

Reality deviated from the gospel in significant ways. While competitive enterprise has always been central to a capitalist economy, the marketplace was far from free. Since 1900, a handful of companies controlled vast sectors of the economy, and these monopolies were rewarded by the visible hand of the state. In steel, public subsidies of capital and markets only encouraged industrialists' complacent indifference to the desires of consumers and even the long-term viability of the industry. Workers did share in this period of unprecedented economic growth. They did so because they were organized, fought steel companies, and won incredible gains. But buying a house, car, or washing machine did not remove steelworkers from the working class. And even in the "golden age" of the American working class, job insecurity was rife, and older, female, and black workers often remained poor. Steelworkers slowly widened the safety net for themselves, particularly for retired steelworkers, and while it was a slow climb out of poverty, progress was steady. While consumerism arguably undermined working-class radicalism, the repression by government, companies, and unions arguably played a more important role. As in the economic realm, government helped to structure the marketplace for ideas by encouraging some political organizations and stifling others.

The Cold War did not end the class struggle in Pittsburgh, but the forces of anti-communism, consumerism, and the healthiest and most equitable economy in living memory blunted its edges and affected its course. While unionized workers fought with corporations, they also cooperated with industrialists in the workplace and through government to provide stability and legitimacy to the overall political and economic system. The class struggle can be seen clearly in the fight between unionists and corporations over how the workplace would be organized, new technology implemented, and the benefits shared from a more productive workplace. While low-level class conflict wracked the workplace, and major strikes regularly broke out, labor law and the political culture of the USWA channeled it into relatively routinized forms such as the grievance process. The union eliminated much of the favoritism of the non-union era, and raised the wages of all laborers, black and white, male and female. Yet the rule of law was frequently corrupt, as many workers, especially women and blacks, discovered in the implementation of the seniority system. Within the union itself, democracy was deeply flawed. Thus, in the struggle for a more perfect union and an end to various kinds of discrimination we can see evidence of a fragmented class struggle. As in the past, workers' struggles for their rights pushed at the central contradictions in the political economy.

As much as any region, Cold War Pittsburgh symbolized the contradictory accomplishments and limitations of a system of political democracy and private control over industrial production. Perhaps that was the reason that when Nikita Khrushchev visited America in 1959, he wanted to see two things: Disneyland and the Mesta Machine Works in West Homestead, Pennsylvania. If the tour had occurred during World War II, local communists, industrialists, trade unionists, and politicians would have received the head of the Soviet Union. But when the world's most powerful communist traveled to Pittsburgh, Pennsylvania's CP was illegal, and the AFL-CIO was as vehemently anti-communist as employers, if not more so. After touring Mesta, Khrushchev proclaimed that this showpiece of American industrial might was "not a modern facility."[376] In the 1980s, one Pittsburgh resident made a wry observation about the visit: "During his tour, some guy, a Mesta worker yelled at him in Russian. Khrushchev gave the man his wristwatch. Now the mills are quiet; the Japanese, instead of the Russians as Khrushchev predicted, are burying us . . ."[377]

Table One
Population of the Pittsburgh Region (SMSA), by Race, 1940–1960

	PITTSBURGH SMSA		PITTSBURGH	
	Total	Black	Total	Black
1940	N/A	N/A	671,659	62,423
1950	2,213,236	137,261	676,806	82,981
1960	2,405,435	163,325	604,322	101,739

Source: Bureau of the Census, Census of Population: 1940 (Washington, D.C.: GPO, 1943), Part 38, 207; Bureau of the Census, Census of Population: 1950 (Washington, D.C.: GPO, 1952), Part 38, 88; Bureau of the Census, Census of Population: 1960 (Washington, D.C.: GPO, 1961), Part 40, 75.

Table Two
Economic Indicators of the Allegheny County Steel Industry

	Capital Invested	Wages	Value Added
1947	29	227	410
1954	40	260	580
1958	136	287	680

Note: All figures in millions of current dollars. Wages are for production workers only.

Source: Bureau of the Census, Census of Manufactures: 1947, Volume III (Washington, D.C.: GPO, 1950), 531; Bureau of the Census, Census of Manufactures: 1954, Volume III (Washington, D.C.: GPO, 1957), Chapter 37, 23; Bureau of the Census, Census of Manufactures: 1958, Volume III (Washington, D.C.: GPO, 1961), Chapter 37, 26.

Table Three
Employment Levels at the Homestead Works

	All Workers	P&M	Clerical	Short Shifts
1944	12,662			
1946		8,981	356	
1947	15,099	7,000		
1949				
1950	13,583			
1953	13,116			
1955		7,747	425	
1956	10,664	8,605		
Oct. 1956		7,798		
1957		8,774		
Feb. 1958		6,667		4,000
Sep. 1958		7,552		2,554
May 1959		7,754	400	
June 1960		7,400		4,600

Employment Levels at the Duquesne Works

	All Workers	P&M	Clerical	Short Shifts
1946	6,274	5,783	491	
1947	6,786			
1948	6,842	6,353	489	
1949		4,150		
Oct. 1949	8,038			2,073 laid off
1950	8,042			
1953	7,588			
1955	4,179	3,856	323	4,179
1956	4,985	4,502		
Oct. 1956		4,993		
1957		3,851		1,445
Feb. 1958		3,307		2,079
Sept. 1958		3,347		1,321
May 1959		5,306		
June 1960		5,000		910 laid off

Note: P&M means production and maintenance (union eligible).
Source: USWA Research Department and Department of Internal Affairs, Bureau of Statistics and Information, *Industrial Directory of the Commonwealth of Pennsylvania* (Harrisburg: Department of Internal Affairs, various issues).

Table Four
Number of Steelworkers, by Occupation and Gender, 1940–1960

MALE

	Professionals, Manager, Technicians	Skilled Crafts/ Foremen	Operatives	Laborers	Clerical	All
1940	7,815	46,255	48,388	67,314	15,710	188,115
1945	1,242	4,333	3,570	7,968	2,317	19,802
1950	7,944	40,200	37,683	37,234	10,450	134,494
1960	10,834	37,867	30,285	25,795	9,505	116,620

FEMALE

	Professionals Manager, Technicnans	Craft/Fore	Operatives	Laborers	Clerical	All
1940	183	157	1,110	477	3,596	5,544
1945	33	14	72	41	723	905
1950	390	257	802	515	5,040	7,042
1960	398	158	378	385	5,661	7,031

FEMALE

	Professionals Manager, Technicnans	Craft/Fore	Operatives	Laborers	Clerical	All
1940	2.3%	0.3%	2.2%	0.7%	18.6%	2.9%
1945	5.3%	0.2%	2.0%	0.5%	23.8%	4.4%
1950	4.7%	0.6%	2.1%	1.4%	32.5%	5.0%
1960	3.5%	0.4%	1.2%	1.5%	37.5%	5.7%

Note: 1940 data for Pittsburgh city only; 1945 for Western Pennsylvania; 1950 and 1960 for Pittsburgh SMSA.

Source: Bureau of the Census, *Census of Population: 1940*, Volume III (Washington, D.C.: GPO, 1943), Part 38, 125–28; Bureau of the Census, *Census of the Population: 1950* (Washington, D.C.: GPO, 1952), Part 38, 370–76; Bureau of the Census, *Census of the Population: 1960* (Washington, D.C.: GPO, 1961), Part 40, 752–54, 869–74.

Table Five
Proportion of Black Males in Steel, 1940–1960

	Laborers	Operatives	Skilled	Overall
1940	13.6%	7.5%	1.5%	7.8%
1945	N/A	N/A	N/A	7.3%
1950	14.2%	7.1%	N/A	6.8%
1960	15.9%	8.2%	N/A	7.4%

Note: 1940 data for Pittsburgh city only; 1945 for Western Pennsylvania; 1950 and 1960 for Pittsburgh SMSA.

Source: Bureau of the Census, *Census of Population: 1940* (Washington, D.C.: GPO, 1943), Part 38, 125–28; 1945, Data for Western Pennsylvania, Districts 15, 16, 19 and 20; 13 February 1945 letter from Harold Ruttenberg to Stanley Granger, National Urban League, Box 1, file 1, Negro, Misc., 1945–1946, CRD, USWA Archives; Bureau of the Census, *Census of Population: 1950* (Washington, D.C.: GPO, 1952), Part 38, 370–76; Bureau of the Census, *Census of Population: 1960* (Washington, D.C.: GPO, 1961), Part 40, 1141–75.

Table Six
Occupational Composition of Steel Workforce, by Race

WHITES				
	Unskilled	Semi-Skilled	Skilled	Non-Specified
1940	40.2%	18.0%	21.9%	19.9%
1950	28.4%	18.9%	N/A	52.7%
1960	24.9%	16.8%	N/A	58.3%

BLACKS				
	Unskilled	Semi-Skilled	Skilled	Non-Specified
1940	71.6%	17.8%	4.3%	6.3%
1950	57.8%	18.6%	N/A	23.6%
1960	50.0%	17.3%	N/A	32.7%

Note: 1940 data for Pittsburgh city only, other data for Pittsburgh SMSA.

Source: Bureau of the Census, *Census of Population: 1940* (Washington, D.C.: GPO, 1943), Part 38, 125–28; Bureau of the Census, *Census of Population: 1950* (Washington, D.C.: GPO, 1952), Part 38, 370–76; Bureau of the Census, *Census of Population: 1960* (Washington, D.C.: GPO, 1961), Part 40, 1141–75.

Table Seven
Occupational Composition of Pittsburgh's
Blue-Collar Workforce in Steel, 1940–1960

	Laborers	Operatives	Craft/Foremen
1940	29.9%	41.6%	28.6%
1950	32.3%	32.7%	34.9%
1960	27.5%	32.2%	40.3%

Note: These figures exclude all clerical, technical, supervisory, and managerial positions.

Source: Bureau of the Census, *Census of Population: 1940* (Washington, D.C.: GPO, 1943), Part 38, 125–27; Bureau of the Census, *Census of Population: 1950* (Washington, D.C.: GPO, 1952), Part 38, 487–88; Bureau of the Census, *Census of Population: 1960* (Washington, D.C.: GPO, 1961), Part 40, 869–72.

Chapter Four

The Road to Deindustrialization: Pittsburgh and the Steel Industry 1960–1977

"To our soldiers out tonight in the jungles of Vietnam, it [the 1965 contract between steel companies and the USWA] means a continued uninterrupted flow of goods . . . The steel industry is a great industry. It has raised great cities. It has brought forth abundance beyond belief. It has forged the weapons of war and the products of peace. Its achievements are the marvel and the mode of the world."

Lyndon Baines Johnson, 1965.[1]

INTRODUCTION:
THE UNRAVELING OF THE AMERICAN CENTURY

At the dawn of the 1960s, the third decade of the "American Century," the United States enjoyed widespread influence over the course of world events. Its political and military alliances spanned the globe, and its industries accumulated healthy surpluses with its trading partners. The U.S. industrial economy provided its owners with considerable profits and many of its workers with a rising standard of living. In addition to moderating the bitter class struggles of the past, and creating a more comfortable way of life for more and more citizens, the "American way of life" was an effective propaganda weapon in the global and domestic struggle against communism. But by the mid-1970s, the American dream had faded as the bill for thirty years of military Keynesianism came due. Despite the most advanced military in the world, the United States suffered a major defeat in Vietnam, and its economy reeled as it absorbed the cost of that war.

Furthermore, the nation's manufacturing base contracted as shoe, textile, steel, and automobile companies—and others outside the "military-industrial complex"—confronted more efficient competitors abroad. American workers' real wages began to decline, and industrial plants began to close. Trade surpluses vanished, and the value of the U.S. dollar fell. The rising price of oil compounded America's economic malaise by fueling serious inflation.[2]

Pittsburgh's steel industry exemplified both the decline of America's industrial strength and the endurance of the American dream. Although eclipsed by Chicago as the largest steel-making district, the Pittsburgh area remained one of the most industrialized regions in the world. Many of its mills produced goods for the military, providing jobs and pride for many workers. When Michael Cimino sought to show the effects of the Vietnam War on the "silent majority," he situated *The Deerhunter* (1977) in a declining Pennsylvania steel town. The movie depicted three young steelworkers-turned-warriors whose unstinting sacrifices were ignored by their country, but not by their community. Cimino's cinematic version of reality ignored the fact that many workers had already begun to quietly criticize the war as a "poor man's fight."[3] The movie also ignored the experiences of black steelworkers and the fact that the mills were on the verge of closing down. The United Steel Workers of America (USWA) continued to enable its members to enjoy a rising standard of living. Yet the union failed to confront either the deterioration of the mills or the discrimination that its owners engendered. The 1960s and 1970s also proved a turbulent time for steel and steelworkers. As in the 1950s, steelworkers fought and won many battles, but the owners of big steel fought for their interests with greater clarity, ruthlessness, and resources than the USWA.

THE CRISIS OF BIG STEEL

During the 1960s, large steel companies confronted increasing competition.[4] After the 116-day strike in 1959, steel imports outstripped exports for the first time since World War II.[5] But imports were just one symptom of a larger malaise. By 1961, the nation's mills were operating at just 39 percent of capacity, their lowest operating rate since 1938. And while steel output soon doubled, big steel steadily lost market share to small domestic steel producers and to glass, plastics, and aluminum.[6] Steel's profits, while still a healthy 8 percent, had begun to fall lower than those of the manufacturing sector.[7] By 1973, steel companies produced record amounts of steel, but profits per sales dollar plummeted to a third of their levels of the 1950s.[8] Steel managers discovered a series of simple solutions to bolster their bottom line—increase prices, lobby for protective tariffs, and seek a greater share of American military spending and foreign aid. The only problem was that none of these "solutions" fundamentally altered the structural forces impinging upon steel.

Big steel's first impulse was to raise prices. In the negotiations over the 1961 contract, Roger Blough, President of U.S. Steel, met with President John F. Kennedy and union President David McDonald, and proposed not to raise prices if the union would settle for a modest wage increase. The union came to an agreement where wage increases roughly equaled the rise in productivity; but a few days after the agreement, Blough announced a price hike. Outraged, Kennedy used the threat of anti-trust lawsuits to force the steel company to back down, quipping, "my father always told me that business men were sons of bitches, but I never believed it till now."[9] Throughout the mid-1960s, other steel companies continued to follow U.S. Steel's lead in raising prices, and seven times between 1962 and 1964 the Justice Department indicted the largest steel firms for price-fixing.[10] The government also threatened to withdraw defense contracts from steel firms. In 1962, a German contractor was awarded a contract for three thousand five hundred tons of armor plate, and a few hundred men were thrown out of work at U.S. Steel's Homestead Works. Only after the intervention of the USWA and Congressman Elmer Holland (D-PA) and Senator Hugh Scott (R-PA) did the navy agree to return to its "buy American" policy.[11] While government lost this round of negotiations, big steel had entered a new era where "jawboning" had acquired some teeth.[12]

Steel companies' appeals for protection fell largely on deaf ears. According to steel executives, imports imperiled "the growth of our own steel industry at a time when America is called upon to defend world peace and the integrity of smaller nations around the globe."[13] But appeals to patriotism or anti-communism failed to sway policy makers from continuing to lower tariffs, and the "great flood of steel imports" continued unabated. Republican steel executives found themselves in the ironic position of requesting that President Kennedy revert to a New Deal policy, abandoned by President Dwight Eisenhower, that permitted the government to buy foreign steel only when it was 25 percent cheaper than American products.[14] Kennedy refused. Similarly, steel's managers sought stricter enforcement of New Deal laws that prohibited dumping goods onto the U.S. market. As U.S. Steel's Roger

Blough explained, "It's unfair competition when steel is sold for much less than the same producer is charging his own native land for the steel." The USWA blamed imports for the loss of thirty-seven thousand jobs, and supported the employers' case. But in 1963, the U.S. Tariff Commission ruled that European and Japanese producers could continue to enter the United States unimpeded.[15]

Steel companies fared little better under subsequent Presidents. During one negotiation session between steel firms and the USWA, steel firms proposed a price raise that President Lyndon Johnson viewed as inflationary. He told the President of U.S. Steel to "tell those nickel bending bastards [on his board of directors] that if they try to bend that nickel on Lyndon Baines Johnson, I'll jam that nickel up their asses in more ways than they can count."[16] In July 1965, U.S. Steel and other large firms pleaded "no contest" to violations of the Sherman Antitrust Act by fixing prices between 1948 and 1961. They were fined a symbolic amount, about $50,000 each.[17] However, the federal government continually sought to lower steel prices, and in 1966, U.S. Steel reversed an announced price increase of structurals after the government threatened to buy from other companies at the "lowest possible price."[18] Such sparring over price hikes ended only when the government refused to buy big steel's products and steel companies moderated their price hikes.[19] When Republican Richard M. Nixon became President, his administration also continued to prevent steel companies from circumventing the market. In 1969, the Justice Department forced U.S. Steel to end its "reciprocating agreements" with suppliers that required each to only buy each other's products.[20] Neither Democratic nor Republican Presidents provided big steel with a painless solution to its declining profitability.

The high prices of American steel attracted more and more imports.[21] In the early 1960s, imports accounted for less than 5 percent of the American steel market, but by 1966 they had doubled.[22] By 1968, foreign producers had seized 17 percent of the U.S. market and would have captured more had steel companies not convinced the federal government to negotiate the Voluntary Restraint Agreement (VRA), which froze imports at roughly 15 percent. Government had achieved its goal of moderating steel prices because imports tempered American steel companies' ability to unilaterally raise their prices. From steel companies' perspective, the VRA possessed faulty "trigger mechanisms," and it failed to cover Canadian and British steel. Nonetheless, the VRA allowed the steel companies to catch their breath and indicated that while the political influence of big steel had waned, it was far from dead.[23]

Throughout the 1960s, steel companies continued to wring profits from their political connections. A case in point was the Vietnam War and the massive economic and military aid packages that the federal government provided to South Vietnam. In 1966, one Democratic Senator from a steel state objected that aid projects for Southeast Asia relied in part on Japanese-made steel.[24] Ultimately, the Senate amended the appropriations bill for Vietnam with a clause that required the government to buy American steel unless "excessive" costs prevented it.[25] A similar measure ensured that 90 percent of the steel used in foreign aid projects was made in the United States.[26] By 1966, 6 percent of American steel production went to Vietnam.[27] (As one steelworker observed, "I don't know if they made all the bombs for the Vietnam war [in the Christy Park Works] but boy they sure made a heck of a lot of them.")[28] Yet federal subsidies for investment or research and development in steel remained relatively modest.[29] At the same time, various European and Asian governments actively promoted the modernization of steel firms—many of whom were owned in part or total by the state.[30] Moreover, for domestic projects, the U.S. government increasingly relied on cheaper foreign-made steel, and steel companies and the USWA pressured state governments to buy American steel for their construction projects.[31] In Pennsylvania, legislators acceded to the unholy alliance of steel companies and unions, but the Republican Governor succumbed to federal pressure and vetoed the measure.[32] As the protected markets for American steel contracted, Pittsburgh's aging mills became increasingly vulnerable.

THE "MODERNIZATION" OF THE MON VALLEY

In an increasingly competitive marketplace, steel companies proved to be their own worst enemies. Their legacy of enormous profits and power reinforced a notoriously conservative corporate culture. One former U.S. Steel manager described the company's management style as "inbred" because supervisors believed that "the only way to do things was the way we did things."[33] Steel companies continued to spend half as much on research as the nonferrous metal industry and only one-seventh the amount of the machinery industry.[34] U.S. Steel maintained that with $4 billion invested in open hearth technology, and modern furnaces that cost $30 to $40 million apiece, the only prudent path of modernization was a slow one.[35] Apparently the high councils of U.S. Steel heeded the stated investment philosophy of Andrew Carnegie ("pioneering don't pay"), rather than the many times he boldly embraced new technology in order to conquer his competitors.[36] The result, as one manager at a major steel company lamented, was that "we were making evolutionary changes when a technological revolution was going on."[37] Consequently, foreign steelmakers perfected the major technological innovations such as the Basic Oxygen Process (BOP), which produced steel faster than open hearths while requiring fewer men and less energy.[38] Not surprisingly, the productivity of foreign steelmakers began to catch up with American producers.

Without adequate investment, Pittsburgh's aging mills were doomed. In the early 1960s, U.S. Steel shuttered its open hearth departments in the Donora and Clairton Works.[39] By 1964, imports accounted for half of the American market for nails, and U.S. Steel closed the door on its nail mill in Donora.[40] In 1966, James & Laughlin (J&L) abandoned the nail-making business after 113 years and closed the nail-related facilities of the Aliquippa Works.[41] The Edgar Thomson Works, or ET, which began as a rail mill, was devastated by the decline of the railroads. The mill only ran full out when a surge of orders made it profitable, and in 1966, ET stopped producing steel rails altogether.[42] Only an aggressive modernization campaign by U.S. Steel could save its mills, yet according to a Bureau of Labor Statistics survey, big steel's investment per worker dropped 6 percent a year from 1966 to 1972.[43] Indeed, steel investment fell sharply after the 1969 VRA; import protections provided companies with a means to bolster profitability, not reinvest.[44]

Yet throughout the 1960s, U.S. Steel executives solemnly proclaimed that the modernization of its mills was well under way.[45] One such "success story" was the Duquesne Works. In 1962, Duquesne's Dorothy Six Blast Furnace came on line. Dorothy was one of the largest iron furnaces in the industry and the most technologically advanced, with some of the first computers used to monitor the production process. The next year, the Corporation built one of its first BOP furnaces at Duquesne (known locally as "the BOP Shop").[46] Duquesne still bled jobs but at a slower pace. Part of the price for Duquesne's "salvation" was a death sentence for the furnaces at National Tube across the river in McKeesport. Following Duquesne's modernization, several hundred furnace workers in McKeesport were gradually terminated.[47] In the long run, Duquesne fell victim to the Corporation's policy of investment triage, and it was closed down in 1984.[48]

Throughout the late 1960s, big steel continued its selective modernization campaign. The main thrust of investment was in Chicago, closer to growing metal markets. For instance, J&L concentrated the lion's share of its modernization efforts in the 1960s in Cleveland, Ohio and Hennepin, Illinois, thereby sealing the fate of its mill on Pittsburgh's Southside.[49] In 1963, Pennsylvania eagerly augmented its tax policies (which already exempted industrial machinery from taxation) to allow companies to deduct new investment from state taxes. Such inducements helped convince U.S. Steel to invest $100 million in Irvin Works in 1966.[50] In 1967, the company invested $100 million in the chemical-making division of the Clairton Works.[51] In 1968, U.S. Steel began the lengthy process of modernizing ET's furnaces and rolling mills.[52] ET's BOP furnaces helped place the company slightly ahead of its European competitors, but well behind the Japanese.[53] The importance of such modernization proved critical. Only those mills that received substantial investments after the late 1960s (Irvin, Clairton, and ET) survived in some form into the 1980s. However, the Corporation was robbing Peter (e.g., the Homestead Works whose furnaces remained outmoded) to pay for Paul (ET).[54] In any case, the public subsidy of private investment proved so successful that U.S. Steel paid no Pennsylvania taxes for both 1966 and 1967, even as its payrolls shrank.[55]

Steel companies also invested a substantial amount of their capital into non-steel ventures. In the 1950s and 1960s, the Corporation invested "in excess of $1 billion" in the extraction and refinement of iron ore throughout the world, and by the 1970s, the company invested half of its new capital into non-steel ventures.[56] As early as 1970, the company reported that "between 15 and 25 per cent" of its revenues derived from real estate, concrete, and chemicals.[57] As U.S. Steel diversified its holdings, other conglomerates bought steel firms whose enormous cash reserves and low profit rates made them attractive acquisitions. Thus in 1969, Ling-Temco-Vaught Corporation (LTV) bought J&L and siphoned off most of its enormous cash flows. The net result of being turned into a cash cow ultimately starved J&L's mills of the capital they needed for modernization and survival.[58] The lack of investment was so pervasive that when Allegheny Ludlum spent $50 million on its mill in Brackenridge, the *Pittsburgh Post Gazette* called it a "welcome sign of confidence in the Pittsburgh region."[59] Steel

companies' disinvestment from steelmaking proved a national phenomenon. Mike Davis has shown how Kaiser Steel, rather than investing in its
Fontana, California, facility, invested in supplying the Japanese with iron
ore and coal. In the 1970s, after Kaiser "allow[ed] its own industrial plant
to become obsolete," Fontana could no longer compete with the more
modern Japanese mills that Kaiser supplied with raw materials.[60] The logic
of market economics led steel companies to eschew investments in steel
and indeed to supply their competitors with raw materials.

   But despite big steel's strategy of disinvestment, many observers and
middle-class Pittsburghers faulted the "greed" of unionized workers for
destroying the industry. In popular parlance, the union killed the goose that
laid the golden eggs.[61] Without question, relatively high American labor
costs disadvantaged American companies vis-à-vis their foreign competitors, although workers' wages in the 1960s only kept pace with inflation.
(Over the decade, improved benefits raised steel's labor costs by a third.)[62]
Yet even in the 1970s, American labor and environmental costs rose no
faster than in Japan.[63] Critically, productivity advances failed to keep pace
with producers abroad. In 1964, American mills used roughly half as much
labor (measured by man-hours per ton at actual operating rates) to produce
a ton of steel as in Germany or Japan. In the next eight years, American
productivity improved just 20 percent while the West German steel industry improved its productivity by 45 percent and Japan by 60 percent. As
late as 1972, American firms still produced steel more efficiently than foreign competitors, on average. But in the next eight years, American productivity improved by less than 3 percent while West Germany's industry
improved by 28 percent and the Japanese by 56 percent.[64] Stagnant American investment resulted in stagnant American productivity growth, and
ultimately contributed to the shuttered mills in the late 1970s.

   Available plant data reveal that by the late 1960s, U.S. Steel had
already abandoned some of its Mon Valley mills. At Duquesne, the Corporation's highest levels of investment came in 1963, when the company disclosed that it spent $24 million to finish its BOP shop. In 1969 and 1970, the
last available dates for this mill, the company invested nothing. In the 1960s,
the Duquesne Works cut 15 percent of its workforce and paid out between
$34 million and $41 million in wages while the value added ranged between
$76 million and $147 million. A similar pattern prevailed at Homestead.
Employment fluctuated throughout the 1960s, and the company's total wage
bill ranged from $58 million to $70 million. In the 1970s, wages doubled

over 1960s levels and ranged between $130 million and $143 million. However, with minimal new investment, the value added trebled from $63 million in 1962 to $207 million in 1977. Although the higher wages of steel-workers—and their success in retaining many workers' jobs—undoubtedly cut into the profits of U.S. Steel, its bottom line (at least as can be ascertained from this data) actually improved in the 1970s.[65] But without substantial reinvestment, these levels of profits could not be sustained. In the face of more efficient producers in the U.S. and around the world, U.S. Steel apparently decided to throw Homestead and Duquesne to the wolves.

In the early 1970s, big steel paid a premium for labor peace, so it could modernize some mills and allow others to die. Steelmakers believed consumers bought imported steel primarily as a hedge in case contract negotiations with the USWA ended in a strike. As a result, before each contract expired, steel mills ran full out and then after the contracts were signed, the mills shut down until customers exhausted their supplies.[66] Steel companies believed that demand for steel would explode in the 1970s, so in 1973 companies signed the Experimental Negotiating Agreement (ENA) with the union. In exchange for a national no-strike clause even after the contract expired (in favor of arbitration) unionized workers were guaranteed a 3 percent annual wage increase plus cost of living adjustments. Ray Anderson, the President of the Homestead local, observed that "I'm no dove, but I've seen a lot of people laid off in the last three years and I'm more than willing to give this plan a try."[67] While locals were allowed to call strikes over local grievances, such "peace in the valley" was supposed to have turned the 1970s into steel's "golden years."[68] Events proved both the union and management wrong.

After 1973, steel markets went into steep decline. Steel firms had hoped to recapture markets lost to plastic, aluminum, and glass, but in the face of rising gasoline prices, auto manufacturers aggressively replaced steel with lighter materials.[69] Big steel companies lost additional market share in wire rod, bar, and light structurals to domestic mini-mills that used non-union labor and ultra-modern furnaces. By the late 1970s, mini-mills produced between 30 percent and 90 percent of the rods, bars, and light structurals.[70] Further pressure came as imports surged to 20 percent of the market.[71] With the urban infrastructure and interstate highway system largely complete, Bethlehem closed its fabricating division (bridges and skyscrapers) in 1975, and U.S. Steel's American Bridge Company followed it in 1984.[72] Yet the return of relatively high profits in some years led punch-drunk companies into the belief that each year would bring a reversal of fortune. Big steel only abandoned the ENA in the early 1980s.[73] By 1986, steel companies had closed major mills in Homestead, Duquesne, McKeesport, Aliquippa, and Pittsburgh, throwing the vast majority of the Pittsburgh region's steel-workers onto the street.

STEELWORKERS' STRUGGLE FOR SECURITY

The steel industry's reentry to the free market, admittedly one filled with better-subsidized private firms or state-owned concerns, wrought disastrous results. While few analysts in the early 1960s could have predicted that the extent to which the industry would bleed, trade unionists would have predicted whose blood would flow. Even at the onset of the "booming" 1960s, steelworkers confronted a lengthy recession and layoffs compounded by automation and imports. Between 1959 and 1962, steel companies through-out the country reduced their payrolls by one-fifth.[74] On the shop floor and at the bargaining table, trade unionists maintained their struggles against steel companies for a measure of security and higher wages. In terms of jobs, they held their ground tenaciously, and gained better wages and bene-fits with each contract. But holding the line at the bargaining table required a shift in political tactics for the union. Amidst Democratic victories in the early 1960s, the USWA helped ensure passage of federal legislation on questions of unemployment, civil rights, and social security. Yet the union also increasingly supported its employers' quest for tax credits and protec-tion from foreign competition. The union's shift in emphasis from union's political cooperation with managers helped some of its members hold onto their jobs, at least for a while, but it failed to restrain management's cease-less efforts for greater efficiency at workers' expense.

When the 1960s began, the issue of crew sizes and work rules remained unresolved. The USWA ended its 116-day strike in January 1960, and while it defeated the companies' attempts to eliminate Section 2-B from the national contract, the union agreed to send the issue of work rules to a special joint committee: the Human Relations Committee (HRC). The HRC never amounted to much; in fact, on the date that it was supposed to have issued its final report, it had not yet agreed upon a chairman.[75] Steel companies were happy to talk about Section 2-B, but on every other matter, the union found it "got a lot of talk."[76] David McDonald, President of the USWA, recalled that the HRC "never came to grips with the problem [of work rules and overmanning] at the plant level" because managers wanted to protect their power, which derived from the number of workers they supervised.[77] Although some observers such as John Hoerr and John Strohmeyer portrayed the union as adamant in its protection of past practices, it was in fact willing to exchange Section 2-B for more control over incentives or protection against new technology. That is because, according to the contract, "the Company shall have the right to change or eliminate any local working condition if . . . the basis for the existence of the local working condition is changed or eliminated"; new technology invariably changed the basis for local working conditions.[78] That is why in a secret report to union members of the HRC, the USWA explained that abandoning Section 2-B would indeed be wise as "arbitrators are handing down decisions that virtually eliminate the protection of crew sizes and rearrangement of work duties in all areas outside of crafts."[79] However, management refused to commit to any tradeoff, and the issue of crew sizes and workrules was thrown back to the mills. Here compromise proved even less likely, and workers and managers merely returned to the grueling "war of position" that led to the 1959 strike and the HRC in the first place.

Workers had little incentive to compromise, as throughout the early 1960s they confronted massive unemployment, and the threat only grew if they gave ground on work rules. Each mill had its own particular causes for hard times—either the machinery was too old or too modern—but everywhere steelworkers faced the reality or the prospect of long-term layoffs. By 1961, two-thirds of the six thousand steelworkers at the aging Clairton Works experienced temporary layoffs; but many feared that they would never work again.[80] In April 1960, Homestead shut down its Open Hearth Number 4 or OH 4, and furloughed five hundred men. U.S. Steel did not reopen that facility for three years.[81] All steel at Homestead was now produced at OH 5, a "modern" complex of open hearths built in 1943 and updated in the 1950s with oxygen lances that sped production.[82] In June of 1962, over six hundred remained laid off.[83] By June 1963, that figure was one thousand. Barney Shields, the head of the grievance committee, was pessimistic: "if we get 800 back, we'll be lucky. When things level off, they never level off where they were before."[84] Indeed, it was 1965 before employment at Homestead returned to the levels of the late 1950s.[85] The situation was no better at J&L; as Nick Mamula quipped, "automation comes in the front door and the steelworkers go out the back door!" When Mamula visited the newly automated 44 Inch Strip Mill in J&L's Southside Works, he remarked that the new facility was virtually empty of workers, and its few rollers did not work on the floor but sat in air conditioned cages, with their eyes "glued to the television screens."[86]

For their part, managers continued to discipline workers with one of the most powerful weapons in their arsenal, the ability to control workers' access to jobs. Supervisors contracted out the construction of new facilities and the routine maintenance of existing machines. This incensed unionists, who objected to the fact that many maintenance workers remained on short shifts while hundreds of "free lancers" (generally unionized contractors) worked in the plant. One management-union survey found that in the 1960s, contracting out cost large locals at least two hundred jobs a year.[87] Robert McClure, the Superintendent of the Homestead Works, defended the use of contractors in the language of pure power, telling unionists that "we have contracted in the past. We will contract in the future. This is our plant to operate as we see fit."[88] Although Homestead's maintenance workers convinced an arbitrator that they deserved compensation when management contracted out "their work" when they were laid off, workers still had to prove they were directly injured before they could be awarded back pay. Three years later, the union admitted it "had a very difficult assignment trying to pinpoint these situations." No back pay was ever remitted.[89]

Over the next decade, contracting out intensified. Management's refusal to negotiate on the matter contributed to Homestead's craft workers picketing U.S. Steel headquarters in 1970, demanding an end to contracting out when so many in the mill did not have full-time work.[90] While managers came out to listen to workers' concerns, the company later decried their "illegal picketing" and noted that "economic conditions dictate the necessity for curtailing employment . . . the company is as anxious as the men to return to full employment."[91] Proclamations of "shared sacrifice" aside, by the end of the 1970s, management admitted that contracting out had risen by at least 50 percent.[92]

New technology afforded managers another means to wrest additional concessions from unionists. For instance, the computerized blast furnace at the Duquesne Works (Dorothy Six) allowed management to replace a full crew of twenty-seven men with seven workers. Furthermore, the company won its demand that "old-timers" would not maintain the computerized furnace. The union agreed that supervisors could choose two new motor inspectors in the blast furnace if supervisors would recall three laid-off men. Although the union had made the deal, it did not sit well with workers in the blast furnace. One of the new maintenance workers, the first new hire in eighteen years, Mike Bilsic, recalled that "nobody talked to me for quite a while, they gave me the cold shoulder."[93] While employment ultimately leveled out, it did so at lower levels than before. In 1968, William Petrisko, President of Duquesne Local 1256, complained that since the 1950s, "our mill has gone from 7,000 men to 4,000, and I've been floating around the mill in a labor pool like a Gypsy."[94]

Growing structural unemployment pushed the USWA to try to achieve greater job and financial security for its members. According to President McDonald, the union sought to give steelworkers "total job security, patterned . . . on the Japanese plan that guarantees a job for life."[95] What the USWA actually won was contract language that allowed laid-off workers with enough seniority to transfer into new jobs in that mill or elsewhere in the company. However, one management survey found that most of the 300 workers from Donora and Clairton who had found jobs at the Irvin Works under this program had been laid off and many would eventually lose their new jobs.[96] The USWA found that almost 4,400 workers at U.S. Steel requested a transfer, but only 400 received it. Furthermore, if workers transferred out of their district (e.g, from Pittsburgh to Chicago), they risked losing all of their departmental and plant seniority.[97] In some instances, such contractual protections worked well enough. In 1965, U.S. Steel replaced Duquesne's twelve-furnace open hearth department with a BOP shop. It rehired 220 of the 250 workers it had displaced, although many of them earned lower wages than before.[98] Affected furnace workers at National Tube proved less fortunate. A hundred displaced men relocated to other mills, about 200 men entered the labor pool, and 300 workers were laid off.[99] (U.S. Steel claimed that its National Tube Works was not shut down, but was merely on standby.)[100] Anthony Cerino, who worked at National Tube, remained skeptical that he would ever work again. As he put it, "the Donora plant shutdown was also 'temporary,' and 4,000 men never went back to work."[101]

In the face of eroding job security, the union bolstered its members' financial security by increasing their pensions. In the 1965 negotiations, the USWA forced the companies to increase pensions so that workers over sixty-five received at least $5 a month times their number of years of service. Four years later, pensions improved by 30 percent, and for the first time, surviving spouses of pensioners obtained rights to half of their partners' pensions.[102] Yet even improved pensions left retirees at the poverty level and enticed few into retirement. Most steelworkers relied on pensions as a kind of "displacement insurance."[103] For instance, of the several hundred men laid off at National Tube in the 1960s, only twenty to twenty-five workers retired. One of them was Leonard Pocuinas, who at fifty-one earned about $160 a month—hardly an extravagant amount, though almost twice the pension of his father who had put in fifty-two years in the mill.[104] Pensions steadily improved; by 1974, a worker with thirty years would receive $350 monthly.[105] Combined with Social Security, most retired steelworkers enjoyed an income that enabled them to meet the federal government's minimum budget for elders.[106] Nonetheless, many Pennsylvania steelworkers agreed with a Chicago steelworker who angrily observed that "twenty million people in this country are on the rag heap because of the pensions in this country. My dad, who's 74 now, spent 37 years in steel. That company used him up. But he gets $260 a month to live on. He can't even slip his son a fiver like a father wants to. Listen, our local gives pensioners picnics. If you watch close when they put out the sweet rolls, the old guys always take an extra one for tomorrow. We should be fucking ashamed."[107]

The USWA won ground on achieving the old union goal of a shorter work week without loss of pay.[108] In 1963 the union won a plan that gave half of all steelworkers a thirteen-week vacation once every five years.[109] Union officials argued that the vacation plan cut the work week of senior steelworkers by an average of two hours per week on top of the three hours a week of paid holidays and vacations.[110] President McDonald expected this vacation plan to create twenty thousand to twenty-five thousand new jobs, but most companies decided it cost less to offer more overtime to their existing workforce (including those men "on vacation") rather than hire new workers.[111] The thirteen-week vacations, while enjoyed by those who received them, created few new jobs. As one worker observed, the company was "working them double shifts instead of hiring new men.[112]

As in the 1950s, steelworkers lost numerous jobs as a result of the incentives that the steel industry extended to workers who met production targets. Incentives proved highly successful in increasing output without adding new workers, particularly in older departments where workers had learned to coax more production out of familiar equipment. At the Duquesne Works in the early 1960s, managers convinced workers at the Number 4 Blast Furnace to increase the number of casts from five to six a turn without adding a man to their crew.[113] Incentives remained a touchy issue, especially for many workers who remained ineligible for bonuses or received less than men in other departments or mills. In 1965, *Business Week* quoted one high-ranking steel executive who said, "the two biggest things involved in the present negotiations are the redesigning of jobs and the building of a new incentive system within the framework of our new technology."[114] Accumulating dissatisfaction with the inequalities in the system of incentive pay almost led to a national strike in 1968, and the union won a victory in 1969 when an arbitrator ruled that big steel firms had to have at least 85 percent of their employees covered by incentive programs.[115] The USWA negotiated with U.S. Steel for over a year on the issue before, like with workrules several years previously, it threw the problem back to the locals.[116] Also in 1969, the USWA re-negotiated its supplement unemployment benefits (SUB) so that steelworkers received up to 85 percent of their average pay if they were demoted or laid off by new technology. (Workers could draw from the fund indefinitely—or more likely, until it was depleted by mass unemployment.) Managers viewed the "Earnings Protection Plan" as a way to "cool down the workers' militancy" and head off another major strike.[117] Although the union won important victories on incentives, it fought for gains within a system that worked to management's strategic advantage.

Perhaps because so many production workers lost jobs to automation and incentives, many craft workers stiffened their resistance when managers attempted to dilute their job descriptions. In 1967, the district negotiator for U.S. Steel observed that "carpenters and bricklayers were always complaining when any other employees handled lumber or bricks."[118] Long experience taught the members of steel's skilled trades that job dilution led to job loss. As a result, many workers extended solidarity to craft workers by refusing to work outside of their job descriptions. Carl Denne, a pipefitter and then a foreman at the Duquesne Works, recalled how the ethos of "each craft did their own work" frustrated management. In 1970, management attempted to form a "bull gang" who would work across craft lines on simple jobs; however, even production workers refused to perform obvious repairs and waited for craft workers to complete "their own work."[119] Of course, in the face of constant managerial pressure, other workers folded. Another Duquesne worker recalled that when he urged workers to stand up for their rights under the contract, "lo and behold, the guys started sticking together." However, he was then fired, albeit ultimately rehired, and "that scared the rest of them so nobody else went by the contract. They went by what the company wanted them to do."[120] Even at the height of union power, building solidarity was tough work.

NEW DEAL POLITICS IN DECLINE

As in previous decades, the USWA mobilized its members politically to shore up its strength on the shop floor. According to its top leaders, the strategy worked. David McDonald observed that after the "the Kennedy-Blough confrontation . . . the right man was in the White House, doing all the right things. . . . [M]y steelworkers were the highest paid, most secure industrial employees in the history of the world."[121] While McDonald overstated the job security of his members, the political influence of the USWA within the Democratic Party remained considerable. Kennedy chose Arthur Goldberg, chief counsel for the USWA, as his Secretary of Labor and later appointed him to the Supreme Court.[122] Kennedy's successor, Lyndon Johnson, also helped the union to negotiate two major contracts with steel companies. But while Democratic Presidents aided the union, they also forced the union to moderate its demands in order to dampen inflation.[123]

Although the union maintained forward momentum in its contract negotiations, the tide was slowly running out on the New Deal. The union's alliance with the Democratic Party remained strong enough to pass unemployment legislation, but too weak to make it meaningful. In the early 1960s, the USWA worked with its close political ally, Congressman Holland, and passed a job-training bill which helped some redundant workers find new jobs.[124] For instance, when a foundry shut down in Blawnox, Pennsylvania, a third of the workers received retraining and ultimately new jobs.[125] However, many steelworkers failed to find jobs with comparable pay and benefits. Joe Lichman, a laid-off worker with thirty-eight years at National Tube, was fifty-four. As such he was too young to die and too young to retire. Lichman believed that teaching "the worker who is obsolete to repair appliances in an age where it is cheaper to discard such appliances and buy new ones is a questionable undertaking."[126] Similarly, in 1962, Congress passed the Trade Expansion Act that enabled workers who lost their jobs due to imports to receive up to 65 percent of their previous wages for eighteen months. Yet the burden of proof rested on workers who had to prove to the U.S. Tariff Commission that imports accounted for more than half of the reason that their facility closed down. The first steelworkers to collect any benefits came only after the USWA's seven-year lawsuit on behalf of steelworkers in Pittsburgh and California.[127]

Furthermore, during the Kennedy-Johnson years, the Democratic Party began to reverse key aspects of the New Deal. Beginning with Kennedy,

Democrats lowered taxes on the wealthy (from 91 percent to 70 percent) and instituted a broad tax deferment policy for new investment that "helped the steel industry very directly," according to Lyndon Johnson.[128] In the short run, the Democrats shored up their electoral support and stimulated economic growth, but the party's slow retreat from progressive taxation meant the tax burden increasingly fell on workers' shoulders. (Court rulings from the 1930s barred Pennsylvania lawmakers from enacting progressive taxes on income, and Pennsylvania enacted a flat tax in 1971.)[129] Furthermore, while automated plants made American mills more productive and protected American jobs from imports, the number of jobs there were to protect steadily declined. Moreover, industrialists retained control over where to invest their capital and increasingly invested outside of Pittsburgh or indeed, outside of steel.[130]

Step by step, the USWA redefined its political agenda away from concerns with the working class as a whole towards a kind of bread-and-butter trade unionism that bolstered some of the interests of the steel industry. In terms of international affairs, the USWA echoed steel's pleas for tariff protection and its "buy American" programs. For instance, in 1965, David McDonald agreed with management on the need "to bring home to both [the union and the public] the importance of foreign competition."[131] The marriage of convenience between steel companies and unionists continued throughout the 1960s. The union staunchly supported the Vietnam War in spite of the fact that workers bore the brunt of its cost and its fighting. (By contrast, the UE soon opposed the Vietnam War, and disputes over the war bitterly divided liberals and social democrats within the United Auto Workers.)[132] Of course every union fought to preserve its workers' jobs, but the USWA adopted management's positions to a remarkable extent. For instance, when one Pittsburgh foundry closed down in 1969, the local union's president did not blame the company but the repeal of a federal tax deferment program for capital investment that allegedly dried up business.[133]

While the Democratic Party pursued its détente policy with the rich, steel's legacy of bitter class conflict precluded any reciprocity on the part of industrialists or the middle class. Steel companies continued to actively support the Republican Party, and its white-collar employees were regularly "maced" for contributions to the Republican Party.[134] Democratic support for steel's interests did little to stem U.S. Steel's opposition to the New Deal's programs (such as Social Security) or its political philosophy (such as progressive taxation and redistributive social programs). Corporate executives such as U.S. Steel's Roger Blough warned of the consequences of domestic "legis-lated labor costs." In 1976, his successor David Roderick warned that federal loans and tariff protections "would be a step towards ultimate nationali-zation." Generally, however, steel executives justified tax subsidies by citing the fact that they carried the banner of free enterprise against Communist and nationalized steel companies throughout the world.[135] For its part, the USWA continued to staunchly support the Democratic Party, but the union's untiring support of free trade and the free enterprise system in general pre-vented it from articulating a coherent critique of the Democrats, many of whom had begun to retreat from the New Deal.[136] The rise of conservatism constrained the political choices of the labor movement as a whole, although a few unions, notably the UAW and the UE, sought to open new political possibilities by vigorously supporting the civil rights movement and Stu-dents for a Democratic Society, in the case of the UAW, or the progressive movement more generally, in the case of the UE.[137]

Within Pittsburgh's house of labor, political alternatives remained scarce, a legacy of that region's strident anti-communism. The govern-ment's campaign against the Communist Party reduced it to a shadow of its former strength. By 1961, when federal legislation (the Internal Security or McCarran Act) required party members to register with the government as agents of a foreign government, all of Pittsburgh's communist leaders from the 1950s had died, moved from the region, or left the party.[138] Even after several years of growth in the 1960s, by 1973 the party claimed just one hundred members. Communists and independent radicals remained decidedly unwelcome within the USWA.[139] The USWA expelled Eugene Dennett from a Seattle local in the mid-1950s, and barred him from participation in the union until he retired in 1966, as much because he continued to combine trade unionism and radicalism as for his past membership in the CP (he was expelled from the Party in 1947).[140] The USWA also boycotted radical unions. Although the UE retained thousands of members in Western Penn-sylvania, the USWA shunned the union.

Political alternatives sporadically popped up from the USWA's grass-roots but remained isolated. For example, in the mid-1960s, trade unionists from McKeesport, Homestead, Clairton, and ET complained that the pri-mary federal programs for displaced steelworkers were variations on unem-ployment or poverty programs such as Food Stamps. In one meeting, trade unionists asked Congressman Holland to arrange federal subsidies for the steel industry akin to those for farmers.[141] Anthony Tomko, president of

Local 1408 (National Tube) took the logic a step further and proposed that the federal government should "have to buy up all the stocks of our industry . . . to satisfy the needs of our Labor Force and its people."[142] The leaders of the USWA viewed Tomko as a dangerous crank and never articulated such an ambitious plan. Yet British steelworkers, facing many of the same pressures, fought for and won the re-nationalization of their industry in 1967. (The Conservative Party had privatized the steel industry in 1953, but in 1967, the British Labor Party fulfilled its promise to put the steel industry back under public control.)[143] In Canada, trade unionists proved too weak to win the wages won by American workers, but in part due to the agitation of the New Democratic Party (the Canadian equivalent of a labor party), they proved politically powerful enough to help win universal health insurance for all citizens in the mid-1960s.[144] One reason for the political atrophy of the USWA lay in its internal union politics.

UNION POLITICS IN THE 1960S

In terms of USWA politics, Pittsburgh remained a bastion of both conformity and rebellion. Nagging unemployment and a top-down leadership that turned a blind eye to workplace problems and stolen elections made Pittsburgh a stronghold of the union's rebels.[145] Paul Hilbert observed that widespread unemployment in Pittsburgh contributed to the rise of "demagogues" such as in the Dues Protest Committee (DPC).[146] Yet the union's leadership was also based in Pittsburgh, and with their enormous power and scores of staff they generally isolated dissidents and disrupted their movements. Working to the advantage of the USWA's administration was the fact that anti-communism had sunk deeper roots in Pittsburgh's political culture than in Youngstown or Chicago, where networks of radicals and socialists often dominated the leadership of union locals or dissident movements.[147] While Pittsburgh's "labor priest" Charles Owen Rice abandoned his anti-communism for the civil rights and anti-war movements, many steelworkers remained steadfast to Rice's earlier passion.[148] In one typical instance, the president of Local 1397 at Homestead told workers that "anybody who votes for [Anthony] Tomko" against Paul Hilbert in the 1960 election for Director of District 15 "should go down to Cuba with Castro."[149] The persistent culture of red-baiting within the USWA helped prevent many rebels from becoming leftists.[150] When communists leafleted workers at the mills, several workers attacked them and only stopped when women handed out the leaflets.[151] One son of a steelworker recalled that when one of his father's co-workers called him a hippie, his father chased his accuser through the mill with a sledgehammer.[152]

Dissidents failed to build from their bases of support in the large locals such as National Tube, Aliquippa, and Irvin. At the 1960 national union convention, rebels were outvoted on every point by overwhelming majorities, and were roughed up and denounced by former confidants like Joseph Murray (the son of Philip Murray), who had promised to run as their vice presidential candidate.[153] As I.W. Abel recalled, "Dave [McDonald] was not above making deals and [many members of the union] were not above accepting them."[154] Nonetheless, one district director from the Pittsburgh region warned that "any illusion that any of us may have that the Dues Protest organization is disorganized is based on a false premise." Each director closely tracked the publications, networks, and political progress of the DPC in his region.[155] Fortunately for McDonald, the rebel's slate never made it on the national ballot, due to what the USWA IEB termed "irregularities" in the nomination process.[156]

After the convention, McDonald launched an offensive against the "bedbugs" that forced dissidents to fight to retain control of their local unions.[157] The USWA leadership placed the local at National Tube (Local 1408) under trusteeship, ostensibly for overspending its treasury during the 1959 strike. Other local unions had gone further into debt without requiring the USWA to run their internal affairs, but McDonald worried that this local was building a rival machine.[158] The unionists from Local 1408 appealed to the IEB but did not expect justice; it was simply "a formality we have to go through." Anthony Tomko, the former president of 1408, admitted that "we are all logical men, we know what this is . . . labor is no longer a bunch of hunkies that came over from the old country."[159] The USWA succeeded in temporarily defeating another rebel, Nicholas Mamula, who briefly lost control over Local 1211, which represented almost twenty thousand workers at J&L in Aliquippa.[160] In other locals, such as Homestead, rebels captured local offices, but by 1962 they were turned out of office.[161] By that point, even Donald Rarick (the 1957 Presidential candidate for the Dues Protest Committee or DPC) had lost control of Local 2227 in the Irvin Works.[162] Dissident politics failed to move beyond the locals and remained a loose affair based on personal contacts more than organization and ideology.[163]

Rebels failed to consolidate their base of power even when their nemesis, the McDonald administration, finally crumbled. In 1965, I.W. Abel,

McDonald's secretary-treasurer, ran for president and blamed McDonald for the "drift and destruction [that] have been growing within this union of ours." Abel promised to "return the union to its members," a message that enjoyed broad support among steelworkers.[164] In a palace coup (half of the union's district directors supported Abel), the "outsider" bested the incumbent. McDonald's supporters claimed that district directors and their staff had done "all they could to steal the election."[165] Although McDonald accused Abel of being a leader whose philosophy was "there goes the mob, I must lead them," reform from above failed to open the path for rebellion from below.[166] In District 15, Director Paul Hilbert faced Donald Rarick and two other challengers who accused him of ignoring the needs of workers in the face of automation, layoffs, and contracting out. Hilbert charged that members of I.W. Abel's "Rank and File Payroll Committee" bankrupted their locals while accusing national leaders of financial improprieties. Hilbert charged that John Hughey received two thousand eight hundred dollars a year; in fact, he served as an unpaid officer of his local. Rarick and other dissidents finally obtained an injunction to stop the handbills from circulating, arguing that in fact a number of Hilbert backers received salaries and expenses from the district. But despite the rebels' legal victory, and strong support for Abel throughout Pittsburgh, Hilbert's forces controlled the ballot boxes and carried the day.[167]

By 1969, reformers finally wrested control of District 15 from Hilbert. That year, Joe Odorcich and George Kutska, both staff men for District 15, and Coleman Conroy, the Financial Secretary of Local 1397, contested Hilbert's re-election. As in 1965, the dissident candidates promised to revitalize the union by involving its members and rooting out incompetence and corruption. Although Odorcich ended the race with a narrow lead, there were widespread reports of fraud, including one involving the switching of ballots at Homestead.[168] Amid rumors of a payoff, long-time dissident Anthony Tomko effectively switched his support to Hilbert when he allowed the ballots at National Tube to be disqualified because of alleged voting irregularities.[169] The International USWA declared Hilbert the winner. He then resigned and accepted another union post, and the USWA International Executive Board appointed Lester H. Thornton as temporary Director. Odorcich termed the move "the biggest steal since Jesse James," and the USWA's decision stirred up massive protest by Mon Valley unionists.[170] One unionist asked "how stupid do you think we are? We're not old-timers who you could bluff and kid. . . . we're going to get a government investigation."[171] After the

U.S. Department of Labor pressured the USWA, Odorcich eventually won the rematch held in 1970. While Odorcich cleaned up the worst abuses within the district, cynicism remained widespread and dissidents as disorganized as before.[172] When Odorcich faced an insurgent in the early 1970s, the contender cited numerous instances of alleged irregularities; as always, the IEB dismissed the charges against the incumbent.[173]

In the 1969 election for USWA president, rebels once again failed to capitalize on their widespread support. USWA President I.W. Abel was challenged by perennial rebel Rarick, who blamed him for the slow increases in wages of steelworkers throughout the 1960s. Rarick died before the election, and the mantle of protest was picked up by one of the USWA's lawyers: Emil Narick.[174] The fact that the rebels ran a staff lawyer for President rather than a rank-and-file steelworker indicated the degree of disorganization amongst "rank-and-filers." Black protest groups backed Abel, and Narick benefited from a growing backlash against civil rights among white workers.[175] Narick ran a surprisingly strong campaign, beating Abel two to one in Pittsburgh and collecting 40 percent of the national vote.[176] In the Homestead Works, Narick collected all but a handful of the votes.[177] But coming close in a national election did not improve the rebels' position, and the rank-and-file movements entered the 1970s as far from power as ever.

THE 1970S: GROWING MILITANCE

In the late 1960s and the early 1970s, the steel industry witnessed a resurgence of labor militance, particularly among younger workers. By 1969, at the peak of the Vietnam War, the steel industry had largely recovered from its doldrums. The President of the Irvin Works' local union observed that for the first time in "ten or twelve years . . . everybody who's been working here before has been called back."[178] Workers led a few wildcat strikes to protest poor working conditions. Another factor spurring militancy was that younger workers' pay did not rise as fast as their family obligations. Strikers even included white-collar workers at mills like J&L's Pittsburgh Works.[179] Spurring these strikes were tougher company policies on drug use, absenteeism, and poor workmanship. For instance, in four months in 1971, almost half of the eight hundred open hearth workers at the Homestead Works received discipline slips.[180] (In 1958, Duquesne gave out just under three hundred slips for the entire mill.)[181] Homestead's chief grievanceman told managers that workers "are so bitter about working conditions that they want to strike."[182] Companies also worried that workers' militance resulted not from legitimate grievances but from "literally hundreds of different organizations active in a subversive plot" to infiltrate the steel industry. According to management, radicals had infiltrated steel in order to "create unrest among our workers" and further their cause of "tearing down our democratic society." The danger signs that managers told foremen to look for, such as young workers who expressed interest in union politics or racial discrimination, indicate that at least in management's view, "normal" steelworkers had become extremely depoliticized.[183]

Workers responded to management's get-tough policies by electing younger and tougher-talking leaders in several local unions. In 1970, workers at J&L's Southside Works, the Aliquippa Works, and Homestead elected relatively young militants to lead their locals. Homestead's new president was Raymond Anderson, a thirty-two-year-old pipefitter who credited management's get-tough attitude regarding layoffs and discipline to his victory. Following his election, Anderson publicly announced that "if we had the right to strike, we'd have something the company would listen to. Now they're laughing at us." Anderson also advocated stronger support for civil rights and the union's black caucus. The *Wall Street Journal* observed that such talk, on top of the union's previous history of strikes, made managers nervous and helped convince them to embrace the ENA.[184]

But while the ENA put more money into workers' pockets, it failed to eradicate many tensions between workers and managers. Young workers often responded to their boring jobs and tough-nosed foremen by skipping work.[185] In the 1990s, after the mills had closed, many older workers emphasized that the poor work habits of younger workers helped to bankrupt the steel industry. One foreman recalled that "I'd get a report that two [workers] would be working, two sleeping . . . they'd be smoking pot, actually."[186] A few younger steelworkers agreed; one recollected that he didn't do anything in the mills except "sleep and marijuana . . . that's why there aren't no more steel mills."[187] Other workers agreed that many workers slept on the night shift, but wondered where management was when those incidents occurred.[188]

Much of workers' "laziness" was not a generational attribute but a variation on defensive shop-floor tactics designed to protect the jobs of other workers.[189] Many new workers recalled being told by full-time steelworkers to slow down the pace of their work.[190] Indeed, the widely held view that steelworkers didn't work very fast was accepted by a group of steelworkers interviewed by Staughton Lynd in the early 1970s. One worker noted that "many days I've worked two hours out of eight." An older worker remarked that no steelworker would admit the work pace was slow; "I know myself, I don't mind admitting how easy it is; but if my wife or somebody else starts to make a joke out of it, I get mad." Yet this group of workers agreed that without such tactics and the union's defense of work rules, many more workers would be laid off.[191] Yet while most workers agreed that these strategies saved jobs, some workers argued that they also limited workers' political vision. As one steelworker pointed out: "people are very defeatist in a lot of ways. . . . Everybody is trying to figure out their own little way to get out of it. I think that's good in a lot of ways. But it makes it harder to get together, and stick together, and really change things."[192]

FROM NEW LEFT TO THE SADLOWSKI CAMPAIGN: THE LEFT'S LAST HURRAH?

In the late 1960s, numerous movements tried to "really change things." Throughout the house of labor, rank-and-file movements challenged their leaders to return to "old-school" union politics. The case of the United Mine Workers was particularly dramatic. Miners in Pennsylvania and elsewhere in Appalachia organized to improve working conditions, press for legislation to aid disabled workers with black lung, and restore union democracy. Many miners supported the Pittsburgh-based Jock Yoblonski, who ran for President of the UMWA in 1969. However, the UMWA's President Tony Boyle ordered Yoblonski murdered, and Boyle was ultimately removed from office and convicted for murder.[193] In some cases, reform movements intersected with the New Left, many of whom abandoned campus radicalism and set out to organize amongst the working class. To paraphrase one Detroit organization: One class conscious worker is worth a thousand radical students. Just as in the early days of the Communist Party, left-wing parties sent organizers into basic industries where they sought to ready themselves for the next insurgency of industrial workers. Similar to the 1920s, communist cadre established shop newspapers, set up rank-and-file organizations, and in some cases developed a measure of credibility. The most successful examples of "colonizing" arose in Detroit. Black automobile workers, tired of the unkept promises and machinations of the United Automobile Workers, organized the Revolutionary Union Movement in a number of factories. In the early 1970s, the RUM and its successors sought to extend its organization into other industrial centers.[194]

But the RUM wrote off Pittsburgh. As two members who spent a couple of years in the city put it: "The 'left' in Pittsburgh is virtually non-existent to the public eye." Apart from occasional anti-war demonstrations or the remnants of the Communist Party, the left remained overwhelmingly white and restricted to academics or tiny Leninist groups. RUM members hoped their own organization would fill this vacuum but cautioned against the commitment of resources. They observed, "The Pittsburgh situation is somewhat in a state of limbo. Twenty years ago, we would have advised anyone to go immediately to the steel mills if they were to organize for socialist revolution. Today, steel is rapidly dying due to obsolete and archaic machinery and mills, and the price of Japanese steel. . . . [B]ig steel will have a role of decreasing importance in the years to come and may well be gone in twenty years."[195] As it turned out, RUM's analysis of steel proved prescient, but this did not deter other radicals from attempting to turn Pittsburgh into an American Petrograd.

Given the weaknesses of Pittsburgh's labor left, many progressive observers were pleasantly surprised by the widespread support steelworkers offered to Edward Sadlowski's campaign for President of the USWA in 1977. In 1973, Sadlowski won the office of Chicago's District Director despite widespread red-baiting and ballot-stuffing. Sadlowski freely admitted his socialist beliefs and appealed to members who were convinced their union's leaders had, in Sadlowski's view, "lost touch with the membership. Their big statement on the woman's issue was an example. Almost 20 percent of the members are women, so they figured they'd get that vote by promising that they'd appoint a woman to the union staff. But here they've been in office for 36 years and now that one of their staffers in the District will be a woman. In a way that sums it up right there."[196] Sadlowski positioned himself for national office by launching a "Fight Back" movement that sought to unite the different networks of dissidents and give expression to those steelworkers who were angry about layoffs, inflation, and corruption.[197] In Chicago, rank-and-filers took over several locals but "experienced [rank-and-file] activists [elsewhere] remind each other that I.W. Abel, too, ran for President with promises to preserve the right to strike, get away from 'tuxedo unionism,' and give the union back to the members."[198]

Sadlowski offered a stark contrast to Lloyd McBride, Abel's chosen successor for the Presidency of the USWA. Sadlowski argued that the ENA compromised the union's "historic adversarial role." As he put it, "I don't find anything compatible with the Steelworkers union and United States Steel, nothing whatsoever." Such views were anathema to McBride, who staunchly defended the ENA and USWA's strategy to help make the industry more competitive: "I don't think that anyone who is an implacable enemy of industry can competently represent the best interests of our membership. This is [a] totally biased, unreasonable attitude. . . . There is a place for industry in our free economy system. . . . I would certainly be an implacable enemy of anything that would run counter to the best interests of our membership."[199] When U.S. Steel announced a price increase, Sadlowski denounced it as against the interests of steelworkers and consumers. Big steel had "no one to blame [but] itself for the inroads being made by foreign steel" while McBride called for quotas on imported steel.[200]

McBride derived support from the entire USWA administration and even the leaders of the AFL-CIO. McBride won the support of virtually all of the USWA's District Directors and consequently their staffs, who campaigned for him and provided the bulk of his money for his campaign. Sadlowski's support came from the leaders and activists in basic steel locals, and he obtained some money from progressives outside of the union. For that reason, George Meany, the president of the AFL-CIO, criticized Sadlowski as an unwitting tool of radicals bent on taking over the union.[201] Indeed, McBride sponsored a group called SMART (Steelworkers Mad About Radical Takeover) who accused Sadlowski of putting liberal chic issues (such as gun control) ahead of steelworkers' interests. As in the past, the USWA staff exercised strong control over the elections in the smaller shops. But in locals where workers put in the time and effort to lobby support, such as putting leaflets regularly on workers' cars, workers overwhelmingly supported Sadlowski.[202] But whether Sadlowski failed to win support outside of basic steel locals or staff members stole the election, Sadlowski still lost the election.[203]

At the time, some analysts viewed the widespread support for Ed Sadlowski as an indication of the growing radicalism of steelworkers.[204] Sadlowski did not hide his socialist politics and his campaign, and the widespread support it received helped weaken the strident anti-communism amongst steelworkers. Sadlowski promised members the opportunity for greater involvement in their union, notably the right to vote on contracts combined with a more adversarial relationship to their employers. He refused to simply defend jobs, telling one interviewer that automation was inevitable, and the union should work to make it work for steelworkers. As he put it, "I think that the ultimate aim of the labor leader . . . has to be one of taking a guy out of a coal mine and off an open hearth floor. And I strongly advocate that we find ways of making steel on an open hearth floor with machines, and the people that were there be benefited monetarily . . . so they can go out and find out what the hell the good life that a lot of public people talk about is all about."[205] If Sadlowski had won, he might have transformed the political culture of the USWA, perhaps refashioning it to something like the early CIO.[206] But Sadlowski lost, and while a number of socialists and rank-and-filers went on to play a major role in large steel locals in the late 1970s and early 1980s, they fought to transform the political culture of their union just as the sand was eroding beneath their feet.

In the mid-1970s, many steelworkers chose to believe that the mills were a permanent feature of life. From 1960 to 1977, workers had given ground in terms of employment levels but had gained far better compensation. Between 1958 and 1967, as a result of contracting out, new technology, and incentives, steel companies boosted production by 30 percent with the same number of workers. However, wages also increased by 25 percent. As noted previously, companies carefully guarded the data that revealed the profitability of each mill, but one government study found that steel companies' price increases far exceeded what were needed to cover their labor costs.[207] Ten years later, big steel had increased its output by 50 percent, cut one-quarter of its workforce, and raised its labor costs by 80 percent.[208] From workers' perspective, the USWA won them more money—3 percent a year above and beyond that decade's considerable inflation—and lessened the pain of layoffs. For instance, in 1975, workers laid off from J&L's Pittsburgh Works observed that between unemployment compensation and SUB pay, unemployment "isn't too bad a deal." But one black worker cautioned that "you don't know if you are going back or when you are going back."[209] Moreover, the USWA's system of benefits was always predicated on the assumption that the mills would remain open, albeit at lower levels of employment; when the mills disappeared in the early 1980s, so would workers' wages, benefits, and pensions. When the mills began to close in the 1970s, they swept away most of workers' organizational strength and ability to extract concessions from corporations. The workers who bore the heaviest burden of that transition were women and African Americans. We now turn to their story.

NEW OPPORTUNITIES, OLD BARRIERS:
BLACK MEN ON THE SHOP FLOOR

As the 1960s got under way, big steel maintained its discriminatory policies against African Americans. Personnel offices hired black men for jobs
in blast furnaces and open hearths and prevented them from obtaining
work in cleaner, lighter, or better-paid departments. One survey found that
in mills without furnace departments (such as the Irvin Works), whites
made up 99 percent of the workforce. At large mills with blast furnaces and
open hearths (such as Homestead, Duquesne, Aliquippa, and Hazelwood)
blacks comprised around 9 percent of the workforce, but 80 percent of them
remained sequestered in the furnaces, Masonry Department, or the track
gangs.[210] Another survey found that black men escaped these "man-killing
jobs" only "at rare intervals" and only when an individual proved unusually persistent.[211] Thus as late as 1973, blacks made up 32.9 percent of the
National Tube Works' Blast Furnace Department but only 1.6 percent of its
Maintenance Department.[212] As in the past, employers' racial stereotyping
limited the employment opportunities of African Americans before they
made it through the door of the personnel office.

As in the 1940s and 1950s, most African Americans rose to skilled
positions in "black departments." At National Tube, the mill's only black
vicing (temporary) foreman worked in the blast furnace, as did nineteen of
the mill's twenty-seven skilled black workers. Even so, whites held half of
that department's skilled jobs.[213] Moreover, black departments suffered
from lower pay and weaker incentive plans than comparable white departments.[214] For instance, Homestead's Masonry Department possessed fewer
better-paying jobs than the overwhelmingly white Electric Shop. Because
of the different incentive plans, blast furnacemen at ET made considerably
less than that mill's open hearth workers where the "top jobs were mostly
white."[215] Thus even after the passage of civil rights laws, the racial division
of labor relegated black workers to smaller paychecks and slower occupational advancement than white workers.[216]

In white departments, black men advanced into skilled positions only
after years of dedicated persistence. One of the first black rollers in the Mon
Valley was Alfred Macon. In 1965, Macon worked in ET's foundry where he
"caught pure hell." Two years later, by a "stroke of God's goodness," he was
laid off and rehired to the slab mill. Now he was in the right place at the
right time. As people retired, he advanced, and by 1970 he could work turns

as a roller. However, his foreman manipulated the schedule so that he was never scheduled for turns. As he noted in a deposition, "I have paid my dues and what is mine is mine. . . . I do not want to hurt no one. But I don't want no one to shit on me and tell me it is candy and I got to like the taste."[217] Such resistance to black "outsiders" was common practice. When Otis Bryant moved into a skilled job in the BOP shop, his foreman told him many times to sit on a bench for an entire turn while "they did my work [in order] to keep from teaching me how to do it."[218] When Frank Moorefield transferred into the 160 Inch Mill in the Homestead Works, many whites acted like he was trespassing on their "private property." When Moorefield would try to speak to them, the older workers would ignore him and ask another white, "What is this nigger doing?"[219]

Of all the jobs and departments that managers reserved for white workers, the most plainly white jobs were those of craftsmen and maintenance workers. These skilled workers made up about a quarter of a mill's workforce and generally enjoyed steady, well-paid, and relatively easy work. In 1961, the USWA's Civil Rights Committee (CRC) complained that management "continue[d] to exclude Negro workers" from apprenticeship programs and thus few blacks obtained maintenance jobs.[220] In 1966, there were twenty-three thousand craftsmen in employed in the Pittsburgh steel industry, of whom 3 percent were black.[221] Despite the presence of hundreds of black workers in the Clairton Works, its local union President estimated that out of eight hundred maintenance workers in the mill, only fifteen were African American.[222] That same year a management survey of National Tube revealed that only 6 percent of its black workers held skilled jobs compared to 35 percent of white men. Conversely, 40 percent of black workers worked as laborers or janitors, but just 11 percent of white men stayed in these "entry-level" positions.[223] As in the past, skilled jobs were effectively labeled "whites only."

Under the Abel administration, the union weakened the institutional barriers to black advancement, but they remained largely intact. In 1968, the USWA won contract language that allowed minority workers greater access to apprenticeship programs and the ability to bid on jobs outside of their departments.[224] However, the number of black craftsmen increased at a painfully slow rate. In 1973, although 11 percent of the Homestead Works were black, they made up 5.8 percent of that mill's apprentices.[225] As a result, most black workers could only fume about the persistence of the racial division of labor. John Hughey recalled that at the Carrie Furnaces, black workers labored in the dust and the smoke of the blast furnace where it was "2,200 degrees, and you faint in the fire. [Managers] didn't hardly want to give you a coffee break. And you see four [skilled] whites come up there to fix one job . . . and they work three hours to put up one rail. And you could not work in that crew. And they could get all the overtime they wanted. That's why they bought boats and two homes and why blacks stayed in Braddock."[226]

If steel companies resisted moving blacks into skilled positions, managers remained adamantly opposed to hiring African Americans for white-collar jobs. In 1968, there were 6,000 steel executives in Pittsburgh, and only 10 of them were black.[227] In 1970, the National Tube Works had 56 male supervisors of whom 1 was African American.[228] In 1966, blacks made up just 2.5 percent of U.S. Steel's clerical workforce.[229] The company told *Business Week* that it had tried to hire more black women as clerical workers but that "few qualified."[230] A closer examination of U.S. Steel's hiring and promotion policies reveals that the most important standard for white-collar employment remained skin color. The only black clerical workers at U.S. Steel's National Tube mill in McKeesport were men like Henderson Thomas, who transferred his seniority from the mill into a unionized white-collar job. At this mill, there were few black unionized clerks, just 4 percent of the total, but not 1 among the 372 non-union office workers.[231]

Despite such pervasive racial discrimination, steel companies continued to promote themselves as "color blind employers," while the government and union proved slow to act and quick to proclaim victory. In 1961, in response to John F. Kennedy's Executive Order 10925, David McDonald ordered the USWA Publicity Department to ask twenty-nine hundred companies to work with the USWA to "stamp out the evils of discrimination in employment."[232] Although both companies and union issued a flurry of press releases, little of substance changed. At one Pittsburgh-area mill, federal anti-discrimination guidelines did not prevent this defense contractor from keeping 85 percent of its black employees as laborers.[233] In another mill, a black worker complained that the administration of the seniority agreement resulted in widespread discrimination. The Office of Federal Contract Compliance largely agreed with him, but pointed out that it was limited to monitoring government contractors.[234] Nonetheless, in 1964, U.S. Steel and the USWA solemnly announced that they had agreed to work with the federal Committee on Equal Employment Opportunity (EEO) to ensure fair employment.[235] Yet when unionists requested data on the employment status of minorities, the company insisted that its commitment to affirmative action meant it did not keep records on its employees' race, nationality, or religious preference.[236] Of course the EEO required the company to maintain data on race and gender, but it did not require companies to share it with the union.[237] One black trade unionist offered a pungent assessment of the company-union "partnership" in this regard: steel firms "have only given us tokenism in the crafts and trades. They have only given us tokenism in the personnel office, and we cannot do anything."[238]

"I SEE A WHOLE LOT OF WORDS AND NOTHING BEING DONE": CIVIL RIGHTS RHETORIC AND REALITY IN THE MCDONALD ADMINISTRATION[239]

In the 1960s, black steelworkers began to break free from the ideological straightjacket of the 1950s and agitated for greater power in their union and equality in the workplace. In 1960, black trade unionists ran for major offices in every major local in the Pittsburgh region.[240] On paper, blacks possessed the votes to win. Cleo Bender observed that there were almost two thousand black members at Homestead, twice as many as elected the last President.[241] The *Pittsburgh Courier* sardonically observed that although black steelworkers "turned out *en masse*," Bender received less than half as many votes as his running mate.[242] However, several African Americans won office at small, even "predominantly white" locals, while at larger mills such as ET, Eugene "Golf Balls" Dirl and Charles "Bill" Davis were elected as Grievance Committeemen. Needless to say, these results were not the dramatic breakthrough that black activists had hoped for.[243] As in the past, black activists had a difficult time overcoming the apathy and cynicism of black steelworkers and the antipathy of many white workers.

Fresh from the hustings, black unionists met in Homestead and formed a "permanent organization for action." In September 1960, "sick and tired of getting promises that are never filled," veteran trade unionists such as Carl Dickerson and Vernon Sidberry from Duquesne, Eugene Dirl from ET, Al Everett and Albert Reid from Homestead, and John Hughey from the Carrie Furnaces united "groups and factions which had been opposed to each other over the years."[244] Such solidarity was inspired by A. Philip Randolph's organization of the Negro American Labor Council (NALC). In May 1960, NALC brought together one thousand black unionists from a variety of industries including steel, auto, and rubber in order to win greater power within individual unions and the AFL-CIO and to widen economic opportunities for black workers.[245] Yet black solidarity failed to elect a single black steelworker to national office despite the fact that both the McDonald and rebel factions in the USWA supported black candidates. In 1961, the successor to the DPC, the Organization for Membership Rights (OMR), endorsed Curtis Strong for the national office of trustee while McDonald backed James DeBow, the President of Pittsburgh's NALC, for the same office. Ultimately the OMR failed to appear on the ballot, but while McDonald was re-elected, DeBow lost to a white candidate.[246] DeBow's failure testified to the duplicity of white liberals and the disorganization of African Americans in the USWA. In the coming years, black activists made little headway against either problem.[247]

While protest organizations rose and fell, at the core of every civil rights group were elected black officials. In the early 1960s, several groups formed to force unions and employers to live up to their civil rights rhetoric: the NALC (1960), the United Negro Protest Committee (1963), and the Ad Hoc Committee of Concerned Black Steelworkers (1964). In each case, the men who won and held local union office proved their most important constituents.[248] John King's assessment of Eugene Dirl, his grievanceman at ET, typified many veteran trade unionists: "I didn't like him," King said, "I told him to his face. A lot of guys didn't like him, but Golf Ball was hell on those bosses."[249] In 1965, both white and black workers elected James Sharpley as a grievanceman because the corruption in his department was so bad that "the foreman would pick his nephew. . . . [E]veryone got bypassed." Within a few years, a few blacks became cranemen, and a few others were trained for skilled craft jobs.[250] Curly McLaughlin recalled that Sharpley "did the job for us—black and white."[251]

Yet the obstacles to forming a cadre of experienced black union leaders remained formidable. Getting elected to office remained one obvious hurdle, but pitfalls also awaited the more successful. Management sometimes co-opted competent leaders. Alex Powell observed that when a black unionist "would speak up," management "would make a supervisor out of him."[252] Booker Kidd, a black worker who later entered management, recalled that management bought off the black grievanceman in Duquesne's blast furnaces: "He was so powerful in the blast furnace" that U.S. Steel "got him out of the mill" and set him up in his own business.[253] Other black officials calculated that in a majority white union they should cultivate a less confrontational style. Several unionists agreed that one of Duquesne's most respected black trade unionists "was not the kind to *fan* trouble. He'd go to that spot if necessary."[254]

Another barrier to the organization or empowerment of black steel-workers was the conservative political culture of the USWA. Black union-ists like John Hughey tired of white leaders who "preached liberalism to us," invariably citing their membership in the NAACP as proof of their good intentions, but failed to act on issues of discrimination.[255] Debates over civil rights carried the potential to crack the facade of liberalism, as one debate in the union's IEB reveals. In 1961, when John F. Kennedy signed executive order number 10925 requiring government contractors to prove they were not discriminating, David McDonald approached the IEB to approve a series of educational conferences to help the union's staff to better understand the new guidelines. McDonald also believed that such a move would steal some of the civil rights thunder from steel companies who had recently hired, amidst much publicity, several token black employ-ees. McDonald clearly expected yet another pro forma endorsement of the union's liberal program, yet underestimated that civil rights agitation within the union had produced a backlash amongst the District Directors. The vast majority of the District Directors in the North and South proved heartily sick and tired of hearing that "we are not doing a job in the mills" for the "colored people." A clearly surprised McDonald begged the men to "not get too involved in this . . . simple recommendation that we have a series of staff conferences of which I approve." But the IEB stood firm, and in a rare move for the board, refused to accept a proposal from their Presi-dent. After the battle was clearly lost, McDonald called upon Boyd Wilson, a prominent black staff member, to respond to various allegations raised by the directors. Wilson's first task was to prove his anti-communist creden-tials. Wilson assured the directors that he "never [advocated] any subver-sive activity. . . . I will challenge any man to say that he has been a more loyal union man than I." Only then did Wilson defend the right of black members to advocate for more opportunity in the union, the issue that lay behind the acrimonious discussion. In the end, the Directors allowed McDonald to issue a press release, but with the clear understanding that he would leave their staff members alone.[256]

African American steelworkers who fought the union to appoint more black staff often found themselves forced to fight with the black unionists who had been appointed to office as a result of such agitation.[257] The man most often caught between the aspirations of black steelworkers and the realpolitik of the USWA remained Boyd Wilson. In February of 1960, black steelworkers in Duquesne asked Wilson to attend a planning meeting for the upcoming Democratic primary. Wilson refused (allegedly under pressure from the Director of District 15) to attend a segregated or black-only meeting. One member of the "Jefferson Vanguard" chided Wilson, saying that "we don't want any cowards in Duquesne," and the group helped upset the Democratic machine in that city.[258] Steelworkers who planned to sue the USWA for its part in racial discrimination in their plant accused Wilson of revealing their plans to the union. They balked at joining the NALC because Wilson was one of its vice presidents.[259] Indeed, John Thornton, an officer of NALC and fellow USWA employee, accused Wilson of sabotaging the organization.[260] When asked about Wilson, one veteran black trade unionist refused "to speak ill of the dead."[261] After talking with many black steelworkers, Pittsburgh's labor priest, Charles Owen Rice, reluctantly concluded that the USWA only "promoted the pliable" to positions of authority.[262]

The union's close relationship with civil rights organizations further constricted potential criticism.[263] The case of James McCoy, an unusually blunt and independent staff member, reveals the support that civil rights groups offered to the leaders of the USWA.[264] In 1963, McCoy founded the NAACP's Labor and Industry Committee, which picketed local businesses in order to encourage them to hire more African Americans. McCoy helped organize demonstrations that urged construction unions to admit black workers and put them on the list of workers that contractors hired. According to some white USWA officials, including Francis Shane (the head of the union's Civil Rights Committee) this ran counter to the policy that all unionists should advocate "equal opportunity for all people." McCoy refused to desist from participating in demonstrations and blasted two pillars of Pittsburgh's civil rights establishment, the city's FEPC and the Pittsburgh Urban League for refusing to back him. McCoy alleged that "I've been covering up the wrongs that these guys have been doing for years."[265] A few weeks later, the Pennsylvania NAACP formed a new Labor Committee, causing the *Pittsburgh Courier* to speculate that McCoy was being punished for his candid statements.[266]

As in the past, the USWA's civil rights organization did little to combat discrimination. After 1961, David McDonald reorganized the CRC into a full-time department with a paid staff, but he retained Francis Shane as its head. Black workers and staff members of the International USWA urged

McDonald to "integrate" the CRD and to end Shane's "one-man operation," which they argued was "the oddest and most contradictory" in the labor movement.[267] Boyd Wilson spoke for many when he observed that "so far as the union is concerned, we have been sort of hiding our heads in the sand."[268] Although the 1964 USWA constitution convention required that all locals establish a CRC, less than a quarter of all locals did so.[269] Local CRCs could neither file nor monitor grievances, and most white unionists preferred that these committees focus on community problems rather than on discrimination in the mills.[270] Moreover, most union presidents in Pittsburgh and elsewhere typically appointed "*his* Negroes to local CRCs."[271] The culture of "promoting the pliable" to stymie more aggressive civil rights activism remained a pervasive phenomenon throughout the USWA.

The most pressing problem regarding discrimination remained the administration of the seniority agreements. The 1960 U.S. Steel-USWA labor agreement established "labor pools" whereby laid-off workers could "bump" workers with less seniority. For instance, between April and June 1963, 1,000 men at the Homestead Works were laid off, and displaced workers could not qualify for the labor pool unless they had been hired before March 4, 1942.[272] Because the labor pools contained primarily unskilled positions, they generally contained more "black jobs" than "white" ones. For instance, at Duquesne, 60 percent of all jobs in the general service department were in the labor pool, because most of those positions were unskilled, but none of the highly skilled jobs in the maintenance department.[273] Whether by accident or design, in times of severe unemployment, labor pools allowed skilled white workers to bump black laborers with less plant seniority—a situation that caused black workers to complain to their union.[274] During the depth of the recession between 1958 and 1963, the Homestead Works hired just 218 men but just 7 blacks. (The mill either refused to hire black workers during hard times or newly-hired blacks failed to survive the labor pool.)[275] Blacks at other mills also bore the brunt of layoffs. Over the course of 1967, the National Tube Works laid off 11.5 percent of its workforce but furloughed 38 percent of its black workers.[276] For many white workers, the labor pool was a last resort in hard times, whereas for blacks it was often the only job they would ever have.

Progress on the issue of seniority came at a painfully slow rate. In 1962, the USWA inserted a stronger non-discrimination clause into the national contracts with U.S. Steel and J&L. If they desired it, local unionists could now implement plant-wide seniority if they could force management to agree.[277] In a tacit acknowledgment of the ineffectiveness of the CRC, Francis Shane confessed that "it took eleven years to get those four lines" in the contract.[278] Even mild-mannered Boyd Wilson caustically observed that the CRC "seem[s] to lack either courage or insight" as the addition of non-discrimination clauses to contracts had had "little effect."[279] While only a handful of mills changed their seniority agreements, the union proclaimed that racial discrimination in steel was a thing of the past.[280] Yet black workers in locals like Homestead continued to protest their inability to break out of "black jobs."[281] Even when one of Homestead's grievance men wanted the CRC members to attend grievance hearings, U.S. Steel refused to allow them entry, observing that "the Civil Rights Committee was not intended to function in the manner desired by [the] Union representative."[282] For its part, U.S. Steel claimed that minorities "are guaranteed the same opportunity as any other employee. . . . Moreover, the labor agreement between management and the union provides equal opportunity for advancement through promotional sequences."[283]

As in the past, the USWA ignored the problems in the mills and emphasized the path of legislative reforms. The union urged its members to support the passage of Pennsylvania's "fair housing" bill. Like many past efforts, the bill was well-intentioned and largely toothless.[284] The CRC mobilized USWA members to support national legislation such as the 1964 Civil Rights Act—the most significant civil rights legislation in decades.[285] The law provided important protections for black and female workers, and the USWA, other unions, and liberal Democrats took much of the credit for this victory. But just as the Wagner Act responded to labor agitation, so too did the Civil Rights Act respond to years of civil rights agitation. Ironically, Title VII of the Civil Rights Act would eventually provide steelworkers with the legal grounds to sue both company and union for racial discrimination. Few members of the CRC should have been surprised that two former members of Homestead's CRC, John Turner and Jimmy Rogers, charged that Local 1397's and U.S. Steel's administration of the local seniority agreements discriminated against black workers.[286]

BLACK PROTEST AND THE CRISIS OF LIBERALISM:
THE ABEL YEARS, 1965–1977

Throughout the 1960s, civil rights issues and organizations affected the outcome of union politics. In the hotly contested 1965 election for USWA

President, Ad Hoc endorsed I.W. Abel, and black votes were widely believed to have delivered him the margin of victory.[287] Everyone on McDonald's slate went down to defeat except Nathaniel Lee, who became the first black steelworker elected to a national office—that of International Teller.[288] Subsequently, Abel fulfilled a number of Ad Hoc's demands. He forced Francis Shane to resign as the Director of the CRC and placed Alex Fuller, a founding member of Ad Hoc, in his place.[289] Abel appointed three staff members to the CRD, including Ernest Clifford, and removed Shane as its head.[290] Abel proved a far more capable trade unionist than McDonald, but he inherited an organization whose political culture discouraged membership involvement on such touchy issues as civil rights. Thus, even in retirement, Shane managed to bring more shame to the tarnished reputation of the CRC by filing a complaint with the Pennsylvania Human Relations Commission, claiming that his ouster was the result of reverse discrimination.[291] Shane also blamed the CRC's shortcomings on his lack of authority over district directors or local union presidents.[292] Most black steelworkers agreed with Harold Keith, the labor reporter for the *Pittsburgh Courier*, who argued Shane had "stalemated" the civil rights struggle in the USWA.[293]

As with previous liberal leaders of the USWA, Abel continued to support civil rights legislation. In 1965, the union supported the national Voting Rights Act and lobbied to strengthen Pennsylvania's FEPC. In 1967, the union supported the drive to strengthen Pittsburgh's FEPC.[294] Unfortunately, most civil rights activists believed the latter measure was entirely too toothless to be of any real use.[295] The achievements of the USWA in this regard were best summed up by the firebrand James McCoy, who remarked that the USWA "played a tremendous part in the passage of every piece of social legislation now on the books at the state and federal level." His praise was qualified, however, by his observation that his union still had "to make such legislation meaningful."[296] Nonetheless, A. Philip Randolph argued that as a result of such gains, and other reforms within the AFL-CIO, black trade unionists should moderate their demands.[297] The mantle of protest passed from NALC to the UNPC and Ad Hoc who fought for wider hiring and promotion practices by companies and their own union.[298] Ad Hoc developed into a network of several hundred members throughout the country, although its formal membership in each mill was sometimes minimal.[299] Nonetheless, John Hughey was typical of many black local officials who were empowered by the knowledge that their struggle "wasn't local anymore."[300]

The 1968 battle over black representation on the IEB revealed the limits of Abel's liberalism and the organizational power of black steelworkers. Led by Ad Hoc, African American unionists maintained that the union should create the position of second Vice President so that the IEB could at long last be racially integrated.[301] Joseph Molony, the new Chairman of the CRD, reasserted the old "reverse discrimination" argument against creating a second Vice President position for a black steelworker. President Abel agreed with Molony and in a cynical allusion to *Brown v. Topeka Board of Education*, claimed that blacks don't want equal but separate treatment.[302] (The issue of a "black Vice President" in the USWA was resolved in September 1976, at the end of Abel's Presidency, when the IEB appointed Leon Lynch as Vice President for Human Affairs.)[303] In 1977, both slates for International USWA offices had an African American running for that office.[304] By contrast, in the United Auto Workers (UAW), black auto workers had succeeded in getting one black officer appointed onto their IEB in 1962 and a second one in 1968.[305] Black automobile workers occupied a more strategic position within the industry and the union; thus the UAW labored hard to win black workers' loyalty even as it bitterly fought the black reform and radical movements. While black workers did not get very far in auto, they proved far better placed and better organized than their counterparts in steel.[306]

Throughout the 1960s, black unionists pressed for reform within the union and made little headway. Although most locals possessed a CRC, these committees could simply "keep an eye on the work of the Grievance Committee" in order to make sure blacks' contractual rights were not being abrogated.[307] In 1965, Robert Nelson, the Chair of Local 1557's (Clairton) CRC, protested that the local seniority agreement discriminated against black workers. At the urging of a black staff representative, Nelson agreed to "withhold from going to any outside agency for the good of the Union" as long as changes were made.[308] Although the Abel administration appointed more blacks to staff jobs, steelworkers felt the struggle against discrimination in the mills "was at a standstill."[309] One black steelworker wondered whether the black official in her district was "a real person living in our city or a myth from afar."[310] In 1968, Joseph Molony (the Chair of the CRC and Vice President of the USWA) promised that the union would negotiate a plant-wide seniority agreement in its next contract. The promise was never kept.[311] (Plant seniority was already enjoyed by steelworkers in many fabricating plants.)[312] At a few mills, black trade unionists enacted long-overdue reforms. By 1970, black unionists at Carrie Furnace had replaced departmental seniority with a plant-wide system.[313] However, when black grievancemen at J&L's Southside mill charged that management and the union manipulated labor pools to keep blacks out of desirable departments, the CRC refused to intervene because "many of our own people in J&L prefer" this racist arrangement.[314]

In the late 1960s and early 1970s, black workers increasingly turned to the courts for redress. Black steelworkers, often members of Ad Hoc, filed lawsuits in Homestead, Youngstown, Alabama, and Baltimore. All the lawsuits charged that companies and union locals colluded in order to deny black workers their seniority rights.[315] (In one case, a worker simply observed "that something is not right in the union 1397.")[316] After decades of inaction, the NAACP joined Ad Hoc in excoriating the USWA for allowing steel companies and the union to manipulate labor pools.[317] Some threatened to decertify from the USWA and join other unions.[318] As discontent amongst black steelworkers mounted, a coalition of African American labor and civil rights groups, including the NAACP and the National Organization for Women, pressured the U.S. Justice Department to sue major steel firms and the USWA.[319] Faced with certain defeat, most major companies and the USWA capitulated and signed the Consent Decree, capping years of struggle by black workers.

CIVIL RIGHTS TRIUMPHANT?
THE CONSENT DECREE AND BLACK MEN

The high water mark for the civil rights movement in the steel industry, the Consent Decree went a long way in eradicating discrimination in steel. The result of an out-of-court settlement in 1974, the Consent Decree required steel companies to pay $31 million in damages to black, Hispanic, and women workers. (Steel companies "generously" paid the union's share of the damages.)[320] Furthermore, in order to rectify past discrimination, one-fifth of all newly-hired workers would have to be women or racial minorities. In one sense, the USWA and steel companies benefited from making these concessions because they never admitted to violating anyone's civil rights and were exempted from further class action lawsuits. As one activist queried, how could a Southern judge have the best interests of black steelworkers at heart?[321] Furthermore, representatives from the union and companies joined the government on local and national audit committees to ensure that the provisions of the Consent Decree were carried out.[322] The cynical design and administration of the Consent Decree, combined with a devastating loss of jobs—thirty thousand in the 1970s alone—hampered the task of dismantling decades of discrimination.[323]

Yet the Consent Decree helped to weaken patterns of discrimination. When jobs became vacant, management was required to post notices throughout the mill so that any interested worker could bid on them. For purposes of bidding and layoffs, job and departmental seniority were replaced with plant seniority. As a result, the Consent Decree transformed the effective seniority rights of minorities. The Valley Machine Shop, or the Big Shop in the Homestead Works, had traditionally been off-limits to blacks, but by 1982, 19.5 percent of its workers were black. Older black men narrowed the gap with their white contemporaries. The lengthy plant seniority of black men hired in the 1940s and 1950s enabled them to advance to the head of seniority lists for semi-skilled jobs. For instance, of the forty-eight semi-skilled machinist helpers in the Big Shop eleven were black men, most of whom began work before the Korean War.[324] Thus just before Homestead closed, older black employees finally achieved occupational parity with whites.

Yet the Consent Decree failed to completely transform the seniority system so that it could undo the pervasive gender and racial stratification of steelworkers. While plant seniority superseded job seniority for all jobs that became open, the priority for jobs went to workers in each plant's LOP. Only if no one from that LOP wanted the job could workers in that department bid on the open position. Only if no one from a department bid on a job could workers transfer into that job from elsewhere in the plant.[325] As a consequence, incumbent workers in an LOP or department still retained many of their traditional privileges. At the Clairton Works, craft apprenticeships were bid on a plant-wide basis, but incumbent workers in the maintenance department were able to bid first on jobs as helpers. Therefore, a worker hired off the streets into the "brick gang" could, after six months, "out-bid" a worker with thirty years' seniority from another department to become a helper to a Motor Inspector. Consequently, the overwhelmingly white and male members of the maintenance department retained the best chance to train for craft jobs. As a result, the system of racial and gender segregation and stratification of jobs remained largely in place.[326]

The Consent Decree also protected incumbent workers against people with high plant seniority from "leapfrogging" over them. In practice, this favored white men in good LOPs. For instance, in November of 1974, several switchmen in Homestead's Transportation and General Services Department complained that management had "leapfrogged" ten men ahead of them on the seniority roster. Management agreed that these ten new men might well hurt the job incumbents, and in exchange for adding the new men to the switchmen's "board," or seniority roster, management added an extra position to the aggrieved workers' LOP. This would "enabl[e] Switchmen to stop at another job before bumping into the labor pool in forced reduction situations."[327] During layoffs, the extra position in the LOP proved invaluable. Consequently, although the Consent Decree weakened discriminatory patterns of promotion, it did so carefully, cautiously, and sometimes not at all.

Because of the limitations of the Consent Decree, the NAACP and many black unionists remained skeptical about it. They observed that the USWA and steel companies still controlled the implementation, direction, and pace of change.[328] One black activist observed that "we didn't ask for the Consent Decree. We asked for our rights. How come every time black people demand our rights we get something [like the Consent Decree] that we cannot even understand?"[329] Finally, if unionists accepted cash payments as a result of the Consent Decree, they were barred from filing their own lawsuits. Many workers thought that a couple of hundred dollars' compensation for years of discrimination was a humiliating joke and refused to endorse their checks.[330] From the perspective of many black men, the Consent Decree was an incomplete victory.

DRAMATIC CHANGE:
THE CONSENT DECREE AND WOMEN'S EMPLOYMENT

The Consent Decree would bring enormous changes in the status of female workers and reverse the marginalization they had suffered during the "liberal" 1960s. Throughout the Pittsburgh region, women comprised only 1.5 percent of all steelworkers in 1960, and that proportion fell to 1.3 percent by the end of the decade. Only a handful of women remained in nonproduction jobs in the large mills like the Duquesne and Homestead Works. In any given year in the 1960s (the only decade when gender data for individual plants is available), between 2 and 4 women worked at Duquesne. Between 1961 and 1966, Homestead management added at least 1,000 workers to its payroll, but the number of female production workers dropped from 101 to 79.[331] Many of these women of steel had been hired during World War II. That was the case with Mary Zoran, Alma Rall, and Betty Eunice, who worked at Homestead transporting samples of steel from the open hearths to the metallurgical laboratories.[332] Because managers preferred men for production jobs, they hired few women. When Bethlehem's nail mill hired Joy Wilkins in 1923, she had "held her own with any man" alongside 40 other women. When she retired in 1969, just 1 was left.[333]

The only growth area of women's employment was in clerical work. Women comprised 37.5 percent of all clerks in 1960 and 42 percent in 1970. One supervisor at a Mon Valley mill rationalized hiring women for these jobs: "with clerical jobs, it's no problem, you could move a woman on. It's a natural thing."[334] However, it was not "natural" to hire black women for white-collar jobs. In 1960, only 160 black women were white-collar workers in the entire American steel industry, a minuscule 0.1 percent of the 165,164 white-collar workers. The handful of black women in steel overwhelmingly worked as laborers and janitors, almost always in traditionally black departments.[335] In Pittsburgh and throughout the United States, steel companies simply refused to hire or promote African American women in appreciable numbers.

The position of women on the shop floor continued to deteriorate despite passage of the 1964 Civil Rights Act. In 1971, women made up just .05 percent of all skilled steelworkers throughout Pennsylvania.[336] Although by 1972 U.S. Steel claimed that it did not discriminate against hiring or promoting married women, few of the company's mills in the Mon Valley actually hired women for anything except secretarial work. U.S. Steel claimed that it was willing to consider women for professional white-collar jobs, but reported that none were available, though women were in abundant supply for clerical and service jobs.[337] There was little to compel steel companies to hire women for production, craft, or supervisory positions as there was an ample reserve army of underemployed men. Furthermore, managers viewed women as poor substitutes for men. As one supervisor in a Mon Valley mill said, "in the steel industry, they usually hire men. There are some jobs women can handle, just like some handicapped person could handle, or even do it better than a regular worker."[338]

The Consent Decree forced companies to hire women in 1973 and 1974, and male attitudes slowly changed.[339] One observer, Leslie Posner, noted that male mill workers were frequently surprised that women they knew would take "their" jobs; male mill workers had expected female applicants to be "feminists" from outside the area. However, some men viewed the Consent Decree as an opportunity for their family members to gain a lifetime of economic security and dignity. One Italian American woman recalled with humor how her father, traditional as he was, literally badgered her to get a mill job. For him, this represented "security for me, my kids, and his grandkids."[340] Once women began to earn a family wage, the change in their lives was immediate.[341] Sheryl Johnson, an African American woman, recalled that "anytime your income goes from $90 a week to $350 a week, there are some changes in your life." Because of the union's health plan, she didn't worry about the cost, "I just lined 'em [her five kids] up" and took them to the dentist.[342] Mary Pat Manso took the traditional male path of going straight from Steel Valley High into the mill. Manso was in the mill "for the money," and explained "I'm not a 'Women's Libber' but I feel that if a woman thinks she is capable of doing a job it shouldn't be held back from her."[343] This widespread sentiment, "I'm not a Women's Libber but . . ." was echoed by many Mon Valley women who entered the mills and enjoyed the wages and benefits that steelworkers had won.

Many women hired in the wake of the Consent Decree initially faced widespread harassment. Many men resented their "preferential" hiring. Consequently, few were upset that companies often hired women on a revolving door basis. After all, the Consent Decree monitored hiring patterns more closely than retention.[344] According to Denise Weinbrenner Edwards, one of the first female millwrights in the Mon Valley, the millwright she worked with "called me dummy every day for two years." Still, the money was great, and she loved her job. After several years, she was able to overcome the millwright's sexism and became his friend.[345] Sheryl Johnson remembered that her supervisor tried to scare her out of applying for an apprenticeship. His "fear tactic" backfired; it made her angry, and she became a craft worker.[346] LaJuana Deanda, a black worker at the Homestead Works, said, "the major problem for females is probation. Some of the foremen propositioned the women. If they don't go, the women get their walking papers." She refused to play any games: "The foreman who pinched me on my behind—I didn't even speak to him. I just punched him. You got to stop the men before they get started."[347]

Male workers and supervisors also aided women workers. One woman remembered that when she started as a millwright's helper, "I didn't know a come-along from a wrench." Eventually, she became a skilled worker and said, "I have two guys to thank, who showed me."[348] In 1977, Ginny Hilde-brand became a laborer in J&L's Hot Coil Department in its Hazelwood mill. A college-educated socialist, she recalled that male workers' consciousness was "contradictory." They would make crude sexist remarks and racist jokes, but frequently transcended those limitations. The best worker in that shop was black, and "everyone treated him with the utmost respect." Hildebrand aspired to become a welder. Her foreman consulted the general foreman, who consented to her bid for a welding job, but only after she "carried the yoke." Hildebrand recalled that "The yoke was the worst job in the shop, no one wanted it." It was a heavy bar that allowed the overhead crane to carry coils to the pickling pits. "This was no formal requirement, but I said yes." The day arrived, and she was able to do the job only if she used her legs to help her lift the bar. Every man in that department, 250 in all, came to watch her "carry the yoke." Forty-five minutes from the end of her shift, Gino, the general foreman, watched her, shook his head and then left. Another worker, "a real Archie Bunker type," came over and told her to take a rest, that he'd finish the job. "He didn't do it because I was inferior. He knew I'd finish the job, but I'd proved my point."[349]

WHITE BACKLASH

If many minorities viewed the Consent Decree as half a loaf, many white steelworkers viewed it as a humiliating defeat. With the ink still wet on the Consent Decree, three hundred USWA members picketed their Pitts-burgh headquarters. Some protested that they were never given a chance to vote on the agreement. Others complained of reverse discrimination. One unionist noted that before the Consent Decree, "after 20 years in the mills, I was making $15,000 a year." After the Consent Decree, "I'm making $10,000. How am I supposed to take that?"[350] One unionist went so far as to file a complaint with the Equal Employment Opportunity Commission. Michael Bonn, an Assistant Grievance Committeeman at the Irvin Works, said he was passed over for the job of motor inspector apprentice because of his "race (white) and sex (male)."[351] Bonn argued he was not a bigot, but believed that since he had been waiting for years to get an apprentice-ship, the nineteen-year-old black woman who got the position should have to "wait her turn."[352]

The fight against the Consent Decree became a ghostly echo of past rank-and-file movements. Frank O'Brian, former President of Local 1843 in

Hazelwood and past DPC leader, railed against the agreement, arguing that it was "a sellout" of the seniority rights of most steelworkers: "The Decree wipes out departmental seniority as well as job security, I can't understand any union going along with such an agreement." Furthermore, steelworkers were never allowed to vote on the agreement.[353] O'Brian and other local presidents founded the Steel Workers for Justice Committee in order to fight the agreement; they denied that there was any racial motivation to their ultimately unsuccessful legal challenge to the Consent Decree.[354]

Black unionists such as Ray Henderson were indignant that local union presidents spent their locals' funds to fight the Consent Decree when they had rarely fought to protect minorities from discrimination. Of course, steel companies could have stopped discrimination "any time [they] wanted. . . . [I]t wouldn't have cost them a cent. But they were controlling two labor forces, black and white, and pitting one against the other."[355] As bleak as the situation was within the steel industry, steelworkers deserve credit for what they did accomplish, as the situation elsewhere in Pittsburgh was invariably worse. That story is the subject of the next section.

RENAISSANCE PITTSBURGH?

The declining fortunes of the steel industry stunted the economic, demographic, and political development of Pittsburgh. In 1960, steel companies employed 131,000 workers, about 30,000 fewer than in 1953, when postwar employment hit its peak. In the region as a whole, there were 776,000 employed workers, 70,000 fewer than in 1953, and Pittsburgh's employment would not return to Korean War levels until 1968. During the Vietnam War boom, area economists opined that Pittsburgh had finally broken free of its dependence on the steel industry and that the region's chronic employment crisis would ease.[356] This prediction proved somewhat true for the next ten years because steel's employment had stabilized at around 100,000 workers, and the total number of workers in the region expanded to 956,000. After 1978, however, a devastating round of plant closings plunged Pittsburgh into a recession from which it has yet to fully recover.[357]

In the 1960s and 1970s as heavy industry slowly bled jobs, Pittsburgh's population dwindled as well. Within the city limits, the population fell from 604,000 in 1960 to 520,000 in 1970 and to just 424,000 in 1980. Throughout the 1960s, the population of the region remained constant at about 2.4 million, but lost about 150,000 in the 1970s. Even during the Vietnam-era "boom," between one-fifth and one-third of young workers in the Mon Valley, the sons and daughters of industrial workers, moved to other regions in search of jobs that could support a family.[358] While all industrial cities lost population in these years to their suburbs, Pittsburgh's overall decline bespoke its bleak regional fortunes. Virtually alone among major urban areas, Pittsburgh attracted almost no immigrants from Latin America or Asia; its largest non-native immigrant group consisted of 4,000 Italians.[359] Southern black migrants also bypassed Pittsburgh. Even as agricultural mechanization decimated the ranks of Southern farm laborers and population in Northern industrial cities mushroomed, Pittsburgh's black population grew by a modest 3.5 percent a decade.[360] The transition to a "post-industrial" economy also had political consequences as the decline of heavy industry eroded the number and power of union members.

The owners of steel companies, in concert with other economic and political elites in Pittsburgh, continued to reshape Pittsburgh's economy through the Allegheny Conference on Community Development (ACCD). The ACCD continued to limit its membership to corporate, financial, and political elites; not until the late 1960s did it open its membership to include any black, female, or trade union members.[361] Not surprisingly, given its composition, despite the wide range of economic and social problems that beset Pittsburgh, the ACCD focused its attentions on revitalizing the downtown on terms that favored its landowners. In order to expand the amount of available office space for corporate headquarters, the ACCD sponsored initiatives to relieve downtown traffic congestion and improve Pittsburgh's cultural facilities. As in the past, public moneys financed most of the projects, clearing black "slums" in favor of parking facilities, stadiums, and highways. As in the past, private interests realized most of its gains.[362] On its own terms, this aspect of the Renaissance succeeded. By 1967, Pittsburgh was the third largest corporate center in the United States.[363]

Pittsburgh's "Renaissance" as a corporate headquarters resulted largely through the consolidation of existing businesses rather than attracting new industries or companies. The largest development in the "golden triangle" came in the late 1960s when U.S. Steel relocated its offices from New York to a new sixty-four-story office building located in downtown Pittsburgh.[364] Similarly, the rise of Pittsburgh as a center for corporate research resulted from the fact that Pittsburgh-based corporations closed regional research facilities around the country in favor of consolidated ones located in suburban Pittsburgh. This was the case with U.S. Steel, whose Monroeville facility expanded until by 1969 it had eighteen hundred employees.[365] Similarly, J&L's research facility employed about two hundred staff.[366] By 1968, Alcoa's New Kensington research facility was one of the world's most modern.[367] The Renaissance undoubtedly attracted additional jobs to the region that prevented a more rapid economic decline that would otherwise have occurred.[368] But the modest numbers of high-technology jobs did not offset the rapid decline of heavy industry. Pittsburgh's working class shouldered most of the pain and costs of the Renaissance, and none more so than black workers, who benefited least from the "booming" 1960s.

THE CIVIL RIGHTS CHALLENGE TO ELITES

The leaders of the ACCD generally ignored black workers, even as they tore down their neighborhoods to make room for Pittsburgh's downtown Renaissance. Frozen out of job markets, and suffering from high rates of unemployment, black workers periodically launched protests to achieve some benefits from the rebuilding of Pittsburgh's economy. One major protest came after black workers formed a local chapter of NALC; they targeted the new Civic Arena, which was located in what had been the Lower Hill District.[369] Prior to urban renewal in the 1950s, the Lower Hill had been a poor black neighborhood, but the contractors who ran the new Civic Arena hired just eight blacks out of a total workforce of several hundred. NALC and the NAACP staged a mass picket as the "awakening event" for Pittsburgh's black community.[370] The mass pickets won promises of jobs for black men and sparked a modest resurgence of community and union-based activism for equal employment.[371]

Despite such victories, jobs in Pittsburgh's downtown remained in sight of blacks but always out of reach. Pittsburgh's major corporations, including its steel companies, banks, and utilities, claimed that they would hire any "qualified Negro"—but most hired only token numbers of African Americans for white-collar jobs. For instance, U.S. Steel's research laboratories in Monroeville remained 99 percent white and employed even fewer blacks on the company's sales staff.[372] In 1963, the *Courier* discovered that such "rigorous" hiring standards at the U.S. Steel, Alcoa, and Koppers headquarters resulted in each company's employment of just two black female clerical workers.[373] Koppers (who manufactured coke ovens) proudly made its downtown board room available for civil rights meetings but employed just three African Americans in non-janitorial positions. The company explained that its "hiring standards" required that virtually all of its black employees push a broom.[374]

In the context of rising unemployment, and the escalation of the Southern civil rights struggle, it is hardly surprising that black workers attempted to alter the hiring practices of the region's major corporations. In 1963, black trade unionists within the NAACP formed the United Negro Protest Committee (UNPC), which served as that group's protest arm. The UNPC attempted to embarrass large companies like Duquesne Light into changing their hiring practices by organizing picket lines and a letter writing campaign.[375] While the UNPC attracted a small cadre of marchers, its protests fared no better than larger efforts that the black community had launched in the late 1940s. One indication that the UNPC jangled the nerves of elites was that the Pittsburgh Police developed its infamous "tactical squad" to deal with black protesters. The tactical squad included the city's largest cops, armed in riot gear, who were massed at each demonstration in order to intimidate picketers. Even black policemen believed that the cops "take particular offense to black people picketing for equality and young people protesting against the Vietnam war."[376] One UNPC official admitted that "boycotting companies like Alcoa, Dravo [shipbuilding] and U.S. Steel is pretty difficult, so we may ask the federal government to look into violations of the Civil Rights Act . . . and cut off those big money contracts many of the companies are holding."[377]

As in the past, only the federal government possessed the economic leverage or legal authority to alter the behavior of corporations. The only question was whether the civil rights movement possessed the strength to give government the requisite will to take on corporations. The test would come in the construction industry.

BLACK POWER AND THE PITTSBURGH PLAN

The fight over the desegregation of the construction industry revealed the limitations of Renaissance Pittsburgh (and the New Deal more generally) for black workers. Far more than in the steel industry, the collusion between white executives and unionists hindered the occupational advances of African American construction workers. While the USWA allowed everyone whom companies hired to join the union, construction unions chose their members and then found them work with the unionized contractors who built most of the large projects in the region. As one black electrician observed, "They have so many doors to keep Negroes out of the craft unions, they might as well be using steel bars."[378] In 1968 and 1969, Pittsburgh experienced a massive building boom. Corporations such as U.S. Steel spent $200 million to expand their office space, and the city of Pittsburgh built a new stadium for the Pittsburgh Steelers and the Pirates. Although most of the construction was within sight of the predominantly black Hill District, few blacks worked at these construction sites; in fact, many of the employed white workers were brought in from out of state. A few blacks were visible "lifting or wheeling or carrying but not . . . doing any skilled work other than a token here and there."[379] In 1969, eighteen organizations formed the Black Construction Coalition (BCC) and negotiated with contractors and unions to get blacks jobs in the construction industry. The BCC also supported these negotiations with demonstrations at construction sites throughout downtown Pittsburgh. At one of the first demonstrations, white construction workers pelted BCC demonstrators with rocks.[380]

Although the BCC, the city, and police agreed to coordinate future demonstrations in an effort to avoid violence, at one of the next demonstrations the police themselves turned violent. On August 25, 1969, thousands of demonstrators chanting "jobs now" marched past closed downtown construction sites. (The city had ordered construction workers off the sites to prevent further clashes.) As the protesters approached the job site at the Three Rivers Stadium, the tactical squad brutally dispersed the march.[381] One marcher, Aurelia Diggs, watched helplessly as a "burly sadist bigot garbed in a policeman's uniform straddled a young black woman and beat her like an animal."[382] Although the BCC, contractors, unions, and the city agreed to a five-day moratorium on demonstrations and building, angry white construction workers stormed the mayor's office demanding that he reopen work sites and compensate them for lost time. The city eventually paid the workers.[383]

Amidst massive white resistance, the BCC mobilized to cut off federal aid for building projects. The Pittsburgh Human Relations Commission halted $4 million worth of construction until the BCC and contractors agreed to a solution. Out of these negotiations emerged the controversial "Pittsburgh Plan," which allocated federal moneys to train blacks for construction jobs.[384] Contractors and unions promised that by 1973, twelve hundred blacks would be trained and hold union cards.[385] Because the plan lacked guarantees, several members of the BCC refused to sign onto the plan. Moreover, several black administrators of the Pittsburgh Plan won the federal training contracts.[386] As early as 1971, the *Pittsburgh Post-Gazette* indicated that few workers had been trained, while much of the federal money disappeared into bogus companies owned by the black administrators of the Pittsburgh Plan.[387] By 1972, the Pittsburgh Plan had fallen at least 50 percent behind schedule, and the *Pittsburgh Courier* disputed whether more than a handful of men had found construction jobs.[388] The Office of Federal Contract Compliance found that one-half of the unions failed to comply with the plan and therefore risked a three-year ban from work that relied on federal funding. However, black members of the Pittsburgh Plan urged that federal funding continue. Sadly, no union or contractor was ever punished.[389] Only in 1977 did Mayor Pete Flaherty remove those members with the most serious conflicts of interest. But the damage to the civil rights movement had already been done.[390] Nonetheless, the Pittsburgh Plan was hailed by the Nixon Administration, construction unions, and contractors as a success.[391] On the foundations of such "successes," Renaissance Pittsburgh built a post-industrial economy whose class inequalities were only exceeded by its institutionalized racial disparities.

CONCLUSION

In the face of a deeply divided working class, Pittsburgh's ruling elites relied on the ACCD to rebuild Pittsburgh into a Renaissance city. The ACCD succeeded in physically transforming Pittsburgh's downtown and reduced the city's notorious pollution problems, all of which encouraged such powerful corporations as U.S. Steel, Westinghouse, Alcoa, and Koppers to keep their headquarters in the city. As these companies closed many of their manufacturing plants, corporate headquarters and research parks provided post-industrial Pittsburgh with its most important (albeit far smaller) economic engine. Yet in the "new" economy, the tried and true tactic of "divide and conquer" would dominate the distribution of jobs. The saga of the construction workers and the "Pittsburgh Plan" reveals the unwillingness of capital, government, and many unions to ameliorate the racial discrimination within their institutions. The sad tale of the Pittsburgh Plan occurred when the USWA and its model of industrial unionism remained the dominant labor organization in the region and could have affected its outcome. The USWA's unwillingness to intervene in this case, or to lead by example, helped to doom Pittsburgh's working class to a future of racial tension. The USWA's inability to counter the flight of capital from heavy industry ensured that racial tension occurred within the context of a precipitous decline in workers' standard of living. That tragic tale is the subject of the next chapter.

Table One

Population of Pittsburgh and Its SMSA, by Race, 1960–1980

| | PITTSBURGH SMSA | | PITTSBURGH | |
	Total Population	Blacks	Total Population	Blacks
1960	2,405,435	163,325	604,322	101,739
1970	2,401,245	169,884	520,117	104,904
1980	2,263,894	175,603	423,938	101,813

Source: Bureau of the Census, *Population Census: 1960* (Washington, D.C.: GPO, 1961), Part 40, 75, 104; Bureau of the Census, *Population Census: 1970* (Washington, D.C.: GPO, 1972), Part 40, 115; Bureau of the Census, *Population Census: 1980* (Washington, D.C.: GPO, 1983), Part 40, 40.

Table Two

Economic Indicators of the Allegheny County Steel Industry

	Capital Invested	Wages	Value added
1958	136	287	680
1963	75	295	690
1967	116	357	980
1972	58	391	741
1977	103	643	1600

Source: Bureau of the Census, *Census of Manufactures: 1958*, Volume III (Washington, D.C.: GPO, 1961), Chapter 37, 26; Bureau of the Census, *Census of Manufactures: 1963*, Volume III (Washington, D.C.: GPO, 1966), Chapter 39, 29; U.S. Bureau of the Census, *Census of Manufactures: 1967*, Volume III (Washington, D.C.: GPO, 1971), Chapter 39, 32; Bureau of the Census, *Census of Manufactures: 1972*, Volume III (Washington, D.C.: GPO, 1976), Chapter 39, 32; Bureau of the Census, *Census of Manufactures: 1977*, Volume III (Washington, D.C.: GPO, 1981), Chapter 39, 41. Wages for production workers only.

Table Three
Profitability of the Duquesne Works, 1961–1970

	Wages	Capital	Value	Value Added
1961	34	N/A	N/A	N/A
1962	34	19	177	76
1963	36	24	212	92
1964	38	7	273	131
1965	39	6	331	149
1966	39	4	327	165
1967	38	3	313	124
1968	40	8	325	129
1969	41	0	351	147
1970	38	0	351	87

Source: Department of Internal Affairs, Bureau of Statistics, *County Industry Report: Allegheny County*, 1961–1975 (Harrisburg: Department of Internal Affairs, 1962–1976).

Table Four
Profitability of the Homestead Works, 1961–1977

	Wages	Capital	Value	Value Added
1961	59	N/A	N/A	N/A
1962	61	30	320	63
1963	61	41	345	68
1964	66	53	405	146
1965	71	47	420	242
1966	72	120	425	162
1967	70	N/A	373	84
1968	70	21	398	77
1969	77	31	387	123
1970	72	23	487	207
1974	133	7	698	230
1976	135	4	744	236
1977	143	N/A	814	207

Source: Department of Internal Affairs, Bureau of Statistics, *County Industry Report: Allegheny County*, 1961–1975 (Harrisburg: Department of Internal Affairs, 1962–1976).

Table Five
Workers at the Duquesne, Homestead, and Irvin Works, 1961–1968

DUQUESNE WORKS

| Year | Total | PRODUCTION AND MAINTENANCE | | CLERICAL AND TECHNICAL | |
		Male	Female	Male	Female
1961	4481	3439	3	921	118
1962	4442	3398	3	917	124
1963	4461	3521	2	800	138
1964	4768	3743	2	891	132
1965	4850	3794	2	905	149
1966	4864	3764	2	969	129
1967	4460	3449	2	899	110
1968	4418	3460	4	846	108

HOMESTEAD WORKS

| Year | Total | PRODUCTION AND MAINTENANCE | | CLERICAL AND TECHNICAL | |
		Male	Female	Male	Female
1961	7976	6108	101	1531	236
1962	7690	6019	91	1344	236
1963	7851	6401	93	1142	215
1964	8175	6644	95	1223	213
1965	8956	7432	76	1298	150
1966	9175	7604	79	1293	199
1967	8644	6937	66	1441	200
1968	9265	7590	67	1407	201

IRVIN WORKS

| Year | Total | PRODUCTION AND MAINTENANCE | | CLERICAL AND TECHNICAL | |
		Male	Female	Male	Female
1961	3415	2625	57	607	126
1962	3709	2921	71	587	130
1963	3569	2850	82	486	151
1964	4044	3365	44	491	144
1965	4153	3410	99	485	159
1966	4182	3423	106	633	20
1967	4172	3380	81	558	153
1968	4124	3384	75	554	161

Source: Commonwealth of Pennsylvania, Department of Internal Affairs, *County Industry Report*, "Allegheny County" (Harrisburg: 1961–68). 1961, 7–20; 1962, 7–26; 1963, 7–23; 1964, 7–23; 1965, 9–25; 1966, 10–27; 1967, 22–39; 1968, 23–40.

Table Six
Number of Steelworkers, by Occupation and Gender, 1960–1980

MALE

	Professionals, Managers, Technicians	Skilled Crafts/ Foremen	Operatives	Laborers	Clerical	All*
1960—Pgh	10,834	37,867	30,285	25,795	9,505	116,620
1971—PA	30,944	46,927	81,317	30,230	10,982	201,826
1980—Pgh						68,217

FEMALE

	Professionals, Managers, Technicians	Skilled Crafts/ Foremen	Operatives	Laborers	Clerical	All
1960—Pgh	398	158	378	385	5,661	7,031
1971—PA	616	25	1,086	939	7,929	10,664
1980—Pgh						8,579

MALE

	Professionals, Managers, Technicians	Skilled Crafts/ Foremen	Operatives	Laborers	Clerical	All
1960—Pgh	96.5%	99.6%	98.8%	98.5%	62.7%	94.3%
1971—PA	98.0%	99.9%	98.7%	97.0%	58.1%	95.0%
1980—Pgh						88.8%

FEMALE

	Professionals, Managers, Technicians	Skilled Crafts/ Foremen	Operatives	Laborers	Clerical	All*
1960—Pgh	3.5%	0.4%	1.2%	1.5%	37.5%	5.7%
1971—PA	2.0%	0.1%	1.3%	3.0%	41.9%	5.0%
1980—Pgh						11.2%

*Number of all workers includes sales, service, and plant protection.
Source: Bureau of the Census, *Population Census: 1960*, Part 40, 96; Equal Employment Opportunity Commission, *Equal Employment Opportunity Report—1971: Job Patterns for Minorities and Women in Private Industry, Volume 3*, 177; Bureau of the Census, *Population Census: 1980*.

Table Seven
Number of Workers at the Duquesne Works

	Total	P&M	Clerical	
June 1960		5,000	N/A	910 laid off
August 1960		3,600	N/A	1,800 short shifts
1961	4,481	3,442	1,040	
1962	4,442	4,001	1,035	
1963	4,461	3,523	924	
1964	4,768	3,745	1,029	
1965	4,850	3,796	1,037	
1966	4,864	3,766	1,118	
1967	4,460	3,451	899	
1968	4,418	3,464	846	
1969	4,272	3,378	894	
1970	3,862	3,071	791	
1971	3,569	2,852	717	
1972	3,637	2,959	678	
1973	3,737	3,117	620	
1974	3,867	3,236	631	
1975	3,607	2,920	687	
1976	3,360	2,715	645	
1977	3,452	2,827	625	

Source: USWA Research Department; Bureau of Statistics, Pennsylvania Department of Internal Affairs, *Industrial Directory of the Commonwealth of Pennsylvania* (Harrisburg: 1961–77). P&M are Production and Maintenance workers.

Table Eight
Number of Workers at the Homestead Works

	Total	P&M	Clerical	
June 1960		7,655	N/A	4,600 short shifts
August 1960		7,400	N/A	2,941 short shifts
1961	7,976	6,209	1,767	
1962	7,690	6,110	1,580	
1963	7,851	6,494	1,357	
1964	8,175	6,739	1,436	
1965	8,956	7,508	1,448	
1966	9,175	7,683	1,492	
1967	8,644	7,003	1,641	
1968	9,265	7,657	1,608	
1969	9,293	7,724	1,569	
1970	9,250	7,940	1,310	
1971	8,047	6,526	1,521	
1972	8,161	6,790	1,371	
1973	8,714	7,265	1,449	
1974	9,212	7,697	1,515	
1975	7,931	6,352	1,579	
1976	6,807	5,488	1,319	
1977	7,217	5,880	1,337	

Source: USWA Research Department; Bureau of Statistics, Pennsylvania Department of Internal Affairs, *Industrial Directory of the Commonwealth of Pennsylvania* (Harrisburg: 1961–77).

Table Nine
Occupational Composition of Steel Workforce in Pittsburgh by Race

WHITES

	Unskilled	Semi-Skilled	Skilled
1963	14.4%	36.5%	23.8%
1966	16.4%	38.8%	24.4%
1971 (PA)	12.5%	32.3%	24.0%
1974	10.6%	40.6%	24.3%
1978	9.7%	36.9%	23.6%

BLACKS

	Unskilled	Semi-Skilled	Skilled
1963	29.3%	55.9%	10.2%
1966	32.8%	51.8%	10.4%
1971 (PA)	23.5%	54.1%	13.4%
1974	28.8%	55.6%	14.3%
1978	17.6%	52.2%	16.2%

Source: Bureau of the Census, *Census of Population: 1960* (Washington, D.C.: GPO, 1961), Part 40, 1141–75; Bureau of the Census, *Census of Population: 1970* (Washington, D.C.: GPO, 1972), Part 40, 971, 986–92, 1017–19; Bureau of the Census, *Census of Population: 1980* (Washington, D.C.: GPO, 1983), Part 40, 346, 400.

Chapter Five

⚛

The Lean Years: 1978–2000

"Remove the voice, the votes, the numerical strength, the financial
strength and the proven social track record of organized labor from
America's economic and political life, and the clock would be inevitably turned back. Some of the worst economic and political excesses in
America would surface and discover a friendlier climate for survival.
Some of the dignity gained for workers and the elderly and the less fortunate would be stripped away, layer by layer. The scales would once
again be tilted against the workers."

I.W. Abel, 1976.[1]

COMING TO TERMS WITH DEINDUSTRIALIZATION

By the mid-1970s, few major cities in the United States remained as
dependent upon heavy industry as did Pittsburgh. Consequently, the plant
closings of the 1970s and 1980s that affected the American working class
eviscerated workers in the Steel City. The region lost so much of its manufacturing base that by 1990 it had proportionally fewer industrial workers
than the national average.[2] So many young and middle-aged adults migrated
from Pittsburgh's job holocaust that the city possessed a higher geriatric proportion of its population than any city outside of Florida. This demographic
profile presented a stark contrast with Pittsburgh in its heyday of industrialization. In 1900, when steel enjoyed rapid growth, Pittsburgh possessed so
many working age adults that its proportion of elderly residents was half that
of most American cities.[3] Many of these workers at the turn of the century

joined the vast industrial armies mobilized by capitalists to produce their wealth. By the 1920s and for decades thereafter, the captains of industries discharged their troops in favor of machines. By the late 1960s, industrialists' pursuit of wealth dictated that they abandon the old battlegrounds and troops, and their capital stole away to new arenas of commerce. Although Pittsburgh in the late 1990s remained a center of steel production, the industry employed a fraction of its former workforce. Steel continues to shape the region today, but largely in terms of lost jobs, squandered opportunities, and a legacy of politics whose style approximates that of a coal camp or a colonial city.[4]

Such massive economic upheaval requires an explanation. Many middle-class observers in Pittsburgh concluded that the dismantling of heavy industry, what scholars have termed deindustrialization, was a natural part of the transition to an economy based upon services and high technology. One of Pittsburgh's premier historians, Roy Lubove, termed steel and other heavy industries part of a "dinosaur economy" whose demise was painful but inevitable.[5] In the wake of deindustrialization, the *Pittsburgh Press* editorialized that "this time we must build new industries, new jobs, new outlooks. . . . [W]e must reinvent Pittsburgh."[6] The call for "new thinking" became a mantra that permeated and redefined Pittsburgh's politics. For Senator Rick Santorum (R-PA), a native of the region, the blame for deindustrialization should be shared equally by owners, workers, and the community at large. "The steel industry changed and we didn't change with it. . . . [N]ow once thriving mills stand as monuments to our lack of vision and our unwillingness to change."[7] In particular, many ostensibly "public" policy analysts have concluded that the unwillingness of unionized workers to accept lower pay scales and more flexible work rules hastened the demise of steel, coal, railroads, and electrical machine manufacturing. Consequently, policy makers such as Santorum have sought to counteract the region's reputation for "chronic labor problems" which ostensibly made the region "a difficult place to do business." Whatever its cause, capital investment per manufacturing worker remains amongst the lowest of any major city in the country. In the fevered imaginations of elites, the specter of "big labor" haunts the region, and weighs like a nightmare on the brains of the living.[8]

Such views ignore the fact that industrialization in Pittsburgh was anything but a natural economic process—and one that even in the heyday of industrial unionism was controlled by big business. By the mid-nineteenth century, railroads, steel companies, and large banks acquired enormous economic and political power that enabled them to enlist the state to help it disorganize labor. Pittsburgh's rapid industrialization depended heavily on its "pro-business climate"—where neither workers nor the state could impose costs (such as decent wages and working conditions, taxes, or environmental controls) on industrialists. Furthermore, the centralization of steel production in Pittsburgh after 1901 owed as much to U.S. Steel's desire to circumvent the market via the "Pittsburgh-plus" system as to the region's proximity to coking coal. Finally, the health and profitability of steel relied in no small part on its ability to ensure that its political influence resulted in military contracts.[9]

Only in the 1930s did workers organize sufficient political strength to contend with that of their employers. The resulting New Deal compromise supported the formation of unions and forced employers to pay more taxes, but the state also funneled considerable capital to industrialists via the "warfare state." While riddled with contradictions, this political compromise held long enough for liberal and pro-labor politicians to weaken the coercive power that employers had exercised for decades. No longer could employers rely upon armies of private police or labor spies. Furthermore, labor won legislative victories that promoted unionism (the Wagner Act) and ensured the prosperity that workers would enjoy after World War II (Social Security, the forty-hour week, and unemployment insurance). Workers' political organization soon weakened, an early victim of employers' political counter-offensive and the Cold War, but their unions retained considerable power and allowed their members to receive a greater share of the wealth that they created—more so than for most wage earners.[10] Labor certainly altered power relations in Pittsburgh—and the economics of steel—but the industry remained profitable for decades, and capital always retained control of its investment decisions and indeed most shop-floor policies regarding workers.

The rapidity and thoroughness of the final stages of deindustrialization in the early 1980s blinded many observers—and not a few workers—to the fact that the efficiency of the steel industry and the efficacy of New Deal compromise had both deteriorated for years. The two phenomena were interrelated, as steel's declining productivity resulted from political as well as economic forces. Beginning in the 1950s, the federal government shifted its military subsidies from steel to more strategic industries such as aerospace, computers, and electronics. Other federal programs initially offset this decline (notably the interstate highway program), although the most lasting benefits accrued to motor vehicle manufacturers and related industries. Steel's profitability was decided in part by the federal government that in the Cold War weighed its obligations for a strong national economy against its responsibilities as the manager of the international economy. In the 1950s, the federal government not only opened steel markets to its allies but it helped underwrite their capital investment programs. Consequently, American steel industrialists confronted an increasingly competitive market (where their competitors received substantial state assistance) without their traditional federal subsidies or strong tariff protections. Higher labor costs simply compounded big steel's problems.[11] Thus throughout the post-World War II period, managers shifted capital into non-steel ventures while they also pursued labor efficiencies in steel.

Steelworkers relied on their political power and ability to disrupt steel production to win a measure of job security and a substantial rise in their standard of living. From its first contract with U.S. Steel in 1937, steel unionism was part and parcel of the political turmoil and deal-making of the New Deal. Each subsequent contract that steelworkers negotiated with steel firms often required strikes and the intervention of the President of the United States, anxious to avoid general economic disruption. Yet throughout the early period of the Cold War, neither liberals nor labor enjoyed sufficient political strength to pass broad legislation as in the 1930s. Indeed, labor never succeeded in overturning the Taft-Hartley amendment to the Wagner Act, which helped to stymie mass unionization and stifled labor's political organization. By the early 1960s, the Democratic Party began to abandon the progressive taxation of the rich. (Admittedly, the origins of such taxation owed as much to the efforts to pay for World War II as much as liberal or pro-labor sentiments.) Such trends were obscured by the Indian summer that New Deal liberalism enjoyed in the mid-1960s. Again, in a few short years, legislators abolished racial segregation, began a war on poverty, and broadened the Social Security system to include health coverage for the aged and indigent. These victories were due in no small part to the political support of CIO unions such as the USWA and the United Auto Workers. Ultimately, the Democratic Party failed to prioritize social spending or redistributive programs over the Cold War or the hot war in Vietnam. Furthermore, liberalism's accomplishments on civil rights seemed too little too late for many black activists and too far too fast for many white workers.[12]

The legislative victories of the liberal-labor alliance in the mid-1960s obscured the USWA's increasing emphasis on specific public policies for its members and employers rather than legislation that benefited workers as a whole. Since the late 1950s, big steel argued that it needed protection from foreign producers, and from the early 1960s onwards, the USWA echoed its pleas.[13] Unsurprisingly, deindustrialization proved to be as political a process as industrialization or the operation and demise of the New Deal. Unfortunately, in both economic and political terms, deindustrialization impoverished workers and the region.

CONCESSIONS AND CORPORATIONS

Throughout the late 1970s, big steel firms sought concessions from government and the USWA. Failing that, big steel searched for a plausible scapegoat. Decades of lackluster investment prevented steel companies from competing with more modern facilities abroad, but American firms blamed the environmental regulations of the early 1970s for ostensibly preventing modernization.[14] Edgar Speer, the chairman of U.S. Steel, referred to the Environmental Protection Agency (EPA) as "those nuts in Washington" opposed to free enterprise and economic growth. In 1976, U.S. Steel took out full-page ads in Pittsburgh that threatened to lay off forty thousand workers because the company said that it could not meet the new environmental regulations for the Clairton Works.[15] U.S. Steel adamantly resisted implementing even simple, low-cost changes in steelmaking that would have resulted in less pollution, leading John R. Quasler, a senior EPA official, to conclude that "U.S. Steel has compiled a record of environmental recalcitrance that is second to none." U.S. Steel ultimately convinced the EPA to impose less stringent pollution controls, complied with those regulations, and then laid off most of its workforce in the 1980s.[16]

Government requirements that the mills clean up their egregious pollution definitely imposed substantial costs on steelmakers, although the regulations were no less costly than those born by Japanese companies.[17] Moreover, given that steel firms had already begun to shift capital into non-steel ventures *before* the 1970s, it seems unlikely that the steel companies would have fundamentally altered the trajectory of their investments just because of environmental regulations. However, big steel generally succeeded in winning the union and workers to its point of view on the environment and imports. As one retired worker explained, "Nobody used to complain about the smoke. Now everybody complains. If there's no smoke, you ain't got no job."[18] The USWA often mobilized workers to oppose environmental controls on steel companies. In the early 1980s, big steel promoted a major advertising campaign with the cooperation of the USWA that promised workers that "the threat is *real* from foreign steel: it's a job-robbing deal." David Roderick, the head of U.S. Steel, blamed foreign producers for "predatory," "discriminatory," and "illegal" trading practices.[19] At the USWA headquarters and in the bastions of some rank-and-file locals, union leaders banned imported cars from the union's parking lots.[20] Thus Pittsburgh's deindustrialization occurred within the context of corporate hegemony over the political analysis and agenda of the USWA.

Even as steel began to collapse as an employer, big steel exerted enormous control over how workers understood deindustrialization. A case in point was Johnstown, Pennsylvania. Beginning in 1973 and continuing throughout the decade, Bethlehem began to close its massive mill in Johnstown. Rather than comply with new environmental regulations for the mill's aging open hearths, the company sought regulatory relief until its old furnaces wore out and it could install modern electric furnaces. In the early 1970s, Bethlehem planned to lay off a third of its workforce of twelve thousand workers. Over the next several years, the union helped Bethlehem pressure environmental agencies and mobilized to urge the government to protect steelmakers from imports. Jack Metzgar, who grew up in Johnstown, summarized the situation: "what is most remarkable . . . is the almost total submission of the steelworkers and the community to the will of Bethlehem Steel. There has been no organized effort to stop the cutback, no plant occupations, no protest demonstrations. . . . [N]o one has suggested that Bethlehem has any less than an absolute right to decide the fate of this western Pennsylvania community."[21] By the end of 1982, just over two thousand workers remained on the job, and another five thousand were laid off.[22] By 1983, fed-up workers at another Johnstown mill rejected the third set of concessions to U.S. Steel that would have cost each worker ten thousand dollars a year. The company immediately closed the plant.[23]

In Youngstown, Ohio, steelworkers challenged the right of corporations to unilaterally decide their fate. For much of the 1970s, the Lykes conglomerate diverted capital from its steel division (formerly Youngstown Sheet and Tube) and funneled it into its electronics division. In 1977, Lykes announced that it would completely shut down the Campbell Works located in Youngstown. At first, residents of Youngstown "rail[ed] about

Lykes, foreign imports or the EPA—which was the line adopted initially by local politicians . . . [and] the USWA and by many steelworkers." But radical rank-and-file workers and community activists advocated that local government exercise its power of eminent domain, take over the facility, and run it in the public interest. Rather than let Lykes make the decision about the fate of their town, workers commissioned an economic feasibility study that showed that with $15 million in government grants and $400 million in loans, the facility could remain open and preserve several thousand jobs. The national leaders of the USWA gave the plan little support (the union staunchly supported "free enterprise"), and the federal government, then headed by Democratic President Jimmy Carter, refused to release the needed money. Staughton Lynd, a key community activist, pointed out that the "tightfisted" Carter Administration allocated over $20 billion for cost over runs on the F-18 fighter and could have easily found the moneys to aid steelworkers.[24] Instead, the Justice Department agreed to let LTV buy Youngstown Sheet and Tube and proceed to replicate the process of disinvestment and mill closures on a far larger scale.[25]

In 1979, U.S. Steel announced that it would close its facilities in Youngstown and lay off three thousand five hundred workers. The company told workers that imports and environmental regulations forced them to close the plant. Bob Vasquez, the local President of the Ohio Works replied that in three separate rulings "the government says that [imports] don't apply here." When he asked the company "what new EPA rules go into effect in 1980, they admitted there weren't any."[26] Building off their experiences with the shutdown of the Campbell Works, local trade unionists filed a lawsuit to prevent U.S. Steel from closing any additional plants. (Workers began to put their own spin on the company's campaign to blame imports for layoffs: "The threat is real—from U.S. Steel.")[27] Initially, a federal judge issued an injunction to keep the mill open, but then ruled in favor of the company. The judge noted that "United States Steel should not be permitted to leave the Youngstown area devastated after drawing from the life blood of the community for so many years. Unfortunately, the mechanism to reach this ideal settlement, to recognize this new property right [of workers to their jobs or communities to the dominant industries] is not now in existence in the code of laws of our nation." U.S. Steel refused to bargain with local trade unionists who sought to buy the plant, and early the following year hundreds of workers occupied the plant. Local management agreed to sell them the mill if workers obtained the necessary capital, and workers ended their sit-in. But the top management of U.S. Steel refused to consider a sale to any worker-owned firm that received government assistance.[28]

Instead, steel firms raised the specter of plant shutdowns to garner enormous concessions from the federal government. In May 1979, U.S. Steel wrested exemptions from the EPA that halved the costs of complying with environmental regulations. David Roderick promised that "U.S. Steel can now act aggressively to revitalize our Pittsburgh area operations." But according to Staughton Lynd, "Two and a half years later, the company has made no major new investments in its facilities in the Pittsburgh area."[29] While steel companies may have profited from the military buildup begun under Carter and vigorously continued by Reagan, higher levels of military spending did little to increase steel employment. As with the environment, so with taxes. In the early days of the Reagan Administration, steel firms won substantial tax breaks in order to deal with imported goods. Instead of modernizing their mills, big steel shifted even more capital out of steel and into more profitable areas. In March 1982, U.S. Steel took its concessions and paid $1.4 billion in cash and $4.7 billion in loans for Marathon Oil. (U.S. Steel anticipated that oil's business cycles would offset that of steel.) Furthermore, U.S. Steel saved approximately $500 million in taxes through the merger. The architect of tax concessions to steel firms, Senator Arlen Specter (R-PA), was dismayed. Specter complained that "we go out on a limb in Congress and we feel they should be putting it in steel."[30] The concessions were enough to have allowed U.S. Steel to modernize several mills, but lawmakers had bailed out steel companies, not steel mills. In the midst of a tide of imported metal and red ink (steel firms collectively lost $5.5 billion in 1982–83), the company sought to save itself, not steel. Steel executives simply exercised their right to invest where profits seemed most promising—which apparently was anywhere but Pittsburgh and often as far from aging steel mills as possible.[31]

While U.S. Steel's merger with Marathon cheered businessmen who thought the firm showed "good sense" to further diversify from steel, it angered trade unionists who suspected that they would pay the bill for such investments. Many workers simply did not believe the company's statement that the merger would "not diminish the company's commitment to steel." At Homestead, Frank Domagala told one reporter that "U.S. Steel is a big farce. This mill has been a profit maker for them and they have not put a dime into it." Another echoed Domagala's analysis: "They still need to make repairs in the mill. It's decrepit and falling apart. They've been promising to fix it up since 1970."[32] But over the next year, Marathon absorbed 80 percent of U.S. Steel's capital expenditures ($1.2 billion) and over $900 million in interest charges.[33] Modernization of this sort all but guaranteed the shutdown of steel in Pittsburgh.

U.S. Steel apparently learned from its Youngstown experiences to avoid a single announcement of mill closures in Pittsburgh.[34] Instead, U.S. Steel promised Pittsburgh's steelworkers that it would keep open profitable facilities, which allowed it to wrest concessions from local unions and to close the rest one piece at a time. The net economic result devastated workers and communities as badly as in Youngstown, but this method of plant closings impeded mass mobilization. By 1987, U.S. Steel had closed more than two-thirds of its steelmaking capacity in the Pittsburgh region, and about 85 percent to 90 percent of its former production workers lost their jobs. The Corporation shuttered the Carrie Furnaces (1982), Duquesne (1984), the steel mill at Clairton (1984), Homestead (1986), National Tube (1987), and the fabricating division in Ambridge (American Bridge, 1987).[35] U.S. Steel began to assemble its new Mon Valley Works from the remains of Clairton (its coke ovens and chemical processing facilities), ET (primarily the BOP shop and primary mill), and the Irvin Works (its rolling mills). Initially, the Corporation added Homestead and Duquesne-National Tube to the Mon Valley Works but then closed those facilities.[36] As one steelworker later complained, "the union did not do enough to keep Homestead open. The union let management close the mill piece by piece. . . . Dorothy Six at Duquesne set a production record but yet was closed down."[37]

A similar process of disinvestment and deindustrialization occurred at LTV (formerly J&L). Despite a new electric furnace installed at the Southside Works in 1978, LTV had not kept pace with its competitors. Consequently, in the early 1980s, the company began shutting down its older departments.[38] One trade unionist recalled with bitter irony that "we worked in a brand new facility and we were shut down regardless" because the "steel industry became part of the finance industry." High interest rates burdened capital investments in steel with substantial interest payments, and even with a modern furnace, LTV thought that it would earn more money by shifting new investment into non-steel industries.[39] By 1985, LTV shuttered all but one department at the Aliquippa Works and then all of the Southside Works.[40] The next year, the company won "drastic" reductions in wages and benefits.[41] A year later, the company defaulted on its pension, forcing the government to take it over at a cost of hundreds of millions of dollars.[42]

Even as they led a fight against imported steel, the major steel companies moved substantial amounts of their capital and business abroad. In many cases, steel firms continued their longstanding pattern of buying mines throughout the world. Throughout the 1970s and 1980s, U.S. Steel invested extensively in steel-related mining operations in South Africa where apartheid ensured that black miners earned extremely low wages. As a result, the profits from what the *Economist* termed "King Solomon's Other Mines" remained high.[43] Sometimes the companies undercut their American operations through joint partnerships with foreign companies. In March 1983, U.S. Steel announced plans to buy 3.5 million tons of steel slabs from British Steel for its Fairless Works outside of Philadelphia. Ironically, Roderick had led steel's lobbying of the federal government for protection from imports. The head of Bethlehem Steel complained that U.S. Steel's plan was "unacceptable and irresponsible" because it imperiled further federal action on imports. The news seemed calculated to rub salt in workers' wounds as it shortly followed the first round of concessions by the USWA to steel companies. (The deal ultimately collapsed.)[44] In 1985, U.S. Steel agreed to buy steel slabs from a South Korean firm rather than produce them in its mill in Utah.[45] In the early 1980s, when the market for steel pipe exploded, U.S. Steel bought tubes from an Italian steelmaker. When the Texas oil boom ended, so did the market for steel pipe, and the net result was that U.S. Steel honored its contract with the Italian company and shut down its tube mill in McKeesport.[46]

The case of nearby Weirton, West Virginia, showed what course steel's history might have taken had worker ownership and capital investment proceeded on a mass scale. In 1984, National Steel sold its mill to its workers who remained in an unaffiliated union (workers were not members of the USWA, nor was the union a member of the AFL-CIO). Workers granted the new company extensive wage concessions but initially saved most of the seven thousand remaining jobs. The new ESOP (Employee Stock Ownership Plan) invested far more in the mill than most comparable mills and still turned a profit. The ESOP stopped short of giving workers the extensive control of the company envisioned by radical workers in Youngstown or in Weirton, and over the next fifteen years, the new ESOP eliminated about half of the jobs of its member-owners. Nonetheless, the ESOP at Weirton proved far more efficient, in both economic and social terms, than the big steel firms, who managed the meltdown of the Mon Valley.[47]

STRUGGLING AGAINST DEINDUSTRIALIZATION

In the late 1970s, radical steelworkers gradually increased their foothold within the USWA. Dissidents gained control of large local unions at Homestead, Duquesne, and Irvin and a few smaller ones.[48] In some respects, the latest upsurge of protest resulted from the influx of socialists, many of whom entered steel shortly before and after the 1977 campaign of Ed Sadlowski.[49] Yet left-wingers sometimes held back mass struggle as they bitterly vied with each other for leadership of rank-and-file movements. Steffie Domike recalled that at the Clairton Works there were about ten communists from four different groups, and "we didn't talk to each other, we hated each other." By 1978, many of the radical groups had collapsed or their cadre moved on to new industries, but those that remained had learned to cooperate with each other and gained some credibility among the workers. As Bob Anderson recalled, "You know, all that stuff was kind of coming together in the early 1980s and then it was all over."[50]

Yet socialists helped facilitate steelworkers' unprecedented levels of organization. In the face of ongoing sexual harassment, female cadre helped organized a women's caucus in the union and a newsletter, *Women of Steel*.[51] The socialist organizers of the *Mill Hunk Herald* created a unique magazine that drew on both "radical chic" and blue-collar culture. Workers submitted prose, poems, and cartoons, helped lay out the journal, and raised funds through disco parties (Mill Hunk Funk) or basketball games (Mill Hunk Dunk).[52] As unemployment grew, rank-and-file locals organized food pantries and supported the formation of the Mon Valley Unemployed Committee. One steelworker recalled that after years of conservative trade unionism, "all of a sudden there's this giant movement taking place . . . it was pretty wild."[53]

Yet even on the brink of deindustrialization, activists engaged in bitter fights over the leadership of the new mass organizations. Infighting tore apart one of the most promising groups, the Mon Valley Steelworkers Unemployed Committee (MVSUC). Hearkening back to the movements of the 1930s, workers mobilized so much resistance to foreclosures that the Sheriff of Allegheny County refused to seize the houses of the unemployed who could no longer pay their mortgages. But the movement began to implode, in large part due to suspicions that individuals who belonged to different groups sought to take over the organization.[54] Personality conflicts led to expulsions, and two socialist parties set up their own Unemployed Committees, which soon collapsed. The MVSUC all but expelled certain members, who organized the Rainbow Kitchen, that, like its "parent" body, organized political campaigns as well as providing food and various services to the community. For its part, the MVSUC (now Mon Valley Unemployed Committee) evolved into a social service organization that continues to mobilize unemployed workers, albeit on a more modest scale.[55] Looking back on all the tumult of the 1980s, one participant wished that fellow activists "would have realized that the enemy was looking at them and laughing at their divisions."[56]

Nonetheless, workers and community activists established an impressive array of community organizations. The Steel Valley Authority (SVA) grew out of efforts to save some viable departments of mills such as Dorothy Six in the Duquesne Works or the Electric Furnace in LTV's Pittsburgh Works. As in Youngstown, U.S. Steel preferred to demolish its older mills rather than sell them to workers. Since steel, auto, and other large corporations would have been the mill's largest customers, such hostility proved fatal to SVA's plans. Nonetheless, the SVA succeeded in its lobbying efforts and convinced several municipalities (with their powers of eminent domain) to join the SVA and keep alive the dream generated in Youngstown of worker- and community-ownership of basic industry. Although the SVA ultimately helped to save some non-steel factories in the region, the organization failed to convince capitalists or government to invest in its large steel mills.[57]

Amidst the widespread anger and frustration of the early 1980s, some workers joined the Denominational Ministry Strategy (DMS). DMS quickly became the most controversial organization in the Mon Valley, as its members held individual executives and bankers responsible for the "corporate evil" that laid waste to the region. Led by charismatic religious activists, DMS members gained widespread media attention by depositing dead fish in safety deposit boxes at banks that refused to extend loans to American steel firms but lent to foreign companies. When DMS began to protest in churches, and in one case threw skunk oil on churchgoers, popular support for the organization quickly dissipated. While DMS remains an intensely controversial organization, its tactics grew out of widespread frustration with more traditional forms of protest.[58]

While workers' response to plant closings generated several new organizations, deindustrialization greatly weakened the power of unions. As recently as the late 1960s, strikes in steel garnered the national attention of politicians and businessmen. No more: In 1986, when workers refused to grant the concessions demanded by USX, the new "parent" corporation of U.S. Steel, the company locked out its 22,000 unionized employees across the country for 184 days. Unlike the 116 day strike in 1959, in 1986–87 the country was awash in steel, and thus the conflict barely affected the national economy.[59] At the end of the conflict, workers agreed to additional wage concessions of approximately $2.50 an hour.[60] In exchange, workers forced USX to agree to invest $250 million at Edgar Thomson and build a continuous caster that helped keep the mill open.[61] But four days after the union settled the lockout, the company closed another four mills, resulting in 3,500 lost jobs.[62]

STRUGGLING WITH THE CONSEQUENCES OF DEINDUSTRIALIZATION

Deindustrialization crippled the health of working-class communities throughout the region. Between 1982 and 1987, U.S. Steel, LTV, and other manufacturing firms eliminated almost 100,000 jobs. The economic "ripple effect" swamped manufacturers that formerly serviced the mills and small businesses patronized by industrial workers, resulting in thousands of additional lost jobs.[63] Even before the mills completely closed, mill towns such as Aliquippa, Homestead, Duquesne, McKeesport, and Braddock had become amongst the poorest in the region. Once vibrant blue-collar cities, former mill towns evolved into ghettoes for the poor, the elderly, and minorities.[64] When the mills closed, these communities lost their largest employers and much of their tax base. According to one resident of the Mon Valley, "Braddock is like the land that time forgot. It looks like somebody just bombed it and didn't clean it up. . . . People look like zombies."[65] Mon Valley municipal governments slashed their payrolls and services. At one point Clairton laid off its entire police and fire department.[66] The Mayor of West Homestead played the state lottery in a hapless attempt to reverse the borough's fortunes.[67] A 1986 survey estimated that a fifth of Duquesne remained unemployed, and half of the borough's households earned less than fifteen thousand dollars a year.[68] Almost a third of Duquesne's high school graduates admitted that their fathers were unemployed or underemployed, and most graduates planned to relocate.[69]

The region generated few new jobs, and most of those that were created paid a third of what the mill had paid.[70] When Ronald Reagan toured the Pittsburgh region, touting the "fact" that high-technology jobs were available, one resourceful ex-steelworker, fed up with a year of retraining and no job, handed his resume to the President. Reagan made a phone call, and Ron Bricker landed a job repairing computers at $6.50 an hour. Reagan was soon inundated with resumes and quickly responded that "I didn't expect that all of the unemployed were suddenly going to ask me to be the employment agency."[71] More than a dozen years after the incident, one former Homestead employee observed that "job training . . . is a joke. . . . Few workers have found jobs in their field of training. The majority are underemployed as part-time school bus drivers, security guards, bartenders. . . . Their wages are far below what they earned in the mills."[72] Even retrained workers like Ron Bricker agreed. Before he moved to Florida (where he still dreamed of returning to his old job in the mill), he became active in Pittsburgh's unemployed movement. At one point, a reporter asked him if he could put her in contact with homeless ex-steelworkers. "And that tore me up. . . . [S]he was not interested in people that lost their jobs, lost their homes, and were getting divorced because they could not handle all this pressure. . . . That's how bad our country was that she wanted to interview people living in a boxcar, so that people would pay attention."[73]

In the midst of a deep national recession, and an even deeper regional one, most ex-steelworkers floundered. One survey sponsored by unions and local universities asked laid-off workers to describe their situation. In the vast majority of cases, workers could not find comparable employment and suffered enormous loss of self-esteem. One worker described it this way: "There isn't enough paper to express what you go through when you lose your job after eighteen years."[74] One steelworker analyzed his chances on the job market: "who is going to want a 41 year old steelworker with a chronic back problem? U.S. Steel used me until I was spent and then cast me aside. For the past seven months we have been living off my wife's secretarial salary. . . . Now I know how a Vietnam vet feels."[75] A few wrote that they had found decent jobs but "it took me about four years to get back to the same income level that I had when I worked at the Duquesne Works." [76] Another simply wrote, "I need a good job. Tell me how I can find one."[77]

While some displaced steelworkers found good jobs, most did not. One 1990 survey found that over half of displaced workers earned seven dollars an hour less than they had in the mill. Many, like Jim Paluti, who had worked at Clairton, held two full-time minimum wage jobs.[78] Almost half of the ex-steelworkers remained unemployed, and most of the rest earned about 60 percent of their former wages.[79] Another survey two years later found the situation largely unchanged. One job counselor admitted, "I can get people jobs at McDonald's. I can't get them jobs that would make them self-sufficient and make a change in their lives."[80] Lackluster job growth continued throughout the 1990s as Pittsburgh employers created new jobs at half the national rate.[81] In the period between 1970 and 1990, Pittsburgh's job growth even lagged behind hard-hit cities like Detroit.[82]

Black workers confronted even bleaker prospects. Throughout the 1980s, black employment in manufacturing fell by 50 percent, and the vast majority of the decent jobs in the service sector went to whites. Steel companies had largely denied black workers access to the skilled trades in the mills. With the mills gone, few black ex-steelworkers could find work as plumbers, electricians, or millwrights.[83] Consequently adult black unemployment remained almost 19 percent, with considerably higher levels among youth. In terms of black joblessness, only Detroit, Cleveland, and Toledo surpassed Pittsburgh.[84] The local media, ever eager to trumpet good news, put the best face on news such as the fact that in the early 1990s Allegheny County's black infant mortality fell, but was forced to admit that black infants remained three times more likely to die than white ones.[85] Throughout the 1990s, Pittsburgh's white poverty and unemployed rates remained among the worst in the country, but black poverty rates were four times higher and overall income levels half that of whites.[86]

Deindustrialization also devastated female steelworkers. By the early 1980s, most of the women who had entered steel mills in the 1970s had lost their jobs. Between 1980 and 1984, the USWA lost over 75 percent of its female members. Most female ex-steelworkers, like their male counterparts, found lower-paid jobs in the service sector that provided no benefits. According to one former steelworker, "those jobs are gone and we're back to where we started" as low-paid workers in the service economy.[87] For instance, Sheryl Johnson lost her job in the Irvin Works as a millwright's apprentice and found a new job as a receptionist that paid a third of her former wage. For female heads of families, the loss of income was no less economically devastating than for men.[88] The loss of relatively stable "breadwinner" jobs forced male and female ex-steelworkers and their spouses to accept whatever jobs they could find.[89] In an economy where employers paid low wages and provided few benefits, female wages increasingly proved no less important for the families of even those male ex-steelworkers lucky enough to keep their jobs.[90]

In the midst of such fundamental change, workers' anger was palpable but often unfocused. In 1981, lines at unemployment centers ran into the streets, but "steelworkers never thought that they would be laid off forever."[91] Plant closings helped spark mass mobilizations akin to those of the 1930s. For instance, when Ronald Reagan visited Pittsburgh, several thousand members of "middle America" stood outside his hotel in the rain, many with rocks in their hands, chanting "fuck you Reagan."[92] But for former steelworkers, "the stress [of sustained unemployment] was tremendous" and anger generally devolved into depression akin to "almost a catatonic state."[93] According to one steelworker, deindustrialization blindsided many workers who thought that "my father worked at this plant, my grandfather worked here, I've worked here for seven or eight years and I'm going to work here until I die." Workers like that "can hate a black guy real easy. If you say that a Jap got your job, he's going to hate the Japanese. . . . [Y]ou know, it's confusion."[94] Despite the political subordination of the USWA to big steel companies, radical and community organizations countered what Bob Anderson of the Rainbow Kitchen called the "anti-foreign scapegoating of the root of the crisis by the steel companies and the international union."[95] But given that radical alternative organizations remained relatively weak, steelworkers' anger and frustration flared, simmered, and then faded.

LABOR AND CIVIL RIGHTS

In the past, black workers—and some white ones—had fought to create a reality in which racial discrimination would have no place. The USWA was an important vehicle for such hopes, and "foreigners" and blacks proved the most enthusiastic advocates of steel unionism in the 1930s. Given a long history of discrimination, immigrants, their children, and African Americans deeply desired a seniority system that would provide a non-biased system of job security and promotion. Even in the late 1940s, the most outspoken white advocates of civil rights, left-wing steelworkers, were sometimes "foreigners" such as Zigmunt Paszkowski or Anthony Salopek or African Americans such as Sonny Robinson. The triumph of anti-communism in the union helped ensure that aggressive fights against discrimination became suspect. While anti-communism alienated many blacks from the union, some black workers joined the crusade against the left. Indeed, a few black unionists at Duquesne joined the fight to deny Salopek a role in the union. During the Cold War, the union organized its civil rights campaigns through a toothless Civil Rights Committee that was designed to fail. While the CRC helped promote civil rights legislation, it did nothing to promote a more equitable seniority system, the highest priority of minority steelworkers.

The history of workers' civil rights campaigns in the steel industry and Pittsburgh reflected the broad patterns of civil rights activism throughout the country. Black workers supported legal efforts to desegregate American institutions and peaceful mass protests such as the threatened march on Washington in 1941. During the 1940s, black workers pressed for the desegregation of the workplace by leading wildcat strikes in steel and conducting large-scale boycotts of Pittsburgh's department stores. Black protest waned in the harsh political climate of the 1950s, although some black steelworkers continued to press for their "Fair Share" of economic opportunity. These workers ran afoul of the company, the union, and the FBI. In the workplace, black workers employed multiple strategies, ranging from conservative to radical, to gain improved conditions. In the 1960s, black workers organized mass protests to gain wider access to jobs and housing; the riots of the late 1960s were an indication of the frustration with the slow pace of change. However, in the 1980s, blacks organized no major protest organizations such as Fair Share or the Ad Hoc Committee of Black Steelworkers. In part this reflected greater efforts by whites at inclusion as well as greater levels of disorganization in the face of the most dire economic problem in decades.[96]

Some readers may wonder what difference it would have made to black steelworkers if the USWA had adopted different policies. Of course, had steel companies been willing to forego long-standing policies of "divide and conquer" along the lines of race and ethnicity, the union would not have much to do. Consider also the difference it would have made to the civil rights movement if the federal government boycotted the products of lawbreakers, as it did in the winter of 1936–37 with regards to the Walsh-Healey Act. (Had the federal government continued such boycotts, American history would surely be far different than today.) The only example of a federal "boycott" came in 1969, during the controversy over the exclusion of African Americans from the building trades, and in this case, the government's inaction suggested that they simply hoped the protesters would go home. If government had upheld its own laws with the power of the purse, it would have greatly strengthened the causes of civil rights and workers' rights.

STEEL'S REBIRTH

Amidst the turmoil of deindustrialization, in the late 1980s, the steel industry began to rebound. As companies closed mills and eliminated jobs, they achieved enormous productivity gains. In the 1980s, U.S. Steel closed fifteen facilities and eliminated in excess of 120,000 steelworkers' jobs throughout the country (over 70 percent of its workforce). With relatively modest investments, man-hours per ton at U.S. Steel fell from 10.8 in the early 1980s to 3.8 in 1989.[97] Indeed, American steel companies returned to their position as some of the world's most efficient (measured by man-hours per ton produced), if not lowest-cost producers.[98] Veteran steelworkers, with their intimate knowledge of steel production and the quirks of the mill's equipment, what Jack Metgzar has termed "metal sense," proved invaluable.[99] However, big steel firms continued to lose ground to imports and just as importantly, lost market share to domestic mini-mills resulting in slim profit margins.[100] Indeed, throughout the 1990s, USX's energy division outperformed its steel division leading stock market analysts to urge the company to sell its former namesake.[101]

The "rebirth" of U.S. Steel's Mon Valley Works indicates the dynamics behind steel's resurgence. By the mid-1990s, U.S. Steel had realized substantial productivity gains, 29 percent over five years, at what had been the Edgar Thomson Works, Irvin Works, and Clairton Works. Part of the credit was due to new equipment, notably the continuous caster that came on line in 1990. (The USWA had forced the company to modernize the mill in order to settle the 1986–87 lockout.) However, most of the productivity was due to an incentive and quality control program termed APEX ("all people, all process, all product excellence"). The mill's general manager explained that a lot of their productivity gains "has to do with the investments we are making in plant and equipment. But more of it is the people." Workers were encouraged to help solve problems, and the result was a dramatic reduction in defects and even a weakening of the rigid divisions between workers and management. According to one unionist, "At first, APEX was top-driven, but eventually it did flow into a partnership."[102] More so than in the past, the real fear of job loss, by management and workers, encouraged this shotgun marriage. One study found that only 6.5 percent of steel's productivity gains resulted from new technology and that just over half resulted from old-fashioned speedup and outsourcing.[103]

In other words, in the 1980s and 1990s, steel firms continued further down the path of low-cost modernization that they had embarked upon in the 1950s, but in the context of ever-stiffer competition. More so than in the past, low profits resulted in fairly stringent capital restraints, which precluded technological breakthroughs and required ever-greater emphasis on labor economies. As one analyst observed, "The nation's integrated steelmakers cannot build new mills because they're too expensive. Any industry that cannot build new mills is in long-term trouble."[104] Indeed, Christoph Scherrer observed that "for many years, every major investment project of steel mills in the United States has been supervised or carried out by foreign engineers."[105] "Metal sense" and speedup, as much as new technology, have helped American steel companies return to their position as extremely efficient producers.[106]

Indeed, American steel companies found it more convenient to buy other steel companies than to build new mills at home. In March 2000, USX announced that it planned to buy Slovakia's state steel firm because its mills were in good condition and close to Western European markets.[107] Whereas the company had once imported Slovak workers to work in their mills in Pittsburgh, now the company exported American capital to purchase mills and hire workers in Slovakia. Such news did little to cheer USX's ex-workers in Pittsburgh, but it helps explain why the region suffers from such chronically low investment.

THE RENAISSANCE IS DEAD, LONG LIVE THE RENAISSANCE: CLASS AND RACE POLITICS IN AMERICA'S "MOST LIVABLE CITY," 1985–2000

Amidst the most savage and prolonged recession in fifty years, Pittsburgh economic elites and the media maintained that the city remained poised on the verge of yet another Renaissance. Even in the mid-1980s, the *Pittsburgh Post-Gazette* editorialized that the massive population loss due to deindustrialization, while painful, was "a blessing that should be accepted and built upon." Indeed, plant closings substantially improved the air quality in the once Smoky City, and many visitors to Pittsburgh found the city a surprisingly green and pleasant place. The largest media providers focused on upbeat news such as the fact that in 1985 Rand McNally ranked Pittsburgh as the "most livable city" in the United States.[108] By the 1990s, the city fathers celebrated the "fact" that Pittsburgh was a "prosperous city" that had completely recovered from deindustrialization. Concerned to bury Pittsburgh's industrial past, journalists searched in vain for a suitably high-tech (and even remotely plausible) nickname to replace the Steel City. Contenders included "Tech City," seeking to draw attention to the corporate research done in the region, or more ludicrously, "Roboburgh" (in honor of Carnegie Mellon's leading role in field robotics research).[109] If regions could rise on a tide of boosterism alone, Pittsburgh would be a world-class city.[110]

As in the past, Pittsburgh's public-private partnership focused primarily on the private interests of the regional economic elites. The Allegheny Conference on Community Development (ACCD) remained the organization of choice for the owning class and politicians to plan and coordinate their policies. The ACCD, in conjunction with Carnegie Mellon University, outlined elites' goals for the region in a 1993 study nicknamed the "white paper."[111] (Its nickname derived from the color of the report's cover, but could have also derived from its committee members who were all white, mostly corporate executives, and with one exception all male.) While acknowledging the major problems that resulted from deindustrialization, the report's recommendations ignored corporations and instead urged reforms upon government and the public: eliminating Pittsburgh's image in the national media as one of "chronic labor problems," streamlining local government and lowering corporate taxes, and creating a "shared economic vision." The most substantial burden urged upon employers was that they take the "Pittsburgh pledge" that bound companies and unions to avoid strikes.[112] The most eloquent evidence of the role of workers in the new economy came at the hands of the titular author of the report, Robert Mehrabian, President of Carnegie Mellon. Even as Mehrabian urged labor and community leaders to "share" in the ACCD's "economic vision" for Pittsburgh, he forced food workers at Carnegie Mellon, already the lowest-paid workers at the region's premier university, to accept even lower wages for entry-level workers. The university also forced workers to make co-payments for their health benefits. Apparently the "shared vision" of the new Renaissance required steadily decreasing wages for low-wage, and largely female and/or African American, workers.[113]

Non-elite surveys found that workers in Pittsburgh confronted substantial poverty exacerbated by pervasive racial discrimination. Researchers from the University of Pittsburgh analyzed data from the U.S. Census that showed that while Pittsburgh had recovered much economic ground, its poverty—and especially black poverty—remained worse than most American cities. The "most livable city" enjoyed by the city's mostly white upper and middle classes coexisted with or rather rested upon a city where a third of its workers labored below the poverty line.[114] The large pool of unemployed and under-employed workers helped maintain labor discipline and depress compensation rates for blue-collar service workers. Perhaps the most revealing response to these studies was how many middle-class whites refused to abandon the vision of Pittsburgh as a "livable" world-class city free from significant poverty or racial stratification.[115]

Yet confronting the reality of Pittsburgh's increasingly polarized economy helps explain the strained relations between workers—especially black workers—and the police. As in the past, questions of economics, labor discipline, and policing remain deeply intertwined, if unacknowledged, in the mainstream media and political discourse. In the heyday of Pittsburgh's industrialization, private spies and police maintained the system of industrial feudalism, and private and public police targeted trade unionists, radicals, and immigrant workers. In the 1930s, labor's growing political power ended most of the police and corporate violence against unionists and immigrants, although federal surveillance of radicals and increasingly civil rights activists took its place.[116] In the post-industrial economy, a new form of industrial policing has emerged. Public police, responsible for maintaining order between increasingly economically polarized neighborhoods, often brutalized the poor, and especially black youth. Since the 1960s, black activists and even black police had complained that the police exhibited a pervasive anti-black and anti-civil rights bias.[117] Throughout the 1990s, so many black and white citizens complained about police misconduct that the NAACP began to monitor complaints against the police, and the ACLU filed a class action lawsuit on their behalf.[118] In 1996, suburban police killed (many Pittsburghers say murdered) Johnny Gammage in a routine traffic stop.[119] In March 1997, the city agreed to allow the Justice Department to monitor the police in order to avoid contesting a federal lawsuit it seemed certain to lose.[120] The plan proved deeply unpopular with the Mayor and police, both of whom quickly proclaimed success at eradicating any trace of racial bias or problems with police brutality. The Mayor and the police argued that such "success" should enable them to escape from federal over-sight. By contrast, the ACLU argued that the police were not "anywhere near compliance" with the terms of the consent decree.[121] Galvanized by the Gammage case, the next year the voting public passed a civilian review board over the objections of the city's media, police, and major politi-cians.[122] It was one of the most important popular victories over city hall in a decade, but the victorious organizations did not have the resources to ensure that the board was granted the proper funds or authority to fulfill its mission.[123]

Labor has proved unable to reverse workers' declining wages and politi-cal power. A case in point has been the "living wage campaign." The most significant coalition of progressive labor and community organizations in the region, the Alliance for Progressive Action, has been stymied in its attempts to pass a countywide ordinance that would require government subcontrac-tors to pay a "living wage." According to research completed by Ralph Bangs at the University of Pittsburgh, lifting workers out of poverty requires wages of nine dollars an hour for individuals and eighteen dollars an hour for single parents. Even in the "booming" economy of the late 1990s, the media and politicians dismissed such demands as utopian, or at least better suited to Steel City than "Roboburgh."[124] According to the *Pittsburgh Post-Gazette*, government intervention for workers would "subvert the public subsidies . . . extended to private developers to locate their operations here." The contro-versy indicates that the direction of public policy in the birthplace of the CIO has moved relentlessly towards public largesse (what the newspaper termed "sweeteners") for "hotels, stores, offices and other employers." In the name of regional, if not global, competitiveness, workers are expected to tighten their belts and open their wallets.[125]

The latest phase of Pittsburgh's renaissance has focused on bolstering the health of downtown businesses through modernizing the region's sports stadiums. As in the past, the public underwrote most of the costs of this public-private "partnership" while private interests realized most of the gains. Throughout the mid- to late 1990s, the *Pittsburgh Post-Gazette* warned of the dire economic consequences that would befall downtown if either the Pittsburgh Pirates or the Pittsburgh Steelers relocated to a new city. (What is rarely disclosed is that the newspaper is one of the owners of the Pirates.) The chronically low attendance at Pirates games was attributed to a wide-spread lack of civic pride instead of high-priced seating and concessions or the economic distress of most workers. The Chairman of PNC Bank warned that without the stadium, the city would become "a minor-league town in a world of major-league competitors."[126]

Consequently, local statesmen put together an $800 million bond package to build separate stadiums for the baseball and football teams. Local media conducted a one-sided debate in which proponents of the measure carefully explained how important it was to downtown businesses and civic pride, while opponents enjoyed the forum of the letters to the editor.[127] Indeed, here was a chance for the region to endorse the "shared economic vision" touted by the ACCD which had proposed publicly financed stadiums several years before.[128] The construction unions backed the plan, despite the fact that it was funded via taxes on workers, because it would provide work for its members for two years. Nonetheless, the measure lost handily, particularly in working-class wards. The *Post Gazette*'s reporter found that "Pittsburgh's corporate elite . . . used to eager cooperation from local politicians" was defeated because the plan collided with "the politics of class resentment."[129] Undaunted by what the Mayor termed the "inertia" of voters, local statesmen turned to "Plan B," which raised the public funds from school districts and a "regional assets board."[130] Plan B never required a public vote, which would have surely failed, but taxpayers nonetheless footed the bill for the stadium plan. In short, modernization of this sort revealed the extent to which elites share their economic vision, or at least costs, with taxpayers; it also spoke volumes about the health of democracy in post-industrial Pittsburgh.

Although Pittsburgh still suffers from all manners of problems left over from, or at least reminiscent of, its industrial past, the city fathers are eager to bury the memory of Pittsburgh as the Steel City. Steel has become a shorthand phrase for the era when blue-collar workers enjoyed relatively high wages and secure jobs, pensions, and benefits. Boosters of the stadium plan tried to link it to the heyday of "steel" by reminding residents that in the 1970s, Pittsburgh was often known as the "City of Champions."[131] One plan for the new football stadium involved building a faux blast furnace that would generate a smoke and light show if the Steelers scored a touchdown.[132] The Mayor worried that this image would "send the wrong message" about Pittsburgh, apparently by reminding visitors—and residents—of the region's industrial and unionized past. This author heard one radio talk show where fans debated the merits of the Mayor's concern. One fan ironically suggested that Pittsburgh's "image problem" could be solved by changing its name to a cipher (à la Prince) and then request everyone to refer to it as "the city formerly known as the Steel City."

TOWARD LABOR-CENTERED PUBLIC POLICY

For better or for worse, Pittsburgh has joined the ranks of America's post-industrial cities. Of course, even at this late date, wealth extraction of the old-fashioned sort still remains in place. The region still mines prodigious amounts of coal and remains a major producer of steel.[133] In general, however, Pittsburgh has been normalized in the terms of wealth extraction, in that it (like all American cities) offers tax breaks and cheap labor to high-tech firms, sports arenas, and downtown department stores.[134] The ideology of the Renaissance or the fervor of its boosters may mask the extent of Pittsburgh's decline from many of its middle-class and elite residents, but the region seems certain to lose both well-paid blue-collar jobs and population. Further manufacturing decline seems likely because the region's chief natural assets, enormous coal reserves, and access to the Ohio River valley do not confer significant competitive advantages in the face of either extremely capital intensive manufacturing (as in the case of Germany or Japan) or extremely low-wage manufacturing (as in the case of Mexico and China). Nonetheless, numerous publicists and journalists have praised Pittsburgh's high-technology and sports-driven Renaissance because it marks a departure from the Steel City. Yet what is even remarkable about Pittsburgh's post-industrial economy is how closely its politics and power relations resemble those of its industrial predecessor.

From the mid-nineteenth century until the 1930s, industrialists turned Pittsburgh into a center for heavy industry because the region enjoyed (in the terminology of business and public policy) a remarkably "favorable business climate." Pittsburgh had much to offer industrialists: abundant natural resources such as coal and rivers, amenable politicians, and cheap non-union labor. By 1900, Pittsburgh was one of the most thoroughly industrialized regions in the world. By the 1920s, industrialists' investment in the region began to lag, but their extraction of wealth continued. The rise of industrial unions in the 1930s, and their considerable political organization, turned Pittsburgh into a stronghold of union power and workers began to enjoy some of the fruits of their labor. Private investment remained remarkably low, but profits (and public subsidies of private industry) remained high enough to ensure that the basic framework of heavy industry remained intact until the early 1980s. Even at that late date, the public and workers sought to protect their jobs by improving Pittsburgh's business climate. Government and trade unionists deferred environmental regulations, tax obligations, and contractual agreements regarding wages and benefits in order to provide enormous amounts of investment capital to capitalists. The strategy succeeded in bolstering the bottom line of steel companies, but because the largest steel firms invested most of their profits elsewhere (i.e. USX and Marathon Oil), in terms of preserving the industrial economy, the strategy proved a spectacular failure. "Public-private partnerships" of this sort failed to stop, and may have hastened, the closure of mills. As in the past, workers—and especially black workers—continue to shoulder most of the burdens in order to make possible the process of private accumulation of wealth.

At present, workers enter most policy debates as a "problem," a source of tax revenues or a very junior partner (e.g., the building trades) in the so-called public-private alliance. In the day-to-day world of Pittsburgh and other American cities, workers are encouraged to compete with each other for jobs and individual advancement rather than cooperate to improve conditions of all workers. Not surprisingly, our governments, ostensibly the extension of the collective will of citizens, primarily function to compete with other cities, counties, states, and countries. Any truly new public-private partnership would have to put workers' interest at the center of the public interest. One trade unionist aptly summarized workers' problems in this regard more than a century before: "centralization of wealth is all the rage, and a very bad rage it is . . . to meet it is a simple problem in theory: Workmen must concentrate more closely in union."[135] In practice, workers have had enormous problems building effective "union" in the workplace and in politics.

Indeed, if the history of Pittsburgh's class struggle teaches us anything, it is just how many working-class militants have tried, in such a large variety of ways, to combat the power of big business and their political allies. Pittsburgh possesses a history of crushing defeats, yet also the important saga of how workers in the 1930s, and for decades after, forced the owning class to concede enormous resources back to them. Indeed, to the extent that Pittsburgh is livable today, it is due to the legacy of labor's victories.

Of course, much remains to be done before workers' interests define the public interest. The struggle to build a political economy that is truly pro-labor requires first a struggle for political vision and will. Scholarship and study can play a role in that struggle, although as in the past, organizing political and industrial solidarity remains more difficult, and ultimately more important.

Notes

A NOTE ON HISTORIOGRAPHY

1. David Brody, *Steelworkers in America: The Nonunion Era* (Cambridge: Harvard University Press, 1960). Francis G. Couvares, *The Remaking of Pittsburgh: Class and Culture in an Industrializing City, 1877–1919* (Albany: State University of New York Press, 1984). Paul Krause, *The Battle for Homestead, 1880–1892: Politics, Culture and Steel* (Pittsburgh: University of Pittsburgh Press, 1992), 15–38, 237–38. David Montgomery, *Workers' Control in America: Studies in the History of Work, Technology, and Labor Struggles* (Cambridge: Cambridge University Press, 1979).

2. Ronald L. Filippelli, "The History Is Missing," in *Forging a Union of Steel: Philip Murray, SWOC, and the United Steelworkers*, ed. Paul F. Clark, Peter Gottlieb, and Donald Kennedy (Ithaca: ILR Press, 1987).

3. Robert Asher and Ronald Edsforth, eds., *Autowork* (Albany: State University of New York Press, 1995). Steven Tolliday and Jonathan Zeitlin, eds., *Between Fordism and Flexibility: The Automobile Industry and Its Workers* (New York: Berg, 1992).

4. Staughton Lynd, "The Possibility of Radicalism in the Early 1930s: The Case of Steel," *Radical America* 6 (November-December 1972): 37–64.

5. James Douglas Rose, "The United States Steel Duquesne Works, 1886–1941: The Rise of Steel Unionism" (Ph.D. diss., University of California-Davis, 1997), 4–9.

6. John Hoerr, *And the Wolf Finally Came: The Decline of the American Steel Industry* (Pittsburgh: University of Pittsburgh Press, 1988), 20. Paul Tiffany, *The Decline of American Steel: How Management, Labor and Government Went Wrong* (New York: Oxford University Press, 1988). Barry Bluestone and Bennett Harrison, *The Deindustrialization of America: Plant Closings, Community Abandonment and the Dismantling of Basic Industry* (New York: Basic Books, 1982). Dennis Dickerson, *Out of the Crucible: Black Steelworkers in Western Pennsylvania, 1875–1980* (Albany: State University of New York Press, 1986). Staughton S. Lynd, *The Fight against Shutdowns: Youngstown's Steel Mill Closings* (San Pedro, CA: Steeple Jack Press, 1982). Lynd, "The Genesis of the Idea of a Community Right to Industrial Property in Youngstown and Pittsburgh, 1977–1987," in *The Constitution and American Life,*

ed. David Thelen (Ithaca: Cornell University Press, 1988), 266–96. Thomas Fuechtmann, *Steeples and Stacks: Religion and Steel Crisis in Youngstown* (New York: Oxford University Press, 1989). Dale A. Hathaway, *Can Workers Have a Voice? The Politics of Deindustrialization in Pittsburgh* (University Park: Pennsylvania State University Press, 1993). Jack Metzgar, "Plant Shutdowns and Worker Response: The Case of Johnstown, Pa.," *Socialist Review* 53 (September-October 1980): 9–49. William Serrin, *Homestead: The Tragedy and Glory of an American Steel Town* (New York: Times Books, 1992). Michael Frisch and Milton Rogovin, *Portraits in Steel: Photographs and Oral Histories of Buffalo's Steelworkers* (Ithaca: Cornell University Press, 1993). John Strohmeyer, *Crisis in Bethlehem: Big Steel's Struggle to Survive* (New York: Viking Penguin, 1987). David Bensman and Roberta Lynch, *Rusted Dreams: Hard Times in a Steel Community* (New York: McGraw-Hill, 1987).

7. Judith Stein, *Running Steel, Running America: Race, Economic Policy and the Decline of Liberalism* (Chapel Hill: University of North Carolina Press, 1998). Another work that pushes labor historians to investigate the political dimensions of trade unionism is Kevin Boyle, *The UAW and the Heyday of American Liberalism 1945–1968* (Ithaca: Cornell University Press, 1995).

8. Bruce Nelson, *Divided We Stand: American Workers and the Struggle for Black Equality* (Princeton: Princeton University Press, 2001), 208.

9. Jack Metzgar, *Striking Steel: Solidarity Remembered* (Philadelphia: Temple University Press, 2000).

10. Thomas Sugrue, *The Origins of the Urban Underclass: Race and Inequality in Postwar Detroit* (Princeton: Princeton University Press, 1996).

CHAPTER 1. THE SECRET OF INDUSTRIALIZATION IN PITTSBURGH

1. Lucy Eldine Parsons, *Life of Albert R. Parsons, With Brief History of the Labor Movement in America* (Chicago: L.E. Parons, 1889), 48–49.

2. In November, 1881, the Federation of Organized Trades and Labor Unions met in Pittsburgh. Out of this organization came the formation of the AFL in 1886. "The Labor Congress," *National Labor Tribune*, 19 November 1881, 1 (hereafter cited as *NLT*).

3. White Paper Committee for the Allegheny Conference on Community Development, "Toward a Shared Economic Vision for Pittsburgh" (Pittsburgh: Carnegie Mellon University, 1993), 6.

4. Steve Massey, "Economy Leaves Blacks Behind," *Pittsburgh Post Gazette*, 18 October 1994, 1, 8 (hereafter cited as *PPG*). University Center for Social and Urban Research, "Black and White Economic Conditions in the City of Pittsburgh" (Pittsburgh: University of Pittsburgh, 1995), 5–7. U.S. Department of Commerce, *Statistical Abstract of the United States, 1992* (Washington: GPO, 1992), 30–32. U.S. Department of Labor, Bureau of Labor Statistics, *Employment, Hours and Earnings, States and Areas, 1939–1975* (Washington: GPO, 1975), Bulletin 1370–12, 631–37. U.S. Department of Labor, Bureau of Labor Statistics, *Employment, Hours and Earnings, States and Areas, 1972–1987* (Washington: GPO), Bulletin 2320, 1431–33.

5. David McDonald, *Union Man* (New York: E.P. Dutton and Co., 1969), 102–04. Melvyn Dubofsky and Warren Van Tine, *John L. Lewis: A Biography* (New York: Quadrangle, 1977), 228–79. Irving Bernstein, *Turbulent Years: A History of the American Worker,*

1933–1941 (Boston: Houghton Mifflin, 1970), 465–73. Myron C. Taylor, *Ten Years of Steel* (U.S. Steel, Hoboken, NJ: 1938), 40–44. Walter Galenson, *The CIO Challenge to the AFL: A History of the American Labor Movement, 1935–1941* (Cambridge: Harvard University Press, 1960), 93–96. Steel Workers Organizing Committee (hereafter cited as SWOC), *Reports of Officers to the Wage and Policy Convention in Pittsburgh* (Indianapolis, 1937), 8. "SWOC Release," 5 November 1936, *The CIO Files of John L. Lewis*, ed. Randolph Boehm and Martin Schipper (Frederick, MD: University Publications of America, 1988), microfilm, reel 12, 640–42, 651.

    6. Philip Murray to SWOC, 29 September 1936, *The CIO Files of John L. Lewis*, Reel 12, 543–44. U.S. Senate, Subcommittee of the Committee on Education and Labor, *Violations of Free Speech and Rights of Labor: Supplemental Hearings*, 77th Congress, 1st session, 1941, 208, 318–20, 396, 582. Jerold S. Auerbach, *Labor and Liberty: The La Follette Committee and the New Deal* (Indianapolis: Bobbs-Merrill, 1966), 72–90.

    7. Joseph Frazier Wall, *Andrew Carnegie* (1970; reprint, Pittsburgh: University of Pittsburgh Press, 1989), 646–48.

    8. "Cramp a Witness, Talks of Subsidy," Andrew Carnegie-Charles M. Schwab Papers, box 1, file 4, PSU. Report of Secretary of the Navy Daniels for 1914, in George Seldes, *Iron, Blood and Profits: An Expose of the World Wide Munitions Racket* (New York: Harpers Brothers, 1934), 381–82, see also 18–19, 236–37. U.S. House of Representatives, Committee on Naval Affairs, *Violations of Armor Plate Contracts*, 53rd Congress, second session, 1894, H. Report 1468, 1; H. Doc. 160, I–XI.

    9. Benjamin Franklin Cooling, *Gray Steel and Blue Water Navy: The Formative Years of America's Military-Industrial Complex* (Hamden, CT: Archon Books, 1979), 119–33, 224–29. E.A. Silsby, *Navy Yearbook 1920–1* (Washington: GPO, 1922), 916–19. Thomas J. Misa, *A Nation of Steel: The Making of Modern America, 1865–1925* (Baltimore: Johns Hopkins University Press, 1995), 104–05, 126–30. Andrew Carnegie to Charles Schwab, 11 August 1900, Andrew Carnegie-Charles M. Schwab Papers, box 1, file 4, PSU.

    10. U.S. Senate Special Committee on Investigating the Munitions Industry, *Munitions Industry*, 74th Congress, 1st session, 1935, 12212–15. "Want Government to Make Munitions," *New York Times*, 21 April 1936, 16 (hereafter cited as *NYT*). "Steel Shortage Holds Up 9 New Navy Ships as Producers Balk at Walsh-Healy Law," *NYT*, 13 February 1937, 1. "Labor Men Firm on Steel Bidding," *NYT*, 16 February 1937, 41. "Here and There NRA," *NYT*, 18 February 1937, 20. "Use of Navy Plant for Steel Studied," *NYT*, 25 February 1937, 1. "U.S. Steel Points Way Out of Bids"; "Steel Wage Rises Step against CIO," *NYT*, 26 February 1937, 9. "Walsh Explains Steel Navy Stand," *NYT*, 20 February 1937, 20. "Bethlehem Hints at 40-Hour Week," *NYT*, 28 February 1937, 17. "Carnegie-Illinois Confers with CIO, Others Raise Pay," *NYT*, 2 March 1937, 1. "Carnegie Steel Signs CIO Contract for Pay Rise, 40-Hour Week, Recognition; Deadlock on Naval Orders Broken," *NYT*, 3 March 1937, 1. "40,000 More Steel Mill Jobs Predicted; Trade Editor Also Sees $3.25 a Ton Rise," *NYT*, 4 March 1937, 2. "Steel Prices Put Up to Offset Outlay for Higher Wages," *NYT*, 5 March 1937, 3. "Navy Buys More Steel," *NYT*, 25 March 1937, 3. Raymond Patrick Kent, "The Development of Industrial Unionism in the American Iron and Steel Industry" (Ph.D. diss., University of Pittsburgh, 1938), 104–05. Buford Rowland and William B. Boyd, *U.S. Navy Bureau of Ordnance in World War II* (Washington: GPO, n.d.), 37–43.

11. For Roosevelt's willingness to use selective anti-trust enforcement to force corporations to comply with his policy aims, see James R. Zetka, *Militancy, Market Dynamics and Workplace Authority* (Albany: State University of New York Press, 1995), 22. The crucial role played by national governments in promoting industrial unionism in the United States and Europe is discussed in Steven Tolliday and Jonathan Zeitlin, "Introduction: Between Fordism and Flexibility," in *Between Fordism and Flexibility: The Automobile Industry and Its Workers*, ed. Tolliday and Zeitlin (New York: Berg, 1992), 1–27, especially 7–11.

12. Melvyn Dubofsky, *The State and Labor in Modern America* (Chapel Hill: University of North Carolina Press, 1994), 166.

13. Mark McColloch, "Consolidating Industrial Citizenship: The U.S.W.A. at War and Peace, 1939–1946," in *Forging a Union of Steel: Philip Murray, SWOC, and the United Steelworkers*, ed. Paul F. Clark, Peter Gottlieb, and Donald Kennedy (Ithaca: ILR Press, 1987).

14. Secretary of the Interior, *Manufactures of the United States*, 8th Census (Washington: GPO, 1865), clxxi–clxxiii. James M. Swank, "Statistics of the Iron and Steel Production of the United States," in the Secretary of the Interior, *Report on the Manufactures of the United States*, 10th Census (Washington: GPO, 1883), 71–88. Carmen DiCiccio, *Coal and Coke in Pennsylvania* (Harrisburg: Pennsylvania Historical and Museum Commission, 1996), 21–38. John N. Ingham, *Making Iron and Steel: Independent Mills in Pittsburgh, 1820–1920* (Columbus: Ohio University Press, 1991), 21–46. Leland D. Baldwin, *Pittsburgh: The Story of a City, 1750–1865* (Pittsburgh: University of Pittsburgh Press, 1937), 129–53, 218–30. Richard Oestreicher, "Working-Class Formation, Development, and Consciousness in Pittsburgh, 1790–1960," in *City at the Point: Essays on the Social History of Pittsburgh*, ed. Samuel P. Hay (Pittsburgh: University of Pittsburgh Press, 1989), 111–20. Marcellin C. Adams, "The Charcoal Iron Furnace at Shadyside Station in Pittsburgh," *The Western Pennsylvania Historical Magazine* (June 1937): 101–12.

15. Secretary of the Interior, *Manufactures of the United States*, 8th Census, clxxi–clxxiii, 492–94.

16. Thomas Lloyd, "History of J&L Corporation," 3, 1938, in J&L Steel Corporation, "Historical Miscellanea, 1871–1953," reel 1.

17. Charles G. Foster, "The Amalgamated Association of Iron and Steel Workers," Pennsylvania Secretary of Internal Affairs, *Industrial Statistics, 1887* (Harrisburg: Department of Internal Affairs, 1887), 1–2, 14.

18. Francis G. Couvares, *The Remaking of Pittsburgh: Class and Culture in an Industrializing City, 1877–1919* (Albany: State University of New York Press, 1984), 9–13. Oestreicher, "Working-Class Formation," 116, 129–30. Ingham, *Making Iron and Steel*, 21–46, 100–02. George Thurston, *Pittsburgh's Progress, Industries and Resources* (Pittsburgh: Eichenbaum, 1886), 166–7. James Meyers, *Pittsburgh: Its Industries and Commerce* (Pittsburgh: n.p., 1870), 23.

19. William E. Zeiter, "Foreword," in *Purdon's Pennsylvania Statutes Annotated*, Title 15 (St. Paul: West Publishing, 1992), 57–58. Philip S. Klein and Ari Hoogenboom, *A History of Pennsylvania* (University Park: Pennsylvania State University Press, 1973), 218.

20. Wall, *Andrew Carnegie*, 114–15.

21. John H. Thompson, "Pittsburgh's Worst Crisis in Municipal Finance: The Railroad Bond Affair (1859–1864)," *Pennsylvania History* 17 (July 1950): 215–20. "Railroads—

Atlantic and Pacific," *The National Era*, 10 May 1849. Klein and Hoogenboom, *A History of Pennsylvania*, 218, 287. George Rogers Taylor, *The Transportation Revolution*, 1815–1860 (New York City: Holt, Rinehart-Winston, 1951), 43–45, 86–93. Zeiter, "Foreword," 56–58, 73–74. George H. Burgess and Miles C. Kennedy, *Centennial History of the Pennsylvania Railroad Company, 1846–1946* (Philadelphia: The Pennsylvania Railroad Company, 1949), 47, 53–57.

22. Pennsylvania Secretary of Internal Affairs, *Industrial Statistics, 1881–2* (Harrisburg, 1882), 190. Secretary of the Interior, *Manufactures of the United States*, 8th Census, clxxii, clxxviii. Couvares, *The Remaking of Pittsburgh*, 10.

23. Klein and Hoogenboom, *A History of Pennsylvania*, 209.

24. DiCiccio, *Coal and Coke*, 13, 31–41.

25. Klein and Hoogenboom, *A History of Pennsylvania*, 287, 357.

26. William A. Russ Jr., "The Origins of the Ban on Special Legislation in the Constitution of 1873," *Pennsylvania History* 11 (October 1944): 262.

27. Krause, *Battle for Homestead*, 15–38, 237–38. J.P. Shalloo, *Private Police: With Special Reference to Pennsylvania* (Philadelphia: American Academy of Political and Social Science, 1933), 185–88. J. Bernard Hogg, "Public Reaction to Pinkertonism and the Labor Question," *Pennsylvania History* 11 (July 1944): 177, 180–81. "Company Towns Put under Ban by Governor Earle of Pennsylvania," *United Mine Workers Journals*, 15 January 1937, 20 (hereafter cited as *UMWJ*). "Company Coal Towns Are Disappearing," *PPG*, 12 November 1948, Section 2, 1.

28. "The End Not Yet," *NLT*, 7 July 1877, 1.

29. *Purdon's*, Title 15, 56–60, 73–74, 131.

30. "Pittsburgh Cordwainers, 1815, Commonwealth vs. Morrow," in John R. Commons et al., *A Documentary History of American Industrial Society* vol. 4 (Cleveland: A.H. Clark Co., 1910–11), 15–87.

31. Hyman Kuritz, "Criminal Conspiracy Cases in Post-bellum Pennsylvania," *Pennsylvania History* 18 (October 1950): 298–99. Victoria C. Hattam, *Labor Visions and State Power: The Origins of Business Unionism in the United States* (Princeton: Princeton University Press, 1993), 150–51.

32. "The Courts against Us," *NLT*, 16 June 1877, 2.

33. Pennsylvania Secretary of Internal Affairs, *Industrial Statistics, 1872–3* (Harrisburg, 1874), 160–61.

34. Philip S. Foner, *The Great Labor Uprising of 1877* (New York: Monad Press, 1977), 13–14. Matthew Josephson, *The Robber Barons: The Great American Capitalists, 1861–1901* (New York: Harcourt Brace and Company, 1934), 102–03, 116–18. Alfred D. Chandler, *The Visible Hand: The Managerial Revolution in American Business* (Cambridge: Harvard University Press, 1977), 79–142.

35. Hyman Kuritz, "The Pennsylvania State Government and Labor Controls from 1865 to 1922" (Ph.D. diss., Columbia University, 1954), 2–4, 77, 83–84. Foner, *1877*, 66. "To Mankind," *NLT*, 28 July 1877, 1. "The Railroaders," "The Locomotive Brotherhood," *NLT*, 14 July 1877, 1. Pennsylvania Secretary of Internal Affairs, *Industrial Statistics, 1872–3* (Harrisburg: Department of Internal Affairs, 1874), 160–61.

36. Robert V. Bruce, *1877: Year of Violence* (1959, reprint; Chicago: Elephant Books, 1989), 125, 115–58.

37. 24 July, 1877, Diary of B.F. Jones, 1875–1899, box 1, J&L Corporation Papers, UE/Archives of Industrial Society, University of Pittsburgh (hereafter cited as AIS).

38. Foner, *1877*, 58–59. "Sowing the Wind, Reaping the Whirlwind," *NLT*, 28 July 1877, 1.

39. Joseph John Holmes, "The National Guard of Pennsylvania: Policeman of Industry, 1865–1905" (Ph.D., diss., University of Connecticut, 1970), 60–94. Foner, *1877*, 67–77.

40. 24 July 1877, Diary of B.F. Jones, 1875–1899, box 1, J&L Corporation Papers, AIS.

41. 26 July 1877, Diary of B.F. Jones, 1875–1899, box 1, J&L Corporation Papers, AIS.

42. 12 August 1877, Diary of B.F. Jones, 1875–1899, box 1, J&L Corporation Papers, AIS.

43. 13 August 1877, Diary of B.F. Jones, 1875–1899, box 1, J&L Corporation Papers, AIS.

44. 4 and 18 September 1877, Diary of B.F. Jones, 1875–1899, box 1, J&L Corporation Papers, AIS.

45. Kuritz, "Labor Controls," 2–4, 77, 83–84. Foner, *1877*, 66.

46. Major William P. Clarke and Captain Charles J. Hendler, *Official History of the Militia and the National Guard of the State of Pennsylvania* (n.p.: 1909, 1912), 489.

47. "A Railroad Daily," *NLT*, 4 August 1877, 1.

48. Holmes, "Policeman of Industry," 166–200, 252.

49. Holmes, "Policeman of Industry," 256–81; Kuritz, "Labor Controls," 234–42. Pennsylvania Federation of Labor, *American Cossack* (n.p.: 1915), 6. Philip M. Conti, *The Pennsylvania State Police: A History of Service to the Commonwealth, 1905 to the Present* (Harrisburg: Stackpole Books, 1977), 28–35.

50. Holmes, "Policeman of Industry," 225–26, 234–35. Ronald G. Gephart, "Politicians, Soldiers and Strikes: The Reorganization of the Nebraska Militia and the Omaha strike of 1882," *Nebraska History* 45 (March 1965): 90. Martha Derthick, *The National Guard in Politics* (Cambridge: Harvard University Press, 1965), 16–20.

51. Nell Irvin Painter, *Standing at Armageddon: The United States, 1877–1919* (New York: W.W. Norton, 1987), 14–24.

52. Josephson, *Robber Barons*, 102. Wall, *Andrew Carnegie*, 113–227.

53. Couvares, *The Remaking of Pittsburgh*, 10. Burgess and Kennedy, *Centennial*, 81. Alfred D. Chandler Jr., *The Railroads: The Nation's First Big Business* (New York: Harcourt, Brace and World, 1965), 31–35. Chandler, *The Visible Hand*, 245. Harold C. Livesay, *Andrew Carnegie and the Rise of Big Business* (Boston: Little, Brown, 1975), 163. David Brody, *Steelworkers in America: The Nonunion Era* (Cambridge: Harvard University Press, 1960), 4.

54. Andrew Carnegie to J.A. Leishman, 21 August 1896, 1, Andrew Carnegie-Charles M. Schwab Papers, box 1, file 1, PSU. Livesay, *Andrew Carnegie*, 159, 163. Wall, *Andrew Carnegie*, 614–17, 775–76.

55. Livesay, *Andrew Carnegie*, 99–106, quotation on 101. Wall, *Andrew Carnegie*, 307–60. Chandler, *The Visible Hand*, 261–69. Ingham, *Making Iron and Steel*, 48–49.

56. Livesay, *Andrew Carnegie*, 106. Brody, *Steelworkers in America*, 4–5.

57. James Howard Bridge, *The Inside History of the Carnegie Steel Company: A Romance of Millions* (1903; reprint, Pittsburgh: University of Pittsburgh Press, 1991) 159, 179. Misa, *A Nation of Steel*, 1–90.

58. John N. Ingham, "Introduction," *Inside History*, xix.

59. Ingham, *Making Iron and Steel*, 70–73.

60. Wall, *Andrew Carnegie*, 589–613.

61. Livesay, *Andrew Carnegie*, 128, 166. Fitch, *Steel Workers*, 127.

62. Each partner signed an "iron clad" agreement to sell their stock to Carnegie, the majority shareholder, at any time for the stock's book value.

63. Wall, *Andrew Carnegie*, 329, 491–93, 721, 747–60. Bridge, *Romance of Millions*, 316–57.

64. Abraham Berglund and P. Wright, *The Tariff on Iron and Steel* (Washington: The Brookings Institute, 1929), 116.

65. Andrew Carnegie to Charles Schwab, 11 August; 15 August; 22 August; 5 October 1900, Andrew Carnegie-Charles M. Schwab Papers, box 1, file 4, PSU.

66. Cooling, *Gray Steel*, 119–33, 224–29. Silsby, *Navy Yearbook 1920–1*, 916–19. U.S. House of Representatives, *Capital and Labor*, 354. Misa, *A Nation of Steel*, 104–05, 126–30. U.S. House of Representatives, *Committee on the Investigation of the United States Steel Company*, Report 2447. Hearings, 8 vols., 62 Cong., 2nd session, 1911–12.

67. H.C. Lackey, "Homestead Forgings, The Past Present and Future," 17 November 1952; No author, "History of Homestead District Works," n.d., box 1, file "Homestead History," William Gaughan Papers, AIS. Historic American Engineering Record, National Park Service and Mon Valley Steel Industry Heritage Task Force, "Homestead Steel Works and Carrie Furnaces," (Homestead: August 1990), vi. Cooling, *Gray Steel*, 125–26. For the technical benefits of rolling armor, see Misa, *Nation of Steel*, 130–31.

68. Kenneth Warren, *The American Steel Industry, 1850–1970: A Geographical Interpretation* (Pittsburgh: University of Pittsburgh Press, 1973), 134–38. S.J. Kleinberg, *The Shadow of the Mills: Working Class Families in Pittsburgh, 1870–1907* (Pittsburgh: University of Pittsburgh Press, 1989), 4. William T. Hogan, S.J., *Economic History of the Iron and Steel Industry of the United States*, vol. 3 (Lexington, MA: Lexington Books, 1971), 813.

69. For a different view of independent steel firms, see Ingham, *Making Iron and Steel*, 94–95.

70. David Montgomery, *The Fall of the House of Labor: The Workplace, the State and American Labor Activism, 1865–1925* (Cambridge: Cambridge University Press, 1987), 40.

71. "Consolidating Iron Manufactures," *NLT*, 6 August 1881, 1.

72. Fitch, *Steel Workers*, 77, 108. Elbaum and Wilkinson, "Industrial Relations," 285.

73. Foster, "The Amalgamated Association," 1–14. Ingham, *Making Iron and Steel*, 100–02.

74. Theodore Jay Hess, "Industrial Relations in the Iron and Steel Industry" (master's thesis, University of Pennsylvania, 1937), 2.

75. 22 November 1876, 25 April 1878 (Copy of rollers' sliding scale contract of April 1872), Diary of B.F. Jones, 1875–1899, box 1, J&L Corporation Papers, AIS.

76. Pennsylvania Secretary of Internal Affairs, *Industrial Statistics*, 1874–5, (Harrisburg: Department of Internal Affairs, 1875), 530. Pennsylvania Secretary of Internal Affairs, *Industrial Statistics, 1876–7* (Harrisburg: Department of Internal Affairs, 1877), 59–63.

77. Pennsylvania Secretary of Internal Affairs, *Industrial Statistics, 1874–5*, 530. Pennsylvania Secretary of Internal Affairs, *Industrial Statistics, 1876–7*, 59–63.

78. Couvares, *The Remaking of Pittsburgh*, 9–13. Oestreicher, "Working-Class Formation," 116, 129–30. Ingham, *Making Iron and Steel*, 96–127.

79. 22 November 1876, Diary of B.F. Jones, 1875–1899, box 1, J&L Corporation Papers, AIS. Fitch, *Steel Workers*, 99. Bernard Elbaum and Frank Wilkinson, "Industrial Relations and Uneven Development: A Comparative Study of the American and British Steel Industries," *Cambridge Journal of Economics* 3 (1979): 283.

80. "What May Be Done," "The Negro Puddlers," *NLT*, 13 March 1875, 2. "Rolling Mill Reports," *NLT*, 20 March 1875, 1. "Pittsburgh," *NLT*, 27 March 1875, 1. "More Help Offered," *NLT*, 27 March 1875, 2. "The Situation," *NLT*, 3 April 1875, 1. "Ended," *NLT*, 17 April 1875, 1. Krause, *Battle for Homestead*, 112–18. "The Amalgamated Association," *Amalgamated Journal*, 27 August 1942, 10 (hereafter cited as *AJ*).

81. 26 May; 2 June; 3 June; 7 June 1879, Diary of B.F. Jones, 1875–1899, box 1, J&L Corporation Papers, AIS. "The Lockout," *Pittsburgh Commercial Gazette*, 3 June 1877.

82. Elbaum and Wilkinson, "Industrial Relations," 288–89.

83. The organization did bar lawyers, liquor dealers, and Asian workers from membership.

84. Krause, *Battle for Homestead*, 121.

85. John Fitch, *The Steel Workers* (1910; Pittsburgh: University of Pittsburgh Press, 1989), 93–95.

86. Holmes, "Policeman of Industry," 60–94. Foner, *1877*, 67–77.

87. Bridge, *Romance*, 8.

88. "Dividing Nationalities," *NLT*, 16 June 1877, 1. Montgomery, *Fall of the House*, 25–26.

89. John A. Garraty, ed., *Labor and Capital in the Gilded Age; Testimony Taken by the Senate Committee upon the Relations between Labor and Capital: 1883* (Boston: 1968), 93–94.

90. Krause, *Battle for Homestead*, 215–26. Montgomery, *Fall of the House*, 14–28.

91. Peter J. Rachleff, "Black, White, and Gray: Working-Class Activism in Richmond, Virginia, 1865–1890" (Ph.D. diss., University of Pittsburgh, 1981), 27–29, 195–211, 551–52.

92. "Interview with F.J. Amormes," n.d., box 3, file 157, PUL, AIS.

93. "The Negro in Mill and Mine," *NLT*, 13 August 1881, 1. "Amalgamated Association," *NLT*, 18 February 1882, 4. "Interview with F.J. Amormes," n.d., box 3, file 157, PUL, AIS. Horace R. Cayton and George S. Mitchell, *Black Workers and the New Unions* (Durham: University of North Carolina Press, 1939), 73–87. Sterling D. Spero and Abram L. Harris, *The Black Worker: The Negro and the Labor Movement* (New York: Columbia University Press, 1931), 249–54. Peter Gottlieb, *Making Their Own Way: Southern Blacks' Migration to Pittsburgh, 1916–1930* (Urbana: University of Illinois Press, 1987), 152–64. Dennis Dickerson, *Out of the Crucible: Black Steelworkers in Western Pennsylvania, 1875–1980* (Albany: State University of New York Press, 1986), 7–18.

94. 4 January 1883; 7 January 1885; 6 January 1886; Diary of B.F. Jones, 1875–1899, box 1, J&L Corporation Papers, AIS. Montgomery, *Fall of the House*, 14–16. Krause, *Battle for Homestead*, 67–77, 141.

95. "The Amalgamated Association," *AJ*, 27 August 1942, 11. Hess, "Iron and Steel," 4. J.S. Robinson, "Amalgamated Association of Iron, Steel, and Tin Workers," John Hopkins University Studies in Historical and Political Science, Series 38, No. 2, Baltimore, 1920, 19–21.

96. David Jardini, "From Iron to Steel: The Recasting of the Jones and Laughlin's Work Force between 1885–1896," *Technology and Culture* 26 (1995): 277–94. Krause, *Battle for Homestead*, 140–46.

97. "The Homestead Strike," *NLT*, 18 February 1882, 4. Pennsylvania Secretary of Internal Affairs, *Industrial Statistics, 1883*, 171–74. Krause, *Battle for Homestead*, 179–92.

98. Pennsylvania Secretary of Internal Affairs, *Industrial Statistics, 1892* (Harrisburg: Department of Internal Affairs, 1893), D1–11.

99. "Oppression," *NLT*, 13 November 1875, 2. Krause, *Battle for Homestead*, 120–33. John D. French, "Reaping the Whirlwind: The Origins of the Allegheny County Greenback-Labor Party of 1877," *Western Pennsylvania Historical Magazine* 64 (April 1981): 97–119. Pennsylvania Department of Internal Affairs, *Pennsylvania Statistic Abstract* (Harrisburg: Department of Internal Affairs, 1975), 222.

100. Lincoln Steffens, *The Shame of the Cities* (1904, reprint; New York: Hill and Wang, 1957) 105, 115. "The Cameron Corruption," *NLT*, 1 September 1877, 1. Harvey O'Connor, *Mellon's Millions: The Biography of a Fortune* (New York: The John Day Company, 1933), 257–58. Paul Kleppner, "Government, Parties and Voters in Pittsburgh," in *City at the Point*, 166–73. Michael P. Weber, *Don't Call Me Boss: Pittsburgh's Renaissance Mayor* (Pittsburgh: University of Pittsburgh Press, 1988), 10–15. Krause, *Battle for Homestead*, 136–39.

101. Blair, "Quay," 81–82.

102. Steffens, *The Shame*, 106–22.

103. "Cameron's Boomerang," *NLT*, 25 August 1877, 1.

104. Krause, *Battle for Homestead*, 138–39.

105 Fitch, *Steel Workers*, 106–07. Krause, *Battle for Homestead*, 195–96, 252–66.

106. Paul B. Beers, *Pennsylvania Politics Today and Yesterday: The Tolerable Accommodation* (University Park: Pennsylvania State University Press, 1980), 43, 54.

107. "Still in Slavery," *NLT*, 18 November 1876, 1.

108. Beers, *Pennsylvania Politics*, 43

109. Act of June 1, 1889, P.L. 420. See also *Purdon's*, Title 72, part 2, *Taxation and Fiscal Affairs*, 252–71. Statement of H.S. Keil, representative of Jones and Laughlin, in Joint Committee of the Senate and House of Representatives of the Commonwealth of Pennsylvania, *Report to Consider and Report a Revision of the Corporation and Revenue Laws*, 1909, 730–32.

110. Beers, *Pennsylvania Politics*, 43, 54.

111. O'Connor, *Mellon's Millions*, 102, 257. William Alan Blair, "A Practical Politician: The Boss Tactics of Matthew Stanley Quay," *Pennsylvania History* 56 (April 1989): 83.

112. Fitch, *Steel Workers*, 95.

113. Krause, *Battle for Homestead*, 15–38, 237–38. Shalloo, *Private Police*, 1933. 185–88. Hogg, "Pinkertonism," 177, 180–81.

114. *Purdon's*, Title 43, 142. Krause, *Battle for Homestead*, 284–314, 348–50. Brody, *Steelworkers in America*, 58–60. Montgomery, *Fall of the House*, 36–43. Charles P. Neill, *Report on Conditions of Employment in the Iron and Steel Industry*, 62nd Congress, 1st session, Senate Document No. 110, 1913, III, 112–21. Fitch, *Steel Workers*, 86–89.

115. Pennsylvania Secretary of Internal Affairs, *Industrial Statistics, 1892*, D1–11.

116. Pennsylvania Secretary of Internal Affairs, *Industrial Statistics, 1893* (Harrisburg: Department of Internal Affairs, 1894), 635–39.

117. Jardini, "From Iron to Steel," 277–94. Misa, *A Nation of Steel*, 172–210, 253–82. Fitch, *Steel Workers*, 153–56. Brody, *Steelworkers in America*, 8–22, 57–58.

118. Thomas Bell, *Out of This Furnace: A Novel of Immigrant Labor in America* (1941; reprint, Pittsburgh: University of Pittsburgh Press, 1976), 167.

119. U.S. Senate, *Report on Conditions of Employment in the Iron and Steel Industry in the United States*, vol. 1, 62nd Congress, Senate Document 110, 1911, xiv–xv.

120. Horace B. Davis, *The Condition of Labor in the American Iron and Steel Industry* (New York: International Publishers, 1933), 67. Charles A. Gulick, *Labor Policy of the U.S. Steel Corporation* (New York: Columbia University Press, 1924), 57.

121. Crystal Eastman, *Work-Accidents and the Law* (New York: Russell Sage Foundation, 1910), 13–14.

122. Fitch, *Steel Workers*, 13. Eastman, *Work-Accidents*, 49–75.

123. "New Labor Laws in This State," *NLT*, 23 May 1907, 1. Brody, *Steelworkers in America*, 165–68.

124. Pennsylvania Department of Labor and Industry, *Biennial Report, 1937–8* (Harrisburg: 1938), table A-18. Mark Aldrich, *Safety First: Technology, Labor and Business in the Building of American Work Safety, 1870–1939* (Baltimore: The John Hopkins University Press, 1997), 129, 309–10. "Personnel Department Annual Report, Jan 1. 1922," 2, box "Historical Sketches," file "Lost Time Accidents, General Information," USX National Tube Papers, AIS.

125. See note 125 for citations.

126. Fitch, *Steel Workers*, 141–42. Katherine Stone, "The Origins of Job Structures in the Steel Industry," *The Review of Radical Political Economics* 6 (summer 1974): 61–97. Richard Edwards, *Contested Terrain* (New York: Basic Books, 1979). David M. Gordon, Richard Edwards, and Michael Reich, *Segmented Work, Divided Workers* (New York: Oxford University Press, 1982).

127. Bureau of the Census, *Comparative Occupational Statistics of the United States, 1870–1940*, 16th Census (Washington: GPO, 1945), 160. Pennsylvania Department of Labor and Industry, *Production, Immigration, Unemployment* (Harrisburg: Department of Labor and Industry, 1914), 174–75, 246–47. Pennsylvania Department of Internal Affairs, *Report on the Productive Industries of the Commonwealth of Pennsylvania for 1916–1919* (Harrisburg: Department of Labor and Industry, 1920), 222–23. Montgomery, *Fall of the House*, 42.

128. Fitch, *Steel Workers*, 9–21, 139–47, 350–53. Ingham, *Making Iron and Steel*, 53.

129. Couvares, *The Remaking of Pittsburgh*, 90. Paul Kellogg, *Wage Earning Pittsburgh* (New York: Arno Press, 1974) 33–60. John Bodnar, Roger Simon, and Michael P. Weber, *Lives of Their Own: Blacks, Italians, and Poles in Pittsburgh, 1900–1960* (Urbana: University of Illinois Press, 1982), 263–66.

130. Anton Cindrich, 25 June 1974, no. 17–2, Pittsburgh Oral History Project, Pennsylvania State Archives (hereafter cited as POHP and PSA). Adam Janowski, interview by Jim Barrett, 14 June 1976, transcript, 8–9, Homestead Oral History Project, AIS (hereafter cited as HOHP). U.S. Senate Committee on Labor and Education, *Investigation of the Strike in the Steel Industry*, 2 vol., 66th Congress, 1st session, 1919, vol. 2, 551, 601. Eastman, *Work-Accidents*, 65.

131. Bureau of the Census, *Comparative Occupational Statistics*, 160. Pennsylvania Department of Labor and Industry, *Annual Report of the Commissioner of Labor and Industry: Statistics of Production, Wages, Employees, 1915* (Harrisburg: Department of Labor and Industry, 1916), 3, 450–51. Pennsylvania Department of Internal Affairs, *Productive Industries, 1916–1919*, 222–23. "Interview with F.J. Amormes," n.d., box 3, file 157, PUL, AIS.

132. Robert Asher, "Painful Memories: The Historical Consciousness of Steel Workers and the Steel Strike of 1919," *Pennsylvania History* 45 (January 1978): 66.

133. Fitch, *Steel Workers*, 10–12. Brody, *Steelworkers in America*, 99, 119–21, 136, 265–67. John Bodnar, *Immigration and Industrialization: Ethnicity in an American Mill Town, 1870–1940* (Pittsburgh: University of Pittsburgh Press, 1977), 38. Cayton and Mitchell, *Black Workers*, 73–87. Spero and Harris, *The Black Worker*, 249–54. Gottlieb, *Making Their Own Way*, 152–64.

134. Fitch, *Steel Workers*, 214–20, 230. "A Homestead Worker Tells a Sad Story," *AJ*, 29 July 1909, 11. "Here It Is," *NLT*, 8 August 1901, 3. Brody, *Steelworkers in America*, 82–84. Krause, *Battle for Homestead*, 358. Kuritz, "Labor Controls," 176–78. Steven Cohen, "Steelworkers Rethink the Homestead Strike of 1892," *Pennsylvania History* 41 (April 1974): 165–66, 172–73. Bodnar, *Immigration and Industrialization*, 102–26. Bernstein, *Turbulent Years*, 648. Charles H. McCormick, *Seeing Reds: Federal Surveillance of Radicals in the Pittsburgh Mill District, 1917–1921* (Pittsburgh: University of Pittsburgh Press, 1997), 46–87. Shalloo, *Private Police*, 183. "No Company Union at U.S. Steel—Boss Says So"; note 4003 "Workers' Enemies Exposed"; Steel and Metal Notes, June 1934, box 24, file "Spies," Harvey O'Connor Papers, Archives of Labor and Urban Affairs, University Archives, Wayne State University (hereafter cited as AL&UA). Harvey O'Connor, *Steel-Dictator* (New York: John Day Company, 1935), 253–54, 274–85. Frank L. Palmer, *Spies in Steel: An Expose of Industrial War* (Denver: The Labor Press, 1928), 3–35. For the spy system on the coal fields, see Thomas H. Coode and John F. Bauman, *People, Poverty and Politics: Pennsylvanians during the Great Depression* (Lewisburg: Bucknell University Press, 1981), 26–44.

135. William E. Forbath, *Law and the Shaping of the American Labor Movement* (Cambridge: Harvard University Press, 1989), 103–04, 177–83. "Labor Meetings," *NLT*, 4 August 1877, 4.

136. Hattam, *Labor Visions*, 112–79. Forbath, *Law and the Shaping*, 37–57.

137. Robert Asher, "Experience Counts: British Workers, Accident Safety and Compensation and the Origins of the Welfare State," n.p., n.d., 101–12.

138. U.S. House of Representatives, *Report of the Industrial Commission on the Relations and Conditions of Capital and Labor*, vol. 17, Document 186, 57th Congress., 1st session, 1901, 461. "Court Hearing on Arbitration," *NLT*, 26 August 1909, 8. "Arbitration Law Unconstitutional," *NLT*, 12 September 1909, 12. Edwin Witte, *The Government in Labor Disputes* (New York: McGraw Hill, 1934), 84, 234. Charles O. Gregory, *Labor and the Law* (New York: W.W. Norton and Co., 1946), 97.

139. Philip Taft and Philip Ross, "American Labor Violence: Its Causes, Character, and Outcome," in *Violence in America: Historical and Comparative Perspectives*, ed. Hugh Davis Graham and Ted Robert Gurr (Beverly Hills: Sage Publications, 1979), 231. Michael Mann, *The Sources of Social Power* (Cambridge: University of Cambridge Press, 1993), vol. 2, 635. Daniel Lazare, "America the Undemocratic," *New Left Review* 232 (November/ December 1998): 21–22.

140. Elbaum and Wilkinson, "Industrial Relations," 275–303. Charles Docherty, *Steel and Steelworkers: The Sons of Vulcan* (London: Heinemann, 1983), 25–42. Judith Eisenberg Vichniac, *The Management of Labor: The British and French Iron and Steel Industries, 1860–1918* (Greenwich: JAI Press, 1990), 39, 138–42, 149. James Holt, "Trade Unionism in the British and U.S. Steel Industries, 1880–1914: A Comparative Study," *Labor History* 26 (winter 1977): 32–35.

141. Bureau of the Census, *Manufactures, Reports by States*, Volume IX, 13th Census, (Washington: GPO 1912), 1055–56.

142. Martin J. Sklar, *The Corporate Reconstruction of American Capitalism, 1890–1916: The Market, the Law and Politics* (Cambridge: Cambridge University Press, 1988), 223–25. "The Open Shop Strike: Sheet and Tin Plate Company Sues 56 Strikers for $200,000 Damages," *NLT*, 19 August 1909, 8.

143. The Commissioner of Corporations, *Summary of Report on the Steel Industry* (Washington: GPO, 1911), iii–viii, 13–40. Abraham Berglund, *The United States Steel Corporation: A Study of the Growth and Influence of Combination in the Iron and Steel Industry* (New York: Columbia University Studies in the Social Sciences, 1907), 73–78. Warren, *American Steel Industry*, 124–26. Hogan, *Economic History* vol. 2, 470–84.

144. Andrew Carnegie, "Steel in U.S." 12 January 1901, Andrew Carnegie-Charles M. Schwab Papers, box 1, file 4, PSU.

145. Josephson, *Robber Barons*, 417–29. O'Connor, *Steel-Dictator*, 11–16, 35–45. John A. Garraty, "The United States Steel Corporation Versus Labor: The Early Years," *Labor History* 1 (1960): 24.

146. Warren, *American Steel Industry*, 196–216. U.S. Steel, *T.N.E.C. Papers*, vol. III, [Temporary National Economic Committee], (n.p.: U.S. Steel, 1940), 1–15, 46–50, 55–79.

147. *Fortune*, 12 December 1935, 142.

148. *T.N.E.C. Papers* vol. II, 138–42.

149. U.S. Steel, *T.N.E.C. Papers*, vol. II, 13–14. "A Billion Dollar Trust," *NLT*, 22 August 1901, 3. O'Connor, *Steel-Dictator*, 366. Gertrude D. Schroeder, *The Growth of Major Steel Companies, 1900–1950* (Baltimore: Johns Hopkins, 1955), 175, 216. Thomas K. McCraw and Forest Reinhardt, "Losing to Win: U.S. Steel's Pricing, Investment Decisions, and Market Share, 1901–1938," *Journal of Economic History* 49 (September 1989): 597–99. Fitch, *Steel Workers*, 207–12.

150. O'Connor, *Mellon's Millions*, 58–75. U.S. House of Representatives, *Committee on the Investigation of the United States Steel Company*, Report 2447. *Hearings*, 8 vols., 62nd Congress, 2nd session, 1911–12.

151. Asher, "Painful Memories," 81. "Weld Boys Strike"; "A Reprisal Bugaboo"; "McKeesport"; *NLT*, 15 August 1901, 1, 5. "Scene in the Great Strike," *NLT*, 29 August 1901, 1.

152. "Strike of 1901," 1–2, USX National Tube Papers, AIS. Brody, *Steelworkers in America*, 62–68. Gerald G. Eggert, *Steelmasters and Labor Reform, 1888–1923* (Pittsburgh: University of Pittsburgh Press, 1981), 36–40. Cayton and Mitchell, *Black Workers*, 73–87. Spero and Harris, *The Black Worker*, 249–54. Gottlieb, *Making Their Own Way*, 152–64. "Negro Bugaboo," *NLT*, 8 August 1901, 3.

153. "President McArdles's Message to Iron and Steel Workers," *AJ*, 7 October 1909, 1; "Two Days Enough-Heater Issues Statement," *AJ*, 28 October 1909, 1.

154. Brody, *Steelworkers in America*, 71–79. Fitch, *Steel Workers*, 99. Dickerson, *Out of the Crucible*, 14–15. A Son of Vulcan, "Who Is to Blame for Non-Unionism in This District?" *NLT*, 12 September 1907, 8. P.J. McLaughlin, "Refutes," *NLT*, 19 September 1907, 8. Michael Santos, "Between Hegemony and Autonomy: The Skilled Iron Workers' Search for Identity, 1900–1930," *Labor History* 35 (1994): 405–12.

155. "State Constabulary," *AJ*, 19 August 1909, 1. "Six Lives Lost in Strike Riot," *NLT*, 26 August 1909, 18.

156. Melvyn Dubofsky, *We Shall Be All: A History of the Industrial Workers of the World* (Urbana: University of Illinois Press, 1988), 202–08. Michael Nash, *Conflict and Accommodation: Coal Miners, Steel Workers and Socialism, 1890–1920* (Westport, Connecticut: Greenwood Press, 1982), 110–14. Montgomery, *Fall of the House*, 289. Conti, *State Police*, 77. Brody, *Steelworkers in America*, 138–39. John N. Ingham, "A Strike in the Progressive Era: McKees Rocks, 1909," *Pennsylvania Magazine of History and Biography* 90 (July 1966): 353–77. Quotation on 373–74. "Steel Car Strike," *NLT*, 19 August 1909, 1.

157. Carl I. Meyerhuber, Jr., *Less Than Forever: The Rise and Decline of Union Solidarity in Western Pennsylvania, 1914–1918* (Toronto: Associated University Presses, 1987), 20–21. McCormick, *Seeing Reds*, 32–33.

158. Montgomery, *Fall of the House*, 317–27. Meyerhuber, *Less Than Forever*, 17–41. Ronald Schatz, *The Electrical Workers: A History of Labor at General Electric and Westinghouse, 1923–1960* (Urbana: University of Illinois Press, 1983), 37–38, 83–92. "Westinghouse Is Organizing Fast," *Justice*, 14 February 1914, 1. "ACIU Scores Victory," *Justice*, 21 February 1914, 1.

159. U.S. Senate Special Committee on Investigating the Munitions Industry, *Munitions Industry*, 74th Congress, 1st session, 1935, 128–30, 3006, 3014. Interworld Church Movement, *Report on the Steel Strike of 1919* (New York: Harcourt, Brace and Howe, 1920), 13. Hogan, *Economic History*, vol. 2, 518–19. O'Connor, *Steel-Dictator*, 77–85. U.S. Steel claimed its profits were roughly half that claimed by the government; see *T.N.E.C. Papers*, vol. II, 16. Thomas Lloyd, "History of J&L Corporation," 12, 1938, in J&L Steel Corporation, "Historical Miscellanea, 1871–1953," reel 1, J&L Corporation Papers, AIS.

160. Gottlieb, *Making Their Own Way*, 92–93, 107. James D. Rose, "The Problem Every Supervisor Dreads: Women Workers at the US Steel Duquesne Works During WWII," *Labor History* 36 (1995): 24–26.

161. Brody, *Steelworkers in America*, 180–98, 214–30. Frank H. Serene, "Immigrant Steelworkers in the Monongahela Valley: Their Communities and the Development of a Labor Class Consciousness" (Ph.D. diss., University of Pittsburgh, 1979).

162. Conti, *State Police*, 146, 160, 168, 316–17, 370. Shalloo, *Private Police*, 123.

163. Pennsylvania State Police, *Biennial Report of the Pennsylvania State Police, 1927–8* (Harrisburg: Commonwealth of Pennsylvania, 1928), 15. Brody, *Steelworkers in America*, 82–84. Krause, *Battle for Homestead*, 358. Kuritz, "Labor Controls," 176–78. Cohen, "Steelworkers Rethink," 165–66, 172–73. Fitch, *Steel Workers*, 214–20. Bodnar, *Immigration and Industrialization*, 102–26. McCormick, *Seeing Reds*, 46–87. Shalloo, *Private Police*, 183. Irving Bernstein, *The Lean Years: A History of the American Worker, 1920–1933* (Boston: Houghton, Mifflin, 1960), 149–51. See also "Labor Conditions," 7 October 1919, 22 September 1919, "Steel Strike Developments," Reel 11, 989; Reel 13, 100, in *Federal Surveillance of Afro-Americans, 1917–1925: The First World War, The Red Scare and the*

Garvey Movement, ed. Theodore Kornweibel, Jr. (Frederick, MD: University Publications of America, 1986).

164. "Strike Sparks," *AJ*, 25 September 1919, 1.

165. "Statement Issued from the Headquarters of the National Committee for Organizing Iron and Steel Workers," *AJ*, 2 October 1919, 1.

166. "Strike Reports," *AJ*, 2 October 1919, 8. "Westmoreland," *AJ*, 23 October 1919, 23. Senate, *Investigation of Strike*, part 2, 619. Mary Field Parton, ed., *The Autobiography of Mother Jones* (Chicago: Charles H. Kerr, 1972), 218. Roy Lubove, *Twentieth Century Pittsburgh: Government, Business and Environmental Change* (New York: John Wiley and Sons, 1969), 12. See also Eric Leif Davin, "The Littlest New Deal: SWOC Takes Power in Steeltown, A Possibility of Radicalism in the Late 1930s," 2, 21, n.d., mss. in author's possession.

167. John Warady, interview by Larry Gorski, 20 April 1974, 2, PSU.

168. "Judges Back Up Mayor," *AJ*, 30 October 1919, 2. "Strike News," *AJ*, 27 November 1919, 6.

169. Cayton and Mitchell, *Black Workers*, 73–87. Brody, *Steelworkers in America*, 258–61. Interworld Church Movement, *Report on Steel Strike*, 42–43, 176–96. Cindrich, 25 June 1974, no. 17–2, POHP, PSA. Kuritz, "Labor Controls," 254–56. Commonwealth of Pennsylvania, *Annual Report of the Department of State Police for the Year 1919*, 127. Conti, *State Police*, 40–148. "Strike of 1919," 7, USX National Tube Papers, AIS.

170. John N. Grajciar, interview by Arthur S. Weinberg, 2 July 1968, 11, PSU.

171. James Douglas Rose, "The United States Steel Duquesne Works, 1886–1941: The Rise of Steel Unionism" (Ph.D. diss., University of California-Davis, 1997), 46. John Warady, interview by Larry Gorski, 20 April 1974, 4, PSU. David Saposs, interview by Alice M. Hoffman, 17 May 1967, 11–15, PSU.

172. Brody, *Steelworkers in America*, 118–21, 259–61. Interworld Church Movement, *Report on the Steel Strike*, 178.

173. Cayton and Mitchell, *Black Workers*, 134–36.

174. Cayton and Mitchell, *Black Workers*, 73–87. Brody, *Steelworkers in America*, 258–61. Interworld Church Movement, *Report on Steel Strike*, 42–43, 176–96. Cindrich, 25 June 1974, no. 17–2, POHP, PSA.

175. Spero and Harris, *The Black Worker*, 262–63.

176. A. Epstein, "The Negro Migrant in Pittsburgh" (master's thesis, University of Pittsburgh, 1918), 36.

177. Abram Lincoln Harris, "The Negro Worker in Pittsburgh" (master's thesis, University of Pittsburgh, 1924), 49.

178. Mary Heaten Vorse, "Bread Lines and Picket Lines," *AJ*, 27 November 1919, 6. "Interview with F.J. Amormes," n.d., box 3, file 157, PUL, AIS.

179. "National Lodge," "It Is Only a Retreat," *AJ*, 15 January 1920, 1. Interworld Church Movement, *Report on Steel Strike*, 181, 195–96. Edward P. Johanningsmeier, *Forging American Communism: The Life of William Z. Foster* (Princeton: Princeton University Press, 1994), 111–49. David Brody, *Labor in Crisis: The Steel Strike of 1919* (Philadelphia: J.B. Lippincott Company, 1965), 168–79. William Z. Foster, *American Trade Unionism* (New York: International Publishers, 1947), 41–42.

180. Kuritz, "Labor Controls," 113–50. Shalloo, *Private Police*, 129. Meyerhuber, *Less Than Forever*, 139–41.

181. Act of April 18, 1929, P.L. 546. Pennsylvania Federation of Labor, *29th Organized Labor's Official Year Book, Supplement to Pennsylvania's Labor Bulletin* (Harrisburg: Pennsylvania Federation of Labor [hereafter cited as PFL], 1929), 21. Beers, *Pennsylvania Politics,* 88–91. The victory of the mine owners did little to stem Pennsylvania's loss of market share to newer fields in Southern Appalachia. John Gaventa, *Power and Powerlessness: Quiescence and Rebellion in an Appalachian Valley* (Urbana: University of Illinois Press, 1980), 85.

182. Curt Miner, "Mill Towns, 'The Underworld Fraternity,' and the Working Man: Reconsidering Local Politics and Corruption within the Industrial Suburb, Homestead, Pennsylvania, 1921–1937," n.d., mss. in author's possession. Adam Janowski, interview by Jim Barrett, 14 June 1976, 18, HOHP, AIS. Anne M. Barton and Margaret Staudenmaier, "Ethnic and Racial Groups in Rankin, Pennsylvania" (master's thesis, University of Pittsburgh, 1947), 11, 25–26. Mildred Allen Beik, *Miners of Windber: The Struggles of New Immigrants for Unionization* (Harrisburg: Penn State Press, 1996), 327–30.

183. Sally Stephenson, "Michael A. Musmanno: A Symbolic Leader" (master's thesis, Carnegie Mellon University, 1981), 37–47. Martin Duffy and Frank Leach, interview by Jim Barrett, 3 June 1976, transcript, 5, HOHP, AIS.

184. Rowland and Boyd, *Bureau of Ordnance,* 32–35. Seldes, *Iron, Blood and Profits,* 348–51.

185. O'Connor, *Steel-Dictator,* 130–31.

186. Hogan, *Economic History,* vol. 3, 954–59, 975–82, 1196. O'Connor, *Steel-Dictator,* 126–31. "U.S. Steel-Break It Up?" *Fortune* (April 1950): 92.

187. O'Connor, *Steel-Dictator,* 126–29. Warren, *American Steel Industry,* 180–81; Hogan, *Economic History,* vol. 3, 878–83, 886–87, 891–92.

188. Misa, *Nation of Steel,* 253–62. O'Connor, *Steel-Dictator,* 127. Bernstein, *Turbulent Years,* 47. Hogan, *Economic History,* vol. 3, 813. U.S. Tariff Commission, *Iron and Steel,* Report 128, Second Series, 1938, 131–32, 324–25. Caroll R. Daugherty, *The Economics of the Iron and Steel Industry* (New York: International Publishers, 1937), 55–57. Taylor, *Ten Years,* 21.

189. Lubove, *Twentieth Century Pittsburgh,* 5.

190. Bernstein, *Turbulent Years,* 47. Hogan, *Economic History,* vol. 3, 813. U.S. Tariff Commission, *Iron and Steel,* Report 128, Second Series, 1938, 107, 131–32, 324–29. Daugherty, *Economics of the Iron and Steel Industry,* 55–57. Taylor, *Ten Years,* 8–9.

191. U.S. Department of Labor, *Impact of the War on the Pittsburgh, Pennsylvania Area* (Washington: GPO, 1943), 9. Pennsylvania Bureau of Employment and Unemployment Compensation, *Pennsylvania Labor Market Surveys—Allegheny County,* January 1941, 5–6. Warren, *American Steel Industry,* 197, 205. David B. Houston, "A Brief History of the Process of the Capital Accumulation in Pittsburgh: A Marxist Interpretation," in *Pittsburgh-Sheffield Sister Cities: Proceedings of the Pittsburgh-Sheffield Symposium on Industrial Cities,* ed. Joel Tarr (Pittsburgh: Carnegie Mellon University, 1986), 38.

192. U.S. Steel, "An Analysis of the Demand for Steel in the Railroad Industry" (U.S. Steel, 1939), 9, 21. Department of Labor, *Impact of the War,* 1–4, 63.

193. J. Frank Beaman, "Steel Makers Plans Oppose Building New Mills in Pittsburgh," *Pittsburgh Press,* 2 April 1935, 1 (hereafter cited as *PP*). Beaman, "Pittsburgh's Throne of Steel Totters," *PP,* 1 April 1935, 1.

194. Charles Hill, "Fighting the Twelve Hour Day in the American Steel Industry," *Labor History* 15 (1974): 35. Brody, *Labor in Crisis,* 177–78. Eggert, *Steelmasters,* 152–60.

195. Carroll R. Daugherty, Melvin G. de Chazeau, and Samuel S. Stratton, *The Economics of the Iron and Steel Industry* (New York: McGraw-Hill, 1937), vol. 1, 165–66. Elmer Maloy, interview by Don Kennedy, 7 November 1967, 3, PSU.

196. Horace B. Davis, "Hot Mill Worker's Widow Gets Raw Deal," 26 April 1929, Federated Press, box 40, O'Connor Papers, AL&UA.

197. "Personnel Department Annual report, Jan 1. 1922," 18, box "Historical Sketches," file "Lost Time Accidents," USX National Tube Papers, AIS. Eastman, *Work-Accidents*, 160–64, 300–04.

198. U.S. Steel, *Annual Report*, 1923, 5, 30.

199. SWOC, Press Release, 17 September 1936, *The CIO Files of John L. Lewis*, Microfilm, Roll 12, 671. O'Connor, *Steel-Dictator*, 5, 7. Robert Brooks, *As Steel Goes . . . Unionism in a Basic Industry* (New Haven: Yale University Press, 1940), 2–3.

200. Gano Dunn, Office of Production Management, *Second Report to the President of the United States on the Adequacy of the Steel Industry for National Defense* (Washington: GPO, 1941), 38.

201. Bernstein, *Turbulent Years*, 507.

202. Philip Klein and collaborators, *A Social Study of Pittsburgh: Community Problems and Social Services of Allegheny County* (New York: Columbia University Press, 1938), 124, 160. Department of Labor, *Impact of the War*, 63. Warren, *American Steel Industry*, 209. Taylor, *Ten Years*, 5.

203. Phil McGuigan, interview by Rose Givens, 13 June 1983, transcript; Rocky Doratio, interview by James Showalter, 6 August 1983; McKeesport Oral History Project, AIS (hereafter cited as MOHP).

204. Joe Dallet, "'Hold-up' at Jones and Laughlin," 24 May 1929; "Swindler Foremen Escapes with Light Sentence," 8 June 1929, box 23, file, "J&L," O'Connor Papers, AL&UA. Leroy McChestes, 8 August 1974, transcript, POHP, PSA. H.A. Lett, "Work, Negro Unemployment in Pittsburgh," *Opportunity* (March 1931): 80. Davis, *The Condition of Labor*, 96, footnote 5, 276. Martin Duffy and Frank Leach, interview by Jim Barrett, 3 June 1976, transcript, 5, HOHP, AIS.

205. F. Alden Wilson, "Occupational Status of the Negro in the Iron and Steel Industry in Pittsburgh and Environs," *Bureau of Business Research* (March-April 1934): 38–41, 44, PUL Papers, AIS.

206. Phil McGuigan, interview by Rose Givens, 13 June 1983, transcript, MOHP, AIS.

207. Ashton Allen, interview by Tony Buba and Ray Henderson, summer 1992, tape recording. Tony Buba and Ray Henderson have graciously allowed the author access to interviews for their video documentary, *Struggles in Steel: A Story of African-American Steelworkers*, videorecording, dir. Tony Buba and Ray Henderson (San Francisco: California Newsreel, 1996).

208. Cayton and Mitchell, *Black Workers*, 31–33.

209. Michael Zahorsky, 31 July 1974, POHP, PSA.

210. Edmond A. Holmes, interview by Henderson and Buba, summer 1992, tape recording.

211. John Hovanec, interview by Jim Barrett, 14 June 1976, transcript, HOHP, AIS. Freeman Patton, 11 July 1974, tape recording, POHP, PSA. Catherine O'Connor, interview by Jim Barrett, 19 May 1976, transcript, HOHP, AIS.

212. Reginald A. Johnson, "Employment of Negroes in Allegheny County," 2 December 1940, box 3, file 135, PUL papers, AIS.

213. Alden, "Occupational Status," 25–26. Robert J. Norell, "Caste in Steel: Jim Crow Careers in Birmingham, Alabama," *Journal of American History* 73 (1986): 671–79.

214. "Letter from a Carnegie Steel Mill Worker," *Metal Worker*, October 1932. Tony Riccitelli, 9 November 1978, Beaver Valley Labor History Society, (hereafter cited as BVLHS). Harvey O'Connor and Jessie O'Connor, interview by Don Kennedy, March 1976, 6, PSU.

215. "Summary of the Subversive Situation," 1 August 1932, Reel 27, 474, Randolph Boehm, ed., *U.S. Military Intelligence Reports: Surveillance of Radicals in the United States, 1917–41*, 1984.

216. Coode and Bauman, *People, Poverty and Politics*, 158–75.

217. Brooks, *As Steel Goes*, 3. Coode and Bauman, *People, Poverty and Politics*, 139–48, 237–39. Meyerhuber, *Less Than Forever*, 141, 149, 152. Richard Keller, *Pennsylvania's Little New Deal* (New York: Garland, 1982), 50–54, 64.

218. "Push for Probes of Insanity Frameups," Federated Press, 30 October 1934; "Press Release," International Labor Defense, box 23, file "J&L," O'Connor Papers, AL&UA. "Steel Worker Railroaded to Asylum," AJ, 1 November 1934, 1, 3.

219. O'Connor, *Steel-Dictator*, 150–62.

220. Coode and Bauman, *People, Poverty and Politics*, 158–73.

221. *NYT*, 26 November 1933.

222. O'Connor, *Steel-Dictator*, 133–76.

223. Philip Murray to Benjamin Fairless, 16 September 1936, *The CIO Files of John L. Lewis*, Reel 12, 675.

224. Dubofsky and Van Tine, *Lewis*, 132–72. Bert Cochran, *Labor and Communism: The Conflict That Shaped American Unions* (Princeton: Princeton University Press, 1977), 46–57. Meyerhuber, *Less Than Forever*, 91–136. Linda Nyden, "Black Miners in Western Pennsylvania, 1925–31: The National Miners Union and the United Mine Workers of America," *Science and Society* 41 (Spring 1977): 69–101. "Statement concerning the Grand Fizzle"; "District 1 Expels Group . . ." *UMWJ*, 1 October 1928, 3, 5. "Dual Unions Roundly Denounced," *UMWJ*, 15 November 1928, 2.

225. Harriet Woodbridge Gilfillan, *I Went to Pit College* (New York: The Literary Guild, 1934), 19, 25.

226. A. Jakira, "Building the Party during Strikes," *Party Organizer* (May-June 1928) (hereafter cited as *PO*). Party membership rose briefly to 1,200. "For a Proper Utilization during Strikes," *PO* (November-December 1932): 30–32. "Every Factory a Fortress of Communism" and "Rooting the Party in the Shops," *PO* (September-October 1931): 4, 13–15. Nyden, "Black Miners," 96.

227. Theodore Draper, "Communists and Miners, 1928–1933," *Dissent* (spring 1972): 380. Gaventa, *Power and Powerlessness*, 84–121.

228. "Party Functioned Poorly in Mining Strike Districts," *PO* (December 1933): 8. Draper, "Communists and Miners," 382–92. Staughton Lynd, "The Possibility of Radicalism in the Early 1930s: The Case of Steel," *Radical America* 6 (November-December 1972): 52.

229. John Brophy, *A Miner's Life* (Madison: University of Wisconsin Press, 1964), 236. Dubofsky and Van Tine, *Lewis*, 182–200.

230. Bernstein, *Turbulent Years*, 46–61.

231. Frances DiCola and Gene DiCola, transcript, n.d., 3–4, 25–30, PSU. Quotes for DiCola. William Theis, interview by Alice Hoffman and Bob Schutte, 8 May 1969, 15–16, PSU. Taylor, *Ten Years*, 29–31.

232. Coode and Bauman, *People, Poverty and Politics*, 137–48. O'Connor, *Steel-Dictator*, 150–62. Meyerhuber, *Less Than Forever*, 141, 149, 152. Keller, *Pennsylvania's Little New Deal*, 50–54, 64. Taylor, *Ten Years*, 29–33.

233. Dubofsky and Van Tine, "John L. Lewis," in Melvin Dubofsky and Warren Van Tine, ed., Labor Leaders in America (Urbana: University of Illinois, 1987), 197–98. Bernstein, *Turbulent Years*, 434. Keller, *Pennsylvania's Little New Deal*, 101.

234. Coode and Bauman, *People, Poverty, and Politics*, 148–50. Dubofsky and Van Tine, *Lewis*, 373–75.

235. Gertrude Haessler, "The Plus and Minus of Shop Work Since Last Party Convention," *Daily Worker*, 25 February 1929 (hereafter cited as *DW*). "Composition of the Party," *PO* (December 1927): 15. Jack Stachel, "Our Factory Nuclei," *PO* (May-June 1928): 5. "Every Factory a Fortress of Communism" and "Rooting the Party in the Shops," *PO* (September-October 1931): 3, 15. Steve Nelson, James R. Barrett, Rob Ruck, *Steve Nelson: American Radical* (Pittsburgh: University of Pittsburgh Press, 1981), 225.

236. *Crucible Worker*, n.d., Shop Paper no. 1, box 43, "Accidents," O'Connor Papers, AL&UA.

237. "TUUL Board Plans Drive on Steel Octopus," *DW*, box 29, file "TUUL," O'Connor Papers, AL&UA.

238. Brooks, *As Steel Goes*, 46–69. Nelson, Barrett, Ruck, *Steve Nelson*, 22–28. John N. Grajciar, interview by Arthur S. Weinberg, 2 July 1968, 5, PSU. "Task of Organizing Negro Steel Workers Stressed," *DW*, O'Connor Papers, box 24, file "Rank-and-File, 1935," AL&UA. Rose, "Duquesne Works," 105–12, 150–62.

239. "Ambridge Trip," 4–5 November 1933, box 22, file "Ambridge," O'Connor Papers, AL&UA.

240. Jack Johnstone, "How the Steel Union Grows in Pittsburgh Region," "'Daily' Played Part in the Building of the Steel Union," *DW*; John Meldon, "To the District TUUL MWIL Organizers," *DW*, 4 September 1931; "Steel and Metal Workers Join in Trade Union Confab," *Federated Press*, 21 August 1933; all in box 25, file "Steel and Metal Workers," O'Connor Papers, AL&UA. "Struggles Ahead," *Steel and Metal Worker* (August-September 1933): 2 (hereafter cited as *SMW*). Cayton and Mitchell, *Black Workers*, 119.

241. James Matles, interview by Ron Filippelli, 6 May 1968, 3, PSU.

242. Cayton and Mitchell, *Black Workers*, 112–3.

243. "550 Pittsburgh Steel Workers Strike," *Federated Press*, 3 September 1931, box 25, file "SMWIU Strikes," O'Connor Papers, AL&UA.

244. "Steel and Metal Notes," Labor Research Association (September 1933): 4; "Pressed Steel Plant Guarded," *PP*, 22 August 1933; both in box 25, file "Strikes," O'Connor Papers, AL&UA. "Why McKees Rock Pressed Steel Car Workers Struck," *SMW* (October 1933): 5. "Steel Workers Strike," *DW*, 21 August 1933, 1.

245. "Try Jail MWIL Organizers in Canonsburg," *DW*; "Steel and Metal Workers Join in Trade Union Confab," *Federated Press*, 21 August 1933, box 25, file "SMWIU Strikes," O'Connor Papers, AL&UA.

246. "Steel Workers Demand Federal Probe of Terrorism," Federated Press, 12 October 1933, box 22, file "Ambridge," O'Connor Papers, AL&UA. "Greensburg Strike Solid," *SMW* (October 1933): 1. By April 1934, there was no listing of organization in Greensburg, *SMW* (March-April 1934).

247. "Letters from Coroapolis," *SMW* (January 1934): 5.

248. Pennsylvania Department of Labor and Industry, *Report to Governor Gifford Pinchot by the Commission on Special Policing in Industry*, Special Bulletin no. 38, 1934, 11–14. Herbert S. Parmes, "Pennsylvania Labor Legislation Promoting Collective Bargaining, 1933–1940" (master's thesis, University of Pittsburgh, 1941), 67–68. Pete Muselin, "The Steel Fist in a Pennsylvania Steel Town," in *It Did Happen Here: Recollections of Political Repression in America*, ed. Bud Schultz and Ruth Schultz (Berkeley and Los Angeles: University of California Press, 1989), 72–74.

249. "200 Deputies Charge Ambridge Pickets," Federated Press, 9 October 1933; "Report on the Ambridge Riot," League for Social Justice, box 22, file "Ambridge," O'Connor Papers, AL&UA. Harry Gaines, "Spread the Strike," *DW*, 7 October 1933, 1.

250. O'Connor, *Steel-Dictator*, 150–62.

251. "Ambridge Trip," 4–5 November 1933, box 22, file "Ambridge," O'Connor Papers, AL&UA.

252. *Struggles in Steel*, videorecording.

253. John Meldon, "SMWIU 2nd National Convention in February," *SMW* (December 1933): 1, 6. Meldon, "Steel Union Consolidating Gains," *DW*, box 25, file "SMWIU," O'Connor Papers, AL&UA.

254. Jack Johnstone, "How the Steel Union Grows in Pittsburgh Region," *DW*; "'Daily' Played Part in the Building of the Steel Union," *DW*, box 25, file "SMWIU," O'Connor Papers, AL&UA. "Experiences in Shop Work," *PO* (November-December 1932): 4–7.

255. James Egan, "Keynote Speech Views Major Tasks and Shortcomings," *SMW* (August-September 1934): 3.

256. O'Connor, *Steel-Dictator*, 250–52. "Communists Here? Police Aver No," *Duquesne Times*, 28 March 1930, 7. David Lindberg, interview by Jim Barrett, 21 May 1976, transcript, 6, HOHP, AIS.

257. "With Our Locals," *SMW* (November 1933): 8. "With Our Locals," *SMW* (December 1933): 8.

258. "With Our Locals," *SMW* (February 1934): 8. "With Our Locals," *SMW* (April 1934).

259. Cayton and Mitchell, *Black Workers*, 118. John Meldon, "Steel Union Consolidating Gains," *DW*, box 25, file "SMWIU," O'Connor Papers, AL&UA.

260. Cayton and Mitchell, *Black Workers*, 125. William Theis, interview by Alice Hoffman and Bob Schutte, 8 May 1969, 14, PSU. Albert Atallah, interview by Alice Hoffman, 20 September 1967, 8, PSU.

261. Fitch, "A Man Can Talk in Homestead," *Survey Graphic* (February 1936): 75.

262. "Huge Mass Meeting," *AJ*, 18 October 1934, 1.

263. Cayton and Mitchell, *Black Workers*, 126.

264. "J&L Hearing," *AJ*, 22 November 1934, 1. "No Company Union at U.S. Steel—Boss Says So"; note 4003, "Workers' Enemies Exposed"; Steel and Metal Notes, June 1934, box 24, file "Spies," O'Connor Papers, AL&UA. O'Connor, *Steel-Dictator*, 253–54,

274–85. Frank L. Palmer, *Spies in Steel* (Denver: The Labor Press, 1928). "Frank Palmer Gives Specific Facts on Steel Spies in Radio Speech," *DW*, 19 August 1933, 3. Coode and Bauman, *People, Poverty, and Politics*, 26–44. "Steel Company Admits Spy System," Federated Press, 19 November 1934, box 23, file "J&L," O'Connor Papers, AL&UA.

265. "Aliquippa Meeting," *AJ*, 25 October 1934, 7.

266. Cayton and Mitchell, *Black Workers*, 162.

267. Cayton and Mitchell, *Black Workers*, 166, 173–74.

268. "Ft. Dukane Lodge," *AJ*, 18 October 1934, 12.

269. Cayton and Mitchell, *Black Workers*, 128, 165–66, 175–80.

270. Cayton and Mitchell, *Black Workers*, 128.

271. Cayton and Mitchell, *Black Workers*, 189.

272. Cayton and Mitchell, *Black Workers*, 134–38, 452–56. Rose, "Duquesne Works, 105–12.

273. Brooks, *As Steel Goes*, 55. "First District Meeting," *AJ*, 18 October 1934, 20. "AFL Official Lays Strike Talk to Radicals," *NLT*, 18 April 1935, 1.

274. Lynd, "Possibility," 51. Bernstein, *Turbulent Years*, 197–207. Bell, *Out of This Furnace*, 323–24.

275. Brooks, *As Steel Goes*, 69–70. *Metal Workers News*, July 1934. Lynd, "Possibilities," 50–59. Bernstein, *Turbulent Years*, 368–69, 439. Albert Atallah, interview by Alice Hoffman, 20 September 1967, 11–12, PSU.

276. P.C. Patterson, "To Employees," 6 June 1934, box "Historical Sketches," file "ERP," USX National Tube Papers, AIS.

277. "Ft. Dukane Lodge," *AJ*, 1 November 1934, 18. John Chorey, interview by Alice M. Hoffman, October 1966, 6, PSU. Elmer Maloy, interview by Jack Spiese, 25 March 1968, 3, PSU.

278. Taylor, *Ten Years*, 33–37.

279. Bernstein, *Turbulent Years*, 456–57, 460–65, 475–77.

280. "Memorandum," 3 June 1936, Philip Murray to SWOC, 29 September 1936; "Field Representatives as of July 6, 1936"; Philip Murray, "The Problem before the SWOC on June 17, 1936," 8 November 1936, *The CIO Files of John L. Lewis*, Reel 12, 111–12, 543–48, 599–600, 735–40. "List of Names," 21 May 1937, BVLHS, file 109, AIS. Max Gordon, "The Communists and the Drive to Organize Steel, 1936," *Labor History* 23 (1982): 255–65. Harvey O'Connor and Jessie O'Connor, interview by Don Kennedy, March 1976, 19, PSU. Dubofsky and Van Tine, *Lewis*, 200, 288–89.

281. Len De Caux, *Labor Radical: From the Wobblies to the CIO* (Boston: Beacon Press, 1970), 279, 283.

282. Act of June 15, 1935, P.L. 348, Section 1. Kent, "Development of Industrial Unionism," 108.

283. "State Aid Pledged if Unionized Men Lose Steel Jobs," *NYT*, 6 July 1936, 1. Dubofsky and Van Tine, "John L. Lewis," 197–98. U.S. Senate, Subcommittee of the Committee on Education and Labor. *Violations of Free Speech and Rights of Labor: Supplemental Hearings*, 77th Congress, 1st session, 1941, 208, 318–20, 396, 582. Auerbach, *Labor and Liberty*, 72–90. Philip Murray to SWOC, 29 September 1936; Press Release, 7 September 1936; Philip Murray, "The Problem before the SWOC on June 17, 1936," 8 November 1936; *The CIO Files of John L. Lewis*, Reel 12, 543–48, 689–90, 735–40.

284. Joseph Cohen to Major George L. Berry, 29 October 1936; "Report," 5 September 1936; *Labor's Non-Partisan League of Pennsylvania*, 3–7; Pennsylvania Federation of Labor Papers, Labor's Non-Partisan League, box 1, file 1, PSU. Steven Fraser, *Labor Will Rule: Sidney Hillman and the Rise of American Labor* (New York: Basic Books, 1991), 361–64. Eric Leif Davin, "The Very Last Hurrah? The Defeat of the Labor Party Idea, 1934–36," in *"We Are All Leaders": The Alternative Unionism of the Early 1930s*, ed. Staughton Lynd (Urbana: University of Illinois, 1996). Dubofsky and Van Tine, *Lewis*, 248–53.

285. Pennsylvania Federation of Labor, *Fraternally Yours, James L. McDevitt* (Harrisburg: PFL, 1956), 28. 5 November 1936, 17 September 1936, 15 October 1936, Minutes of the Pittsburgh Central Labor Union, AIS. PFL, *Report of the 35th Annual Convention*, 1936, 189–204.

286. "SWOC Release," n.d., "around Nov. 8," *The CIO Files of John L. Lewis*, Reel 12, 635–37. Dubofsky and Van Tine, "John L. Lewis," 197–98. Bernstein, *Turbulent Years*, 434.

287. "Statement of Philip Murray," 7 November 1936; "SWOC Release," 5 November 1936, *The CIO Files of John L. Lewis*, Reel 12, 640–42, 651.

288. Act of June 4, 1937, P.L. 1595. Bernstein, *Turbulent Years*, 434, 648.

289. Philip Murray to SWOC, 29 September 1936, *The CIO Files of John L. Lewis*, Reel 12, 543–44. David Brody, "The Origins of Modern Steel Unionism: The SWOC Era," in *Forging a Union of Steel*, ed. Clark, Gottlieb, and Kennedy, 19–22.

290. Freeman Patton, 11 July 1974, tape recording, POHP, PSA.

291. Charles Bollinger, interview by Alice Hoffman, June 1966, transcript, United Steel Workers of America (USWA) Oral History Project, United Steel Workers of America Archives, PSU. McDonald, *Union Man*, 94. October 28, 1937, minute book of Local 1397, John McManigal Collection, AIS.

292. Frank Miller Keck Jr., "The Development of Labor Representation at the Homestead Steel Works" (Ph.D. diss., University of Pittsburgh, 1952), 43.

293. Bernstein, *Turbulent Years*, 465–73.

294. Bernstein, *Turbulent Years*, 643–45.

295. Bernstein, *Turbulent Years*, 450–51. "Report, 2/24/37," BVLHS, file 88, AIS.

296. Bernstein, *Turbulent Years*, 647–48.

297. "Pact Failure: No Plans Made to Resume Operations at Mills of Corporation," *PPG*, 13 May 1937, 1. "Troopers Look over Aliquippa Scene for Earle," *PPG*, 14 May 1937, 1. "Walk-Outs Here Ended: 35,000 Return to J&L and Other Plants," *PPG*, 15 May 1937, 1.

298. "Steel Workers Hail Governor as Strike Ends," *PPG*, 14 May 1937, 4. "Aliquippa Meeting," *AJ*, 24 October 1934, 7.

299. "Monessen Workers Swell Steel Strike Ranks," *PPG*, 14 May 1937, 1.

300. "Walk-Outs Here Ended," *PPG*, 15 May 1937, 1. SWOC won the union election handily: 17,028 for the union to 7,207 against, see "CIO Wins J&L Victory," *PPG*, 21 May 1937, 1–2.

301. "The 1937 strike in Aliquippa," [Reprint of letters written May 12–14, 1937] (July 1981): 6, 8, BVLHS, box 3, file 1, AIS.

302. James Green, *The World of the Worker: Labor in Twentieth-Century America* (New York: Hill and Wang, 1980), 164–65. See also Dubofsky and Van Tine, "John L. Lewis," 198–99.

303. Donald S. McPherson, "The 'Little Steel' Strike of 1937 in Johnstown, Pennsylvania," *Pennsylvania History* 39 (April 1972): 219–38.

304. George Walcroft to John L. Lewis, 3 August 1937, *The CIO Files of John L. Lewis*, reel 14, 595–96.

305. 5 November 1936; 17 September 1936; 15 October 1936; 18 March 1937; 26 August 1937; 16 September 1937, Minutes of the Pittsburgh Central Labor Union, AIS. PFL, *Fraternally Yours*, 28.

306. "CIO Men Win in Pennsylvania Primary," *Steel Labor* (September 1937): 2 (hereafter cited as *SL*). "Election Returns," 2 November 1937, LNPL, box 1, file 2, PSU.

307. "Steeltown Mayors," *Bulletin Index*, 11 November 1937, 10–12. Davin, "The Littlest New Deal," 2.

308. Beers, *Pennsylvania Politics*, 130–34.

309. Editorial, *New Republic*, 30 March 1938; "Mid City Press," 16 April 1938; "Financial report, Primary Campaign, 1938"; "State Vote at a Glance," LNPL, box 1, file 4, PSU.

310. William J. Kelly, "An Important State of Facts," 25 April 1938, LNPL, box 1, file 4, PSU.

311. Coode and Bauman, *People*, 246–47. "James and Davis Carry State," PPG, 9 November 1938, 1.

312. "List of Names," 21 May 1937, BVLHS, file 109, AIS.

313. USWA International Executive Board (hereafter cited as USWA IEB), 16–17 February 1948, 133–34, box 43, file 9, USWA Archives, PSU. Nelson, Barrett, and Ruck, *Steve Nelson*, 299, 315. David Oshinsky, "Labor's Cold War: The CIO and the Communists," in *Major Problems in the History of American Workers*, ed. Eileen Boris and Nelson Lichtenstein (Lexington, MA: D.C. Heath, 1991), 512. Charles McCollester, ed., *Fighter with a Heart: Writings of Charles Owen Rice: Pittsburgh Labor Priest* (Pittsburgh: University of Pittsburgh Press, 1996), 67.

314. "Names in Third Class Cities on Communist Petitions, PP, 15 June 1940, 1, 7. Rose, "Duquesne Works," 307–15.

315. "Lodge Organizes," *SL* (June 1940): 4.

316. "Steel Workers and Communism," *SL* (July 1939): 1.

317. Pennsylvania State Police, *Biennial Report of the Pennsylvania State Police*, 1942–44, (Harrisburg: Pennsylvania State Police, 1944), 9–10.

318. K.H.M. to W.C.O., 13 July 1944, box 30, file "USWA Locals," USX Duquesne Works Papers, AIS.

319. USWA IEB, 1–2 April 1946, 105–06, 129–30. 4 March 1941, "Monthly Intelligence Reports," reel 27, 951–56. Randolph Boehm, ed., *U.S. Military Intelligence Reports: Surveilliance of Radicals in the United States, 1917–41*, 1984. See also Jim Dolson interview by Bob Anderson, 1 May 1991, Unemployed Steel Workers Oral History Project, Homestead Steel Industry Heritage Project (hereafter cited as USWOHP, SIHP).

320. Rick Halpern, *Down on the Killing Floor: Black and White Workers in Chicago's Packinghouses, 1904–54* (Urbana: University of Illinois Press, 1997), 96–167. Schatz, *The Electrical Workers*, 64–76. Ronald L. Filippelli and Mark McColloch, *Cold War in the Working Class: The Rise and Decline of the United Electrical Workers* (Albany: State University of New York Press, 1995), 13–64. August Meier and Elliot Rudwick, *Black Detroit and the Rise of the UAW* (New York: Oxford University Press, 1969). Sidney Fine, *Sit-Down: The General Motors Strike of 1936–7* (Ann Arbor: University of Michigan Press, 1969).

321. Rose, "Duquesne Works," 4–9.

322. James J. Matles, and James Higgins, *Them and Us: Struggles of a Rank-and-File Union* (New York: Prentice-Hall, 1974), 25–37, 55–56.

323. Matles and Higgins, *Them and Us*, 22–60, 71, 82, 123–25. By 1935, almost all of the news in the SMWIU concerned the metal trades. See *SMW* 1935, passim.

CHAPTER 2. FROM GREAT DEPRESSION TO GREAT FEAR: THE "WARFARE STATE" IN STEEL

1. Harvey O'Connor, *Mellon's Millions: The Biography of a Fortune* (New York: The John Day Company, 1933), 64.

2. Gano Dunn, Office of Production Management, *Second Report to the President of the United States on the Adequacy of the Steel Industry for National Defense* (Washington: GPO, 1941), 106–24.

3. "Production," *Steel*, 30 June 1941, 17. "May Steel Production," *Iron Age*, 12 June 1941, 113. "Steel Industry," *Wall Street Journal*, 3 January 1939, 27 (hereafter cited as *WSJ*). "Recent Activity of the Steel Industry," *Steel Facts* (August 1945): 3.

4. Carroll W. Pursell Jr., ed, *The Military Industrial Complex* (New York: Harper and Row, 1972), 158–59. "Mightiest Navy," *Steel Facts* (1945): 1.

5. Buford Rowland and William B. Boyd, *U.S. Navy Bureau of Ordnance in World War II* (Washington: GPO, n.d.), 41.

6. "Only $650 Millions in War Profits," *SL* (January 1944): 11. "Steel Adds Half Billion," *SL* (April 1943): 2. "Net Profits of Leading Steel Companies," in District 19, box 48, file 21, USWA Archives, PSU.

7. "Steel: Report on the War Years," *Fortune* (May 1945). "A Study of Wartime Steel Industry Expansion," *Iron Age*, 21 June 1945.

8. Gerald White, "Financing Industrial Expansion for War," *Journal of Economic History* 9 (1949): 157–58.

9. Civilian Production Administration, *War Industrial Facilities Authorized, July 1940-August, 1945* (Washington: GPO, 1946). "Navy Department Okays Expansion Here in Armor Plate Mill," *Homestead Messenger*, 14 March 1942 (hereafter cited as *HM*). "New Mill Boosts Steel Production: Open Hearths Already Producing," and "A Mill Is Born," *HM*, 30 November 1943. "First Steel Poured at New Homestead Expansion," *Steel*, 21 June 1943, 83; "New DPC Plant Nears Completion," *Steel*, 24 January 1944, 31; Joel Sabadasz, "Duquesne Works: Overview History" (Homestead: unpublished mss., 1991), 14; Mark Brown, "Technology and the Homestead Steel Works, 1879–1945" (Homestead: unpublished mss., 1991), 64–69.

10. Rowland and Boyd, *Bureau of Ordnance*, 43.

11. Rowland and Boyd, *Bureau of Ordnance*, 42. War contracts were important to the victory of the union at Bethlehem in 1941. Sidney Lens, *The Labor Wars: From the Molly Maguires to the Sitdowns* (New York: Anchor Books, 1973), 386.

12. Dubofsky and Van Tine, *John L. Lewis*, 345. United Mine Workers of America, *Proceedings of the 1940 United Mine Workers of America Convention*, 315.

13. "Roosevelt Sweeps County," *PPG*, 6 November 1940, 1. Dubofsky and Van Tine, *John L. Lewis*, 339–70.

14. "Labor Can Win," 8 October 1940; Comparisons, 1940 Political Platforms; "G.O.P. Spent 3 Million in This State"; Labor's Non-Partisan League, box 1, file 13, USWA Archives, PSU (hereafter cited as LNPL). "Endorsement of Senator Guffey," n.d., LNPL, box 1, file 11, USWA Archives, PSU.

15. USWA IEB, 22 June 1942, 27, box 41, file 2, USWA Archives, PSU. Dubofsky and Van Tine, *John L. Lewis*, 389–414.

16. Pennsylvania Industrial Union Council, Sixth Annual Convention Proceedings (Harrisburg: Pennsylvania Industrial Union Council, 1943), 7 (hereafter cited as PIUC).

17. PIUC, Seventh Annual Convention Proceedings (Harrisburg: PIUC, 1944), 358.

18. 28 April 1942; Vote for Victory! 22 April 1940; LNPL, box 1, file 17, USWA Archives, PSU. "State Primary, 1942," n.d.; LNPL, box 1, file 18, USWA Archives, PSU.

19. SWOC, *Reports of Officers*, in Melvyn Dubofsky and Warren Van Tine, ed., *Labor Leaders in America* (Urbana: Univ. of Illinois Press, 1987), 15–16.

20. Harold J. Ruttenberg and Stanley Ruttenberg, "Live Steel—Dead Jobs," *The New Republic*, 14 October 1940, 519, 522.

21. Harold J. Ruttenberg, "The Big Morgue," *Survey Graphic* (April 1939): 266–69. "J&L Start Operation of $25,000,000 Steel Strip Mill," *Pittsburgh Sun-Telegraph*, 13 December 1937.

22. Philip Murray, *Technological Unemployment: The Social and Economic Consequences of Technology* (Pittsburgh: SWOC, 1940), 42–43.

23. Ruttenberg and Ruttenberg, "Live Steel—Dead Jobs," 519, 522.

24. Nelson Lichtenstein, *Labor's War at Home: The CIO in World War Two* (New York: Oxford University Press, 1982), 24–25, 82–89, 89–98, 108–09. Ronald Schatz, "Philip Murray," in *Labor Leaders in America*, 248–49.

25. USWA IEB, 18–19 November 1942, 60, USWA Archives, PSU.

26. USWA IEB, 18–19 November 1942, 104–37, USWA Archives, PSU. Quotation on 131.

27. USWA IEB, 19–20 May 1943, 102–04, USWA Archives, PSU.

28. Freeman Patton, 11 July 1974, tape recording, POHP, PSA.

29. John Warady, interview by Larry Gorski, 20 April 1974, transcript, USWA Archives, PSU. Albert Reid, interview by Jim Barrett, 16 June 1976, transcript, HOHP, AIS. Anne M. Barton and Margaret Staudenmaier, "Ethnic and Racial Groups in Rankin, Pennsylvania: A Study of Relationships between Them as Expressed through Various Social Forces" (master's thesis, University of Pittsburgh, 1947), 65. F. Alden Wilson, "Occupational Status of the Negro in the Iron and Steel Industry in Pittsburgh and Environs," *Bureau of Business Research* (March-April 1934): 52, PUL Papers, AIS. Horace R. Cayton and George S. Mitchell, *Black Workers and the New Unions* (Durham: University of North Carolina Press, 1939), 159–68. "Honored by Union Men," *SL* (May 1939): 2. Oliver Montgomery in *Struggles in Steel: A Story of African-American Steelworkers*, dir. Tony Buba and Ray Henderson (San Francisco: California Newsreel, 1996).

30. John Chorey, interview by Alice M. Hoffman, October 1966, 7, USWA Archives, PSU.

31. 22 April 1937, 13 May 1937, 10 June 1937, minute book of Local 1397, John McManigal Collection, AIS.

32. Charles Bollinger, interview by Alice Hoffman, June 1966, transcript, USWA Archives, PSU. Robert Lewis Ruck, "Origins of the Seniority System in Steel" (seminar paper, University of Pittsburgh, 1977), footnote 4, 132.

33. Frank Miller Keck Jr., "The Development of Labor Representation at the Homestead Steel Works" (Ph.D. diss. University of Pittsburgh, 1952), 49.

34. Ruck, "Origins," 46. John Warady, interview by Larry Gorski, 20 April 1974, transcript, USWA Archives, PSU.

35. David J. McDonald, interview by Helmut J. Golatz and Alice Hoffman, 20 February 1970, 13, USWA Archives, PSU. Minutes of the Shop Stewards Meeting held at Local Headquarters, 9 September 1937; 14 June 1940, John McManigal Collection, AIS. "Dues Drive Underway at U.S. Steel Mills," *SL* (January 1939): 3. 19 October 1938; 11 December 1938, minute book of Local 1256, USWA Archives, PSU. Local 1256 Shop Stewards Meeting, 28 January 1940; 25 February 1940, USWA Archives, PSU.

36. 30 November 1938, Local 1256 Record Book, Local 1256, box 1, USWA Archives, PSU. 20 April 1937, box 27, "Third Step Minutes," USX Duquesne Works Papers, AIS.

37. Leroy McChestes, 8 August 1974, transcript, POHP, PSA. Martin Duffy and Frank Leach, interview by Jim Barrett, 3 June 1976, transcript, HOHP, AIS. Ashton Allen, interview by Ray Henderson and Tony Buba, summer 1992, tape recording. 26 August 1937, minute book of Local 1397, John McManigal Collection, AIS.

38. John Warady, interview by Larry Gorski, 20 April 1974, 5, USWA Archives, PSU.

39. Barton and Staudenmaier, "Ethnic and Racial Groups in Rankin," 65. John Chorey, interview by Alice M. Hoffman, October 1966, 8, USWA Archives, PSU. Boyd Wilson, interview by Jack Spiese, 23 October 1967, 7, USWA Archives, PSU.

40. 13 February 1940, minute book of Local 1397, John McManigal Collection, AIS. 23 September 1937, minute book of Local 1397, John McManigal Collection, AIS.

41. 8 August 1939, minute book of Local 1397, AIS. Keck, "Development of Labor Representation," 49.

42. A-47-40, 28 June 1940, box 26, USX Duquesne Works, AIS.

43. USWA Local 1256 Duquesne, PA box 1, file "Report of Fees, Dues, Membership," 1939–1940, USWA Archives, PSU.

44. McDonald, *Union Man*, 120–23.

45. Albert Reid, interview by Jim Barrett, 16 June 1976, HOHP, AIS. See also L.M. Gilgore to John L. Lewis, 1 June 1938, *John L. Lewis Papers*, reel 14, 662–64.

46. Alex Powell, interview by Henderson and Buba, summer 1992, tape recording. See also Martin Duffy and Frank Leach, interview by Jim Barrett, 3 June 1976, transcript, HOHP, AIS; Steve Vravel, interview by Jim Barrett, 28 May 1976, transcript, HOHP, AIS.

47. Minutes of the Shop Stewards Meeting held at Local Headquarters, 19 March 1940; 20 April 1940; 4 June 1940; 16 July 1940; 13 August 1940, John McManigal Collection, AIS.

48. Local 1256 Shop Stewards Meeting, 1 November 1941, USWA Archives, PSU.

49. "Steel Union Suspended," *NYT*, 13 June 1942, 22.

50. Thomas Augustine, "The Negro Steelworkers of Pittsburgh and the Unions" (master's thesis, University of Pittsburgh, 1948), 31.

51. USWA IEB, 22 June 1942, 156–57, USWA Archives, PSU.

52. USWA IEB, 18–19 November 1942, box 41, file 3, 7–8, USWA Archives, PSU.

53. John Hovanec, interview by Jim Barrett, 14 June 1976, transcript, HOHP, AIS.

54. Frank Takach, interview by Jim Barrett, 28 May 1976, transcript, HOHP, AIS. Phil McGuigan, interview by Rose Givens, 13 July 1983, transcript, MOHP, AIS.

55. Otis King, interview by author, 25 February 1992, tape recording. William Gaughan, interview by author, 7 June 1992, written notes.

56. Junius Brown, interview by Miracle Davis, 13 July 1983, transcript, MOHP, AIS.

57. Ernestine Holt, "Status of Steelworkers: Negroes Refused Supervisory Jobs," *Pittsburgh Courier*, 24 August 1946, 16 (hereafter cited as *PC*).

58. Milo Manly to G. James Fleming, 7 March 1943, 1–5, Fair Employment Practice Commission Papers, box 404, "Strike Data"; Robert C. Weaver, "Seniority and the Negro Worker," 21–26, FEPC Papers, box 406, file "Miscellaneous"; RG 228, National Archives (hereafter cited as FEPC Papers).

59. Augustine, "The Negro Steelworkers of Pittsburgh," 20–22. Cayton and Mitchell, *Black Workers*, 162–63. Frank and Gene DiCola, n.d., 16, USWA Archives, PSU. John Chorey, interview by Alice M. Hoffman, October 1966, 7, USWA Archives, PSU.

60. Junius Brown, interview by Miracle Davis, 13 July 1983, transcript, MOHP, AIS.

61. Cayton and Mitchell, *Black Workers*, 208. James McCoy Jr., interview by Mark B. Lapping, 7 November 1968, USWA Archives, PSU.

62. Romare Bearden, "The Negro in 'Little Steel,'" *Opportunity* (December 1937): 363–64.

63. Rocky Doratio, interview by James Showalter, 6 August 1983, transcript, MOHP, AIS.

64. Minutes of the Shop Stewards Meeting held at Local Headquarters, 31 April 1940, John McManigal Collection, AIS.

65. Boyd Wilson, interview by Jack Spiese, transcript, 23 October 1967, 7, USWA Archives, PSU.

66. Augustine, "Negro Steelworkers," 43.

67. Junius Brown, interview by Miracle Davis, 13 July 1983, transcript, MOHP, AIS.

68. "Fears Clairton Issues May Affect Job Chances: Hiring Policy at Mills Appears to Be Race Tainted," *PC*, 22 June 1940, 3.

69. Leroy McChestes, 8 August 1974, transcript, POHP, PSA. Augustine, "Negro Steelworkers," 32.

70. USWA IEB, 5 May 1944, 94–103, box 41, file 11, USWA Archives, PSU.

71. Ralph E. Kroger, "When J&L Workers Got off the Job, Management Decided to Get 'On the Ball,'" *PC*, 3 August 1946; "'Unfair' J&L Decision," *PC*, 20 September 1947, 1, 13. Harold Keith, "Who's Who in Labor," *PC*, 11 February 1947, 2. Keith, "Who's Who in Labor," *PC*, 29 March 1947, 34.

72. John P. Davis to Joy P. Davis, 16 May 1944, 1–6, box 404, file "Tension Data," FEPC Papers, National Archives.

73. Milo A. Manly to G. James Fleming, 3 May 1944, "Strike at J&L," FEPC Papers, box 404, file "Strike Data," FEPC Papers, National Archives. "FEPC Called," *PC*, 29 April 1944.

74. "Strike or Work Stoppage Report No. 15," 19 November 1945, box 28, file S-5 (a), USX Duquesne Works Papers, AIS.

75. 4 January 1943, report, box 30, file "USWA Locals," USX Duquesne Works Papers, AIS.

76. K.H.M. to W.C.O., 27 December 1944, regarding "strikes," in box 18, file S-5 (a), USX Duquesne Works Papers, AIS.

77. John P. Davis to Joy P. Davis, 16 May 1944, 1–6, box 404, file "Tension Data," FEPC Papers, National Archives.

78. A-135–42, A-134–42, 15 September 1942, box 12, USX Duquesne Works, AIS.

79. Holt, "Status of Steelworkers: Negroes Refused Supervisory Jobs," *PC*, 24 August 1946, 16.

80. Milo Manly to G. James Fleming, "Memorandum," 7 March 1944; see also "Strikes Occurring over Racial Issues," file "Strike Data," box 404, FEPC Papers, National Archives. "Flash Steel Strike Ends at Clairton," *PPG*, 28 February 1944. "Steel Losses Mount," *PP*, 23 September 1944. "Steel Mill Strike at Clairton Ends," *PP*, 25 September 1944.

81. G.R.L. to C.F.B., "Job Seniority," 15 November 1943, box 2, file S-3 (a), USX Duquesne Works Papers, AIS.

82. E.E.M., "Local Agreements—Restricted," 4 May 1945, 1, and throughout.

83. "Homestead," 12 March 1946; "Clairton," 22 April 1947; in "Local Seniority Agreements," 21 December 1949, 1–3, 9 December 1955; box 2, file S-3 (a), USX Duquesne Works Papers, AIS.

84. E.E.M., "Posting Job Openings," 29 December 1947, box 2, file S-3 (a), USX Duquesne Works Papers, AIS.

85. "Memorandum of Meeting," 9 May 1947, box 2, file S-3 (a); "Present and Proposed Promotional Sequences," February 1947, box 32, file S-3 (b), USX Duquesne Works Papers, AIS.

86. Mark McColloch, "Modest but Adquate: Standard of Living for Mon Valley Steelworkers in the Union Era," in *U.S. Labor in the Twentieth Century: Studies in Working-Class Struggles and Insurgency*, ed. John Hinshaw and Paul Le Blanc (Amherst, NY: Humanity Books, 2000), 247.

87. J.E.L to E.E.M., "Promotional Sequences," 21 February 1947; "Promotional Sequence Changed," 6 August 1947; "Job Seniority No. 6 Bar Mill," 23 February 1949; box 2, file 2–3 (b), USX Duquesne Works, AIS. R. Tilone, "Wage Rationalization Program in U.S. Steel: Agreement with USWA on Classification of Jobs to Eliminate Intra-Plant Wage-Rate Inequities," *Monthly Labor Review* 64 (June 1947): 967–82.

88. "She Came Up through the Mill," *U.S. Steel News* (October 1941): 25 (hereafter cited as *USSN*).

89. *The Radio Story of the Industrial Family That Serves the Nation: United States Steel* (U.S. Steel, n.d., approximately 1946–47), III, I, B2, file "Labor and Industry," American Service Papers, AIS. John Hoerr, *And the Wolf Finally Came: The Decline of the American Steel Industry* (Pittsburgh: University of Pittsburgh Press, 1988), 568. Junius Brown, interview by Miracle Davis, 13 July 1983, transcript, MOHP, AIS. Mark Ruetter, *Sparrow's Point: Making Steel—The Rise and Ruin of American Industrial Might* (New York: Summit Books, 1988), 360–78.

90. "Women in Duquesne Works," 25 June 1942, box 32, file W-3 (a), USX Duquesne Works Papers, AIS. "First Woman Pensioner," *USSN* (October 1946): 43.

91. Bureau of the Census, *Census of Population: 1940*, Volume III (Washington: GPO, 1943), Part 38, 125–28.

92. "Female Employees on Production Jobs," 3 December 1942, box 32, file W-3 (a), USX Duquesne Works Papers, AIS.

93. J.E.L. to CIS President's Staff, 26 December 1942, box 32, file W-3 (a), USX Duquesne Works Papers, AIS.

94. USWA IEB, 14–15 January 1943, 59–60, box 41, file 4, USWA Archives, PSU.

95. "Equal Pay for Equal Work for Women," 2 August 1943, Ruttenberg Papers, box 1, file 16, USWA Archives, PSU.

96. U.S. Department of Labor, Women's Bureau, *Women's Employment in the Making of Steel*, Bulletin 192–5, report prepared by Ethel Erickson (Washington: GPO, 1944), 4.

97. "Women in Production," *USSN* (January 1945): 4–5. "Christy Parks—Arsenal Extraordinary," *USSN* (October 1944): 1–3. James D. Rose, "The Problem Every Supervisor Dreads: Women Workers at the U.S. Steel Duquesne Works during World War Two," *Labor History* 36 (1995): 27–33.

98. "These Women War Workers Know Their Stuff," *HM*, 12 January 1945, 10. "Women in Production," *USSN* (January 1945): 4–5. "Women in U.S. Steel," *USSN* (April 1945): 5.

99. Bureau of the Census, *Census of Population: 1940*, Volume III (Washington: GPO, 1943), 111–28.

100. Women were hired at the Clairton Works in November 1942. Most of the women initially hired were white; see "Taking Over for Their Men Folks," *USSN* (January 1945): 12. Across the river from Homestead, ET hired black women only in May of 1945; see "Local Plants Hiring Negro Men and Women," *PC*, 19 May 1945, 3. Joe Trotter, *Black Milwaukee: The Making of a Black Proletariat, 1915–1945* (Urbana: University of Illinois Press, 1985), 168–73. Jacqueline Jones, *Labor of Love, Labor of Sorrow: Black Women Workers and the Family from Slavery to the Present* (New York: Vintage Books, 1985), 238–40.

101. "Union Wins Job Fight," *PC*, 26 May 1945, 1.

102. Dennis Dickerson, *Out of the Crucible: Black Steelworkers in Western Pennsylvania, 1875–1980* (Albany: State University of New York Press, 1986), 162–65.

103. Inventory of National Defense Program, Identification Card Listings, 1940s Series, USX National Tube Papers, AIS.

104. U.S. Department of Labor, Women's Bureau, *Negro Women War Workers*, Bulletin No. 205, (Washington: GPO, 1945), 5.

105. "Women in Production," *USSN* (January 1945): 2.

106. Erickson, *Women's Employment*, 25. Elizabeth Jones, conversation with author, 15 December 1993, notes. Elizabeth Jones, "For the Duration: Men, Women and Work in World War II" (Ph.D. diss., American University, 1996), 106.

107. "District Labor Pool Exhausted WMC Announces," *HM*, 27 November 1943, 1.

108. "Steel Works Officers Deny Worker Migration," *HM*, 27 May 1943, 1.

109. Ann Marie Draham, "People, Power and Profits: the Struggle of U.S. Steel Workers for Economic Democracy, 1882–1985" (n.d., mss. in author's possession), 153.

110. John Bodnar, Roger Simon, and Michael P. Weber, *Lives of Their Own: Blacks, Italians and Poles in Pittsburgh, 1900–1960* (Urbana: University of Illinois Press, 1982), 239. Jones, "For the Duration," 100.

111. PIUC, Sixth Annual Convention Proceedings, (Harrisburg: PIUC, 1943), 54–55.

112. 27 December 1943; 10 January 1944; 14 February 1944; minute book of Local 1397, John McManigal Collection, AIS.

113. Meeting no. 81, 17 November 1942; Meeting no. 93, 21 September 1943; Meeting no. 94, 19 October 1943; box 32, file W-3 (a), USX Duquesne Works Papers, AIS. USWA IEB, 19–20 May 1943, 4, box 41, file 5, USWA Archives, PSU. Jones, "For the Duration," 77–78.

114. War Production Board, "Equal Pay for Equal Work for Women," 3, 2 August 1943, Ruttenberg Papers, box 1, file 16, USWA Archives, PSU.

115. Jones, "For the Duration," 83–85.

116. 3rd step minutes, general discussion, 17 November 1942; 26 January 1943, box 27, USX Duquesne Works Papers, AIS.

117. 3rd step minutes, general discussion, 21 September 1943; 19 October 1943, box 27, USX Duquesne Works Papers, AIS.

118. Jones, "For the Duration," 96–107, quotation on 100.

119. 3rd step minutes, 45–19, 20 March 1945; 45–24, 17 April 1945; box 33, USX Duquesne Works Papers, AIS.

120. PIUC, Sixth Annual Convention Proceedings (Harrisburg: PIUC, 1943), 57–58.

121. "Irvin Production Is Cut by Strike," *HM*, 9 April 1945, 1.

122. "Suspend Four Girls, 140 Workers Quit," *HM*, 28 April 1945, 1. "Girls End Three Day Walkout," *HM*, 30 April 1945, 1.

123. USWA IEB, 24–26 May 1945, 10–11, 33–39, USWA Archives, PSU.

124. USWA, *The Braddock Steelworker* (Pittsburgh: USWA, 1945), 5–6.

125. Charles R. Walker, "Steel: A Retrospect," *Survey Graphic* (April 1946): 125.

126. "Community Officials Join Picket Lines," *SL* (February 1946): 6.

127. USWA IEB, 23 January 1946, 34, USWA Archives, PSU.

128. "$77,490,375 Is Paid WAA for Plants," *NYT*, 8 August 1946, 28. U.S. Steel paid about $65 million for the parts of the Homestead, Duquesne, and ET Works; the government spent about $110 million to build these facilities.

129. USWA IEB, 24–29 June 1946, 355, USWA Archives, PSU.

130. USWA IEB, 1–4 October 1946, 188–95, USWA Archives, PSU.

131. James Green, *The World of the Worker: Labor in Twentieth-Century America* (New York: Hill and Wang, 1980), 50.

132. "Pennsylvania CIO Bars Commies as Officers," *SL* (May 1947): 11. The Director of District 15 argued that communists were more loyal to the USSR than the United States. According to James Thomas, "two days after Russia was out of the war" communists at Homestead had led "a terrible work stoppage." Thomas did not elaborate, or offer any evidence beyond his word of this strike.

133. USWA IEB, 16–17 February 1948, 245–49, USWA Archives, PSU.

134. USWA IEB, 19–20 April 1951, 189–51, USWA Archives, PSU.

135. Francis McNary, 8 July 1974, POHP, PSA.

136. Milton Macintyre, interview by Henderson and Buba, summer 1992, tape recording.

137. A-138–42, 12 December 1942; Fourth Step Minutes, 19 December 1942; "For Your Information," 12 December 1942; "Sitdown Strike," 11 December 1942; "Plant Protection," 8 December 1942; in box 2, USX Duquesne Works Papers, AIS.

138. 27 March 1944, minute book of Local 1397, John McManigal Collection, AIS. See also "Examples," 6 July 1949, box 2, file S–3 (a), USX Duquesne Works Papers, AIS.

139. USWA IEB, 19–20 May 1943, 35, box 41, file 5, USWA Archives, PSU.

140. Grievance 45–64-D, box 21, USX Duquesne Works Papers, AIS.

141. Walter Alfred Schratz, "Development of and Experience with Industrial Grievance Procedure, with Reference to the Open-End and Closed-End Type" (Ph.D. diss., University of Pittsburgh, 1954), 160–72.

142. "Notes from Meeting," 2–3, 7 November 1945; "Moving of Test Ingots Stripper Cranes," 2–3, 45–70-D, box 21, USX Duquesne Works Papers, AIS.

143. Memo from K.H.M. to W.C.O., 9 October 1945; E.E.M. to W.C.O., 29 March 1946; box 9, file "Grievance Procedure and Correspondence, 1937–1959," USX Duquesne Works Papers, AIS.

144. "Suspended Steel Union Officers," *NYT*, 24 August 1945, 14. "Steel Union Suspended," *NYT*, 29 April 1947, 21.

145. "Let's Have No Unauthorized Strikes," *SL* (December, 1945): 5.

146. Memo from E.E.M. to W.C.O., 29 March 1946; John Stephans to Philip Murray, 28 March 1946, box 9, file "Grievance Procedure and Correspondence, 1937–1959," USX Duquesne Works Papers, AIS. Philip Murray to USWA members, 21 May 1947, box 18, file S-5(A), USX Duquesne Works Papers, AIS.

147. Memo from G.J.C. "Memorandum of Record: Slow-Down," 30 October 1950, box 18, file S-5 (A), USX Duquesne Works Papers, AIS.

148. 46–27-D, box 21, USX Duquesne Works Papers, AIS.

149. "Production of Steel Here at 53%," *HM*, 24 August 1945, 1. Tom Daniels, "Pencil Patter: Retroactive Pay," *HM*, 27 August 1945, 8.

150. 1944 figures from Dickerson, *Out of the Crucible*, 154–55; 1946 figures from memo, "United Steelworkers of America Membership in U.S. Steel," 25 October 1946, box 25, file 28, Research Department Papers, USWA Archives, PSU.

151. Milton Macintyre, interview by Henderson and Buba, summer 1992, tape recording.

152. Sabadasz, "Duquesne Works," 22. Charles Rumford Walker, *Steeltown: An Industrial Case History of the Conflict between Progress and Security* (New York: Harper, 1950).

153. Francis McNary, 8 July 1974, POHP, PSA.

154. Tom Daniels, "Pencil Patter: Victory Variations," *HM*, 20 August 1945, 1, 5.

155. "Vets Want Jobs at Mill on Return," *HM*, 11 August 1945, 1.

156. Jones, "For the Duration," 116–21. Leslie Posner, "Male-Female Worker Relations in a Traditionally Male Industrial Setting: The Case of the First Women Workers in a 'Company–Town' Steel Mill" (Ed.D. diss., University of Pittsburgh, 1979), 69.

157. "Health and Welfare, 1947 Survey," box 65, file 7, Research Department, USWA Archives, PSU. Anonymous, conversation with author, 3 September 1993, notes. Paula Bland, interview, December 1991, transcript, Western Pennsylvania Historical Society.

158. E.E.M., "Super Seniority," 15 November 1943, box 2, file S-3 (a), USX Duquesne Works Papers, AIS.

159. "Production of Steel Here at 53%," *HM*, 24 August 1945, 1.

160. 46–16, 3rd step minutes, 19 April 1946, box 24, USX Duquesne Works Papers, AIS. "Farewell Letter of a Woman War Worker," *USSN* (July 1946): 31–32.

161. 3rd step minutes, 46–12, 16 April 1946, box 24, USX Duquesne Works Papers, AIS. Rose, "Every Supervisor Dreads," 48–49.

162. J.L.P. to Members of the President's Staff, 28 June 1946, box 32, file W-3 (A), USX Duquesne Works Papers, AIS.

163. 25 November 1947, "The CIO Looks at Labor Laws," box 48, file 21, USWA District 19 Papers, USWA Archives, PSU.

164. "Memorandum of Meeting," 12 March 1946, box 32, file W-3 (A), USX Duquesne Works Papers, AIS. See also 3rd step minutes, 46–12, 16 April 1946, box 24, USX Duquesne Works Papers, AIS.

165. John Scott, *Behind the Urals: An American Worker in Russia's City of Steel* (1942; reprint, Bloomington Indiana: Indiana University Press, 1973), 143–45.

166. "Production of Steel Here at 53%," *HM*, 24 August 1945, 1. Daniels, "Pencil Patter: Retroactive Pay," *HM*, 27 August 1945, 8.

167. "Married Women Survey," 11 July 1949, box 32, file W–3 (A), USX Duquesne Works Papers, AIS. Jones, "For the Duration," 114–21. Posner, "Male-Female Worker Relations," 128–29.

168. A.L.N. to D.P.A., "Married Women," 21 July 1949, box 3, file S-3 (f), USX Duquesne Works Papers, AIS.

169. "Family Affair," *USSN* (January 1947): 2–5. "Can Famine Averted by Tinning Process," *USSN* (April 1946): 10.

170. 3rd step minutes, 3, 21 August 1945, USX Duquesne Works Papers, AIS.

171. *PC*, 18 August 1945, 4.

172. Ronald Schatz, *The Electrical Workers: A History of Labor at General Electric and Westinghouse, 1923–1960* (Urbana: University of Illinois Press, 1983), 30–33, 119–27.

173. Ruth Milkman, *Gender at Work: The Dynamics of Job Segregation by Sex during WWII* (Urbana: University of Illinois Press, 1987), 13, 65–152. Nancy Gabin, *Feminism in the Labor Movement*, 210–27.

174. Gabin, *Feminism in the Labor Movement*, 1, 111–13, 126.

175. "USA Picket Lines Strong Everywhere," *SL* (March 1946): 4.

176. Draham, "People, Power, Profits," 157. Interestingly, this march was organized by a communist member of local 1397, Elmer Kish. During the Cold War, pickets were restricted to members only. See also Gordon King, "The Sun Shines in Pittsburgh," *Nation*, 2 February 1946, 122. The *Nation* observed that women ran an honorary two-hour picket at the Homestead Works.

177. "Budget Cut Kills FEPC Here," *PC*, 4 August 1945, 1.

178. Kroger, "Fear Job Famine Here," *PC*, 25 August 1945, 1. Theodore W. Graham, "War Ends! We Face Job Crisis," *PC*, 18 August 1945, 1, 4. Holt, "Vets Prefer Compensation to Low Wage Jobs," *PC*, 17 August 1946, 18.

179. "Fear New Wave of Job Bias Here: Powerless USES and Lack of FEPC 'Protects' Firms," *PC*, 15 September 1945, 1; "Machinist Turned Down at 7 Plants," *PC*, 14 April 1945, 3. Holt, "Status of Steelworkers: Negroes Refused Supervisory Jobs," *PC*, 24 August 1946, 16.

180. *Summary: Race Relations Survey of Allegheny County,* 23–24, box 9, file 2, "Labor and Industry, 1954–1956," NAACP Papers, AIS.

181. Holt, "Status of Steelworkers," *PC,* 24 August 1946, 16.

182. Keith, "Who's Who in Labor," *PC,* 5 April 1947, 16.

183. Kroger, "J&L Workers," *PC,* 3 August 1946, 1, 5.

184. J. William Lloyd, "Long-Term Mortality Study of Steelworkers: V, Respitory Cancer in Coke Plant Workers," *Journal of Occupational Medicine* 13 (February 1971): 53–68. Carol K. Redmond, Antonio Ciocco, J. William Lloyd, and Hugh W. Rush, "Long Term Mortality Study of Steelworkers: VI, Mortality from Malignant Neoplasms among Coke Oven Worker," *Journal of Occupational Medicine* 14 (August 1972): 621–29.

185. R.L. Prattis, "Labor Everywhere," *PC,* 10 August 1946, 14.

186. Holt, "Status of Steelworkers," *PC,* 24 August 1946, 16.

187. Kroger, "J&L Workers," *PC,* 3 August 1946, 1, 5. Prattis, "Labor Everywhere," *PC,* 10 August 1946, 14. Prattis, "Labor Everywhere," *PC,* 24 August 1946, 16.

188. "Union Men Appeal Case," *PC,* 19 July 1947. "See 'Unfair' J&L Decision," 20 September 1947, 1, 13.

189. Keith, "Who's Who in Labor," *PC,* 14 May 1947, 20.

190. Prattis, "Labor Everywhere," *PC,* 10 August 1946, 14.

191. Minutes of the 12 September 1956, USWA Committee on Civil Rights, 3, 12 September 1956; 29 July 1958; box 6, file 5, Hague Papers, USWA Archives, PSU. Francis Shane to Committee on Civil Rights, 2, 2 October 1961, box 6, file 9, Hague Papers, USWA Archives, PSU. "Committee on Civil Rights Participation in USWA District Conferences, 1966," 3, n.d., box 11, file 32, CRD, USWA Archives, PSU.

192. "Steel Men Prefer Carnegie Plant—Writer Finds," *PC,* 31 August 1946, 16. Madison directed a racially mixed crew, see "Steel Making Champs," *PC,* 1 March 1947, 7.

193. Black unionists had filled prominent positions in Local 1256, USX Duquesne Works, since the 1940s, see "Nobody Plays 'Hooky' at District 15 Classes," *SL* (April 1949): 7. Delegates to District Conference, 18 October 1957, box 1, file "District Meetings," District 15 Papers, USWA Archives, PSU.

194. Keith, "Who's Who in Labor," *PC,* 19 April 1947, 2.

195. Keith, "Who's Who in Labor," *PC,* 22 February 1947, 6.

196. Keith, "Who's Who in Labor," *PC,* 5 April 1947, 16.

197. Keith, "Who's Who in Labor," *PC,* 29 March 1947, 34. Keith, "Who's Who in Labor," *PC,* 8 February 1947, 11. Ralph Kroger, "CIO Adviser Says 'Negroes Must Not Seek Special Treatment When Layoffs Come,'" *PC,* 11 August 1945, 3. Keith, "Who's Who in Labor," *PC,* 15 February 1947, 12.

198. Augustine, "Negro Steelworkers," 34–45. Fisk Race Relations Survey, 25 and 27, box 9, file 2, "Labor and Industry, 1954–1956," NAACP Papers, AIS. See also, 8 November 1943, minute book of Local 1397, John McManigal Collection, AIS.

199. Augustine, "Negro Steelworkers," vi, 55.

200. Steve Nelson, James R. Barrett, Rob Ruck, *Steve Nelson: American Radical* (Pittsburgh: University of Pittsburgh Press, 1981), 299, 315. The FBI doubled that estimate. "Cvetic Names Communists Here," *PPG,* 22 February 1950, 1; "District has 550 Reds, Cvetic Says," *PPG,* 23 February 1950, 1. George Edwards, interview by author, 3 March 1992, tape recording. Harvey O'Connor, "Personal Histories of the Early CIO," ed.

Staughton Lynd, *Radical America* 5 (May-June 1971), 54–55. Ronald L. Filippelli, "The History Is Missing, Almost," in *Forging a Union of Steel: Philip Murray, SWOC, and the United Steelworkers*, ed. Paul F. Clark, Peter Gottlieb, and Donald Kennedy (Ithaca: Cornell University Press, 1987), 9. Nathan Glazer, *The Social Basis of American Communism* (Westport, CT: Greenwood Press, 1961), 115, 123.

201. Although precise numbers are not available, the *PP* red-baited very few local union officials during a period when the paper was energetically exposing every communist it could find, see "Local Communist Claims Red Aid to Steel Workers," *PP*, 14 July 1947. Also see remarks of Harvey O'Connor, "Personal Histories," 52–54. Ben Fisher, interview by author, 10 September 1992, notes.

202. USWA IEB, 1–2 April 1946, 108, 140–41, box 42, file 10, USWA Archives, PSU.

203. Jim Allander, "Some Experiences in Recruiting to the Party," *PO* (December 1934): 6–8. Paul Lyons, *Philadelphia Communists, 1936–1956* (Philadelphia: Temple University Press, 1982), 51–61, 164, 201, footnote 11. Dorothy Ray Healey and Maurice Isserman, *California Red: A Life in the American Communist Party* (Urbana: University of Illinois Press, 1993), 131.

204. Ruth Kish, interview by author, 2 March 1992, tape recording. "CIO Men Off to Aid Labor Bills," *HM*, 27 September 1945, 1.

205. Hazel Garland, "Seek Law on Job Bias in Duquesne," *PC*, 16 June 1945, 1. George Powers, *Cradle of Steel Unionism: Monongahela Valley, PA* (East Chicago, Indiana: Figueroa Printers, 1972), 39. William Jacobs, "'Steelworkers for Wallace' Group Out to Beat Leader Phil Murray," *PP*, 26 July 1948, 9.

206. Keith, "Who's Who in Labor," *PC*, 22 March 1947, 13. There were 250 whites and 87 blacks in his department.

207. USWA IEB, 1–2 April 1946, 123–32, box 42, file 10, USWA Archives, PSU.

208. USWA IEB, 1–2 April 1946, 152–64, box 42, file 10, USWA Archives, PSU.

209. USWA IEB, 1–2 April 1946, 123–32, box 42, file 10, USWA Archives, PSU.

210. USWA IEB, 1–2 April 1946, 121–22, box 42, file 10, USWA Archives, PSU.

211. USWA IEB, 1–2 April 1946, 152–64, box 42, file 10, USWA Archives, PSU.

212. USWA IEB, 1–2 April 1946, 132, 144, box 42, file 10, USWA Archives, PSU.

213. Barton and Staudenmeir, "Ethnic and Racial Groups in Rankin," 66.

214. "CIO Warns Communists: Don't Meddle in Unions," *SL* (December 1946): 2.

215. 7 July 1946, Minutes of USWA Local 1000 (Firth Sterling), District 15, box 8, USWA Archives, PSU.

216. Keith, "Who's Who in Labor," *PC*, 11 August 1956, Section 2, 3. John Hughey, interview by author, 5 August 1993, tape recording. "Hypocrisy in Organized Labor," *PC*, 31 May 1958, Section 2, 8. Robert J. Norrell, "Caste in Steel: Jim Crow Careers in Birmingham, Alabama," *Journal of American History* 73 (December 1986): 681–85.

217. Lloyd Ulman, *The Government of the Steel Workers' Union* (New York: John Wiley and Sons, 1962), 130.

218. "Steelworkers Here Defend Two Officers," *PC*, 28 June 1947, 1, 4.

219. N.d., but probably November-December 1948, "Hold for Confirmation," Charles Owen Rice Papers, AIS.

220. USWA IEB, 3 May 1949, 36–49, box 43, file 15, USWA Archives, PSU.

221. USWA IEB, 1–2 April 1946, 152–64, box 42, file 10, USWA Archives, PSU.

222. USWA IEB, 16–17 February 1948, 147–49, box 43, file 9, USWA Archives, PSU.

223. Minute book of Local 1256, 1 September 1948, USWA Archives, PSU. USWA IEB, 16–17 February 1948, 127–53, box 43, file 9, USWA Archives, PSU. McDonald, *Union Man*, 194–95.

224. Kim Moody, *An Injury to All: The Decline of American Unionism* (New York: Verso, 1988), 48.

225. Memo from David J. McDonald to USWA District Directors, 8 October 1948; "Introducing the Progressive Party," 29 July 1948; box 4, file "Progressive Party, 1948," USWA District 15, McKeesport, PA, USWA Archives, PSU. McDonald, *Union Man*, 195–97. 16 August 1944, box 6, file 16, Hague Papers, USWA Archives, PSU. William Jacobs, "'Steelworkers for Wallace' Group Out to Beat Leader Phil Murray," *PP*, 26 July 1948, 9. USWA IEB, 1 September 1948, 5–19, box 44, file 7, USWA Archives, PSU. USWA IEB, 3 May 1949, 14–26, box 43, file 15, USWA Archives, PSU.

226. Curtis D. MacDougall, *Gideon's Army* (New York: Marzani and Munsell, 1965), vol. 3, 616–17, 830–38.

227. James Matles, interview by Ron Filippelli, 6 May 1968, transcript, 70–71, USWA Archives, PSU.

228. C. Edmund Fisher, "'Forceful Methods Employed by Comreds in Holding Control," n.d., *PPG*, box 1, file 3, CRD, USWA Archives, PSU.

229. Ruth Kish, interview by author, 2 March 1992, tape recording.

230. Local 1256 Record Book, 17 July 1948, USWA Archives, PSU.

231. Local 1256 Record Book, 21 September 1948, USWA Archives, PSU. See also, "Weekly Labor Report," 3 February 1949; "CIO Election Set Tuesday," *McKeesport Daily News*, 31 January 1949; "Union Members Faces Hearing," *McKeesport Daily News*; box 30, file "USWA Locals," USX Duquesne Works, AIS.

232. Local 1256 Record Book, 21 September 1948; 19 January 1949; 1 February 1949; 2 February 1949, USWA Archives, PSU. USWA IEB, 23 March 1950, box 4, file 2, USWA Archives, PSU.

233. Schatz, *The Electrical Workers*, 188–244. Ronald L. Filippelli and Mark McColloch, *Cold War in the Working Class: The Rise and Decline of the United Electrical Workers* (Albany: State University of New York Press, 1995), 141–66.

234. A.L.N. to various Superintendents, 8 September 1948, box 10, file P-3 (H), USX Duquesne Works Papers, AIS.

235. A.H.W. to Pittsburgh District Industrial Relations Superintendents, 20 March 1946, box 10, file P-3 (H), USX Duquesne Works Papers, AIS.

236. A.L.N. to K.H.M., 12 May 1948, box 10, file P-3 (H), USX Duquesne Works Papers, AIS.

237. For a list of "suspects," see R.W.G. to W.C.O., re: "Suspects," 21 December 1950, box 10, file P-3 (H), USX Duquesne Works Papers, AIS. George Edwards, interview by author, 3 March 1992, tape recording.

238. Ruth Kish, interview by author, 2 March 1992, tape recording.

239. USWA IEB, 19–20 April 1951, 8–9, USWA Archives, PSU.

CHAPTER 3. COLD WAR PITTSBURGH: 1949–1959

1. I.W. Abel, *Collective Bargaining: Labor Relations in Steel, Then and Now* (Pittsburgh: Carnegie Mellon University Press, 1976), 39–40. "I have not cited two other obvious facts about organized labor as a responsible force for progress within our society—two facts that are either unnoticed or unappreciated. I refer to labor's acceptance and support of the free enterprise system as the system under which our economy should, and does, function. I also refer to labor's ability to function within our two-party political system."

2. "U.S. Steel First Quarter Net Rose 70%," *NYT*, 29 April 1959, 2. U.S. Steel, *Annual Report*, 1957, 31. U.S. Steel, *Annual Report*, 1969, 29.

3. Industrial Union Department AFL-CIO, *Insurmountable Obstacles: An International Comparison of the Path to Union Recognition* (Washington: AFL-CIO, 1995), 5–27. David Knoke, Franz Urban Pappi, Jeffrey Broadbent, Yutaka Tsujinaka, *Comparing Policy Networks: Labor Politics in the U.S., Germany, and Japan* (Cambridge: Cambridge University Press, 1996), 32–56. David Stebenne, *Arthur Goldberg: New Deal Liberal* (New York: Oxford University Press, 1991), 152–53. Philippe C. Schmitter and Gerhard Lehmbruch, eds., *Patterns of Corporatist Policy-Making* (Beverly Hills: Sage, 1982). Roger M. Blough, *The Washington Embrace of Business* (Pittsburgh: Carnegie Mellon University Press, 1975), 22–31.

4. Ann Markusen and Joel Yudken, *Dismantling the Cold War Economy* (New York: Basic Books, 1992), 52–53. Bruce Shelman, *From Cotton Belt to Gunbelt: Federal Policy, Economic Development and the Transformation of the South, 1938–1980* (New York: Oxford University Press, 1991). Ann Markusen, Peter Hall, Scott Campbell, and Sabina Deitrick, *The Rise of the Gunbelt: The Military Remapping of Industrial America* (New York: Oxford University Press, 1991). Roger Lotchin, *Fortress California 1910–1961: From Warfare to Welfare* (New York: Oxford University Press, 1992). Roger Lotchin, ed., *The Martial Metropolis: U.S. Cities in Peace and War* (New York: Praeger, 1984). Military Procurement Hearings Before a Subcommittee of the Committee on Armed Services of the United States Senate, 86th Congress, 1st session, July 1959, 322–23. Thomas Sugrue, *The Origins of the Urban Underclass: Race and Inequality in Postwar Detroit* (Princeton: Princeton University Press, 1996), 140.

5. "Pruning Steel Production Down to Size," *BW*, 20 March 1954, 182. "Budget Halves 1955 Deficit," *NYT*, 18 January 1955, 1. Markusen and Yudken, *Dismantling*, 64.

6. Gilbert Burck, "The Transformation of U.S. Steel," *Fortune* (January 1956): 93. "Pruning Steel," *BW*, 20 March 1954, 182. Warren, *American Steel Industry*, 287.

7. H.C. Lackey, "Homestead Forgings, The Past, Present and Future," 5–16, 17 November 1952, box 1, "History Homestead," William Gaughan Papers, AIS. Historic American Engineering Record, National Park Service and Mon Valley Steel Industry Heritage Task Force, "Homestead Steel Works and Carrie Furnaces (Draft)" (Homestead: unpublished mss., 1990), v., 74.

8. Paul Tiffany, *The Decline of American Steel: How Management, Labor and Government Went Wrong* (New York, 1988), 129–37.

9. House Committee on Expenditures in the Executive Departments, *Certificates of Necessity and Government Plant Expansion Loans*, 82nd Congress, 1st session, H. Report 504, 16021. Joint Committee on Defense Production, *Review of Tax-Amortization Program*,

83rd Congress, 1st session, S. Report 154, 10–13. "Five Year 'Gravy,'" *Fortune* (October 1951): 85, 114. Robert Schlaifer, J. Keith Butts, and Pearson Hart, "Accelerated Amortization," *Harvard Business Review* 29 (May 1951): 113–24. William H. Hogan, *Economic History of the Iron and Steel Industry of the United States*, vol. 4 (Lexington, MA: D.C. Heath and Company, 1971), 1748–49. Tiffany, *The Decline of American Steel*, 129–37, 179.

10. Tiffany, *The Decline of American Steel*, 35, 47, 129–37.

11. U.S. Steel, *Annual Report*, 1957, 31. U.S. Steel, *Annual Report*, 1969, 29.

12. James P. Mitchell, "Background Statistics Bearing on the Steel Dispute," *Monthly Labor Report* 82 (Washington: GPO, 1959), 1107.

13. Anthony Frank Libertella, "The Steel Strike of 1959: Labor, Management, and Government Relations" (Ph.D. diss., Ohio State University, 1972), 5–6, 13.

14. Stebenne, *Arthur Goldberg*, 84.

15. Ronald Schatz, "Battling over Government's Role," in *Forging a Union of Steel: Philip Murray, SWOC and the United Steelworkers*, ed. Paul F. Clark, Peter Gottlieb, and Donald Kennedy (Ithaca, NY: ILR Press, 1987), 96. Tiffany, *The Decline of American Steel*, 84–85, 97–99. Stebenne, *Arthur Goldberg*, 74–75.

16. "Answers to Questions Most Frequently Asked about Social Insurance and Pensions," *SL* (December 1949): 4.

17. The union also sought additional fringe benefits and the union shop which required that all new company employees, after a brief probation period, join the union and pay dues to it.

18. Mary K. Hammond, "The Steel Strike of 1952," *Current History* 23 (November 1952): 285–90. Tiffany, *The Decline of American Steel*, 84–85, 97–102.

19. Ronald Schatz, "Battling over Government's Role," 98–99.

20. John Strohmeyer, *Crisis in Bethlehem: Big Steel's Struggle to Survive* (Bethesda, MD: Adler and Adler, 1986), 64. "President Warns He Is Ready to Act in Steel Strike," *NYT*, 19 July 1956, 1. Stebenne, *Arthur Goldberg*, 139–40.

21. USWA IEB, 16–17 September 1953, 78, box 45, file 6; USWA IEB, 26 January 1954, 15–23, box 45, file 8; USWA Archives, PSU.

22. USWA IEB, 5–6 April 1954, 34–38, quotations on 34, 37–88, box 45, file 9, USWA Archives, PSU.

23. USWA IEB, 9–10 September 1957, 41, box 46, file 3, USWA Archives, PSU.

24. USWA IEB, 6–7 January 1959, box 46, file 9, USWA Archives, PSU.

25. Strohmeyer, *Crisis in Bethlehem*, 66. Blough, *Washington Embrace*, 35–38.

26. USWA IEB, 5 January 1960, 4–30, 7, box 46, file 18, USWA Archives, PSU. Libertella, "Steel Strike of 1959," 232–56.

27. U.S. Department of Commerce, *International Iron and Steel* (Washington: GPO, 1956), 18–19. Stebenne, *Arthur Goldberg*, 150. Tiffany, *The Decline of American Steel*, 103–27. Judith Stein, *Running Steel, Running America: Race, Economic Policy and the Decline of Liberalism* (Chapel Hill: University of North Carolina Press, 1998), 197–203, 207.

28. Benjamin Fairless, "Facing Up to the Competition," *67th General Meeting of the American Iron and Steel Institute*, The Yearbook of the AISI (New York: AISI, 1959), 145.

29. Tiffany, *The Decline of American Steel*, 167–84.

30. "Union Comment on U.S. Steel's Release of Its 1959 Annual Report," box 11, file "Wages, Benefits, Profits, 1960," Miller Papers, USWA Archives PSU.

31. Strohmeyer, *Crisis in Bethlehem*, 85.

32. Reutter, *Sparrow's Point*, 419.

33. Leonard Engel, "Technology Prods Big Steel," *Nation*, 22 January 1949, 94–96. Hogan, *Economic History*, 1543–45, 1564–66.

34. "Continuous Casting: Revolution in Steel Making?" *BW*, 28 August 1948, 21–22.

35. Albert R. Karr, "New Techniques Speed Steel's Open Hearths, Slashing Mills' Costs," *WSJ*, 14 August 1962, 1, 18.

36. Strohmeyer, *Crisis in Bethlehem*, 62.

37. Gilbert Burck, "The Transformation of U.S. Steel," *Fortune* (January 1956): 203. Between 1950–54, steel companies added 28.2 million tons of capacity at a cost of $4.5 billion, and over the next six years they built another 24.3 million tons at a cost of $7.3 billion. Tiffany, *The Decline of American Steel*, 129–37, 179.

38. "Open Hearths Razed," *Blast Furnace and Steel Plant* (January 1954): 105. "Oxygen Speeds Production of Stainless Steels in the Electric Furnace," *Blast Furnace and Steel Plant* (January 1949): 62.

39. Gilbert Burck, "The Transformation of U.S. Steel," *Fortune* (January 1956): 203. "The Goal of the All-Basic Open Hearth Furnace Achieved," *Blast Furnace and Steel Plant* (June 1959): 617–18.

40. In 1940, roughly a third of the male workforce in steel was classified as unskilled. By the end of the 1950s, laborers made up about 22 percent of the total. While the number of skilled workers did not rise, their proportion of the workforce rose from around 25 percent in 1940 to 32.5 percent in 1960. The ratio of semi-skilled, white-collar, and supervisors were unchanged. Bureau of the Census, *Census of the Population: 1940* (Washington: GPO, 1943), Part 38, 125–28; Bureau of the Census, *Census of the Population: 1950* (Washington: GPO, 1952), Part 38, 370-76. Bureau of the Census, *Census of the Population: 1960* (Washington: GPO, 1961), Part 40, 1141–75.

41. For a general discussion of incentives, see Michael Buraway's *Manufacturing Consent: Changes in the Labor Process under Monopoly Capitalism* (Chicago: University of Chicago Press, 1977); Bruce B. Williams, *Black Workers in an Industrial Suburb: The Struggle against Discrimination* (New Brunswick: Rutgers University Press, 1987).

42. USWA IEB, 27–28 June 1951, USWA Archives, PSU.

43. "Behind the Steel Strike," *Fortune* (July 1952): 55–56.

44. A.L.N. to F.A.B., 21 March 1957, box 2, file "Seniority and Continuous Service," Duquesne Works Papers, AIS.

45. John Hughey, interview by author, 5 August 1993, tape recording.

46. "So, You're on Incentive," *The Sentinel* (April 1957): 5. "The Ol' Shell Game," *The Sentinel* (October 1958): 6.

47. Hoerr, *Wolf*, 301–02.

48. Philip Bonosky, *The Magic Fern* (New York: International Publishers, 1961), 24–26.

49. R.W.G. to W.C.O., "Labor Reduction Program," 4 May 1950, box 3, file S-3 (g), USX Duquesne Works Papers, AIS. "Weekly Labor Report," 19 August 1949, and "Crew Reductions Made in Secondary Finishing Yards," 19 September 1949, both in box 3, file S-3 (f), USX Duquesne Works Papers, AIS. Thomas E. Hughes, "Communications in the Steel

Industry," *Iron and Steel Engineer* (April 1955): 109–14. Griffin L. Isaacs, "Automatic Control for Regenerative Soaking Pits," *Iron and Steel Engineer* (February 1953): 75–78. John McManigal, "Your Union: Automation—No Bugaboo," *The Sentinel* (December 1957): 6. "U.S. Steel Installs Electronically-operated Contour Roll Lathe at Homestead," *Iron and Steel Engineer* (March 1953): 173–74.

50. "Memorandum of Meeting with Local No. 1256 Grievance Committee on Assigning Additional Duties to Existing Jobs," 24 May 1950, box 3, file S-3 (g), USX Duquesne Works Papers, AIS.

51. A.L.N. to G.J.C., "Weekly Labor Report," 25 May 1950, box 3, file S-3 (g), USX Duquesne Works Papers, AIS.

52. "Force Reductions," 14 June 1950, box 3, file S-3 (g), USX Duquesne Works Papers, AIS.

53. "Steel Plant Shut by 7 Hour Strike," *NYT*, 21 April 1950, 17.

54. USWA IEB, 16–17 September 1953, 130–32, box 45, file 6, USWA Archives, PSU. Nelson Lichtenstein, "Reutherism on the Shop Floor: Union Strategy and Shop Floor Conflict in the USA 1946–1970," in *Between Fordism and Flexibility: The Automobile Industry and Its Workers*, ed. Steven Tolliday and Jonathan Zeitlin (New York: Berg, 1992), 130–39. See also Rick Halpern, *Down on the Killing Floor: Black and White Workers in Chicago's Packinghouses, 1904–54* (Urbana: University of Illinois: 1997). Roger Horowitz, *"Negro and White: Unite and Fight!" A Social History of Industrial Unionism in Meatpacking, 1930–90* (Urbana: University of Illinois Press, 1997).

55. A.L.N. to G.J.C., "Weekly Labor Report," 10 August 1950, box 18, file S-5 (A), USX Duquesne Works Papers, AIS.

56. A.L.N. to G.H.D., 29 February 1956, box 18, file S-5 (A), USX Duquesne Works Papers, AIS.

57. "Potential Sources of Labor Relations Trouble," 21 February 1952, box 7, file W-1 (b), USX Duquesne Works Papers, AIS.

58. A.L.N. to G.H.D., 29 February 1956; report no. 56; report no. 63, all in box 18, file S-5 (A), USX Duquesne Works Papers, AIS.

59. "Force Reduction History and Status from 1951," 20 May 1952, box 3, file S-3 (g), USX Duquesne Works Papers, AIS. "Strike or Work Stoppage" report no. 56, box 18, file S-5 (A), USX Duquesne Works Papers, AIS.

60. "New or Changed Incentive Plans and Force Reduction Proposals Which Involve Labor Relations Problems," 16 April 1952; 16 May 1952, box 3, file S-3 (g), USX Duquesne Works Papers, AIS.

61. S.M.J. to R.C.C., "Potential Labor Problems Duquesne Works," 2 June 1952, box 3, file S-3 (g), USX Duquesne Works Papers, AIS.

62. "Information for Review," 12 February 1953, box 3, file S-3 (g), USX Duquesne Works Papers, AIS.

63. "Force Reductions," 14 June 1951; "General Laborer—Force Reduction—Blast Furnace Department," n.d., but first entry is dated 19 June 1951; both in box 3, file S-3 (g), USX Duquesne Works Papers, AIS.

64. "Pruning Steel Production Down to Size," *BW*, 20 March 1954, 182.

65. USWA IEB, 19–20 August 1954, 102, box 45, file 13, USWA Archives, PSU.

66. "Operations Cut: Repairs Needed, Shutdown, July 18," *The Sentinel* (July 1954): 1.

67. "It's Your Union," *The Sentinel* (June 1954): 2. "Recession?!?! Operations Here Curtailed," *L.U. 1397 Union News*, later named *The Sentinel* (April 1954): 1.

68. See table 3 at the end of this chapter.

69. Elmer Trapp to Howard Hague, 19 November 1957, box 15, file 10, Hague Papers, USWA Archives, PSU.

70. McManigal, "Your Union: Automation—No Bugaboo," *The Sentinel* (December 1957): 6.

71. Otis Brubaker to David McDonald, "Long-Term Employment Trend in the Basic Steel Industry," 25 March 1953, box 4, file "USWA District 15, McKeesport, PA," Research Department, USWA Archives, PSU. "Impact of Technological Change and Automation on the Basic Steel Industry," 7, n.d., box 2, file "Automation, 1961–1963," Miller Papers, USWA Archives, PSU.

72. USWA IEB, 4 June 1959, 8, box 46, file 12, USWA Archives, PSU.

73. "Least Guilty Could Be Penalized Most in Wildcat Strike," *The Sentinel* (December 1959): 3. A.L.N., "Proposed Agenda Items," 20 March 1957, box 30, file "USWA Locals," USX Duquesne Works Papers, AIS.

74. J.W.S. to all General Superintendents, 1 June 1956; J.W.S. to E.H.G., 21 September 1956; both in box 18, file S-5 (A), USX Duquesne Works Papers, AIS.

75. A.L.N. to G.H.D., "Work Stoppage Data," 29 February 1956, box 18, file S-5 (A), USX Duquesne Works Papers, AIS. "Memorandum on Threatened Work Stoppage," 28 October 1951, 29 October 1951, box 18, file S-5 (A), USX Duquesne Works Papers, AIS.

76. There were at least eleven wildcats at Duquesne between 1947 and 1956. A.L.N. to G.H.D, "Work Stoppage Data," 29 February 1956, box 18, file S-5 (A), USX Duquesne Works Papers, AIS. "Steel—The Money or the Glory," *Fortune* (January 1954): 66.

77. Robert Asher, "The 1949 Ford Speedup Strike and the Postwar Social Compact, 1946–1961," in *Autowork*, ed. Robert Ahser and Ronald Edsforth (Albany: State University of New York Press, 1995), 127–54. Steve Jefferys, "'Matters of Mutual Interest': The Unionization Process at Dodge Main, 1933–9," in *On the Line: Essays in the History of Autoworkers*, ed. Nelson Lichtenstein and Stephen Meyer (Urbana: University of Illinois Press, 1989), 122–23.

78. "Supplementary Is Amended," *The Sentinel* (July 1955): 1, 3. Minutes of Special 3rd Step Meeting, 19 November 1954; "Agreement on Plant-wide Labor Pool," 8 September 1955; "Problems Encountered in Developing and Negotiating Local Seniority Agreements," 23 December 1955, 1–2; both in box 2, file 2, USX Duquesne Works Papers, AIS.

79. "Supplemental Seniority Agreement between U.S. Steel Corporation, Homestead District Works, and USWA Local 1397," 1 November 1962, 30, box 16, USX Duquesne Works, AIS.

80. Anthony Sancosky to I.W. Abel, 20 September 1957, box 1, file "District Meetings," District 15 Papers, USWA Archives, PSU. For discussion of implementing the labor pool at Duquesne, see "Pending," 3 November 1954–16 September 1960, box 16, file S-3 (d), USX Duquesne Works Papers, AIS.

81. "Union Wins Greatest Victory in 20 Years," *The Sentinel* (August 1956): 1. A.H. Raskin, "Pact Settles Steel Strike: Three Years of Peace Assured," *NYT*, 28 July 1956, 1. Hoerr, *Wolf*, 76–77.

82. "SUB Pay at 52.5% during December," and "Operations Up, Job Needs Low," *The Sentinel* (January 1959): 1. "Business Changes Tune on SUB as Unemployment Hits Donora," *The Sentinel* (January 1958): 2.

83. See table 2 and table 4 at the end of the chapter. Pennsylvania Bureau of Statistics and Information, *Industrial Directory of the Commonwealth of Pennsylvania*, (Harrisburg: Pennsylvania Bureau of Statistics and Information, 1947, 1954 and 1958).

84. O.P. "Re: USW Union," 11 March 1957, box 30, file "USWA Locals," USX Duquesne Works Papers, AIS.

85. "Strike Ends"; "U.S. Steel-Union Talks Bar Rarick," *HM*, 9–10 December 1958, 1.

86. Industrial Relations Department, "Number of hourly employees," 4 March 1958, box 9, file P-3 (a), USX Duquesne Works Papers, AIS. 3rd step minutes, 15 January 1958, box 16, file S-1 (d), USX Duquesne Works Papers, AIS.

87. "Operations Up, Job Needs Low," *The Sentinel* (January 1959): 1.

88. "Bars Do Not Always a Prison Make," (Caption) *The Sentinel* (September 1958): 11.

89. U.S. Steel First Quarter Net Rose 70%," *NYT*, 29 April 1959, 2. "U.S. Steel Pledges No Price Rise," *WSJ*, 29 July 1959, 3.

90. "OH 4 Furnaces Relit on February 1"; "Plantwide Recalls Expected"; *The Sentinel* (February 1959): 1.

91. "Union Comment on U.S. Steel's Release of Its 1959 Annual Report," box 11, file "Wages, Benefits, Profits, 1960," Miller Papers, USWA Archives, PSU.

92. USWA IEB, 13–14 April 1959, 66, box 46, file 10, USWA Archives, PSU.

93. "Memorandum of Maintenance Shops and Gangs Meeting," 8 June 1959, box 18, file S (5) B, USX Duquesne Works Papers, AIS. See also McManigal, "Your Union," *The Sentinel* (June 1958): 6. McManigal, "Your Union: You and Section 2-B," *The Sentinel* (December 1959): 6. "Crane Repairmen (Bull Gang) Assigned Linemen's Work," *The Sentinel* (June 1958): 2.

94. "Memorandum of Meeting with Maintenance Shops and Gangs," 22 June 1959, box 18, file S (5) B, USX Duquesne Works Papers, AIS.

95. "Memorandum of Meeting with Union on Pipefitter Strike Disciplinary Action," 28 May 1959, box 18, file S (5) B, USX Duquesne Works Papers, AIS.

96. "Memorandum of Telephone Call from V.S., Grievance Committeeman," 25 May 1959, box 18, file S (5) B, USX Duquesne Works Papers, AIS. Carl Denne, interview with author, 1992.

97. "Imports Worry Steel Men," *BW*, 30 January 1954, 144. "Steel: Never a Peaceful Moment All the Way," *BW*, 4 September 1954, 86.

98. USWA IEB, 13–14 April 1959, 4-20, box 46, file 10, USWA Archives, PSU. Hoerr, *Wolf*, 326. Joel Sabadasz, "Draft of "Duquesne Works: Overview History" (Homestead: 1991), mss. in author's possession, 32.

99. "Do Steelworkers Want a Strike?" *U.S. News and World Report*, 15 May 1959, 44–50. Libertella, "Steel Strike of 1959," 135–37.

100. Harold J. Ruttenberg, "Steel Strike in '59? A Size-Up by One Who Knows Both Sides," *U.S. News and World Report*, 27 February 27, 1959, 66.

101. Jack Metzgar, *Striking Steel: Solidarity Remembered* (Philadelphia: Temple University Press, 2000), 57.

102. "When Steel Closes Down," *U.S. News and World Report*, 27 July 1959, 37.

103. John McManigal, "To be or not to be," n.d. but probably 1959, 2; "Snow Job," n.d., but 1959; both in John McManigal Papers, AIS.

104. Metzgar, *Striking Steel*, 67.

105. Libertella, "Steel Strike of 1959," 232–56. Metzgar, *Striking Steel*, 94–117.

106. James D. Rose, "The Struggle over Management Rights at U.S. Steel, 1946–1960: A Reassessment of Section 2-B of the Collective Bargaining Contract," *Business History Review* 72 (Autumn 1998): 446–77.

107. "Summary of Section 2-B Arbitration Cases," Section X, 27 August 1953, 1, box 16, file "Management Guides: Local Working Conditions," USX Duquesne Works Papers, AIS.

108. A.L.N. to G.J.C., 8 July 1953, box 9, file "Section 2-B," USX Duquesne Works Papers, AIS. Strohmeyer, *Crisis in Bethlehem*, 68.

109. Pike and Fisher arbitration handbook, box 58, unnamed file, Homestead Works Papers, Indiana University of Pennsylvania. McGannon, *Treating*, 663–64. USC–322; A.L.N. to G.J.C., "Local Working Conditions," 8 July 1953 and 23 March 1954; "Grievances Alleging Company Violation of Section 2-B of the 1947 Contract," 1 July 1952; A.L.N. to G.J.C., "Local Working Conditions," 22 September 1953; all in box 9, file "Conditions/Correspondence Reports Involving Section 2-B," USX Duquesne Works Papers, AIS.

110. Metzgar, *Striking Steel*, 95.

111. R.W.M. to G.J.C., 3 December 1958; P.J.K. to E.J.W., 2 December 1958; H.H.F. to G.J.C., 1 December 1958; R.J.F. to R.W.M., "Oral Labor Agreements," 24 November 1958; R.W.M. to G.H.D., 5 May 1960; R.W.M. to G.H.D., 16 May 1960; "Review of Local Working Conditions," 2 December 1959; R.W.M. to G.J.C., 3 December 1958; R.W.M. to G.J.C., 16 March 1967; all in box 9, file "Section 2-B," USX Duquesne Works Papers, AIS. Strohmeyer, *Crisis in Bethlehem*, 68–69.

112. "Statement of Proposal," n.d.; J.M.L. to R.J.F., "Potential Sources of Labor Relations Trouble," 15 May 1958, 23 May 1958, and 20 June 1958; "Work Requirements with the use of 175-ton iron ladles—Blast Furnace," 6, n.d.; all in box 3, file D-1 (b–2), USX Duquesne Works Papers, AIS.

113. Joseph G. Colangelo Jr., "The Second Battle of Homestead," *Reporter*, 18 July 1963, 30.

114. A.L.N. to K.H.M., 2 February 1950, box 2, file S-3 (a), USX Duquesne Works Papers, AIS. Walter Alfred Schratz, "Development of and Experience with Industrial Grievance Procedure, with Reference to the Open-End and Closed-End Type" (Ph.D. diss., University of Pittsburgh, 1954), 164.

115. P.G.K., "Developing and Negotiating a Local Seniority Agreement," 14, 9 December 1955, box 2, file S-3 (a), USX Duquesne Works Papers, AIS.

116. "Problems Encountered in Developing and Negotiating Local Seniority Agreements," 23 December 1955, 2, box 2, file 2, USX Duquesne Works Papers, AIS.

117. James J. Thomas to Philip Murray, 19 July 1951, 1, box 3, file "Misc.," District 15 Papers, USWA Archives, PSU.

118. Blast Furnace LOP, "Addendum 'C,'" 15 December 1958; "Promotional Sequence" for the Blast Furnace, n.d., but probably July 1953; both in box 3, file D-1 (b-2), USX Duquesne Works Papers, AIS. Robert Lewis Ruck, "Origins of the Seniority System in Steel" (seminar paper, University of Pittsburgh, 1977), 67.

119. "'No Discrimination in Employment'—U.S. Steel," *PC*, 9 January 1954, 30. "U.S. Steel Policy: 'No Job Bias!'" *PC*, 16 January 1954, Section 2, 3. Memo from R. Maurice Moss, 13 February 1953, box 4, file 34, Civil Rights Department (CRD), USWA Archives, PSU.

120. See tables at the end of this chapter. Dennis Dickerson, *Out of the Crucible: Black Steelworkers in Western Pennsylvania, 1875–1980* (Albany: State University of New York Press, 1986), 154–55.

121. "Number of Employees by Ethnic Group," 5 October 1973, DW 82, Affirmation Action Compliance Program, USX National Tube Works Papers, AIS. EEOC file, box 179, EEO Report, 6 June 1970 USX National Tube Works Papers, AIS. Dickerson, *Out of the Crucible*, 154–55.

122. Bureau of the Census, *Census of Population: 1950* (Washington: GPO, 1952), Part 38, 472.

123. Pennsylvania Fair Employment Practices Committee, *Third Annual Report*, 3 March 1959, 6.

124. John Hughey, interview by author, 5 August 1993, tape recording. Henderson Thomas, Lee Robinson, interview by Henderson and Buba, summer 1992, tape recording. Joseph Robinson, interview by Larry Evans, 16 December 1986, video recording, Hillman Library, University of Pittsburgh.

125. Memo from A.L.N. to G.J.C., "Re: National Deliverance Day," 12 March 1956, box 18, file S-5 (A), USX Duquesne Works Papers, AIS.

126. Ruck, "Origins," 97.

127. George Henderson, interview by Henderson and Buba, summer 1992, tape recording.

128. "Benefits Seen for Steelmen," *PC*, 26 April 1947, 1, 4.

129. John Hughey, interview by author, 5 August 1993, tape recording.

130. "Problems Encountered in Developing and Negotiating Local Seniority Agreements," 23 December 1955, 1–2, box 2, file 2, USX Duquesne Works Papers, AIS.

131. Jesse Pierce and Alex Powell; Curly McLaughlin; Earl Williams; interview by Henderson and Buba, summer 1992, tape recording.

132. Harold Keith, "Sparks Fly at Steel Union Parley," *PC*, 5 January 1957, 3. Keith, "Workers Defend Albert Everett," *PC*, 12 January 1957, 2. Lee Robinson, interview by Henderson and Buba, summer 1992, tape recording.

133. Ruck, "Origins," 102.

134. Mary Ann Boytim, interview by Sara Sturdevant, 16 August 1992, transcript log, SIHC, interview no. ES92-SS1-C. Milton Macintyre, interview by Henderson and Buba, summer 1992, tape recording.

135. "Family Affair," *USSN* (January 1947): 2. William Serrin, *Homestead: The Glory and Tragedy of an American Steeltown* (New York: Times Books, 1992), 62. Donald Woodington; Rivers; interview by Henderson and Buba, summer 1992, tape recording.

136. John McManigal Jr., interview by author, 16 June 1993, tape recording.

137. In one case, a woman's father had been killed in the Duquesne Works, and the Superintendent of Industrial Relations tried to get her hired at another mill. He noted that she was not a great typist but to her credit had "a nice appearance and appears to be a quite intelligent and a bright young girl." R.W.M. to P.G.K., 11 May 1960, box 9, file P-3 (a), USX Duquesne Works Papers, AIS. Michele McMills, interview by author, 26 August

1992, tape recording. Barbara Posner, "Male-Female Worker Relations in a Traditionally Male Industrial Setting: The Case of the First Women Workers in a 'Company-Town' Steel Mill" (Ed. D. diss., University of Pittsburgh, 1979), 93.

138. Otis King, interview by author, 25 February 1993, tape recording.

139. Milton Macintyre, interview by Henderson and Buba, summer 1992, tape recording.

140. Lee Robinson, interview by Henderson and Buba, summer 1992, tape recording.

141. Anonymous, interview by Henderson and Buba, summer 1992, tape recording.

142. Donald Woodington, interview by Henderson and Buba, summer 1992, tape recording.

143. Jesse Larrington, interview by Henderson and Buba, summer 1992, tape recording.

144. Industrial Relations Department, "Total Number of Men Laid Off Reducing Force," n.d., box 3, file S-3 (f), USX Duquesne Works Papers, AIS.

145. "Duquesne Local 1256, U.S.A.-C.I.O.: To the Carnegie Illinois Steel Corp and to the Citizens of Duquesne, Pa," 2 August 1949, box 3, file S-3 (f), USX Duquesne Works Papers, AIS.

146. Sabadasz, "Duquesne Works," 22.

147. A.L.N. to K.H.M. "Industrial Relations Problems," 12 October 1949, box 2, file S-3 (a), USX Duquesne Works Papers, AIS.

148. A.L.N to G.J.C., "Weekly Labor Report," 28 July, 9; 18 August 1949; "Minutes of Meeting" on Grievances A-49–16 and A-49–17, Industrial Relations Department, "Industrial Relations Problems at Duquesne Works"; all in box 3, file S-3 (f), USX Duquesne Works Papers, AIS.

149. "U.S. Steel Modernizes Duquesne Blast Furnaces," *Iron and Steel Engineer* (December 1950): 150.

150. "Arbitrator Rules Out Moves from OH 4 to OH 5," *The Sentinel* (May 1959): 1–2.

151. "Summary of Force Reduction and Severance Pay Liability," 25 July 1949, box 3, file S-3 (f), USX Duquesne Works Papers, AIS.

152. No title, 9 August 1949, box 3, file S-3 (f), USX Duquesne Works Papers, AIS.

153. Industrial Relations Department, "Industrial Relations Problems at Duquesne Works," 9 August 1949, box 3, file S-3 (f), USX Duquesne Works Papers, AIS.

154. Industrial Relations Department, "Memorandum, Subject: Notice of Vacancies in Swing Frame Grinder Occupation, Conditioning Department," 21 April 1950, box 3, file S-3 (f), USX Duquesne Works Papers, AIS.

155. Ruck, "Origins," 59.

156. "Present and Proposed Promotional Sequences," February 1947, box 32, file S-3 (b), USX Duquesne Works Papers, AIS.

157. R.W.M. to G.J.C., "Treatment of Employees Displaced as the Result of Abandoned Facilities and Major Technological Advances," 21 December 1959, box 3, file D-1 (b-2), USX Duquesne Works Papers, AIS.

158. Henderson Thomas, interview by Henderson and Buba, summer 1992, tape recording.

159. R.W.G. to R.H.G., "Maintaining Continuous Service of Laid-Off Employees with Long Service," 8 November 1954, box 3, file S-3 (g), USX Duquesne Works Papers, AIS. R.W.M. to G.J.C., "Treatment of Employees Displaced as the Result of Abandoned Facilities

and Major Technological Advances," 21 December 1959, box 3, file D-1 (b–2), USX Duquesne Works Papers, AIS.

160. See table 4 at the end of this chapter. U.S. Department of Labor, Women's Bureau, *Women's Employment in the Making of Steel*, Bulletin 192–5, report prepared by Ethel Erickson (Washington: GPO, 1944), 4.

161. "Courier Asks Steelworkers How Strike Affects Them," *PC*, 6 June 1952, 1, 17. "Homestead Steelworkers Hold Annual Conference," *SL* (December 1948): 12. Keith, "Who's Who in Labor," *PC*, 29 March 1947.

162. "Plant Survey Dead-End Positions for Female Employees," 4 January 1951, box 32, file W-3 (a), USX Duquesne Works Papers, AIS.

163. USWA IEB, April 19–20, 1951, 174–77, USWA Archives, PSU.

164. R.W.G. to J.H.E., 10 January 1951, box 32, file W–3 (A); "Agreement Affecting Seniority Rights of Women," 20 February 1951; both in box 32, file W-3 (A), USX Duquesne Works Papers, AIS.

165. "Females Employed since January 1, 1951," 14 April 1954, box 32, file W-3 (A), USX Duquesne Works Papers, AIS.

166. "Memorandum on Meeting Regarding Four-Day Week Schedule," 15 July 1954, box 3, file S-3 (f), USX Duquesne Works Papers, AIS.

167. Halpern, *"Negro and White, Unite and Fight!"* 165–66.

168. "Clerical Workers Reap Benefits in New Steel Pact," *SL* (September 1954): 4.

169. C.D.F. to R.W.M., 29 April 1959, box 32, file w-3 (a), USX Duquesne Works Papers, AIS.

170. Bureau of the Census, *Census of Population: 1960* (Washington: GPO, 1961), Part 40, 931–32. Richard L. Rowan, *The Negro in the Steel Industry* (Philadelphia: University of Pennsylvania Press), 47.

171. Ruck, "Origins," 68–70.

172. G.J.E., n.d. but probably March 1963, 1–2, box 16, file S-3 (d), USX Duquesne Works Papers, AIS. USWA IEB, 19–20 August 1954, 47–50, box 45, file 13, USWA Archives, PSU.

173. P.G.K., "Developing and Negotiating a Local Seniority Agreement," 9, 9 December 1955, box 2, file S-3 (a), USX Duquesne Works Papers, AIS. See also J.W.S. to E.B.S. "Confidential," 11 September 1962, 8, box 16, file S-3 (d), USX Duquesne Works Papers, AIS.

174. "Agreement on Accounting Department Transfer with Salaried Workers Union Grievance Committeeman, H.O.G.," 29 August 1950, in box 3, file S-3 (g), USX Duquesne Works Papers, AIS.

175. Jesse Pierce and Alex Powell, Curly McLaughlin, Earl Williams, interview by Henderson and Buba, summer 1992, tape recording.

176. Ruck, "Origins," 98.

177. Otis King, interview by author, 25 February 1992, tape recording.

178. Notes from Employment Cards, USX Duquesne Works, AIS. Donald Woodington, interview by Henderson and Buba, summer 1992, tape recording.

179. Ernestine Holt, "Steel Men Prefer Carnegie Steel Plants," *PC*, 31 August 1946, 16.

180. Albert Reid, interview by Jim Barrett, 16 June 1976, transcript, HOHP, AIS. George Suber, interview by author, 9 March 1992, tape recording.

181. HD 65–173, USX Duquesne Works Papers, AIS.

182. Bureau of the Census, *Population Census: 1950* (Washington: GPO, 1952), Part 38, 370–74, 472–75.

183. Memo from R. Maurice Moss to Administration Files, 13 February 1953, box 4, file 34, CRD Papers, USWA Archives, PSU. "Blast Furnace Crew," *PC*, 14 January 1956, 6.

184. Thomas Walker, interview by Henderson and Buba, summer 1992, tape recording.

185. Otis Bryant, interview by Henderson and Buba, summer 1992, tape recording.

186. Donald Woodington, interview by Henderson and Buba, summer 1992, tape recording.

187. Keith, "Sparks Fly," *PC*, 5 January 1957, 3. Keith, "Workers Defend," *PC*, 12 January 1957, 2. Keith, "USWA Local Defies," *PC*, 19 January 1957, 2. "Discrimination in Homestead Works," *PC*, 9 February 1957, Section 2, 3. Keith, "Clobbering Jim Crow," *PC*, 16 February 1957, 6.

188. John Hughey, interview by author, 5 August 1993, tape recording.

189. Bureau of the Census, *Population Census: 1950* (Washington: GPO, 1952), Part 38, 370–75.

190. Bureau of the Census, *Population Census: 1960* (Washington: GPO, 1961), Part 40, 931–32, 752–54.

191. Lee, Taliferro, and Wilson, interview by Henderson and Buba, summer 1992, tape recording.

192. Bureau of the Census, *Population Census: 1950* (Washington: GPO, 1952), Part 38, 370–75, 472.

193. Keith, "Sparks Fly," *PC*, 5 January 1957, 3; Keith, "Workers Defend Albert Everett," *PC*, 12 January 1957, 2; Keith, "USWA Local Defies Fair Job Policy," *PC*, 19 January 1957, 2. "Discrimination in Homestead," *PC*, 9 February 1957, Section 2, 3; Keith, "Clobbering Jim Crow," *PC*, 16 February 1957, 6.

194. "Monthly Activities Report," 10 April 1954, box 6, PUL Papers, AIS. "Balance Sheet: A News Letter from the Urban League of Pittsburgh," winter 1957, box 9, file 3, CRD Papers, USWA Archives, PSU.

195. Bureau of the Census, *Population Census: 1960* (Washington: GPO, 1961), Part 40, 931–32, 752–54.

196. Otis King, interview by author, 25 February 1992, tape recording.

197. Booker Kidd, interview by Henderson and Buba, summer 1992, tape recording.

198. *Struggles in Steel: A Story of African-American Steelworkers*, video recording, dir. Tony Buba and Ray Henderson (San Francisco: California Newsreel, 1996).

199. "'Fair Share' Group Eyes Braddock Area," *PC*, 19 January 19, 1957, 3. Ruck, "Origins," 95. Otis King interview by author, 25 February 1992, tape recording.

200. Edmond Holmes, interview by Henderson and Buba, summer 1992, tape recording.

201. Anonymous, interview by Henderson and Buba, summer 1992, tape recording.

202. Keith, "Sparks Fly," *PC*, 5 January 1957, 3. Keith, "Workers Defend," *PC*, 12 January 1957, 2. Keith, "USW Local Defies," *PC*, 19 January 1957, 2. "Discrimination in Homestead," *PC*, 9 February 1957, Section 2, 3. Keith, "Clobbering Jim Crow," *PC*, 16 February 1957, 6.

203. John Hughey, interview by Henderson and Buba, summer 1992, tape recording.

204. Bureau of the Census, *Population Census: 1950* (Washington: GPO, 1952), Part 38, 370–75, 472. Bureau of the Census, *Population Census: 1960* (Washington: GPO, 1961), Part 40, 752–54.

205. Dickerson, *Out of the Crucible*, 186, 206.

206. "Vicious Prejudice Seen as Roadblock to the Employment of Skilled Negroes," *PC*, 19 December 1959, 3–4.

207. Industrial Report No. 4, 10 March 1954; 14 April 1954; Industrial Report No. 5, October 1955; Industrial Report No. 6, April 1956; all in box 6, file "Monthly Activities Report," PUL, AIS.

208. Industrial Report No. 5, October 1955, box 6, file "Monthly Activities Report," PUL, AIS.

209. Industrial Report No. 6, June 1956, box 6, file "Monthly Activities Report," PUL, AIS. Dickerson, *Out of the Crucible*, 210.

210. Keith, "Sparks Fly," *PC*, 5 January 1957, 3. Keith, "Workers Defend," *PC*, 12 January 1957, 2. Keith, "USW Local Defies," *PC*, 19 January 1957, 2. "Discrimination in Homestead," *PC*, 9 February 1957, Section 2, 3. Keith, "Clobbering Jim Crow," *PC*, 16 February 1957, 6.

211. James A. Jordan, 31 January 1958, box 20, file 5, NAACP Papers, AIS.

212. Monthly Report for September 1961, box 38, NAACP Papers, AIS.

213. Ralph E. Kroger, "Oldest Employee of Union Railroad Ousted from Job," *PC*, 24 August 1946.

214. Milton Macintyre, interview by Henderson and Buba, summer 1992, tape recording. LaRue Frederic, "NAACP report for Station WAMO," 18 April 1959, in author's possession. Bureau of the Census, *Population Census 1960* (Washington: GPO, 1961), vol. I, Part 40, 953–55.

215. "To Secure These Rights," *SL* (July 1948): 5.

216. Phyl Garland, "From the Soil to the Shop," 11 June 1960, *PC*, Magazine Section. Dickerson, *Out of the Crucible*, 180–81. Minutes of CRC, 3 February 1959, 1, box 6, file 7, Howard Hague Papers, USWA Archives, PSU.

217. 27 August 1957, minutes of CRC Regular Quarterly Meeting, 7, box 9, file 5, Civil Rights Department, (CRD), USWA Archives, PSU.

218. Dickerson, *Out of the Crucible*, 195.

219. John Hughey, interview by author, 5 August 1993, tape recording. Jesse Walker, interview by Henderson and Buba, summer 1992, tape recording.

220. "USA's Civil Rights Campaign Hits Peak at Four Conferences," *SL* (March 1950): 5. ". . . At the Pittsburgh Civil Rights Conference," *SL* (March 1950): 6. "Pittsburgh Conference—Delegate List, 1950," box 2, file 8, CRD Papers, USWA Archives, PSU. Transcript of Proceedings, USWA Civil Rights Conference, 29 January 1950, box 2, file 9, CRD Papers, USWA Archives, PSU.

221. Ben Fisher, interview, 23 June 1977, transcript, USWA Archives, PSU. "Committee on Civil Rights Petitions, USWA, 1950," box 2, file 1, CRD Papers, USWA Archives, PSU. "USA's Civil Rights Campaign," *SL* (March 1950): 5. "Steel Union to Co-Sponsor Series of Civil Rights Meetings Planned by CIO," *SL* (September 1950): 11.

222. "To Secure These Rights," *SL* (July 1948): 5.

223. "FEPC Law Would Benefit All Citizens," *SL* (July 1951): 11. "Communism—What's That?" *SL* (March 1951): 1. "Steel Union to Co-Sponsor," *SL* (September 1950): 11.

224. "USA-CIO Aids in Passage of FEP[C] Ordinances in Pittsburgh, River Rouge," *SL* (February 1953): 10. "'We Have Just Begun to Move Ahead,' Abel Tells District 15 Conference," *SL* (April 1953): 2.

225. A Union Man, "The Mill," *Steel Voice* (June 1949): box 1, file "Communists, 1948–1949," District 15 Papers, USWA Archives, PSU.

226. Keith, "Negro Workers Declared Wary of 'Commie' Label," *PC*, 31 May 1952, 17.

227. George Edwards, interview by author, 3 March 1992, tape recording.

228. Keith, "Who's Who in Labor," *PC*, 12 March 1949, 16.

229. Keith, "Who's Who in Labor," *PC*, 11 August 1956, Section 2, 3. John Hughey, interview by author, 5 August 1993, tape recording. "Hypocrisy in Organized Labor," *PC*, 31 May 1958, Section 2, 8. Robert J. Norrell, "Caste in Steel: Jim Crow Careers in Birmingham, Alabama," *Journal of American History* 73 (December 1986): 681–85. For a different perspective, see Judith Stein, "Southern Workers in National Unions: Birmingham Steelworkers, 1936–1951," in *Organized Labor in the Twentieth Century South*, ed. Robert H. Zieger (Knoxville: University of Tennessee Press, 1991), 183–221.

230. Keith, "Who's Who in Labor," *PC*, 23 April 1949, 16.

231. Keith, "Who's Who in Labor," *PC*, 14 May 1949, 20.

232. USWA, *Proceedings of the Fifth Constitutional Convention of the United Steelworkers of America* (Pittsburgh: USWA, 1950), 167. Boyd L. Wilson to Francis C. Shane, 20 November 1957, box 10, file 11, CRD Papers, USWA Archives, PSU.

233. Keith, "Who's Who in Labor," *PC*, 14 July 1956, Section 2, 10.

234. "John Duch and Celosky Not Guilty," *The Sentinel* (November 1954): 4. "Commission Upholds Ruling in Duch Trial," *The Sentinel* (July 1957): 5.

235. Keith, "Sparks Fly," *PC*, 5 January 1957, 3. Keith, "USW Local Defies," *PC*, 19 January 1957, 2. Keith, "USW Trial Board Holds Up Verdict as Everett Backers Yell, 'Kangaroo!'" *PC*, 9 February 1957, 3. Ruck, "Origins," 90.

236. Keith, "Clobbering Jim Crow," *PC*, 16 February 1957, 6.

237. Keith, "Sparks Fly," *PC*, 5 January 1957, 3. Lee Robinson, interview by Henderson and Buba, summer 1992, tape recording.

238. "Plant Rules Out Local Company FEPC Meetings," *The Sentinel* (April 1959): 5.

239. Minutes of Special Meeting, 3 February 1959, box 6, file 7, Hague Papers, USWA Archives, PSU. USWA, *Proceedings*, 1960, 350. Minutes of CRC, 9 December 1964, box 6, file 11, Hague Papers, USWA Archives, PSU.

240. "Labor and Industry Committee, Correspondence," box 42, file 1, NAACP, AIS. "Minutes of the September 12, 1956, USWA Committee on Civil Rights," 3; "Minutes— Regular Quarterly Committee Meeting," 29 July 1958, 3; both in box 6, file 5, Hague Papers, USWA Archives, PSU. Francis Shane to CRC, 2 October 1961, 2; "Minutes of CRC," April 17, 1961; both in box 6, file 9, Hague Papers, USWA Archives, PSU. "Committee on Civil Rights Participation in USWA District Conferences, 1966," 3, box 11, file 32, CRD Papers, USWA Archives, PSU. "Charge J&L-Union with Bias," *PC*, 3 January 1970, 1 and 4.

241. Stebenne, *Arthur Goldberg*, 144.

242. USWA, *Proceedings*, 1950, 169–73.

243. Keith, "Who's Who in Labor," *PC*, 1 November 1952, 13.

244. Keith, "Who's Who in Labor," *PC*, 24 January 1954, 16.

245. Keith, "Who's Who in Labor," *PC*, 10 October 1953, 20.

246. "Courier Asks Steelworkers How Strike Affects Them," *PC*, 21 June 1952, 1. "FEP[C] Ordinances in Pittsburgh," *SL* (February 1953): 10. Dickerson, *Out of the Crucible*, 212. "FEPC Review: Events and Trends in Pittsburgh Fair Employment Practices," July-August 1954, 2; June 1955, 1; both in box 10, file 5, NAACP Papers, AIS.

247. USWA, *Proceedings*, 1954, 167.

248. Francis Shane to District Directors, 14 March 1956, box 6, file 5, Hague Papers, USWA Archives, PSU. "Keystone State Gets Fair Housing Bill," *SL* (February 1961): 6. The "Fair Housing Law" was signed into law on February 28, 1961. It combined the old FEPC into a Pennsylvania Human Relations Commission. It also expanded the scope of the 1939 public accommodations law, see Pennsylvania Equal Rights Council, 17 March 1961, box 38, file "PA Equal Rights Council," NAACP Papers, AIS.

249. Keith, "Who's Who in Labor," *PC*, 25 February 1956, 10. "FEPC Review," October 1954, 1, box 10, file 5, NAACP Papers, AIS. "Where to Go for Help," box 20, file 3, NAACP Papers, AIS. Workshop Summaries, box 12, file 1, NAACP Papers, AIS.

250. "Curly" McCloughlin, interview by Henderson and Buba, summer 1992, tape recording.

251. Dickerson, *Out of the Crucible*, 212. Oliver Montgomery, interview by Henderson and Buba, summer 1992, tape recording. See also Committee on Fair Employment Practice, *First Report, July 1943-December 1944* (Washington: GPO, 1945), 81–82. Herbert Hill, "Black Workers, Organized Labor and Title VII of the 1964 Civil Rights Act: Legislative History and Litigation Record," in *Race in America: The Struggle for Equality*, ed. Herbert Hill and James E. Jones Jr. (Madison: University of Wisconsin Press, 1993), 311.

252. Memo from A.L.N. to G.J.C., "re: National Deliverance Day," 12 March 1956, box 18, file S-5 (A), USX Duquesne Works Papers, AIS.

253. Keith, "Sparks Fly," *PC*, 5 January 1957, 3. Keith, "Workers Defend," *PC*, 12 January 1957, 2. 6 June 1957, USWA IEB, box 15, file 35, USWA Archives, PSU.

254. Keith, "USW Local Defies," *PC*, 19 January 1957, 2.

255. Keith, "Clobbering Jim Crow," *PC*, 16 February 1957, 6.

256. 20 March 1957, Albert Everett et al. to I.W. Abel; "Report and Recommendation," 6 June 1957; "Supplementary Seniority Agreement," 1 June 1955; all in 6 June 1957, USWA IEB box 15, file 35, USWA Archives, PSU.

257. "Fair Share Asks Homestead Workers to 'Have Humility,'" *PC*, 23 February 1957, 6.

258. Minutes of the CRC, 10 November 1958, box 6, file 6, Hague Papers, USWA Archives, PSU.

259. John Hughey and Jesse Larrington, interview by Henderson and Buba, summer 1992, tape recording. John Hughey, interview by author, 5 August 1993, tape recording.

260. John Hughey, interview by author, 5 August 1993, tape recording.

261. "Fair Share Asks," *PC*, 23 February 1957, 6.

262. "Acquittal of John Duch Irks Negro Members of Steel Union," *PC*, 2 March 1957, 3. Ruck, "Origins," 90.

263. "'Rebel with a Cause' Hilbert Runs Again," *PC*, 19 November 1960, Section 3, 1. Ray Henderson, interview by author, 6 August 1993, tape recording.

264. Keith, "Who's Who in Labor: Backer Sets Precedent, Wins Post in USW Local," *PC*, 31 August 1957, Section 2, 1.

265. Keith, "Clobbering Jim Crow," *PC*, 16 February 1957, 6.

266. John Hughey and Jesse Larrington, interview by Henderson and Buba, summer 1992, tape recording.

267. Walter Maxwell, interview by Henderson and Buba, summer 1992, tape recording.

268. Interview with Tommy Walker, by Henderson and Buba, summer 1992, tape recording. Bob Morgan, interview by Henderson and Buba, summer 1992, tape recording.

269. Williams, *Black Workers in an Industrial Suburb*, 167–71.

270. Lee Robinson, interview by Henderson and Buba, summer 1992, tape recording.

271. Charles Lee Jr., interview by Henderson and Buba, summer 1992, tape recording. Edmond Holmes, interview by Henderson and Buba, summer 1992, tape recording.

272. Jesse Walker, interview by Henderson and Buba, summer 1992, tape recording.

273. Henderson Thomas, interview by Henderson and Buba, summer 1992, tape recording.

274. Keith, "Who's Who in Labor," *PC*, 1 January 1949, 16.

275. "Key Union Policy Job for Negro," *PC*, 12 August 1961, 21. The unionist who was elected in 1961 was Vernon Sidberry.

276. Keith, "Who's Who in Labor," *PC*, 1 January 1949, 16.

277. "Goney Wins USW District 17 Election," *PC*, 12 February 1949, 3. Keith, "Who's Who in Labor," *PC*, 19 February 1949, 16.

278. Keith, "Who's Who in Labor," *PC*, 14 October 1950. Keith, "Who's Who in Labor," *PC*, 5 February 1949, 16. "USW District 17 Incumbent Holds 'Special' Conference," *PC*, 5 February 1949, 2. Keith, "Who's Who in Labor," *PC*, 24 January 1954, 16.

279. Carl Dickerson and others to David J. McDonald, 22 May 1958, box 10, file 11, Howard Hague Papers, USWA Archives, PSU.

280. Keith, "USW Local Defies," *PC*, 19 January 1957, 2.

281. Jesse Walker, interview by Henderson and Buba, summer 1992, tape recording. See also Kathryn Close, "Steel Makers: 1937–1947," *Survey Graphic* 36 (March 1947): 219.

282. John King, interview by Henderson and Buba, summer 1992, tape recording.

283. John Hughey, interview by author, 5 August 1993, tape recording.

284. "Race Men Aspire to Union Office," *PC*, 7 July 1956, 3.

285. Albert Reid, interview by Jim Barrett, 16 June 1976, transcript, HOHP, AIS.

286. Keith, "Who's Who in Labor: A Steelworker Writes a Letter," *PC*, 12 January 1957, Section 2, 3.

287. Gwendolyn Young Richburg, interview by Henderson and Buba, summer 1992, tape recording.

288. Anonymous, interview by Henderson and Buba, summer 1992, tape recording.

289. Henderson Thomas, interview by Henderson and Buba, summer 1992, tape recording.

290. Edmond Holmes, interview by Henderson and Buba, summer 1992, tape recording.

291. Otis King, interview by author, 25 February 1992.

292. Statement by Alfred B. Macon, 14 February 1980, in author's possession (courtesy of Denise Weinbrenner Edwards).

293. George Suber, interview by author, 9 March 1992, tape recording.

294. Henderson Thomas, interview by Henderson and Buba, summer 1992, tape recording. Bob Morgan, interview by Henderson and Buba, summer 1992, tape recording.

295. George Henderson, interview by Henderson and Buba, summer 1992, tape recording.

296. Anonymous, interview by Henderson and Buba, summer 1992, tape recording.

297. "USW Trial Board Holds Up Verdict," *PC*, 9 February 1957, 3.

298. Edmond Holmes, interview by Henderson and Buba, summer 1992, tape recording.

299. Anonymous, interview by Henderson and Buba, summer 1992, tape recording.

300. John Hughey and Jesse Larrington, interview by Henderson and Buba, summer 1992, tape recording.

301. "Force Reduction, Part-Timing and Furloughing during Curtailed Operations," 30 November 1949, box 3, file S-3 (f), USX Duquesne Works Papers, AIS.

302. John Hughey and Jesse Larrington, interview by Henderson and Buba, summer 1992, tape recording.

303. Bob Morgan, interview by Henderson and Buba, summer 1992, tape recording.

304. Robert Rivers, interview by Henderson and Buba, summer 1992, tape recording.

305. George Henderson, interview by Henderson and Buba, summer 1992, tape recording.

306. Charles Lee Jr., interview by Henderson and Buba, summer 1992, tape recording.

307. "Don Rarick Cleared of 'Dual Unionism,'" *HM*, 22 December 1958, 1. 16 April 1952, 34; 1 August 1956; 21 January 1953; 20 January 1954; 16 July 1958; 19 November 1958; USWA Meeting Attendance Book, Local 1256 Papers, USWA Archives, PSU.

308. David Caute, *The Great Fear: The Anti-Communist Purge under Truman and Eisenhower* (New York: Simon and Schuster, 1978), 216–23. Sherley Uhl, "Communists Go Far Here—Underground," *PP*, 19 November 1961, 1, 7. Paul Lyons, *Philadelphia Communists, 1936–1956* (Philadelphia: Temple University Press, 1982), 164.

309. The case of Frank Svoboda was one of the only communist trials in the Pittsburgh region in the 1950s. USWA IEB, 19–20 August 1954, 41–42, box 45, file 13, USWA Archives, PSU. "Ouster Upheld," *Advance Leader*, 3 June 1954, 9.

310. USWA IEB, 2–4 March 1955, 169–73, box 45, file 15, USWA Archives, PSU.

311. Filippelli and McColloch, *Cold War in the Working Class*, 141–66.

312. Lloyd Ulman, *The Government of the United Steel Workers' Union* (New York: John Wiley and Sons, 1962), 155–56.

313. Ed Mann, *We Are the Union: The Story of Ed Mann*, ed. Alice and Staughton Lynd (Pittsburgh: Solidarity USA, n.d.), 19–20.

314. Mike Bilsic, interview by author, 19 March 1992, tape recording. HH 66-212, box 18, Homestead Local 1397 Papers, Indiana University of Pennsylvania (hereafter cited as IUP). Schratz, "Grievance Procedures," 172. Ulman, *Government*, 8–13, 18–21, 40–41, 44–49, 81–82, 172. Close, "Steel Makers: 1937–1947," 183–84. Nelson Lichtenstein, *Labor's War at Home: The CIO in World War II* (Oxford: Oxford University Press, 1982), 187–88. Mark McColloch, "Consolidating Industrial Citizenship: The U.S.W.A. at War and Peace, 1939–1946," in *Forging a Union of Steel: Philip Murray, SWOC, and the United Steelworkers*, ed. Paul F. Clark, Peter Gottlieb, and Donald Kennedy (Ithaca: ILR Press, 1987), 80.

315. Ulman, *Government*, 143.

316. John Herling, *Right to Challenge: People and Power in the Steelworkers' Union* (New York: Harper and Row, 1972), 23–35. Ulman, *Government*, 100–10.

317. Ulman, *Government*, 129.

318. USWA IEB, 17 November 1946, 23–103, USWA Archives, PSU. De Caux, *Labor Radical*, 507–08. "Bill of Complaint," April 1953, box 3, file "George Ponist," District 15 Papers, USWA Archives, PSU. Serrin, *Homestead*, 261.

319. Thomas Geogehan, *Which Side Are You On? Trying to Be for Labor When It's Flat on Its Back* (New York: Plume, 1992), 62.

320. Herling, *Right to Challenge*, 25–26.

321. Philip Nyden, *Steelworkers Rank-and-File: The Political Economy of a Union Reform Movement* (New York: Praeger Publishers, 1984), 38.

322. *The Maloney Campaigner*, 19 October 1955, box 30, file "USWA Locals," USX Duquesne Works Papers, AIS.

323. Herling, *Right to Challenge*, 33–40.

324. Nyden, *Steelworkers Rank-and-File*, 39–42. Dickerson, *Out of the Crucible*, 225.

325. "United Steelworkers, Do You Like Dictatorship?" n.d.; "Hilbert is the One for Us," 5 February 1957, box 30, file "USWA Locals," USX Duquesne Works Papers, AIS.

326. Stebenne, *Arthur Goldberg*, 171.

327. Anthony Tomko, interview by author, 2 June 1993, tape recording. Hoerr, *Wolf*, 253. Stanley Aronowitz, *False Promises: The Shaping of American Working Class Consciousness* (New York: McGraw-Hill, 1973), 377. Herling, *Right to Challenge*, 61.

328. Nyden, *Steelworkers Rank-and-File*, 37–42; Ulman, *Government*, 140–75. Other centers of DPC activism were Local 1408 (National Tube), Local 1843 (J&L's Hazelwood mill), Local 1211 (J&L's Aliquippa mill).

329. USWA IEB, 11–12 August 1958, box 46, file 7, USWA Archives, PSU.

330. Ulman, *Government*, 145–47. "Boos Greet Rarick," *HM*, 17 September 1958, 1. "Rarick Faces Ouster," *HM*, 19 September 1958, 1. "McDonald Asked," *HM*, 15 December 1958, 1. "Mamula Won't Bring Accusers up on Charges," *HM*, 19 December 1958, 1. "Don Rarick Cleared of 'Dual Unionism,'" *HM*, 22 December 1958, 1. "'Rebel with a Cause' Hilbert Runs Again," *PC*, 19 November 1960, Section 3, 1.

331. USWA IEB, 6 January 1961, 62–120, box 47, file 3, USWA Archives, PSU.

332. Durable goods operator is the closest the Census comes to identifying steelworkers. Bureau of the Census, *Census of Population: 1960* (Washington: GPO, 1961), Part 40, 953–55. These figures do not include steelworkers' incentive pay or benefits such as medical insurance that most workers did not enjoy.

333. Bureau of the Census, *Population Census: 1950* (Washington: GPO, 1952), Part 38, 514–15, 953–55.

334. Mark McColloch, "Modest but Adequate: The Standard of Living for Mon Valley Steelworkers in the Union Era," in *U.S. Labor in the Twentieth Century: Studies in Working-Class Struggles and Insurgency*, ed. John Hinshaw and Paul Le Blanc (Amherst, NY: Humanity Books, 2000). See also Oliver Montgomery, interview by Henderson and Buba, summer 1992, tape recording. Barrett Franklin, "Family Automobile History," 1–3, mss. in author's possession.

335. Reutter, *Sparrow's Point*, 378–79.

336. Warner Bloomberg, Jr., "Five Hot Days in Gary, Indiana," *Reporter*, 11 August 1955, 36.

337. Otis King, interview by author, 25 February 1992, tape recording.

338. "Steelworkers Need," *SL* (August 1949): 4–5. "Industry Case is Based on Greed for Profits," *SL* (September 1949): 8–9. "Big Pensions for Corporation Heads—Non-Contributory," *SL* (November 1949): 1, 4. "Is Your Wife Going to Work When You Retire?" *SL* (November 1949): 4.

339. "His 61c Pension 'Lumped,'" *Homestead District Sun*, 22 September 1949, 1.

340. David Dempsey, "Steelworkers: 'Not Today's Wage, Tomorrow's Security,'" *New York Times Magazine*, 7 August 1949, rpt. in Melvyn Dubofsky, *American Labor since the New Deal* (New York: New York Times Books, 1971). Edwin Beachler, "Steelworkers Hope Strike Truce Continues," *PP*, 16 July 1949, 1.

341. "Health Survey, Homestead, PA, 1954," box 64, file 7, David McDonald Papers, USWA Archives, PSU.

342. "Homestead Steelworker Tells World of Union Won Benefits," *The Sentinel* (April 1958): 5. Mary Ann Boytim, interview by Sara Sturdevant, 16 August 1992, notes, SIHC, interview no. ES92-SS1-C.

343. McColloch, "Modest but Adequate," 253–54.

344. "The Women in Steel," *SL* (October 1951): 1.

345. "Who Says It's a Man's World?" *SL* (March 1951): 5. "Pensioned Steelworkers Take the Spotlight," *SL* (June 1953): 12.

346. "The Families' Needs Are the Real Issue at the Bargaining Table," *SL* (June 1954): 1.

347. "There's a Good Reason," *SL* (August 1954): 1.

348. "Is Your Wife Going to Work When You Retire?" *SL* (November 1949): 4.

349. "Basic Steel Pensions," *SL* (January 1969): 4–5. McColloch, "Modest but Adequate," 255.

350. Anonymous, conversation with author, 3 September 1993, notes.

351. Judith Modell, conversation with author, 20 December 1993, notes.

352. Beckman and Associates, *Steel Valley Area Regional Development Plan* (Wexford, Pennsylvania: The Associates, 1974), 59–67. Pittsburgh Regional Planning Association, *Steel Valley District: A Long-Range Development Plan for the Boroughs of Homestead, Munhall, West Homestead, West Mifflin, Whitaker: A Technical Report* (Pittsburgh: The Association, 1961), 98.

353. Warren, *American Steel Industry*, 262–328.

354. U.S. Department of Labor, Bureau of Labor Statistics, *Employment, Hours and Earnings: States and Areas, 1939–1974*, Bulletin 1370-11 (Washington: GPO, 1975), 631–32.

355. During the 1940s, Chicago's black population grew by 80 percent, Detroit's by 101 percent, and Philadelphia's by 50 percent; Pittsburgh's center-city black population expanded only by a third, or at half the rate of all Northern American cities. Morton Grodzins, *The Metropolitan Area as a Racial Problem* (Pittsburgh: University of Pittsburgh Press, 1958), 2. During the 1950s, 1.5 million black Southerners moved to cities in the North, Midwest, and West, but only twenty thousand of those migrants came to Pittsburgh. Jacqueline Jones, *The Dispossessed: America's Underclass from the Civil War to the Present* (New York: Basic Books, 1992), 230.

356. "Allegheny Conference on Community Development: Officers and Members of the Executive Committee," 1 October 1955, in box 5, file 5, USWA President's Office Papers, USWA Archives, PSU.

357. Bruce M. Stave, *The New Deal and the Last Hurrah: Pittsburgh Machine Politics* (Pittsburgh: University of Pittsburgh Press, 1970), 23.

358. Roy Lubove, *Twentieth Century Pittsburgh: Government, Business and Environmental Change* (New York: John Wiley and Sons, 1969), 106–76. Weber, *Don't Call Me Boss*, 208–76. See also Shelby Stewman and Joel A. Tarr, "Four Decades of Public-Private Partnership in Pittsburgh," in *Public-Private Partnership in American Cities: Seven Case Studies*, ed. R. Scott Fosler and Renee A. Berge (Lexington, MA: Lexington Books, 1982).

359. Weber, *Don't Call Me Boss*, 304–09.

360. Ray Sprigle, "What's Wrong with Our Police? Sprigle Tells How Ward Bosses Dictate Selection of Inspectors," *PPG*, 23 February 1950, 1, 7. Sprigle, "Homestead Vice Raids Tougher: Detectives Find Themselves in Midst of Hot Primary," *PPG*, 27 April 1953. "Sprigle Goes to Bat for Officer Benny Buford," *PC*, 8 January 1955, 1. Weber, *Don't Call Me Boss*, 71–72.

361. Weber, *Don't Call Me Boss*, 294.

362. Kroger, "Negro Police Get None of the 'Gravy' in the Hill District," *PC*, 21 June 1947, 32. Serrin, *Homestead*, 288–92.

363. Edward Greer, *Big Steel: Black Politics and Corporate Power in Gary, Indiana* (New York: Monthly Review Press, 1979), 27–38.

364. Bureau of Labor Statistics, *Employment and Earnings, States and Areas, 1939–1974*, Bulletin 1370–11, (Washington: GPO, 1979), 636.

365. Weber, *Don't Call Me Boss*, 277–78, 287–90.

366. Weber, *Don't Call Me Boss*, 59, 62.

367. Bureau of the Census, *Census of Population: 1960, Detailed Characteristics*, Vol. I (Washington: GPO, 1961), Part 40, 931.

368. In 1950, the U.S. Census reported that 548 African Americans worked amongst 10,329 local and state government workers in the Pittsburgh SMSA. Bureau of the Census, *Census of Population: 1950*, Vol. II (Washington: GPO, 1952), Part 38, 472. Keith, "Democrats Owe Us Plenty: Here's What We Have," *PC*, 1 November 1952, 1, 4.

369. "Fire Department Jim Crow Killed," *PC*, 16 January 1954, 1. Kroger, "Negro Firemen Not Promoted, They Continue to Sleep in Segregated Beds," *PC*, 22 August 1959, 2. "NAACP Claims City Using Racist Hiring Practices," *PC*, 5 January 1974, 28.

370. Kroger, "Craft Unions Want Pay Raises but Few Have Negro Members on Public Payroll," *PC*, 5 December 1959, 2.

371. George E. Barbour, "25 out of 53 County Departments Have No Negro Employees," *PC*, 10 June 1961, 2.

372. Arthur J. Edmunds, *Daybreakers: The Story of the Urban League of Pittsburgh, the First Sixty-Five Years* (Pittsburgh: Pittsburgh Urban League, 1983), 114–15. "Department Store Fight Won," *PC*, 1 February 1947, 1. K. Leroy Irvis, "Summary Report on the Campaign to Secure a Non-Discrimination Hiring Policy in the Major Pittsburgh Department Stores," 25 January 1947, *Inside Facts*, vol. 2, no. 2; both in Series 13, box 23, file "Printed Material, Pittsburgh, 1947–1949," NUL Papers, Library of Congress. James Hackshaw, "The Committee for Fair Employment in Pittsburgh Department Stores: A Study of the Methods and Techniques Used by the Committee in Their Campaign to Secure a Non-Discriminatory Hiring Policy in the Department Stores of Pittsburgh" (master's thesis, University of Pittsburgh, 1949).

373. Edmunds, *Daybreakers*, 114–15.

374. Bureau of the Census, *Census of the Population: 1950* (Washington: GPO, 1952), Part 38, 373. Bureau of the Census, *Census of the Population: 1960* (Washington: GPO, 1961), Part 40, 752.

375. 13 May 1961, minutes of the Executive Board Meeting, NUL Papers, Part 2, Series 2, box 18, file "Pittsburgh, 1960–1961."

376. Serrin, *Homestead*, 293–95.

377. Robert Qualters, "Homestead," mss. in author's possession. (Courtesy of Randy Harris.)

CHAPTER 4. THE ROAD TO DEINDUSTRIALIZATION: PITTSBURGH AND THE STEEL INDUSTRY, 1960–1977

1. "Johnson's Announcement and Steel Settlement," *NYT*, 4 September 1965, 1.

2. Bennett Harrison, *The Great U-Turn: Corporate Restructuring and the Polarizing of America* (New York: Basic Books, 1990). Makoto Itoh, *The World Economic Crisis and Japanese Capitalism* (New York: St. Martins, 1990).

3. George Gallup, "Union Members Split on Vietnam," *Washington Post*, 3 January 1968, in DR office box 51, file "War Protest," UE Papers, AIS. "Poll Finds Drop in War Support," *NYT*, 12 April 1970, 30. Harlan Hahn, "Dove Sentiment among Blue-Collar Workers," *Dissent* (May-June, 1970): 10–15. Peter B. Levy, *The New Left and Labor in the 1960s* (Urbana: University of Illinois Press, 1994), 46–63. Tony Buba, interview by author, 15 January 2000, notes.

4. John Hoerr, *And The Wolf Finally Came: The Decline of the American Steel Industry* (Pittsburgh: University of Pittsburgh Press, 1988), 31–37. John Strohmeyer, *Crisis in Bethlehem: Big Steel's Struggle to Survive* (New York: Viking Penguin, 1987), 27–35.

5. Donald F. Barnett and Louis Schorsch, *Steel: Upheaval in a Basic Industry* (Cambridge: Ballinger Publishing Company, 1983), 47–49. Paul Tiffany, *The Decline of American Steel: How Management, Labor and Government Went Wrong* (New York: Oxford University Press, 1988), vii. William Scheuerman, *The Steel Crisis: The Economics and Politics of a Declining Industry* (New York: Praeger, 1986), 46. "Big Furlough Announced by U.S. Steel," *HM*, 15 June 1962, 1.

6. "Steel Operating Rate Dropped to 22-Year Low Last Week," *NYT*, 14 January 1961, 43. "Steel Production Rises Again to Reach Highest Level in Year," *NYT*, 23 May 1961, 55.

7. "Johnson's Statement and Steel Summary," *NYT*, 4 May 1965, 49. Robert Crandall, *The U.S. Steel Industry in Recurrent Crisis: Policy Options in a Competitive World* (Washington: The Brookings Institution, 1981), 113.

8. William Wylie, "Big Steel Wrestles with Low Profit," *PP*, 8 May 1973.

9. Strohmeyer, *Crisis in Bethlehem*, 78–82. Hoerr, *Wolf*, 290. David McDonald, *Union Man* (New York: E.P. Dutton and Co., 1969), 292–306. "Steel: a 72-Hour Drama with an All-Star Cast," *NYT*, 23 April 1962, 1, 23.

10. "8 Steel Companies and 2 Executives Are Indicted Here as Anti-Trust Violators," *NYT*, 8 April 1964, 68.

11. "Chamber, Union Hit Steel Deal," *HM*, 20 June 1962, 1. "300 Furloughs Due at Mill," *HM*, 28 June 1960, 1. "Planners Get Report on Navy Steel Buys," *HM*, 6 July 1962, 1.

12. Jawboning was the process by which politicians brought public pressure on corporations, hoping to force them to voluntarily change their economic behavior.

13. "Foreign Import Steel Levy Urged by USS President," *PP*, 8 February 1967, 2. "USW Backs Steel Import Fight," *PP*, 9 February 1967, 25.

14. "Steel Production Gained Last Week," *NYT*, 28 March 1961, 51.

15. "Imports of Steel Called Unfair," *NYT*, 21 August 1963, 11.

16. Strohmeyer, *Crisis in Bethlehem*, 74.

17. Franklin Whitehome, "8 Steel Concerns Fined $50,000 Each over Price Fixing," *NYT*, 24 July 1965, 1.

18. Edwin C. Dale Jr., "U.S. Curbs Buying of Steel to Fight Price Increase," *NYT*, 4 January 1966, 1. Dale, "U.S. Accepts Steel Compromise," *NYT*, 6 January 1966, 1.

19. Dale, "Johnson Assails Bethlehem for 5% Price Rise," *NYT*, 1 August 1968, 1. Dale, "Pentagon Limits Buying of Steel in Price Dispute," *NYT*, 2 August 1968, 1. Neil Sheehan, "Johnson Extends Curbs on Steel to All Agencies," *NYT*, 4 August 1968, 1. Robert A. Wright, "U.S. Steel Ends 7-Day Price War, Rises Cut in Half, Rest of Industry Accedes Back to 2.5%," *NYT*, 8 August 1968, 1.

20. "U.S. Steel Is Hit by Anti-Trust Suit," *PPG*, 17 June 1969, 1, 4. "Buy Power Monopoly by U.S. Steel Halted," *PPG*, 26 August 1969.

21. Eileen Shanahan, "Panel Says Steel Could Raise Pay and Hold Prices," *NYT*, 4 May 1965, 1.

22. "Congress Is Warned over Steel Imports," *NYT*, 4 June 1966, 41. "Johnson's Statement," *NYT*, 4 May 1965, 49.

23. Barnett and Schorsch, *Upheaval in a Basic Industry*, 47–49. Tiffany, *The Decline of American Steel*, vii. Scheuerman, *The Steel Crisis*, 46.

24. "Robert A. Wright, "US Buying Rules Irk Steel Trade," *NYT*, 20 February 1966, Section III, 1.

25. "Senate Approves 2 Vietnam Funds," *NYT*, 11 March 1966, 13.

26. "Congress Votes $2.9 Billion Aid," *NYT*, 8 October 1966, 14.

27. "More Steel Ordered for War in Vietnam," *NYT*, 6 July 1966, 63.

28. Mike Bilsic, interview by Bob Anderson, 25 April 1991, USWOHP, SIHC.

29. "Navy Gives Six Firms $92 Million Bomb Order," *WSJ*, 28 April 1966, 14. "Kaiser Jeep," *WSJ*, 28 June 1966, 8.

30. Thomas R. Howell, William A. Noellert, Jesse G. Kreier, and Alan William Wolff, *Steel and the State: Government Intervention and Steel's Structural Crisis* (Boulder: Westview Press, 1988), 56–250. William H. Chapman, "Competing Interests Create a Minefield," *Washington Post*, 16 October 1977, L–1.

31. "Breakthrough: Seven-Year Fight by USWA Results in U.S. Aid for Job Loss through Imports," *SL* (December 1969): 10–11. Patrick Boyle, "Senate Bill Outlaws Foreign Steel Use in Public Buildings," *PP*, 24 May 1967, 4.

32. Paul B. Beers, *Pennsylvania Politics Today and Yesterday: The Tolerable Accommodation* (University Park: Pennsylvania State University Press, 1980), 325.

33. Jim Card, interview by author, 31 May 1994, notes.

34. William T. Hogan, S.J., *Economic History of the Iron and Steel Industry in the United States*, Volume 4 (Lexington, MA: D.C. Heath and Company, 1971) 1669–71. Barnett and Schorsch, *Upheaval in a Basic Industry*, 59–60.

35. "Faster Furnaces: New Techniques Speed Steel's Open Hearths, Slashing Mills' Costs," *WSJ*, 14 August 1962, 1, 18.

36. Joseph Frazier Wall, *Andrew Carnegie* (1970; reprint, Pittsburgh: University of Pittsburgh Press, 1989), 321. Harvey O'Connor, *Steel-Dictator* (New York: John Day Company, 1935), 41.

37. Strohmeyer, *Crisis in Bethlehem*, 62.

38. Barnett and Schorsch, *Upheaval in a Basic Industry*, 51–60. John Barnett, "Steel Automation: New Equipment Likely to Bring Big Reduction in Mills' Working Force," *WSJ*, 16 September 1966, 1, 22.

39. "U.S. Steel Will Close Its Wire Plant at Donora," *WSJ*, 9 February 1966, 2. Kenneth Warren, *The American Steel Industry, 1850–1970: A Geographical Interpretation* (Pittsburgh: University of Pittsburgh Press, 1973), 285–91.

40. "The Rising Threat of Foreign Steel Imports," *USSN* (May-June 1965): 4–5. "U.S. Steel Will Close Its Wire Plant at Donora," *WSJ*, 2 February 1966, 2. "Phase Out at Donora Works," *USSN* (April 1966): 16.

41. "Jones and Laughlin Ends Nail Making," *NYT*, 3 March 1966, 45.

42. William Allan, "BOFs Slated for Edgar Thomson," *PP*, 19 December 1968, 1, 4. "Big Furlough Announced by U.S. Steel," *HM*, 16 June 1962, 1. Warren, *American Steel Industry*, 288.

43. BLS, *Technological Change and Manpower Trends in Five Industries* (Washington: GPO, 1975), Bulletin 1856, 27. "Steelyard Blues: New Structures in Steel," *NACLA Report on the Americas* 13 (January-February 1979): 11.

44. General Accounting Office, *Economics and Foreign Policy Effects of Voluntary Restraint Agreements on Textiles and Steel* (Washington: GPO, 1974), 16.

45. William Allan, "BOFs Slated for Edgar Thomson," *PP*, 19 December 1968, 1, 4. Rosensweet, "Future of U.S. Steel," *PPG*, 7 July 1967, Daily Magazine Section, 1.

46. Joel Sabadasz, "Duquesne Works: Overview History" (Homestead: unpublished mss., 1991), 24–27. J.M Stapleton and D.H. Regelin, "The New Giant in the Valley," *Blast Furnace and Steel Plant* (January 1959): 55–61. "USS Blast Furnace Has Third Bell," *Steel*, 10 June 1963, 104–06. "U.S. Steel Hails New Oxygen Facility," *Steel*, 25 May 1964, 47–48. "New Look inside Blast Furnaces," *BW*, 22 July 1961, 53–54. Nicholas Knezevich, "Duquesne's 'Dorothy' Dominates," *PP*, 29 May 1963.

47. "USWA Blames Automation in Shutdown," *PP*, 7 October 1965, in box 36, file 2, Research Department Papers, USWA Archives, PSU. Allan, "U.S. Steel Joins Two Mon Valley Plants," *PP*, 16 January 1969.

48. Hoerr, *Wol*, 440–42.

49. "J&L Raises Profit, Plans a Giant Expansion Move," *NYT*, 30 April 1965, 45.

50. "New Cold-Rolled Sheet Mill Will Nearly Double Irvin Capacity," *USSN* (October-November 1966): 14–15. *NYT*, 17 September 1966, 33. "Tooling up for Competition," *USSN* (April-May 1967): 5.

51. Alvin Rosensweet, "Future of U.S. Steel Tied to Pittsburgh, Edwin Gott States," *PPG*, 7 July 1967, Daily Magazine Section, 1. Lawrence Walsh, "$600 Million USS Air Cleanup Okd," *PP*, 11 November 1976, 1, 4.

52. William H. Wylie, "Dream Becomes Reality at Edgar Thomson Works," *PP*, 25 October 1970, Section 3, 8. William Allan, "$500 Million in USS Plans for Braddock," *PP*,

13 March 1968. "Significant Dates in E.T.'s History," *Braddock Free Press*, 25 August 1971, 1. Wylie, "Giant Irvin Works Expansion May Add 350 New Steel Jobs," *PP*, 24 November 1971, 1.

53. Barnett and Schorsch, *Upheaval in a Basic Industry*, 55.

54. Hogan, *Economic History*, 1670–71.

55. William E. Deibler, "Prober Reveals Legal Skip of One US Steel Tax," *PPG*, 28 March 1970. "Paid '67 State Tax, U.S. Steel Insists," *PP*, 26 April 1969, 1, 3.

56. Hogan, *Economic History*, 1660–69. Quotation from 1660. "Steelyard Blues," 15.

57. Markowitz, "US Steel—and Lots of Non-Steel," *PPG*, 21 December 1970, 31. Markowitz, "Big Steel Plans," *PPG*, 7 May 1968.

58. Hogan, *Economic History*, 1760–62.

59. "Editorial," *PPG*, 21 June 1975, 4.

60. Mike Davis, *City of Quartz: Excavating the Future in Los Angeles* (New York: Verso, 1990), 410–20.

61. David R. Francis, "To Save US Steel Jobs: A Huge Pay Cut?" *The Christian Science Monitor*, 7 August 1986, 23. Jim Balanoff and Greg Palast, "Big Steel's Scapegoat," *NYT*, 17 September 1982, 23.

62. U.S. Department of Labor, Bureau of Labor Statistics, *Employment and Earnings: United States, 1939–1972* (Washington: GPO, 1974), x.

63. Office of Technology Assessment, *U.S. Industrial Competitiveness: A Comparison of Steel, Electronics and Automobiles: Summary* (Washington: GPO, 1981), 23. Steel Panel Committee on Technology and International Economic and Trade Issues, *The Competitive Status of the U.S. Steel Industry: A Study of the Influences of Technology in Determining International Industrial Competitive Advantage* (Washington: National Academy Press, 1985), 58–59.

64. Crandall, *The U.S. Steel Industry in Recurrent Crisis*, 55.

65. See tables 7 and 8. Financial data for individual mills of U.S. Steel is difficult to obtain, but disclosures by manufacturers to the state of Pennsylvania in the 1960s and 1970s makes it possible to make crude assessments of the viability of the Duquesne and Homestead Works. This data, while imperfect, gives a general picture of the financial situation of individual mills.

66. Jack Markowitz, "Big Steel Plans: Diversify to Grow," *PPG*, 7 May 1968.

67. John P. Moody, "Harmony Is Chief Aim of Unique Steel Pact," *PPG*, 25 April 1973. Hoerr, *Wolf*, 109–33. Barnett and Schorsch, *Upheaval in a Basic Industry*, 69–70.

68. John Hughey, interview by author, 10 August 1993, tape recording. William Wylie, "Big Steel Wrestles with Low Profit," *PP*, 8 May 1973.

69. Strohmeyer, *Crisis in Bethlehem*, 102. Mark Reutter, *Sparrow's Point: Making Steel the Rise and Ruin of American Industrial Might* (New York: Summit Books, 1988), 415–19.

70. Barnett and Schorsch, *Upheaval in a Basic Industry*, 86–90.

71. Barnett and Schorsch, *Upheaval in a Basic Industry*, 48, 238–39.

72. Strohmeyer, *Crisis in Bethlehem*, 108–19. Barnett and Schorsch, *Upheaval in a Basic Industry*, 41.

73. Hoerr, *Wolf*, 115–33.

74. "Faster Furnaces: New Techniques Speed Steel's Open Hearths, Slashing Mills' Costs," *WSJ*, 14 August 1962, 1, 18. "Johnson's Statement," *NYT*, 4 May 1965, 49.

75. "Steel Unit's Work Rules Issue Report, Is Stalled," *WSJ*, 30 November 1960. William L. Smith, "Steel Unit Fails to Name Head," *American Metal Market*, 30 November 1960, box 6, file 13, Marvin Miller Papers, USWA Archives, PSU. I.W. Abel, interview by Alice Hoffman, 12 June 1979, USWA Archives.

76. USWA IEB, 8–9 August 1960, 140–42, box 46, file 29, USWA Archives, PSU.

77. McDonald, *Union Man*, 292.

78. Jack Metzgar, *Striking Steel: Solidarity Remembered* (Philadelphia: Temple University Press, 2000), 198–201, 102, 94–117. See also "Summary of Section 2-B Arbitration Cases," 27 August 1953, 1, box 16, file "Management Guides: Local Working Conditions," USX Duquesne Works Papers, AIS.

79. Joint Committee on Local Working Conditions, "Draft," n.d., box 6, file 13, "Local Working Conditions, 1960–1961," Marvin Miller Papers, USWA Archives, PSU.

80. Knezevich, "Clairton Hungry as Relief Lags," *PP*, 5 February 1961, 19. "Top Worry Is Job Security," *BW*, 27 January 1962, 121. See also "USWA Hits Job Lag at District Mills," *PP*, 3 December 1961, 1, 6.

81. "Complete Shutdown of OH 4, April 30: Co. Refuses to Move Men into OH 5," *The Sentinel* (April 1960): 1. "OH 4 Resumes Operation Again: 6 Furnaces to Be in Operation by May 5," *The Sentinel* (March-April 1963): 1.

82. "OH 4 Furnaces Relight Feb. 1: Plantwide Recalls Expected," *The Sentinel* (February 1959): 1.

83. "More Work for Fewer Workers?" *HM*, 30 June 1962.

84. Joseph G. Colangelo Jr., "The Second Battle of Homestead," *Reporter*, 18 July 1963, 29–31. Jack Smith, "Smith Explains Local's Finances," *The Sentinel* (January-February 1963): 1.

85. See tables 7 and 8.

86. Nick Mamula, "State of the Union: A Six Hour Day!" *Aliquippa Steelworker* (March 1960): 8.

87. "Report of the Joint Steel Industry-Union Contracting Out Review Commission," 7 November 1979, 54. Folder 10a., BVLHS, AIS.

88. "'Contracting Out' to Continue Here," *The Sentinel* (April 1961): 1–2.

89. Grievances A–60–269; A–60–279; A–60–280; A–60–281; A–60–287; A–60–288; A–60–289; A–60–291; A–60–292, box 17, Homestead Local 1397 Papers, Indiana University of Pennsylvania (IUP).

90. 3rd step minutes, 14 and 20 October 1970, 4, Box 27, Homestead Local 1397 Papers, IUP.

91. "Steelworkers Protest Outsiders Working at Homestead," *PPG*, 19 November 1970.

92. "Report of the Contracting Out Review Commission," 8–18, 41–43, 54.

93. "Promotional Sequence Agreement—Blast Furnace Department," 2 April 1953, box 3, file D-1 (b-2); Industrial Relations Department, "Maintenance Requirements for No. 6 Blast Furnace," 15 January 1963, box 3, file D-1 (b-2), USX Duquesne Works Papers, AIS. Mike Bilsic, interview by author, 19 March 1992, tape recording.

94. "In Steel, A Conflict of Priorities," *BW*, 27 January 1968, 64.

95. McDonald, *Union Man*, 324.

96. J.W.S. to E.B.S. "Confidential," box 16, file S-3 (d), USX Duquesne Works Papers, AIS.

97. USWA IEB, 14–15 February 1963, 124–35, box 48, file 3, USWA Archives, PSU.

98. "How Steel Jobs Are Dwindling," *BW*, 14 August 1965, 80–82. "Contract Improves Protection of Workers Continuous Service," *The Sentinel* (January 1960): 7. This language did allow workers to transfer their seniority from mill to mill. For instance, Mike Bonn transferred between the Fairless Works in Eastern Pennsylvania to the Irvin Works. Michael Bonn, interview by author, 3 September 1993, tape recording.

99. "Old Steel Valley Starts to Shake off Its Grime," *BW*, 22 January 1966, 90–92.

100. "U.S. Steel Will Idle McKeesport Facilities, Starting in November," *WSJ*, 23 September 1965, 21.

101. "When the Mill Closes," *SL* (December 1965): 18.

102. "Basic Steel Pensions," *SL* (January 1969): 4–5.

103. "Early Retirement," *SL* (August 1966): 10–11. "Old Steel Valley Starts to Shake Off Its Grime," *BW*, 22 January 1966, 92. Barnett, "Steel Automation," *WSJ*, 19 September 1966, 1, 22. Hoerr, *Wolf*, 330–32.

104. "Basic Steel Pensions," *SL* (January 1969): 4–5. Metzgar, *Striking Steel*, 198–201.

105. I.W. Abel, *Collective Bargaining: Labor Relations in Steel, Then and Now* (Pittsburgh: Carnegie Mellon University Press, 1976), 60.

106. Mark McColloch, "Modest but Adequate: The Standard of Living for Mon Valley Steelworkers in the Union Era," in *U.S. Labor in the Twentieth Century: Studies in Working-Class Struggles and Insurgency*, ed. John Hinshaw and Paul Le Blanc (Amherst, NY: Humanity Books, 2000), 255.

107. Judith Coburn, "Sadlowski Strides toward Bethlehem," box 2, file 17, Labor Notes Papers, AL&UA.

108. "USWA Urges Job Spread through Shorter Work Week," *SL* (April 1961): 10–11. "USWA Study Emphasizes Technological Change in Steel," *SL* (January 1962): 3. "32 Hours for 40 Pay," *The Sentinel* (March 1955): 4.

109. John D. Pomfret, "Steel and Union Reach Contract for 2-Year Peace," *NYT*, 21 June 1963, 1. McDonald, *Union Man*, 299–300.

110. "The Vanishing 40-Hour Week," *SL* (August 1963): 4.

111. John D. Pomfret, "McDonald Sees More Steel Jobs," *NYT*, 18 June 1963, 18. "McDonald Critical of New Steel Contract," *NYT*, 8 September 1965, 28. "Steel Men Thrive on Sabbaticals," *BW*, 26 November 1966, 166–68. Ruth Kish, interview by author, 2 March 1992, tape recording.

112. "Steel Holiday Plan Fails to Make Jobs," *NYT*, 24 March 1965, 20. "Travel, Hobbies, Projects Occupy 13-Weekers of Sparrows Point," *SL* (July 1964): 10.

113. Industrial Relations Department, "Problems and Proposals with New No. 6 Blast Furnace," 19 March 1962, box 3, file D-1 (b-2), USX Duquesne Works Papers, AIS.

114. "How Steel Jobs Are Dwindling," *BW*, 14 August 1965, 75. John McManigal Jr., interview by author, 7 June 1993 and 16 June 1993, tape recording.

115. "Arbitrator's Decision Extends Incentive Coverage to 65,000 USWA Members," *SL* (August 1969): 10.

116. John P. Moody, "USW Says US Steel Welshed on Offer," *PPG*, 18 February 1970, 1.

117. "Protecting the Paychecks of Victims of Technology," *BW*, 16 August 1969, 98. "Earnings Protection Plan," *SL* (September 1969): 9.

118. Grievance HH–67–52, box 18, Homestead Local 1397 Papers, IUP.

119. Carl Denne, interview by author, n.d., 1992, tape recording. Mike Bilsic, interview by author, 19 March 1992, tape recording. John McManigal Jr., interview by author, 7 June 1993 and 16 June 1993, tape recording. Hoerr, *Wolf*, 324–29.

120. Bob Masey, interview by Bob Anderson, 5 May 1991, USWOHP, SIHC. See also *Women of Steel* (November 1979): 5, no box, file "Women of Steel," Steffie Domike Papers, AIS.

121. McDonald, *Union Man*, 307. Charles E. Morgan, "Rank-and-File Satisfied with New Settlement," *PPG*, 3 April 1963.

122. McDonald, *Union Man*, 279–306.

123. David Jones, "Johnson Reports Accord on New Steel Contract after Suggesting Terms," *NYT*, 4 September 1965, 1. John D. Promfret, "President's Role in Steel Accord Called Decisive," *NYT*, 5 September 1965, 1.

124. "Job Training Set for Nation's Unemployed," *SL* (May 1962): 8–9. "USWA Hits Job Lag at District Mills," *PP*, 3 December 1961, 1, 6. "Impact of Technological Change and Automation on the Basic Steel Industry," n.d., 3–4, box 2, file "Automation, 1961–1963," Miller Papers, USWA Archives, PSU.

125. "Back on the Job," *SL* (July 1969): 9.

126. "When the Mill Closes," *SL* (December 1965): 18.

127. "Breakthrough: Seven-Year Fight by USWA Results in U.S. Aid for Job Loss through Imports," *SL* (December 1969): 10–11.

128. "Depreciation Aids Many Businesses," *NYT*, 20 February 1966, Section III, 1. "Johnson's Statement," *NYT*, 4 May 1965, 49.

129. Beers, *Pennsylvania Politics*, 9, 390.

130. See the first two sections of this chapter.

131. "Contract Talks in Steel Resume," *NYT*, 10 March 1965, 30. "Blough and McDonald Seeking Stricter Curb on Steel Dumping," *NYT*, 17 March 1964, 45.

132. Kevin Boyle, *The UAW and the Heyday of American Liberalism 1945–1968* (Ithaca: Cornell University Press, 1995), 185–256. Ronald L. Filippelli and Mark D. McColloch, *Cold War in the Working Class: The Rise and Decline of the United Electrical Workers* (Albany: State University of New York Press, 1995), 183.

133. "USW Agrees on Shutdown at Blaw-Knox," *PP*, 24 May 1967, 27.

134. George Swetnam and William Allan, "Alleged Macing at USS Faces Test," *PP*, 2 April 1972, 23. See also Strohmeyer, *Crisis in Bethlehem*, 46–52.

135. "Foreign Import Steel Levy Urged by USS President," *PP*, 8 February 1967, 2. Roger M. Blough, *The Washington Embrace of Business* (Pittsburgh: Carnegie Mellon University Press, 1975), passim. See also Howell, Noellert, Kreier, and Wolff, *Steel and the State*. Agis Salpukas, "Steel Plan Gains Guarded Approval," *NYT*, 7 December 1976, 11.

136. Abel, *Then and Now*, 39–40.

137. Boyle, *Heyday*, 185–256. Fillipelli and McColloch, *Cold War*, 172.

138. Sherley Uhl, "Communists Go Far Here—Underground," *PP*, 19 November 1961.

139. Richard Fontana, "Communist Party Hopeful Seeks City Council Seat," *PP*, 31 May 1973.

140. Eugene V. Dennett, *Agitprop: The Life of an American Working-Class Radical* (Albany: State University of New York Press, 1990), 153–97.

141. Ingrid Jewel, "USWA Seeks U.S. Aid on McKeesport," *PPG*, 1 October 1965. "Displaced Steel Help Discussed," *PPG*, 8 October 1965, 6.

142. "To the Honorable Congressman and Senators," 25 September 1965, box 2, file "Automation, 1964–1965," Miller Papers, USWA Archives, PSU.

143. Dana Adams Schmidt, "Commons Votes Labor Bill for Nationalizing of Steel," *NYT*, 26 July 1966, 1.

144. M.G. Taylor, *Insuring National Health Care: The Canadian Experience* (Chapel Hill: University of North Carolina Press, 1990), 7. Elaine Bernard, "Why Unions Matter," in *U.S. Labor in the Twentieth Century: Studies in Insurgency and Struggle*, ed. John Hinshaw and Paul LeBlanc (Amherst, NY: Humanity Press, 2000), 455. Michael Bliss, "Too Healthy for Our Own Good," *Canadian Business* (July 1993): 16.

145. "USW Office Workers Local in Votes, Factions Cause Uproar," *HM*, 22 November 1960, 1. "Local President Reaffirms 'Interference,' Disputes Reply," *HM*, 30 November 1960, 1.

146. USWA IEB, 11–12 July 1962, 46, box 47, file 13, USWA Archives, PSU.

147. Mike Bilsic, interview by author, 19 March 1992, tape recording. Ray Henderson, interview by author, 6 August 1993, tape recording. Ben Fisher, interview by author, 10 September 1992, notes. Larry Evans, interview by author, 25 July 1992, notes. Nyden, *Steelworkers Rank-And-File*, 4–5. Kornblum, *Blue Collar Community*, 110–11.

148. Patrick J. McGeeve, *Reverend Charles Owen Rice: Apostle of Contradiction* (Pittsburgh: Duquesne University Press, 1989), 92–135, 191–93.

149. "Bresko Defends Administration," *HM*, 8 July 1960, 1.

150. Tom Caroll, "Monongahela Valley Ethnographic Case Study Project" (Pittsburgh: Historical Society of Western Pennsylvania, 1992), 25.

151. John McManigal Jr., interview by author, 7 June 1993 and 16 June 1993, tape recording.

152. Tony Buba, "Foreword," in *Overtime: Punchin' Out with the Mill Hunk Herald, 1979–1989* (Pittsburgh: Piece of the Hunk Press, 1990), ii.

153. "Steel Signs a No-Strike Pledge," *NYT*, 20 September 1960, 1, 24. "Steel Insurgents Suffer Setback," 23 September 1960, 7.

154. I.W. Abel, interview by Alice Hoffman, 12 June 1979, 22, USWA Archives, PSU.

155. USWA IEB, 28–29 April 1960, 119–22, box 46, file 28, USWA Archives, PSU.

156. USWA IEB, 6 January 1961, 156–215, box 47, file 3, USWA Archives, PSU.

157. "McDonald Bids Union Fight Rebel Groups," *NYT*, 19 March 1960, 10.

158. Peter Bradley, "Locals Here Up to Ears in Debt to USW," *PP*, 18 September 1960. "Opponents of McDonald Win in McKeesport," *HM*, 27 June 1960, 1. "Ousted Local 1408 Head Fights for Reinstatement," *HM*, 10 September 1960, 1.

159. USWA IEB, 13–15 September 1960, 3–21, quotations on 11, 21–22, box 47, file 1, USWA Archives, PSU.

160. Charles H. Allard, "Biega Gets Mamula's USW Post," *PPG*, 22 July 1961. Allard, "Drive Opens to Regain Job for Mamula," *PPG*, 27 July 1961. "Mamula Makes New Legal Try in Union Fight," *HM*, 16 June 1960, 1. "Veteran Aliquippa J&L Steelworker May Gain $12,000 Local President's Chair," *PC*, 14 October 1961, 2.

161. "1397 May Get Power Struggle," *HM*, 18 May 1960, 1. "Basic New Local 1397 President," *HM*, 2 July 1960, 1. "Smith Elected President of USW Local 1397," *HM*, 25 June 1962, 1.

162. "Candidates for Irvin USW Continue Blasts," *HM*, 13 June 1960, 1. "Rarick Leads in Election," *HM*, 15 June 1960, 1. "'Rebels' Claim Leads in Most 2227 Races," *HM*, 16 June 1960, 1. "Barron Elected New President of Local 2227," *HM*, 15 June 1962, 1.

163. Michael J. Zahorsky, interview by Jack Spiese, 27 July 1967, USWA Archives, PSU.

164. John Herling, *Right to Challenge: People and Power in the Steelworkers' Union* (New York: Harper and Row, 1972), 189, 177–236. I.W. Abel, interview by Alice Hoffman, 12 June 1979, USWA Archives. Campaign literature can be found in box 30, file "USWA Locals," USX Duquesne Works Papers, AIS.

165. Damon Stetson, "Both Sides Charge Irregularities in Steel Voting," *NYT*, 12 February 1965, 35. David McDonald, interview by Helmut J. Golantz and Alice Hoffman, 20 February 1970, 33–43, PSU.

166. USWA IEB, 16–17 November 1964, 113, box 48, file 15, USWA Archives, PSU.

167. Charles Allard, "Four Now in Race," *PPG*, 30 October 1964. Allard, "Rarick Enters Contest for USW Director," *PPG*, 28 October 1964. "Court Bans McDonald Hand-bills," *PPG*, 5 February 1965, 8. "Election Eve Hearing Set in USW Row," *PP*, 2 February 1965. "Hearing Delayed on USWA Handbills," *PP*, 8 February 1965, 2. "Another Hilbert Performance," n.d. but 1965; "Official Returns," 30 April 1965; both in box 30, file "USWA Locals," USX Duquesne Works Papers, AIS.

168. "Odorcich Wins USWA Election in District 15," *PPG*, 4 April 1969, Section 2, 13. John P. Moody, "USWA Voting Probe Starts in Homestead," *PPG*, 11 March 1969, 19.

169. Hoerr, *Wolf*, 331. Verlich, "Odorcich Calls Choice of Hilbert 'Big Steal,'" *PP*, 1 May 1969, 2.

170. Verlich, "Odorcich Calls Choice of Hilbert 'Big Steal,'" *PP*, 1 May 1969, 2.

171. John P. Moody, "USWA Members Fight District 15 Election Ruling," *PPG*, 3 May 1969, 1, 4.

172. Hoerr, *Wolf*, 331–32. Moody, "Five Report Irregularities in USW Election," *PPG*, 25 June 1973. Lynd, "Two Steel Contracts," 61.

173. "Report and Recommendations of International Commission," and various, box 35, files 2–19, USWA IEB Papers, USWA Archives, PSU.

174. "Donald Rarick, Steel Union Rebel, Dies," *PPG*, 18 September 1968. Rosensweet, "Narick to Run against Abel to Head USW," *PPG*, 18 September 1968. "Blacks Back USW Incumbents," *PP*, n.d., copy in author's possession.

175. "Negroes Push to Rise Higher in Unionism," *BW*, 29 June 1968, 125.

176. International Tellers, USWA, "Report on International Election," 18 April 1969, box 5, file 4, Sadlowski Papers, AL&UA. John P. Moody, "Abel Trails Narick in Area Vote," *PPG*, 14 February 1969, Section 2, 17. "Odorcich Wins USWA Election in District 15," *PPG*, 4 April 1969, Section 2, 13. "USWA Vote: Faint Praise for Abel," *BW*, 22 February 1969, 105. Verlich, "Abel, Narick Key on Progress in USWA Battle," *PP*, 2 February 1969, Section 2, 10. Emil Narick, interview by author, 28 June 1993, tape recording. "Beware of New Divide-and-Conquer Tactics," *SL* (December 1969): 15. Serrin, *Homestead*, 316.

177. William B. Kane to John McManigal, 10 March 1969, in author's possession.

178. Michael K. Drapkin, "Steelworkers Become Much Sought After as Mills Expect Continued Strong Activity," *WSJ*, 21 May 1969, 5.

179. "Rash of Local Strikes Plagues Steel Concerns," *WSJ*, 2 August 1968, 3. Ed Verlich, "District Becoming Delirious from Too Many Strikes," *PP*, 2 June 1971. Drapkin, "Steelworkers Become Much Sought After," *WSJ*, 21 May 1969, 5. Frank Fernback to Otis Brubaker, 15 July 1970, box 67, file 1, Research Department Papers, USWA Archives, PSU.

180. John V. Conti, "Talking Tough: Militant New Leaders of Steel Union Locals Challenge Old Policies," *WSJ*, 2 March 1971, 1, 13.

181. "Report of Disciplinary Action," 1958, box 16, file S-1 (d), USX Duquesne Works Papers, AIS.

182. 3rd step minutes, 8 April 1970, 1; 11 and 12 March 1970, 2, box 27, Homestead Local 1397 Papers, IUP.

183. "Confidential: Summer Work-In," n.d., probably 1968–69, box 1, William Gaughan Papers, AIS. William Kornblum, *Blue Collar Community* (Chicago: University of Chicago, 1974), 236.

184. Conti, "Talking Tough," *WSJ*, 2 March 1971, 1, 13. John P. Moody, "Harmony is Chief Aim of Unique Steel Pact," *PPG*, 25 April 1973.

185. Bennett Kremen, "No Pride in This Dust: Young Workers in the Steel Mills," in *The World of the Blue-Collar Worker*, ed. Irving Howe (New York: Quadrangle Books, 1972), 11–22.

186. Hoerr, *Wolf*, 325. Carl Denne, interview by author, n.d., 1992, tape recording.

187. Anonymous, conversation with author, 12 February 1994, notes.

188. Denise Winebrenner, interview by Bob Anderson, 23 April 1991, transcript, USWOHP, SIHC, Homestead PA. SIHC supported the research and transcription of the USWOHP and has graciously allowed me access to these materials.

189. John McManigal Jr., interview by author, 7 June 1993 and 16 June 1993, tape recording.

190. Ginny Hildebrant, interview by author, 18 August 1992, tape recording. Staughton Lynd, "Two Steel Contracts," *Radical America* 5 (September-October 1971): 58–59. See also Jerry Manning, interview by Sara Sturdevant, ES 92-SS4-C, SIHC.

191. Lynd, "Two Steel Contracts," *Radical America* 5 (September-October 1971): 58–59. Bob Masey, interview by author, 9 June 1992, tape recording.

192. Lynd, "Two Steel Contracts," *Radical America* 5 (September-October 1971): 70.

193. Rusticus, "The Sadlowski Campaign," *Radical America* 11 (January-February 1977): 75–76. Alan Derickson, *Black Lung: Anatomy of a Public Health Disaster* (Ithaca: Cornell University Press, 1998).

194. Dan Georgakas and Marvin Surkin, *Detroit, I Do Mind Dying: A Study in Urban Revolution* (Boston: South End Press, 1998). James A. Geschwender, *Class, Race and Worker Insurgency: The League of Revolutionary Black Workers* (Cambridge: Cambridge University Press, 1978). "Great Lakes Steel: Summation of History and Experience," n.d., probably 1973, box 13, file 12, DRUM Papers, AL&UA. "Flint Tribune," n.d., probably 1976, box 16, file 2, DRUM Papers, AL&UA. "J&L RAF," 27 March 1975, box 16, file, DRUM Papers, AL&UA.

195. "Report from Pittsburgh," October 1972, box 15, file 18, DRUM Papers, AL&UA.

196. William Kornblum, "Insurgency in the Steel Union," *Dissent* (Summer 1975): 220. Kornblum, "The Challenge of the Rank and File," *Nation*, 26 January 1974, 114–16.

197. Judith Coburn, "Sadlowski Strides toward Bethlehem," box 2, file 17, Labor Notes Papers, AL&UA.

198. Philip Nyden, "Sadlowski and the New Insurgency," *Nation*, 18 September 1976, 241–44. Rusticus, "The Sadlowski Campaign," *Radical America* 11 (January-February 1977): 75–76.

199. "Sadlowski Contest," in box 2, file 18, Labor Notes Papers, AL&UA.

200. Ralph Nader, "Two Labor Views of Steel Price Hikes," *NYT*, 26 December 1976, box 9, file 22, John Herling Papers, AL&UA.

201. "Insurgent in Union Accused by Meany," *NYT*, 11 January 1977. Joseph L. Rauh Jr., "Outsiders' Assistance in Union Elections," *NYT*, 17 January 1977, 25. Lee Dembart, "Steel Union Leadership Fight," *NYT*, 17 January 1977, 36.

202. Tony Novolsel, interview by Bob Anderson, 29 May 1991, transcript, USWOHP, SIHC. "Pittsburgh Report to the National Steel Fraction," 6 December 1976, box 2, file 18, Labor Notes Papers, AL&UA.

203. "McBride Seems Victor," *NYT*, 10 February 1977, 1. "Sadlowski Charges Fraud," *NYT*, 13 February 1977, 21.

204. Steffie Domike, interview by Bob Anderson, 24 June 1991, USWOHP, SIHC. "Pittsburgh Report to the National Steel Fraction," 6 December 1976; "The Sadlowski Campaign," n.d.; Joel G., "Impressions and Observations," n.d., box 2, file 18, Labor Notes Papers, AL&UA. Robert Anderson, interview by Bob Mast, 1993, USWOHP, SIHC.

205. "Sadlowski Contest," in box 2, folder 18, Labor Notes Papers, AL&UA.

206. *Labor Today* (Sadlowski's campaign newspaper), Labor Notes Papers, box 2, file 17, AL&UA. William Kornblum, "Why the Insurgents Lost in Steel," *Dissent* (Spring 1977): 1935–38.

207. Eileen Shanahn, "Panel Says Steel Could Raise Pay and Hold Prices," *NYT*, 4 May 1965, 1.

208. See table 2.

209. William McCloskey, "Unemployment Nothing New for J&L Steelworkers," *PPG*, 9 June 1975, 1.

210. Richard L. Rowan, *The Negro in the Steel Industry* (Philadelphia: University of Pennsylvania Press), 84–85.

211. Oliver Montgomery, interview by Henderson and Buba, summer 1992, tape recording. "Conference with Weirton Steel Company Employees in Re: Complaint," 2 August 1962, box 42, file "Labor and Industry Committee, 1962," NAACP Papers, AIS.

212. "Number of Employees by Ethnic Group," 5 October 1973, Affirmation Action Compliance Program, National Tube Plant, DW 82, USX National Tube Works Papers, AIS.

213. Affirmation Action Compliance Program, Exhibit 3, 30 June 1970, 1, DW 82, USX National Tube Works Papers, AIS. "The Negro in U.S. Steel," *USSN* December 1966): 3. Otis Bryant; John King; Donald Woodington; Thomas Walker; interview by Henderson and Buba, summer 1992, tape recording.

214. *USA v. USS et al.*, Civil Action 70:906, appendix, from United States District Court, Northern District of Alabama, found in Ruck, "Origins," table 11.

215. Tommy Walker; Otis Bryant, interview by Henderson and Buba, summer 1992, tape recording. See also *Rodgers and Turner v. U.S. Steel*, U.S. Court of Appeals, 3rd Circuit, Joint Appendix v-3, 775a-6a. From Ruck, "Origins," 94.

216. James Sharpley and Jesse Pierce, interview by Henderson and Buba, summer 1992, tape recording. Johnstown CRC, memo, 9 September 1969, box 24, file 23, "District 15, 1970, Civil Rights," CRC, USWA Archives, PSU.

217. Statement by Alfred B. Macon, 14 February 1980, in author's possession. Courtesy of Denise Weinbrenner Edwards.

218. Otis Bryant; Edmond Holmes, interview by Henderson and Buba, summer 1992, tape recording.

219. Frank Moorefield; Donald Woodington, interview by Henderson and Buba, summer 1992, tape recording.

220. Francis Shane to CRC, 2 October 1961, box 6, file 9, "CRC, 1961," Hague Papers, USWA Archives, PSU.

221. Robert Dietsch, "Steel Urged to Increase Negro Staffs," *PPG*, 22 May 1968, box 7, file 20, "Newspaper Clippings, January-August, 1968," CRD, USWA Archives, PSU.

222. Notes by E.L. Clifford, 11 May 1967, box 16, file 28, CRD Papers, USWA Archives, PSU.

223. EEO Report, 30 June 1971, 1–11, box 179, USX National Tube Works Papers, AIS.

224. Dickerson, *Out of the Crucible*, 234.

225. Ruck, "Origins," 97–98.

226. John Hughey and Jesse Larrington, interview by Henderson and Buba, summer 1992, tape recording.

227. Dietsch, "Steel Urged to Increase Negro Staffs," *PPG*, 22 May 1968, box 7, file 20, CRD Papers, USWA Archives, PSU. "No Black Executives at ALCOA, Dravo, WABCO," *PC*, 16 August 1969, 1. "No Black Managers: Mellon Given 10 Days to Respond to UNPC Demands," *PC*, 23 August 1969, 1.

228. Binder "Equal Employment Opportunity Report, Pay Ending 6–20–70," 1–3, box 179, EEOC-1970, USX National Tube Works Papers, AIS. Dickerson, *Out of the Crucible*, 241.

229. "The Negro in U.S. Steel," *USSN* (December 1966): 4.

230. "Negroes Zero in on Steel Industry," *BW*, 10 December 1966, 156.

231. EEO Report, 30 June 1971, 1–11, box 179, USX National Tube Works Papers, AIS. Henderson Thomas, interview by Henderson and Buba, summer 1992, tape recording. United Steelworkers of America, *Proceedings of the 16th Constitutional Convention of the United Steel Workers of America* (Pittsburgh: United Steelworkers of America, 1972), 307.

232. Dickerson, *Out of the Crucible*, 219. Press release, 27 November 1961, box 6, file 9, "Civil Rights Committee, 1961," Hague Papers, USWA Archives, PSU.

233. "Conference with Weirton Steel Company Employees in Re: Complaint," 2 August 1962, box 42, file "Labor and Industry Committee, 1962," NAACP Papers, AIS.

234. Robert R. Hobson to Charlie Hampton, 9 January 1969, box 21, file 17, CRD Papers, USWA Archives, PSU.

235. "Joint Statement on 'Plan for Progress,'" 24 June 1964, box 6, file 11, Hague Papers, USWA Archives, PSU.

236. "First Meeting of the Joint Committee on Civil Rights," 18 December 1968, box 18, file 32, CRD Papers, USWA Archives, PSU.

237. Ben Fischer to Bernard Kleiman, 16 May 1969, box 18, file 32, CRD Papers, USWA Archives, PSU.

238. United Steelworkers of America, *Proceedings*, 1972, 307.

239. Carl Dickerson, in United Steelworkers of America, *Proceedings of the 13th Constitutional Convention of the United Steel Workers of America* (Pittsburgh: United Steelworkers of America, 1966), 343.

240. Phyl Garland, "From the Soil to the Shop: USWA Has Come Far but Can Go Further," *PC*, 18 June 1960, Magazine Section, 1.

241. Keith, "Negro Steelworkers in Local Elections," *PC*, 18 June 1960, 3.

242. Keith, "May Challenge McDonald With Negro Candidate: USWA Heads Feel 'Bedbugs' Bite," *PC*, 2 July 1960, 2. "Basic New Local 1397 President," *HM*, 2 July 1960, 1.

243. Garland, "From the Soil to the Shop," *PC*, 18 June 1960, Magazine Section, 1. Keith, "May Challenge McDonald with Negro Candidate," *PC*, 2 July 1960, 2. John Hughey, interview by author, August 5, 1993, tape recording.

244. Keith, "Negro Steelworkers Show Unrest as Big Convention Opens," *PC*, 24 September 1960, Section 2, 3.

245. "Negro Labor's Giant Step," *PC*, 11 June 1960, 13. Kim Moody, *An Injury to All: The Decline of American Unionism* (New York: Verso Press, 1988), 74–75.

246. Keith, "May Challenge McDonald with Negro Candidate," *PC*, 2 July 1960. Keith, "'Recognition Denied Capable Negro Steelworkers,' Rarick," *PC*, 3 September 1960, Section 2, 3.

247. Harold Keith, interview by author, 15 July 1996, tape recording.

248. Ad Hoc Convention Program, 29 July 1967, box 12, file 54, CRD Papers, USWA Archives, PSU. Francis Shane to David McDonald, 12 November 1964, box 6, file 12 "Civil Rights Committee, 1965," Hague Papers, USWA Archives, PSU.

249. John King; Thomas Walker, interview by Henderson and Buba, summer 1992, tape recording.

250. James Sharpley and Jesse Pierce, interview by Henderson and Buba, summer 1992, tape recording.

251. "Twenty-first meeting of the joint committee on civil rights," 12 August 1970, box 25, file 24, CRD Papers, USWA Archives, PSU.

252. Alex Powell, interview by Henderson and Buba, summer 1992, tape recording.

253. Booker Kidd; Donald Woodington; Charles Lee Jr., interview by Henderson and Buba, summer 1992, tape recording.

254. Edmond Holmes; Booker Kidd; Donald Woodington, interview by Henderson and Buba, summer 1992, tape recording.

255. John Hughey and Jesse Pierce, interview by Henderson and Buba, summer 1992, tape recording.

256. USWA IEB, 4–5 October 1961, 143–66, quotation on 143, 162, 165–66, box 47, file 7, USWA Archives, PSU.

257. USWA IEB, 4–5 October 1961, 143–66, box 47, file 7, USWA Archives, PSU.

258. George E. Barbour, "Did Top Brass 'Gag' Boyd Wilson?" *PC*, 27 February 1960, 3. Barbour, "District 15, USWA, Protested Wilson's Speech in Duquesne," 5 March 1960, 8.

C.B. Clark, "Democratic Campaign Chairman Ignored Warnings of Clairton Negro's Anger," *PC*, 18 November 1961, 3.

259. Trezzvant W. Anderson, "Georgia Steelworkers Say Union Is 'Selling Out,'" *PC*, 23 July 1960, 7. "Wilson's Lips Tight on Atlanta Situation," *PC*, 23 July 1960, 9.

260. Dickerson, *Out of the Crucible*, 219–20. Gwendolyn Young, interview by Henderson and Buba, summer 1992, tape recording. Garland, "From the Soil to the Shop," *PC*, 18 June 1960, Magazine Section, 1.

261. John Hughey, interview by author, 5 August 1993, tape recording.

262. Msng. Charles Owen Rice, "Incident," *The Thrust*, 25 August 1968. Harold Keith, interview by author, 15 July 1996, tape recording. Frank Bolden, interview by author, 7 August 1993.

263. "Labor Head Joins Randolph Tribute," *PC*, 12 March 1960, 8. "Distinguished Guests Awarded Plaques: Over 18,000 Attend Freedom Jubilee Rally," *PC*, 25 June 1960, 3. "McCoy Heads Labor Division in NAACP Drive," *PC*, 24 June 1961, Section 2, 3.

264. Harold Keith, interview by author, 15 July 1996, tape recording. Frank Bolden, interview by author, 7 August 1993.

265. Keith, "'Will Not Quit NAACP,' Declares USWA's McCoy," *PC*, 22 June 1963, 1, 4.

266. Garland, "Is 'Squeeze Play' Aimed at McCoy?" *PC*, 20 July 1963, 1.

267. John Thornton, Joseph Neal, and other Staff Representatives to David McDonald, 14 September 1960, box 6, file 8, Hague Papers, USWA Archives, PSU.

268. "New Frontiers for Negro Steelworkers Opening Up?" 21 May 1961, *The Worker*, Midwest Edition, 1.

269. Minutes of the CRC, 9 December 1964, box 6, file 11, Hague Papers, USWA Archives, PSU. Francis Shane to members of the CRC, 17 April 1961, box 6, file 9, Hague Papers, USWA Archives, PSU.

270. USWA, *Proceedings of the 10th Constitutional Convention of the United Steel Workers of America* (Pittsburgh: United Steelworkers of America, 1960), 350. Minutes of CRC meeting, 18 September 1964, box 6, file 11, Hague Papers, USWA Archives, PSU.

271. Minutes of CRC meeting, 18 September 1964, box 6, file 11, Hague Papers, USWA Archives, PSU.

272. Joseph G. Colangelo Jr., "The Second Battle of Homestead," *Reporter*, 18 July 1963, 29–31. Jack Smith, "Smith Explains Local's Finances," *The Sentinel* (January-February 1963): 1.

273. "Labor Pool Payroll Check," 3 November 1962, box 16, file S-3 (d), USX Duquesne Works Papers, AIS.

274. USDC Northern District of Alabama in Civil Action No. 66–343, *USA v. USS et al.* (subaction of 70–906). Plaintiffs' Pre-Trial brief, 9–11, in Ruck, "Origins," 80. Keith, "USWA Trio Maps New Answers to Old Problems," *PC*, 15 June 1963, 9. Notes by Eugene Arrington, 3 October 1963, box 2, Miller Papers, USWA Archives, PSU. Grievance A-64-39, 1 May 1964, box 17, Homestead Local 1397 Papers, IUP.

275. *Rodgers and Turner v. U.S. Steel*, U.S. Court of Appeals, 3rd Circuit, Joint Appendix v-3, 789a, from Ruck, "Origins," 94.

276. EEO Report, box 82, "Affirmative Action Compliance Program" Binder, USX National Tube Papers, AIS.

277. "Discrimination Banned in New Steel Contracts," *SL* (July 1962): 13. "USWA Signs Non-Discrimination Pact with 11 Steel Firms," *SL* (July 1964): 3.

278. Bill McClinton, "Civil Rights Groups Wage Controversial But Effective Fight," *Pittsburgh Catholic*, 28 March 1963, box 2, file "Civil Rights, Frank Shane, 1961–1965," Miller Papers, USWA Archives, PSU.

279. Minutes of CRC, 3 April 1964, box 6, file 11, Hague Papers, USWA Archives, PSU.

280. "Negroes Push to Rise Higher in Unionism," *BW*, 29 June 1968, 125–26. "Labor's Labyrinth: The Unskilled Negro," *SL* (October 1967): 11.

281. Eugene Arrington, 3 October 1963, box 2, file "Civil Rights—Frank Shane, 1961–1965," Miller Papers, USWA Archives, PSU. Woody L. Tayor, "Negroes Lay Bias to Homestead Union," *PC*, 9 November 1963, 5.

282. 3rd step minutes, 12 March 1969, 2, box 27, Homestead Local 1397 Papers, IUP.

283. "U.S. Steel Disclaims Bias," *PC*, 12 September 1970, 1.

284. John G. Deedy Jr., "Civil Rights and the Steelworkers," *America*, 6 May 1961, 249–51. Frank Bolden, interview by author, 7 August 1993, tape recording.

285. "USWA Lobbying Conference Pushes Civil Rights Goal," *SL* (January 1964): 8. "McDonald Nails Down Lies about Civil Rights Bill in Message Sent to All Steelworker Local Unions," *SL* (June 1964): 2. Press Release, 26 October 1964, box 6, file 11, Hague Papers, USWA Archives, PSU. "U.S. Steelworkers' Abel Adds Emphasis on Civil Rights," *PC*, 4 February 1967, 24.

286. "Discrimination Charged against U.S. Steel Company," *PC*, 29 August 1970, 8. Dwight Casimere, "White Supremacy in Steel Unions," *Muhammed Speaks*, 27 June 1969, 2. Jimmie Rodgers, conversation with author, 8 March 1992, notes. Ruck, "Origins," 93.

287. Dickerson, *Out of the Crucible*, 228. Philip W. Nyden, "Evolution of Black Political Influence in American Trade Unions," *Journal of Black Studies* 13 (June 1983): 389.

288. "The New USWA Executive Board," *SL* (June 1965): 24. Edward Verlich, "New USWA Regime Rings Up 'Firsts,'" *PP*, 30 May 1965, 1, 8.

289. John Hoerr, "Internal Disputes Stirring USWA," *Pittsburgh Point*, 6 July 1967, 1, 4. "U.S. Steelworkers' Abel Adds Emphasis on Civil Rights," *PC*, 4 February 1967, 24.

290. Keith, "USWA Trio," *PC*, 15 June 1963, 9. "U.S. Steelworkers' Abel Adds Emphasis on Civil Rights," *PC*, 4 February 1967, 24.

291. Hoerr, "Internal Disputes Stirring USWA," *Pittsburgh Point*, 6 July 1967, 1, 4. Sherley Uhl, "Ousted Aide Charges Bias in USWA Job," *PP*, 24 May 1967, 38.

292. Hoerr, "Internal Disputes Stirring USWA," *Pittsburgh Point*, 6 July 1967, 1, 4.

293. "Francis C. Shane Retires from Steelworkers' Staff Post," *PC*, 1 October 1966, 8B.

294. "Pennsylvania Steelworkers Join in Bid to Strengthen Rights Laws," *SL* (January 1966): 5. Marguerite I. Hofer to Joseph Molony, 16 June 1967, box 15, file 5, CRD Papers, USWA Archives, PSU. "Pittsburgh Steelworkers Urge Stronger Rights Code in Housing," *SL* (March 1967): 17. Fred Forsythe, 7 February 1967, box 14, file 14, CRD Papers, USWA Archives, PSU.

295. Byrant Artis, "Integration Plan Falls Short, City Told," *PP*, 8 February 1967, 46.

296. "Wipe Out 'Tokenism,'" District 16 Is Urged," *SL* (December 1966): 17.

297. Moody, *An Injury to All*, 75. "U.S. Steelworkers' Abel Adds Emphasis on Civil Rights," *PC*, 4 February 1967, 24. "Honor USWA President at Civil Rights Dinner," *SL* (November 1965): 7.

298. John Hughey, interview by author, 5 August 1993, tape recording. Frank Bolden, interview by author, 7 August 1993. Ray Henderson, interview by author, 6 August 1993, tape recording.

299. Nyden, "Evolution," 379–98. Joseph Hill, "Steel: Changing Workplace," *Dissent* (winter 1972): 41.

300. John Hughey and Jesse Pierce, interview by Henderson and Buba, summer 1992, tape recording.

301. W.V. Deutermann Jr., "Steelworkers Debate Black Representation," *Monthly Labor Review* 91 (November 1968): 16–17. "Discussion," n.d., box 6, file 12, Hague Papers, USWA Archives, PSU. Francis Shane to David McDonald, 12 November 1964, box 6, file 12, Hague Papers, USWA Archives, PSU. USWA, *Proceedings of the 3rd Constitutional Convention of the United Steel Workers of America* (Pittsburgh: United Steelworkers of America, 1946), 217–19.

302. Dickerson, *Out of the Crucible*, 235.

303. "McBride Publicity," n.d., no box, file "Sadlowski Campaign," Steffie Domike Papers, AIS. Donald Woodington, interview by Henderson and Buba, summer 1992, tape recording.

304. "Steel Workers Face Tough Problems," n.d., no box, file, "Sadlowski Publicity," Steffie Domike Papers, AIS.

305. August Meier and Elliot Rudwick, *Black Detroit and the Rise of the UAW* (New York: Oxford University Press, 1979), 221.

306. Heather Ann Thompson, "Auto Workers, Dissent, and the UAW: Detroit and Lordstown," in *Autowork*, ed. Robert Asher and Ronald Edsforth (Albany: State University of New York Press, 1995), 181–208.

307. M. Peter Jackson to Alex Fuller, 7 March 1966, box 12, file 24, CRD Papers, USWA Archives, PSU. "Wipe Out 'Tokenism,'" District 16 Is Urged," *SL* (December 1966): 17. Memo, 4 August 1967, box 12, file 54 CRD Papers, USWA Archives, PSU. "Negroes Push to Rise Higher in Unionism," *BW*, 29 June 1968, 125–26.

308. Robert E. Nelson to Joseph Sabo, 10 December 1965; Robert E. Nelson to Alex Fuller, 7 March 1966; both in box 12, file 24, CRD Papers, USWA Archives, PSU.

309. USWA, *Proceedings of the 16th Constitutional Convention of the United Steel Workers of America* (Pittsburgh: United Steelworkers of America, 1972), 307.

310. Newspaper clipping, n.d., attached to Dorothy Kelly to Alex Fuller, 4 March 1970, box 23, file 23, CRD Papers, USWA Archives, PSU. Alex Fuller to Dorothy Kelly, 9 March 1970, box 23, file 23, CRD Papers, USWA Archives, PSU.

311. "Negroes Push to Rise Higher in Unionism," *BW*, 29 June 1968, 125–26.

312. Judith Stein, *Running Steel, Running America: Race, Economic Policy and the Decline of Liberalism* (Chapel Hill: University of North Carolina Press, 1998), 337.

313. John Hughey, interview by author, 5 August 1993, tape recording.

314. Philip H. Scheiding to Bernard Kleiman, 22 December 1966, box 14, file 2, CRD Papers, USWA Archives, PSU. Ray Henderson, interview by author, 6 August 1993,

tape recording. See also Milton Mcintyre, interview by Henderson and Buba, summer 1992, tape recording.

315. Ruck, "Origins," 84, 93. Robert E. Nelson to Alex Fuller, 7 March 1966, box 10, file 9, "Clifford, Ernest L., 1966," CRC Papers, USWA Archives, PSU. Robert R. Hobson to Charlie Hampton, 9 January 1969, box 21, file 17, CRD Papers, USWA Archives, PSU. Staughton Lynd, remarks at Working Class History Seminar at University of Pittsburgh, winter 1992.

316. Sydney Lee Smith to Ernest Clifford, 8 August 1973, file "Salway Smith Forging Charges"; Melvin Green, file "Charges Filed against Union Local Equal Opportunities" both in box 44, Local 1397 Homestead Records, IUP.

317. Ralph Kroger, "USWA Protest Mapped in 3 Cities, Meets," PC, 1 August 1970, 24.

318. Kroger, "Black USWA National Protesters Pickets Unions Headquarters Here," PC, 18 July 1970, 1.

319. Nyden, "Evolution," 390.

320. Philip Shabacoff, "Steel and Union Adopt a Plan on Job Equality," NYT, 14 April 1974, 1. Shabacoff, "Steel and Union Accept Job Plan," NYT, 16 April 1974, 64.

321. Struggles in Steel: A Story of African-American Steelworkers, videorecording, dir. Tony Buba and Ray Henderson (San Francisco: California Newsreel, 1996).

322. "Audit Committee Guides Rights Decree Implementation," SL (June 1974): 5. John P. Moody, "Civil Rights Panel Costs USWA Officers Here," PPG, 28 October 1974, 21.

323. Bureau of the Census, Census of Population: 1970, (Washington: GPO, 1961), Part 40, 404. Bureau of the Census, Census of Population: 1980, (Washington: GPO, 1983), Part 40, 920–22.

324. Incumbency roster, Valley Machine Shop, 23 April 1982, box 31, file 3, Homestead Local 1397 Records, IUP. "Seniority Rosters—Slab and Plate Division," Homestead Local 1397 Papers, IUP.

325. "Memorandum of Agreement," Homestead Plant, Local Union 1397—District 15, box 28, file "48 inch Shutdown," Homestead Local 1397 Records, IUP.

326. Women of Steel (August 1979): 5, no box, file "Women of Steel," Steffie Domike Papers, AIS.

327. EH-74-221, box 22, Homestead Local 1397 Records, IUP.

328. Ray Henderson, interview by author, 6 August 1993, tape recording.

329. Buba and Henderson, Struggles in Steel, videorecording.

330. John P. Moody, "Blacks Mull Back Pay Offer of USS Here," PPG, 9 June 1975, 2.

331. Commonwealth of Pennsylvania, Department of Internal Affairs, County Industry Report, "Allegheny County" (Harrisburg: Department of Internal Affairs, 1961–68), 1961, 7–20; 1962, 7–26; 1963, 7–23; 1964, 7–23; 1965, 9–25; 1966, 10–27; 1967, 22–39; 1968, 23–40. U.S. Department of Labor, Women's Bureau, Ethel Erickson, Women's Employment in the Making of Steel, (Washington: GPO, 1944), Bulletin 192–5, 19.

332. "Who Says the Mill Is a Man's World? Not These USWA Gals," SL (January 1966): 8.

333. "After 46 Years in Johnstown Mill Lady Steelworker Calls It Quits," SL (April 1969): 18.

334. Leslie Barbara Posner, "Male-Female Worker Relations in a Traditionally Male Industrial Setting: The Case of the First Women Workers in a 'Company-Town' Steel Mill" (Ed.D. diss., University of Pittsburgh, 1979), 163.

335. Richard L. Rowan, *The Negro in the Steel Industry* (Philadelphia: University of Pennsylvania Press, 1968), 50. Bureau of the Census, *Census of Population: 1960* (Washington: GPO, 1961), table 36.

336. Equal Employment Opportunity Commission, *Equal Employment Opportunity Report—1971: Job Patterns for Minorities and Women in Private Industry*, vol. 3, 177.

337. Affirmative Action Compliance Project, 1972, Section D-b, USX National Tube Papers, box 82, AIS.

338. Posner, "Male-Female Worker Relations," 160.

339. Seniority Roster for Valley Machine Shop, 23 April 1982, box 31, file 3, Homestead Local 1397 Records, IUP. Michele McMills, interview by author, 26 August 1992, tape recording.

340. Pittsburgh Filmmakers, Mon Valley Unemployed Committee and Mon Valley Media, *Women of Steel*, videorecording (Pittsburgh: Television Satellite Communications, 1985).

341. Ruth Kish, interview by author, 2 March 1992, tape recording. Ray Henderson, interview by author, 10 August 1993, tape recording.

342. *Women of Steel*, videorecording. For other examples of harassment of black women workers, see LaJuana Deanda, in *Women of Steel*, November 1979, 5, and Gaye Robinson, in *Women of Steel*, November 1979, 4, no box, file "Women of Steel," Steffie Domike Papers, AIS.

343. Mill Hunk Herald, *Overtime: Punching Out with the Mill Hunk Herald*, 172.

344. *Women of Steel*, May 1979, 3, no box, file "Women of Steel," Steffie Domike Papers, AIS.

345. Denise Weinbrenner Edwards, interview by author, 15 June 1992, tape recording.

346. *Women of Steel*, videorecording.

347. LaJuana Deanda, *Women of Steel*, November 1979, 5, no box, file "Women of Steel," Steffie Domike Papers, AIS. Michelle McMills, *Women of Steel*, August 1979.

348. *Women of Steel*, videorecording.

349. Ginny Hildebrand, interview by author, 18 August 1992, tape recording.

350. William Wesser, "Steelworkers Picket 'Union Dictatorship,'" *PP*, 17 June 1975, 7.

351. *McKeesport Daily News*, July 1977, no box, file "Consent Decree," Steffie Domike Papers, AIS.

352. Michael Bonn, interview by author, 3 September 1993, tape recording.

353. Ray Steffans, "USWA Aide Blasts 'Equal Job' Decree," *PP*, 19 May 1975, 3.

354. John Hughey, interview by author, 5 August 1993, tape recording. Verlich, "Steelworkers Here Map Fight over Minority Decree," *PP*, 4 October 1974, 2. Mike Bonn, interview by author, 3 August 1993, tape recording.

355. Ray Henderson, interview with author, 2 December 1993, notes; 6 August 1993, tape recording.

356. Douglas W. Eray, "Pittsburgh: Growth outside Manufacturing," *NYT*, 11 July 1971, Section 3, 13.

357. U.S. Department of Labor, Bureau of Labor Statistics, *Employment, Hours and Earnings, States and Areas, 1939–1975* (Washington: GPO, 1975), Bulletin 1370–12, 631–37. U.S. Department of Labor, Bureau of Labor Statistics, *Employment, Hours and Earnings, States and Areas, 1972–1987* (Washington, D.C.: GPO, 1989), Bulletin 2320, 2847–68.

358. Beckman, Yoder and Associates, Inc., *Steel Valley Area Regional Development Plan* (Pittsburgh, n.d., probably 1974), 22–28.

359. Nora Faires, "Immigrants and Industry: Peopling the 'Iron City,'" in *City at the Point: Essays on the Social History of Pittsburgh*, ed. Samuel P. Hays (Pittsburgh: University of Pittsburgh Press, 1989), 17–18.

360. "Pittsburgh off Course during 1950–62 Exodus," *PC*, 30 October 1965, 3. Bureau of the Census, *Population Census: Detailed Characteristics* (Washington: GPO, 1970), 749–50.

361. David Rosenberg, "Did the Collapse of Basic Industry Really Take the Allegheny Conference by Surprise?" *In Pittsburgh*, 21–27 March 1990, 18.

362. Roy Lubove, *Twentieth Century Pittsburgh: Government, Business and Environmental Change* (New York: John Wiley and Sons, 1969), 123–32.

363. Lubove, *Twentieth Century Pittsburgh*, 128.

364. "Big Steel, Big Spender Here in '67," *PP*, 17 January 1967.

365. Hogan, *Economic History*, 1669–71.

366. Hogan, *Economic History*, 1757–58.

367. George David Smith, *From Monopoly to Competition: The Transformations of Alcoa, 1888–1986* (New York: Cambridge University Press, 1988), 334. See also Margaret B.W. Graham and Betty H. Pruitt, *R&D for Industry: A Century of Technical Innovation at Alcoa* (New York: Cambridge University Press, 1990).

368. Rosenberg, "Surprise," 18–20.

369. "Labor Group Meets, Plans for Future," *PC*, 26 August 1961, 11.

370. News Release, 16 October 1961, box 38, file "News Release—PC, 1961," NAACP Records, AIS.

371. "Courier, NAACP, NALC Mass Protest Wins: Arena to Improve Job-Hiring Policy," *PC*, 28 October 1961, 2.

372. "Negroes Zero in on Steel Industry," *BW*, 10 December 1966, 156. Dietsch, "Steel Urged to Increase Negro Staffs," *PPG*, 22 May 1968, box 7, file 20, CRD Papers, USWA Archives, PSU.

373. Rosensweet, "The Negro in Pittsburgh: Joblessness a Basic Problem Here," *PPG*, 12 September 1963, 1, 8.

374. "Vicious Prejudice Seen as Roadblock to the Employment of Skilled Negroes," *PC*, 12 December 1959, 5.

375. Ed Wintermantel, "Craig Credits Police 5-Year Plant with Keeping Riots Here Bloodless," *PP*, 14 April 1968, Section 3, 1.

376. David Peck, "Picketing Bias Laid to Policemen," *PPG*, 12 February 1971. Ed Wintermantel, "Craig Credits Police 5-Year Plan with Keeping Riots Here Bloodless," *PP*, 14 April 1968, Section 3, 1. Nick Ludington, "Hotel Here Okays Hiring More Negroes," *PP*, 26 May 1964, 4.

377. "No Black Executives at ALCOA, Dravo, WABCO," *PC*, 16 August 1969, 1. Carl Morris, "Comment: Blacks Need United in Quest for More and Better Jobs," *PC*, 19 July 1969, 13. Morris, "Comment: Demonstration Post-Mortem," *PC*, 6 May 1967, 5.

378. Phyllis Garland, "Local Craft Union Color Bar Is Lifted," *PC*, 13 July 1963, 1.

379. Msgr. Charles Own Rice, "Bias in Building," *PC*, 23 August 1969, 13.

380. Diane Perry, "Violence Erupts at North Side Stadium Site," *PC*, 16 August 1969, 1. Philip S. Foner, *Organized Labor and the Black Worker, 1619–1981* (New York: Praeger, 1981), 408–09.

381. Diane Perry, "Golden Triangle Is Hit with Cop Brutality, Mass Arrests," *PC*, 30 August 1969, 1, 15. "Police Lost Respect at Demonstration," *PC*, 8 September 1969, 12. Diane Perry, "Mass March, Boycott Started," *PC*, 13 September 1969, 1. "Job Tensions at New High: Black Coalition Won't Back Down," *PC*, 27 September 1969, 1.

382. Aurelia H. Diggs, "Became Black after Seeing Brutality," *PC*, 6 September 1969, 13.

383. "Blacks Agree to 'Holiday' for Parleys," *PP*, 28 August 1969, 1, 4. John P. Moody, "City's Protester's Taking a Break over Labor Day," *PPG*, 30 August 1969, 1, 3. "Construction Workers Get 'Lost' Pay," *PPG*, 12 September 1969.

384. Verlich, "Builders, Coalition Race July 1 Deadline: $300 Million in U.S. Funds at Stake," *PP*, 21 June 1970. Lawrence Walsh, "Construction Ban Awaits Black Jobs," *PP*, 8 February 1970, 1, 12. "Call Pittsburgh Plan Totally Worthless," *PC*, 12 December 1970. "May 'Freeze' Pittsburgh Plan Projects," *PC*, 18 September 1971, 1, 4.

385. "BCC Never Ratified the Pittsburgh Plan," *PC*, 7 November 1970, 1. "The Pittsburgh Plan," *PC*, 12 February 1972, 8.

386. "Near Riot over Black Union Members: Iron Workers Admit 5 Despite Furor," *PC*, 25 July 1970, 1. "IBEW Accepts First Negro," *PC*, 27 February 1971, 1. "Leaders Rap Pittsburgh Plan: Trainees Take Case to D.C.," *PC*, 8 May 1971, 1, 4. Barbara White Stack, "Minorities Shut Down Hill Job," *PPG*, 12 January 1983, 4. Virginia Linn, "Black Coalition Moves to Gain Minority Work on Airport," *PPG*, 18 April 1987, 5.

387. Ralph Z. Hallow, "War on Poverty Costs Plenty, Goes Nowhere," *PPG*, 21 September 1971, 1–2. Diane Perry, "Black Construction Coalition Backs Pittsburgh Plan Trainees," *PC*, 22 May 1971, 1, 5. "Pittsburgh Plan Trainees Still Out of Work," *PC*, 5 June 1971, 1, 5.

388. "The Pittsburgh Plan," *PC*, 12 February 1972, 8.

389. "U.S. Says Unions Not Complying," *PC*, 12 June 1971, 1. Woody L. Taylor, "Pittsburgh Plan Asks to Place 17 Unions 'in Compliance,'" *PC*, 3 July 1971, 5.

390. Mike Moyer, "Pittsburgh Plan Agrees to Cuts Sought by Pete," *PPG*, 20 January 1977, 13.

391. Verlich, "Most Unions Opening to Blacks, Study Shows," *PP*, 12 December 1971, A-3. Roger Stuart, "Once-Hostile Blacks, Unions Unite on Job," *PP*, 9 September 1973, A-17.

CHAPTER 5. THE LEAN YEARS: 1978–2000

1. I.W. Abel, *Collective Bargaining: Labor Relations in Steel, Then and Now* (Pittsburgh: Carnegie Mellon University Press, 1976), 41.

2. Allegheny Conference on Community Development, *Toward a Shared Economic Vision for Pittsburgh and Southwestern Pennsylvania* (Pittsburgh: Carnegie Mellon University, 1993), 9–10.

3. S.J. Kleinberg, *The Shadow of the Mills: Working-Class Families in Pittsburgh 1870–1907* (Pittsburgh: University of Pittsburgh Press, 1989), 46.

4. Steve Massey, "Economy Leaves Blacks Behind," *PPG*, 18 October 1994, 1, 8. United States Department of Commerce, *Statistical Abstract of the United States, 1992* (Washington: GPO, 1992), 30–32. U.S. Department of Labor, Bureau of Labor Statistics, *Employment, Hours and Earnings, States and Areas, 1939–1975* (Washington: GPO, 1975), Bulletin 1370–12, 631–37. U.S. Department of Labor, Bureau of Labor Statistics, *Employment, Hours and Earnings, States and Areas, 1972–1987* (Washington: GPO), Bulletin 2320, 1431–33.

5. Roy Lubove, *Twentieth-Century Pittsburgh, Volume II: The Post Steel Era* (Pittsburgh: University of Pittsburgh Press, 1996), 3–40, quotation on 25.

6. "A Question of Leadership," *PP*, 11 November 1984.

7. Rick Santorum, "Region Renaissance Initiative," *PPG*, 31 October 1997, 23.

8. *Toward A Shared Economic Vision*, 1–10, quotation on 6. Joyce Gannon, "Why Not Pittsburgh? Taxes, Unions among Reasons Companies Avoid Region," *PPG*, 30 June 1994, B-11. Clarke Thomas, "Union Problem? What Union Problem?" *PPG*, 5 January 1994, C-3. Charles McCollester, "Labor's Pains and Gains," *PPG*, 21 September 1997, B-1.

9. See chapter 1.

10. See chapter 2.

11. See chapter 3.

12. Kevin Boyle, *The UAW and the Heyday of American Liberalism 1945–1968* (Ithaca: Cornell University Press, 1995), 185–256.

13. See chapter 4.

14. Clyde H. Farnsworth, "Study for EPA Finds Rules Are Costly for Steel Industry," *NYT*, 26 September 1980, D-5.

15. "There Is No Known Technology Which Will Bring Cokemaking at Clairton in Compliance with Allegheny County's Air Pollution Code," *PPG*, 10 June 1976, 3. Lawrence Walsh, "$600 Million USS Air Cleanup Okd," *PP*, 11 November 1976, 1. "The United States Is Being Legislated into a No-Growth Society," (advertisement) in Kennedy P. Maize, "Can EPA Clean Up US Steel?" *Environmental Action*, 25 September 1976, 2–8.

16. Advertisement, *PP*, 29 June 1976, 11.

17. Office of Technology Assessment, *U.S. Industrial Competitiveness: A Comparison of Steel, Electronics and Automobiles: Summary* (Washington: GPO, 1981), 23. For the costs of environmental controls, see BLS, *Technological Change and Manpower Trends in Five Industries* (Washington: GPO, 1975), Bulletin 1856, 28.

18. Frank Takach, interview by Jim Barrett, 28 May 1976, transcript, 3, HOHP, AIS. See also "Pollution" (Cartoon), *PPG*, 7 June 1975, 6.

19. Anatole Kaletsky, "U.S. Threat to Fight Japan on Steel Imports," *NYT*, 16 December 1982, 1. Stuart Auerbach, "Steel Executives Step Up Pressure for Import Curbs," *Washington Post*, 25 November 1983, D8.

20. William Serrin, "Steel Union Talks Opening This Week," *NYT*, 6 July 1982, A-11. Michael Bonn, interview by author, 3 September 1993, tape recording. Mike Bilsic, interview by author, 19 March 1992, tape recording.

21. Jack Metzgar, "Plant Shutdowns and Worker Responses: The Case of Johnstown, PA," *Socialist Review* 10 (September-October 1980): 9–26, quotation on 10. Michael K. Drapkin, "Antipollution Laws Are Forcing Steelmakers to Close Old, Dirty Open Hearth Furnaces," *WSJ*, 1 December 1970, 40. Agis Salpukas, "Pennsylvania Eases Pollution Enforcement for Steel," *NYT*, 28 November 1977, 49, 51.

22. William Robbins, "City of Adversity Gets Some News That May Help," *NYT*, 3 January 1983, 8.

23. William Serrin, "Sad Johnstown Awaits Demise of a Steel Plant," *NYT*, 21 April 1984, 7.

24. William Scheuerman, *The Steel Crisis: The Economics and Politics of a Declining Industry* (New York: Praeger, 1986), 203. For a different perspective on the Carter Administration, see Judith Stein, *Running Steel, Running America: Race, Economic Policy and the Decline of Liberalism* (Chapel Hill: University of North Carolina Press, 1998), 253–72.

25. Metzgar, "Plant Shutdowns," 9–14. Staughton Lynd, "What Happened in Youngstown: An Outline," *Radical America* 15 (winter 1981): 37–48.

26. Jerry Knight, "Youngstown Jobless Rate Will Soar," *Washington Post*, 2 December 1979, K–1.

27. Denise Weinbrenner, interview by Bob Anderson, 23 April 1991, USWOHP, SIHC. Staughton Lynd, "Big Steel's Irony," *NYT*, 1 December 1981, A-31.

28. Lynd, "What Happened in Youngstown," 43–44.

29. Lynd, "Big Steel's Irony," *NYT*, 1 December 1981, A–31.

30. Leslie Wayne, "Big Steel's Puzzling Strategy," *NYT*, 10 July 1983, C-1. Karen W. Arenson, "Tax Law's Effect on Mergers," *NYT*, 7 September 1982, D-1. Robert J. Cole, "Marathon Holders Vote Merger with U.S. Steel," *NYT*, 12 March 1982, D-1.

31. Congressional Budget Office, *The Effects of Import Quotas on the Steel Industry* (Washington: GPO, 1984), 29. Jack Metzgar, *Striking Steel: Solidarity Remembered* (Philadelphia: Temple University Press, 2000), 138. "America's Steelmen Yearn to Make Anything but Steel," *The Economist*, 2 November 1985, 71.

32. Lydia Chavez, "Pittsburgh Confronts Oil Bid," *NYT*, 7 December 1981, D-1. Doug Root, "Merger a Misplaced Priority Stunned Steelworkers Say," *PPG*, 18 November 1981, 23. "U.S. Steel Unions Seek to Join Court Battle," *WSJ*, 17 December 1981, 4. Larry Tell, "U.S. Steel's Takeover of Marathon Questioned by Laid-Off Steelworkers," *National Law Review*, 28 December 1981; "Steelworkers Rap Marathon Plan," *PP*, 1 December 1981; box 51, file "Newspaper Clippings," Homestead Local 1397 Papers, IUP.

33. Leslie Wayne, "Big Steel's Puzzling Strategy," *NYT*, 10 July 1983, C-1.

34. Robert Anderson, interview by Bob Mast, 1993, USWOHP, SIHC.

35. "Steel Company Plant Shutdowns, 1974–1982," *USSN* (July 1982): 18–20. Jim McKay, "Banking the Fire," *PPG*, 5 December 1990. 'Music' of a Giant Steel Plant Fades in Pennsylvania Town," *NYT*, 6 April 1984, 19. "The Decline of Steel in Western Pennsylvania," n.d., in author's possession.

36. "Hidden Assets and Hopes of a Harvest," *Metal Producing* (June 1985): 62–63.

37. University of Pittsburgh School of Business and others, "Economic Development Employment Survey: Narrative Responses," spring 1990, 10.

38. Robert Dodge, "Pouring New Hope for LTV," *Washington Post*, 16 December 1979, F-1. "Jones and Laughlin to Close Old Plant," *NYT*, 14 November 1980, D-4. "LTV Shutting Mill," *NYT*, 23 May 1984, D-5.

39. Pete Mamula, interview by Bob Anderson, 29 April 1991, USWOHP, SIHC.

40. Barnaby J. Feder, "Struggle to Survive in Town That Steel Forgot," *NYT*, 27 April 1993, D–1.

41. James Risen, "May Set Trend in Industry," *Los Angeles Times* (hereafter cited as *LAT*), 5 April 1986, D-1.

42. "U.S. Takes Over LTV Pensions," *LAT*, 13 January 1987, 1. "Steelworker's Wife Fights to Assure Full Pension," *LAT*, 12 January 1987, D-2. Len Boselovic, "Study Shows Extent of Government Subsidies to U.S. Steel Industry," *PPG*, 30 November 1999. Kevin G. Hall, "Mexico Clears Steel Firms of Unfair Trade Charges," *Journal of Commerce*, 4 January 1996, 3.

43. "Steel Mineral Reserves," *Mining Week*, 8 May 1981, 353. "King Solomon's Other Mines," *Economist*, 16 May 1981, 106.

44. Wayne, "Big Steel's Puzzling Strategy," *NYT*, 10 July 1983, C-1.

45. Daniel F. Cuff, "U.S. Steel in Korean Import Plan," *NYT*, 17 December 1985, D-1.

46. James Risen, "USX Will Close 4 Mills," *LAT*, 5 February 1987, D-1. Hoerr, *Wolf*, 135–43.

47. Steven Greenhouse, "Employees Make a Go of Weirton," *NYT*, 6 January 1985, C-3. James B. Lieber, *Friendly Takeover: How an Employee Buyout Saved a Steel Town* (New York: Viking, 1995), passim. Cindi Lash, "A Steel Community Faces Its Worst Fears," *PPG*, 24 January 1999, 1. Len Boselovic, "Keeping the ESOP Alive," *PPG*, 31 March 1996, C-1. Leslie Wayne, "Big Steel's Problems Are Home Grown," *NYT*, 29 April 1999, C-1, C-12.

48. Ron Weison, interview by author, 16 June 1993, tape recording. Ginny Hildebrant, interview by author, 18 August 1992, tape recording. Mike Bonn, interview by author, 3 August 1993, tape recording. Larry Evans, interview by author, 25 July 1992, notes. Bob Masey, interview by author, 9 June 1992, tape recording. Michele McMills, interview by author, 26 August 1992, tape recording. Denise Weinbrenner Edwards, interview by author, 15 June 1992, tape recording. Mike Bilsic, interview by author, 19 March 1992, tape recording. Terrence Patrick Gates, interview by Bob Anderson, 22 July 1993; Mike Bilsic, 25 April 1991; Patricia Tanaka Blaney, 6 January 1993; Larry Evans, 8 January 1992; Jim Cottone, 28 April 1991; Linda Stovall, 21 August 1991; all in USWOHP, SIHC. "Our Jobs—The Future at Homestead," 8 October 1981; "Important Meeting"; box 51, file "Newsclippings," Homestead Local 1397 Papers, IUP. Jim McKay, "Ron Weisen," *PPG*, 14 January 1998, B-6.

49. Larry Evans, interview by author, 25 July 1992, notes.

50. Steffie Domike, interview by Bob Anderson, 24 June 1991, USWOHP, SIHC. "Pittsburgh Report to the National Steel Fraction," 6 December 1976; "The Sadlowski Campaign," n.d.; Joel G. "Impressions and Observations," n.d.; box 2, file 18, Labor Notes Papers, AL&UA Archives. Robert Anderson, interview by Bob Mast, 1993, USWOHP, SIHC.

51. Linda Stovall, interview by Bob Anderson, 21 August 1991, USWOHP, SIHC.

52. Larry Evans, interview by Bob Anderson, 8 January 1992, USWOHP, SIHC. The Mill Hunk Herald, *Overtime: Punchin' Out with the Mill Hunk Herald Magazine 1979–1989* (Pittsburgh: Piece of the Hunk Publishers, 1990).

53. Jim Cottone, interview by Bob Anderson, 28 April 1991, USWOHP, SIHC. "Help the Unemployed," box 51, file "Newsclippings," Homestead Local 1397 Papers, IUP. "Steel Union Giving Away Food to Jobless Workers," *NYT*, 6 May 1982, 20.

54. Lois Brown, interview by Bob Anderson, 7 May 1991, USWOHP, SIHC. Bob Anderson, interview by Bob Mast, 1993, USWOHP, SIHC. Tom Hritz, "Born to Be Sheriff," *PPG*, 25 October 1998, B-1.

55. Jan Carlino, interview by Bob Anderson, 12 June 1991, USWOHP, SIHC. Mon Valley Unemployed Committee *Reporter*, various. Jim McKay, "Ready for the Next Downturn," *PPG*, 27 June 1999, C-1.

56. Larry Evans, interview by Bob Anderson, 8 January 1992, USWOHP, SIHC.

57. Dale A. Hathaway, *Can Workers Have a Voice? The Politics of Deindustrialization in Pittsburgh* (University Park: The Pennsylvania State University Press, 1993), 91–130. SVA, "Federation for Industrial Retention and Renewal News," winter 1994.

58. Hathaway, *Can Workers Have a Voice?* 49–90. Ron Weison, interview by author, 16 June 1993. Darrell Becker, interview by Bob Anderson, 3 June 1991; Mike Bonn, 29 April 1991; Mel Packer, 11 May 1991; USWOHP, SIHC. Andrew Sheehan, "Jobless Steel Worker Held in Skunk-Oil Bombing," *PPG*, 25 January 1985. Dan Hopey, "Fanning the Flames: Church, Neighborhood Protests Divide Support for Mon Valley Unemployed," *PP*, 27 May 1984, B-1.

59. James Risen, "Settlement Is Bad News for USX's Rivals," *LAT*, 19 January 1987, D-1.

60. William Serrin, "USX Plants Struck by Steel Workers," *NYT*, 1 August 1986, 10. "Steelworkers Approve Pact with USX," *LAT*, 1 February 1987, 4.

61. Len Boselovic, "Caster to Revive Steel Mill on Mon," *PPG*, 2 September 1990, 1.

62. James Risen, "USX Will Close 4 Mills," *LAT*, 5 February 1987, D-1. "Workers Called Back to USX Steel Plants as Stoppage Ends," *NYT*, 2 February 1987, 14.

63. Morton Coleman, "Decline of the Mon Valley Viewed in a Global Context," in *Steel People: Survival and Resilience in Pittsburgh's Mon Valley*, ed. Jim Cunningham and Pamela Martz (Pittsburgh: School of Social Work, 1986), 4. Steel Valley Authority, "Economic Development Employment Survey," n.d., 1–3.

64. Barnaby J. Feder, "Struggle to Survive in Town That Steel Forgot," *NYT*, 27 April 1993, D-1.

65. Carol Bernick, interview by Bob Anderson, 3 May 1991, USWOHP, SIHC.

66. Lindsey Gruson, "Steel Towns Discharge Police and Reduce Services Sharply," *NYT*, 6 October 1985, 1. Michael Margolis, Robert E. Burtt, and Jeffrey McLaughlin, "Impact of Industrial Decline: Braddock, North Braddock and Rankin," in *Steel People*, 15–17.

67. "Mayor of the Year Nominee," *PP*, 11 July 1991, S-2. William Serrin, *Homestead: The Tragedy and Glory of a Steel Town* (New York: Times Books, 1992), 402.

68. David Biegel, Jim Cunningham, Pamela Martz, "Mon Valley People Speak: The Duquesne Survey," in *Steel People*, 50.

69. Jane Blotzer, "Leaving the Most Liveable City," *PPG*, 18 June 1986, 1, 7.

70. Coleman, "Decline of the Mon Valley," in *Steel People*, 5.

71. "Reagan Rules Out Role as Employment Agency," *NYT*, 15 April 1983, B-8.

72. William M. Fidel, "Steelworkers Know about Job Retraining," *NYT*, 10 May 1995, 22.

73. Ron Bricker, interview by Bob Anderson, 14 May 1991, USWOHP, SIHC.

74. "Narrative Responses," 30.

75. "Narrative Responses," 22.

76. "Narrative Responses," 35.

77. "Narrative Responses," 22.

78. Mary Kane, "Mon Valley: A Rough Road to Recovery," *PP*, 5 March 1990, 1, 6.

79. "Clairton Applicants Survey," *Tri-State Conference Call*, Fall,1990, 1.

80. Maureen Morrissey, "Hard Times: Recession Compounds Misery in Long-Suffering Mon Valley," *PPG*, 6 February 1992, S-1.

81. Patricia Sabatini, "Defining a Record," *PPG*, 30 January 2000, F-1.

82. Karen Joyce Gibson, "Income, Race and Space: A Comparative Analysis of the Effects of Poverty Concentration on White and Black Neighborhoods in the Pittsburgh and Detroit Metropolitan Areas" (Ph.D. diss., University of California-Berkeley, 1996), 60–65.

83. *Struggles in Steel: A Story of African-American Steelworkers*, videorecording, dir. Tony Buba and Ray Henderson (San Francisco: California Newsreel, 1996).

84. Jim McKay, "Blacks Lost Jobs and a Generation with Manufacturing's Demise," *PPG*, 15 November 1994, 6. Jones, "Black Unemployment Nearly Three Times That of Whites," *PPG*, 30 November 1997, 12.

85. "Racial Inequality Infant Mortality Rates Declining but Disparity Remains," *PPG*, 27 March 1993, B-2.

86. Steve Massey, "Economy Leaves Blacks Behind," *PPG*, 18 October 1994, 1. Jim McKay, "Area's Job Woes Cross Color Lines," *PPG*, 28 March 1996, C–6. Gibson, "Income, Race and Space," 66, 72, 85.

87. *Women of Steel,* videorecording.

88. "Women Face Low Pay after Losing Steel Jobs," *NYT*, 17 May 1984, C-11. Ginny Hildebrant, interview by author, 18 August 1992, tape recording. Denise Weinbrenner Edwards, interview by author, 15 June 1992, tape recording.

89. Dale Russakoff, "'Life Was Simple' When Mills Roared," *Washington Post*, 12 April 1987, 13.

90. Dale Russakoff, "Chasing Work Fractures Lives of Steel Families," *Washington Post*, 28 March 1993, 1. Denny Trumbaluak, "Steelworkers' Lament from Beaver County," in *Overtime: Punching Out With the Mill Hunk Herald*, 43.

91. Jerry Laychak, interview by Bob Anderson, 8 May 1991, USWOHP, SIHC. Bob Erickson, interview by author, 3 June 1993.

92. Mel Packer, interview by Bob Anderson, 21 August 1991, USWOHP, SIHC.

93. Lois Brown, interview by Bob Anderson, 7 May 1991, USWOHP, SIHC. Mel Packer, interview by Bob Anderson, 21 August 1991, USWOHP, SIHC.

94. Jim Cattone, interview by Bob Anderson, 28 April 1991, USWOHP, SIHC.

95. Robert Anderson, "Steel Worker Lore," 17 March 1996, USWOHP, SIHC.

96. Pittsburgh Filmmakers, Mon Valley Unemployed Committee and Mon Valley Media, *Women of Steel*, videorecording (Pittsburgh: Television Satellite Communications, 1985).

97. USX, *A Decade of Change* (Annual Report), 1989, 4, 16.

98. "American Steel: Did You Say Deindustrialising?" *The Economist*, 17 December 1988, 75.

99. Jack Metzgar, *Striking Steel: Solidarity Remembered* (Philadelphia: Temple University Press, 2000), 118–41.

100. Steve Dinnen, "Can American Steel Find Quality?" *Industry Week*, 20 January 1992, 36. Leslie Wayne, "Big Steel's Problems Are Home Grown," *NYT*, 29 April 1999, C-1, C-12. Steven Greenhouse, "U.S. Steel's Long Road Back," *NYT*, 5 June 1984, D-1. Christopher G.L. Hall, *Steel Phoenix: The Fall and Rise of the U.S. Steel Industry* (New York City: St. Martin's Press, 1997), 336.

101. Len Boselovic, "Steel Unit Limits USX Potential," *PP*, 12 August 1990, D-17. "USX in Talks to Sell Steel Unit," *PP*, 7 May 1991, B-1.

102. "America's Best Plants," *Industry Week*, 21 October 1996. Alan Wallace, "The Legacy of 'ET' Flourishes in New Era," in "Steelworking," n.d. but probably 1996, 3–4.

103. Christoph Scherrer, "Surprising Resilience: The Steelworkers' Struggle to Hang on to the Fordist Bargain," in *Trade Union Politics: American Unions and Economic Change, 1960s–1990s*, ed. Glenn Perusek and Kent Worcester (Atlantic Highlands, NJ: Humanities Press, 1995), 157.

104. Steven Greenhouse, "U.S. Steel's Long Road Back," *NYT*, 5 June 1984, D-1.

105. Scherrer, "Surprising Resilience," 157. United States International Trade Commission, *Annual Survey Concerning Competitive Conditions in the Steel Industry and Industry Efforts to Adjust and Modernize*, USITC Publication 226 (Washington: USITC, 1989).

106. Hall, *Steel Phoenix*, 336.

107. "U.S. Steel Group Is Set to Buy Steel Assets of Slovakia's VSZ," *WSJ*, 27 March 2000, 10.

108. "No-Growth a Blessing?" *PPG*, 29 May 1985, 8.

109. Ian Rodger, "A City Transformed," *Financial Times*, 5 June 1985, 12. Steve Creedy, "Steel City to Tech City," *PPG*, 24 November 1996, C-2. Ken Zapinski, "From Steel City to Digital Furnace," *PPG*, 2 December 1999, C-1. Teresa Lineman, "Forget Steel City, We're Now Roboburgh," *PPG*, 24 November 1999, C-1.

110. Brukhart Holzner and Jean-Pierre Collet, "Let's Get Global," *PPG*, 6 March 1996, 15. John G. Craig, Jr., "What's Right in Our Region," *PPG*, 29 October 1995, B-3. Julian Borger, "Pittsburgh: From Industrial Wreck to Dot Com Metropolis," *Guardian*, 12 February 2000, 19. Mike Rosenwald, "Pittsburgh Looks Past Steel to Build a Future in High Tech," *Boston Globe*, 28 November 1999, 26. R.W. Apple Jr., "Where Steel Was King a New Spirit Reigns," *NYT*, 30 July 1999, 33.

111. Steve Massey, "Stepping Up to the Plate," *PPG*, 8 December 1996, C-1. Massey, "Reviving the Region's Economy," *PPG*, 7 November 1993, 1.

112. *Toward a Shared Economic Vision*, 1–20. Len Boselovic, "Pittsburgh's Tax Bite 4th Highest of 27 Big US Cities," *PPG*, 5 November 1998, E-7.

113. Tom Kelly, "Robert and Me," *Focus* (December-November 1991): 5. "Labor Dispute Still Unresolved," *Focus* (September 1993): 1, 3. Clarke Thomas, "Union Problem? What Union Problem?" *PPG*, 5 January 1994, C-3.

114. University Center for Social and Urban Research, "Black and White Economic Conditions in the City of Pittsburgh" (Pittsburgh, University of Pittsburgh 1995), 18–30. The report defined poverty by measures such as access to health care and disposable income for entertainment and was thus less restrictive than federal guidelines.

115. *Eyewitness News This Morning*, KDKA Pittsburgh, 5 December 1996, Video Monitoring Services of America.

116. See chapter 1.

117. David Peck, "Picketing Bias Laid to Policemen," *PPG*, 12 February 1971.

118. R. Lamont Jones, "NAACP to Monitor Complaints on Police," *PPG*, 14 December 1993, D-1. Jones, "Rights Suit Targetting City Police," *PPG*, 27 March 1996, 1.

119. Laurent Belsie, "Black–White Divide Deepens Over the Thin Blue Line," *Christian Science Monitor*, 22 October 1996, 3.

120. Johnna A. Pro, "Justice Department Consent Decree Pushes Police to Overhaul Operations," *PPG*, 1 March 1998, C–1.

121. Timothy McNulty, "Mayor Seeks End of Consent Decree," *PPG*, 5 November 1999. McNulty, "Consent Decree Under FOP Fire," *PPG*, 18 September 1998, B–3. Edward A. Kearns, "This Consent Decree Is a Disservice to Pittsburgh and the Police," *PPG*, 6 March 1997, 16. Marjorie Provan, "Civilian Review Board Is Just as Unnecessary Now as in the Past," *PPG*, 15 March 1997, 6. Ervin Dyer, "Give Civilian Review Board Power, Black Leader Says," *PPG*, 21 June 1997, 9.

122. R. Lamont Jones, "200 Start Work on Plan for Police Review Board," *PPG*, 16 January 1996, B-1. Jones, "Citizens Call for Policing the Police," *PPG*, 15 January 1994, B-1. "Policing Police: Civilian Review Is One Option, but Needs Further Study," *PPG*, 19 January 1994, B-2. Douglas Heuck, "March Planned Calling for Police Civilian Review Board," *PPG*, 23 June 1996, B-3. John Bull, "Petition Challenged," *PPG*, 26 February 1997, B-1. Pro, "Mayor's Proposal for Civilian Review Board Draws Fire," *PPG*, 16 July 1997, B-1.

123. Chuck Peters, "A Citizen, Reviewing the Police," *PPG*, 15 January 2000, 9. Marlynne Pitz, "Review Board Proposes Sanctions," *PPG*, 6 November 1999, 11.

124. Jane Blotzer, "Whose Boom?" *PPG*, 1 March 1998, B-1.

125. "Not So Livable," *PPG*, 16 April 2000, E-2.

126. Steve Massey, "Stepping up to the Plate," *PPG*, 8 December 1996, C-1. Tom Waseleski, "Our Ancestors Made Pittsburgh Work, Our Job Is to Keep It Going," *PPG*, 1 November 1997, 14. "Renaissance III," *PPG*, 22 March 1998, 12.

127. Larry Harris, "Pittsburgh Has a Chance to Show the World What It Can Do," *PPG*, 8 December 1998, 24. Rick Santorum, "Region Renaissance Initiative," *PPG*, 31 October 1997, 23.

128. Massey, "Stepping up to the Plate," *PPG*, 8 December 1996, C-1. Bruce Keidan, "City's Concessions Too Late," *PPG*, 7 August 1994, D-1.

129. Dennis B. Roddy, "A Tax Drive That Up Ended Politics," *PPG*, 6 November 1997, 1, C-2. "Election 1997," *PPG*, 6 November 1997, C-3-16. Cindi Lash, "Tracing the Roots of a Renaissance," *PPG*, 5 February 1999, 17.

130. Robert Dvorchak, "'Hero' Murphy Sees Plan B's Potential," *PPG*, 7 February 1999, 1. Timothy McNulty, "Murphy Eyeing a Third Term," *PPG*, 28 December 1999, B-1.

131. Waseleski, "Our Ancestors," *PPG*, 1 November 1997, 14. Rick Santorum, "Region Renaissance Initiative," *PPG*, 31 October 1997, 23.

132. Tom Barnes, "Towers Atop Steelers' Stadium Would Symbolize Region's Past and Future," *PPG*, 12 August 1999, B-1.

133. Steve Massey, "Steel Still King," *PPG*, 13 April 1994, B-9.

134. Greg LeRoy, *No More Candy Stores: States and Cities Making Job Subsidies Accountable* (Washington: Grassroots Policy Project, 1997).

135. "Consolidating Iron Manufactures," *NLT*, 6 August 1881, 1.

Index

Name Index